IAN G. BARBOUR

Carleton College
Northfield, Minnesota

Issues in

Science and Religion

HARPER TORCHBOOK

New York,

To my father
George Brown Barbour

A hardcover edition of this book was originally published in 1966
by Prentice-Hall, Inc.

ISSUES IN SCIENCE AND RELIGION

First TORCHBOOK edition published 1971.

STANDARD BOOK NUMBER: 06–131566–4

Acknowledgments

No author can express the extent of his intellectual and personal dependence on other people; he can only acknowledge those to whom he is most immediately indebted. Professors John Compton (Vanderbilt University), Harmon Holcomb (Colgate-Rochester Divinity School), and Fred Berthold (Dartmouth College) each read the manuscript in an earlier draft and made valuable suggestions; Harold Schilling (Pennsylvania State University), Daniel Williams (Union Theological Seminary), Danner Clouser (Carleton College), and Hugh Barbour (Earlham College) read portions of it. Students in my classes in modern physics, in religious thought, and in a seminar on the relations of science and religion have contributed both indirectly and directly. A fellowship from the American Council of Learned Societies and selection for a Harbison Award from the Danforth Foundation made possible the year's leave during which much of the writing was done. The original publisher of each of the quotations granted permission to include it; each article quoted is used by permission of both its author and the editor of the journal in which it appeared. (Publishers of the British editions of quotations cited are also acknowledged in the footnotes.) The patience of four children during several summer vacations should not go unrecognized; fortunately there is now an answer to the recurrent question: "When will your book be finished, Dad?" (though now the answer should be, "One never finishes a book—one simply abandons it eventually"). Finally, without the constant encouragement and help of my wife, both this project and my life would be immeasurably the poorer, for I owe her more than can be said here or anywhere.

I. G. B.

Contents

1

Introduction

Is the scientific method the only reliable guide to truth? Is man only a complex biochemical mechanism? How can God act if the world is law-abiding? These questions suggest the three types of issues which we will examine: (1) *methods of inquiry* in science and religion, (2) *man's relation to nature*, and (3) *God's relation to nature*.

Concerning methods, most writers today see science and religion as *strongly contrasting enterprises* which have essentially nothing to do with each other. We will find that the reasons for this sharp separation of spheres lie partly in the history of recent centuries. For example, when church leaders attacked Galileo's theory of the solar system or Darwin's theory of evolution, they made pronouncements on scientific issues which they were incompetent to judge. Conversely, Newton and other scientists used God to fill gaps in their scientific accounts—until better data or new theories made divine intervention unnecessary. The "God of the gaps," invoked as a hypothesis to account for scientifically unexplained facts, or introduced as a cause producing effects on the same level as natural causes, retreated further as each of the gaps in human knowledge was closed. But in addition such a picture of God had little relevance to the religious life of man; it was as dubious from the standpoint of religion as from that of science. In the light of these

previous mistakes, theologians now insist on a careful differentiation between scientific and religious questions—not simply to avoid
conflicts with science, but to clarify the distinctive character of
theological assertions.

Moreover, the two schools of thought that are dominant in
contemporary Western theology stress *radically distinctive features
of religion*, which contrast with scientific inquiry. Religion, it is
said, has its own methods totally unlike the procedures of science.
According to some theologians, religious knowledge derives entirely
from God's self-disclosure in historical revelation, not from human
discovery; we must look to particular events in which God has
revealed himself, and such events have no parallel in science.
According to other theologians, religious questions arise in the realm
of personal selfhood, not in the realm of impersonal objectivity
which science studies; religious issues are of ultimate concern and
require a type of personal involvement very different from the detached, objective attitude of the scientist. These theological movements, which are summarized in Chapter 5, tend to portray science
and religion as watertight compartments of human thought. There
is little interest today in looking to nature for support for religious
beliefs; the once-popular arguments of "natural theology"—such as
the claim that evidences of design prove the existence of a Designer—appear dubious logically and, more significantly, reflect a
speculative approach very different from the attitudes characteristic
of religion itself.

This separation of the spheres of science and religion has been
reinforced by the view of many scientists that *science provides
technical knowledge* of a specialized kind, rather than a total philosophy of life. Here again a lesson has been learned from the mistakes of history. Some scientists of the past were too eager to turn
particular theories into cosmic principles or philosophical systems;
for example, evolution was variously taken as evidence for theism
(or naturalism) or for an ethic of cooperation (or an ethic of competition). Today there is greater caution about drawing any such
far-reaching conclusions from scientific data. According to this
"positivistic" view, science provides limited knowledge of a technical kind; we must not expect it to do other jobs, such as providing
over-all world-views or philosophies of life. If science has this more
modest and more specialized role, it can neither help nor hinder

religion, and by the same token it cannot be used to support a naturalistic world-view.

The *limitations of science* are recognized in many recent writings in the philosophy of science (see Chapter 6). The influence of the observer on the data is inescapable in modern physics. The creative role of the human mind in inventing concepts by which to correlate observations has been acknowledged. The theories of physics are highly abstract and symbolic, often only very indirectly tied to experiments. Behavior in the atomic domain is not picturable or even imaginable—no suitable models or analogies can be drawn from ordinary experience. We are warned not to mistake scientific abstractions for the real world. Some authors maintain that theories are not replicas of reality at all, but only "mental constructions" or "useful fictions" for coordinating experimental data. Others speak of the selectivity of the scientist in picking out the particular kinds of relationships in which his interest centers; the choice as to what facts are relevant depends on the context of inquiry. A theory is said to be like a map, valuable for specific purposes, but never exhaustive or complete.

In addition to these currents of thought in theological and scientific circles, the influence of *language analysis* (Chapter 9) in recent philosophy has contributed to the separation of science and religion. Linguistic analysts direct attention to the functions that various types of language serve in human life. Among the characteristic functions ascribed to religious language are the expression and evocation of worship and self-commitment to a way of life—functions very different from those of scientific language (the prediction and control of publicly observable, repeatable phenomena). The religious community uses actor-language, whereas the scientific community uses spectator-language. Science and religion are "complementary languages."

According to these various interpreters, science and religion are *independent and autonomous*, and each should tend to its own affairs. They yield "complementary perspectives" rather than mutually exclusive descriptions; we are enjoined to be content with a plurality of unrelated languages. Both scientist and theologian are told to avoid metaphysics—that is, inquiry concerning the most general categories for interpreting the structure of reality. On this reading, there could be no dialogue between them—except about the personal problems which the scientist faces as a human being (for example, ethical choices, motivation for work, responsibility to society). The theologian may also have something to say to a culture that depersonalizes human existence and treats science as a source of salvation, but to theological ideas as such the findings of science would be irrelevant.

In the chapters that follow we will submit that such a separation of science and religion as *complementary languages* is indeed a valid starting point or "first approximation" for representing the relations between them. Such an approach will avoid some of the mistakes of the past, and it will keep before us the distinctive characteristics of the scientific and religious communities. It will reflect the greater humility displayed by both scientists and theologians in disavowing any sweeping claims of all-inclusive truth. Nevertheless we will maintain that we cannot stop with an absolute separation of spheres, and we will argue that there are significant possibilities for dialogue. Among the considerations that will lead to this conclusion are the following:

First, we will propose that despite the differences between the two fields there are also *significant parallels in their methods.* It will be suggested in Part Two that there are similarities in the interaction of experience and interpretation, in the use of models and analogies, and in the role of the community of inquiry in the two areas. Personal involvement in science and in religion differ in degree, but there is no absolute dichotomy of "objectivity" versus "subjectivity," since the knower makes an important contribution to all knowledge. We will maintain that religious language, although used primarily in the context of worship, does make cognitive claims about reality, in addition to the noncognitive functions it serves. Moreover, revelation cannot be divorced from human interpretation, and the revelatory power of past events is known in their ability to illuminate present experience. We will, in short, argue that science is a more human enterprise, and that theology is a more self-critical undertaking, than is indicated in most of the recent discussions.

Second, it will be urged that we must seek *an integrated worldview.* "Complementary perspectives" are, after all, perspectives on a single world. Both scientific and religious language are realistic and referential in intent; in neither case can one remain satisfied with "useful fictions." The two sets of statements must contribute to a coherent interpretation of all experience, rather than remain as unrelated languages. This search for unity is in part motivated by the desire for coherence of thought in place of compartmentalization and intellectual isolation, which cut off dialogue. But it is also an implication of the biblical conviction that God is Creator and Lord of all that is, and not simply of man's interior life or his future salvation. To be sure, religion must never be identified too closely with a metaphysical system or forced to fit into a neat and final synthesis that claims to encompass all reality. Scientists, for their part, legitimately resist any imposition of alien metaphysical systems imported from outside their own work. But both scientist and theologian inevitably use metaphysical categories whether they intend to or not; and each can contribute to tentative attempts at a coherent view of reality, without any violation of his own integrity.

Third, we will defend the importance of *a theology of nature.* Though theology does indeed start from historical revelation and the realm of personal existence, it should not stop there. Most contemporary theological works say very little about nature. Discussions of providence, for example, refer extensively to God's activity in history but are silent about his activity in nature. What, then, was God's role in the long stretches of cosmic time before man's appearance? Is a sharp distinction between history and nature tenable, if nature itself has a history and if man is rooted in nature? In neo-orthodoxy, nature is the unredeemed setting for man's redemption; but has God as Creator done so little to anticipate his work as Redeemer that the realm of nature is completely separate from the realm of grace? In existentialism, nature is the impersonal stage for the drama of personal existence; but is Christianity to be so radically interiorized that nature is left devoid of meaning? The view we will propose is not a new "natural theology" (that is, an argument for God from the evidence in nature), but rather a "theology of nature," an attempt to view the natural order in the framework of theological ideas derived primarily from the interpretation of historical revelation and religious experience.

Fourth, from the scientific side, *a new view of nature* forces us to reexamine our ideas of God's relation to the world. Tradition pictured a static world, created initially in its present form. In the seventeenth century, after Newton, the image of watch and watchmaker seemed appropriate. Today, the dynamic and temporal character of a growing, evolving universe (of which biological evolution is only one facet) must be taken seriously in theology. We will suggest (Chapter 12) a concept of *"continuing creation"* which, it is hoped, is consistent with both the biblical understanding of God and the scientific understanding of nature. We will examine (Chapter 13) the possibilities and the limitations in using the ideas of the "process philosophy" of Whitehead as a means of describing divine creativity in temporal process; we will find it necessary to adapt (rather than to adopt) his categories of thought to express the biblical view of divine sovereignty, but we will agree with his conclusions concerning the temporality of God. We cannot remain content with the idea of unrelated "complementary languages" if the same natural order studied by the scientist is regarded by the theologian as the object of providential action.

Let us turn now from the issue of methodology to that of *man's relation to nature*. Historically, one of the initial responses to the rise of science was the attempt to preserve the uniqueness of man by postulating within a mechanical picture of nature various gaps in which entities of another kind could operate. Thus Descartes upheld a *mind-body dualism*, with mind as a separate immaterial entity, free and rational, inhabiting and controlling a machine-like body. At a later point the vitalists proposed another type of gap in the physical order, a specific life principle or vital force influencing matter. Traditional religion has often imagined a spiritual soul inside a material body, and has set man apart from the rest of nature.

But with the advance of science, *such gaps in the physical order* have been increasingly difficult to defend. There is no clear line between the living and the nonliving, and there now seems to be nothing in principle to prevent the laboratory synthesis of life from "inert chemicals." In Chapter 11 a number of lines of scientific research are summarized—the discovery of DNA as the "genetic code" that controls life processes, the construction of computers that duplicate certain features of human thought, the design of target-seeking missiles that display "purposeful" behavior, and so forth. Such findings have led some interpreters to conclude that man is essentially a complex deterministic mechanism explainable in physico-chemical terms. Such a viewpoint is *reductionistic*—that is, it assumes that the behavior of any system can be exhaustively explained by the laws governing the behavior of its component parts. Briefly put, reductionism is taken to imply that religion is just psychology, psychology is basically biology, biology is the chemistry of large molecules, whose atoms obey the laws of physics, which will ultimately account for everything!

In this situation, the approach of *"complementary languages"* provides a way of acknowledging both the special characteristics of man and the findings of science, without reverting to dualism. Here *mind* and *brain* are not two separate entities, but the same set of events viewed from two perspectives—from within and from without. *Purpose* and *mechanism* are not mutually exclusive—they are alternative ways of analyzing the same system. An act is *free* when described in actor-language and *determined* when described in spectator-language. Such proposals, which will be elaborated in Part Three, do not posit any gaps in scientific explanations into which "extra" entities might enter. A mechanistic explanation may be complete in its own terms, and may fully answer one set of questions, but it does not answer other types of questions; diverse models and conceptual schemes may be valuable for diverse purposes. In general, "either/or" dichotomies turn out to be not mutually exclusive competitors but alternative types of analysis useful in differing contexts.

But it will be suggested that in each of these cases we must go on to ask how the aspects of man which give rise to such complementary languages are related to each other; we must seek *a unitary view of man* which admits *many-leveled complexity*. We will attempt to reply to reductionism by defending the use of concepts and theories, at higher organizational levels, which are not reducible to lower-level concepts. Thereby we can give specific meaning to the otherwise vague proposition that "the whole is more than the sum of its parts." Our interpretation of living beings is neither mechanistic nor vitalistic but organismic. No elusive entities of the sort postulated by vitalists or dualists are assumed, but the distinctive behavior of integrated totalities and the emergence of new characteristics at higher levels are indicated. We will also maintain that a dualism of body and soul fails to express the unity of the human person which both modern science and the Bible itself assert. We will see man as an integral self, a psychosomatic being incorporating many interrelated levels of activity; hopefully this view can do justice to both biological and theological insights concerning man.

Such an interpretation must allow for both *man's kinship with nature* and *his transcendence of nature*. Until the last century, man was taken to be radically different from all other beings. Darwin's generation stressed the similarities between man and animal life, partly to bolster the case for man's evolutionary ancestry. But contemporary biologists are impressed with the uniqueness of many human capacities (rational decision, symbolic language, cultural evolution). We will propose that the idea of emergence admits genuine novelty in evolutionary history, without requiring any absolute ontological gaps. Moreover, a new understanding of nature is offered in recent science—not as a deterministic mechanism but as a dynamic interactive process, with indeterminacy at the atomic level and alternative potentialities for the future. A responsiveness analogous to a rudimentary mental life exists far down the scale of living beings. We may legitimately interpret the lower in terms of the higher and understand the part in terms of the whole, as well as vice versa. Such considerations will enable us to recognize both continuity and discontinuity between man and nature.

A common pattern will thus appear as we discuss problems of method and as we examine particular scientific theories and their implications for our views of the relation of God and man to nature. First we will note the difficulties in *dualistic* schemes and postulated gaps in the scientific account, on the one hand, and the inadequacies of *reductionistic* interpretations, on the other. Second, the idea of *complementary languages* will allow us to emphasize the differences between scientific and religious questions, and the usefulness of alternative conceptual schemes in talking about man or nature in a variety of contexts. Third, we will explore some categories for analyzing *the structures of reality* to which these complementary languages might be applicable. This exploration will be tentative and partial, and will not yield any neat all-inclusive synthesis; it must recognize the diversity of human experience and the limitations of human understanding. Its immediate goal will be *dialogue between the religious and the scientific communities*, each of which must respect the integrity of the other and resist the temptation to impose its own categories of thought on the other. Because religious and scientific questions have so often been confused in the past, the initial task is to disentangle them; only then can new attempts at synthesis avoid distorting the unique genius of each.

Before starting this undertaking, the objectives and scope of this volume need to be defined:

1. *"Science"* will refer to *the natural sciences*; except for tangential comments, the social sciences are not explored. Although the author is himself a physicist, he has tried to maintain a balance between problems in the physical and the biological sciences. For present purposes we will define *"nature"* as the object of study of the natural sciences; this will leave for further scrutiny broader definitions in which all aspects of man are considered part of nature, or in which nature includes nonscientific characteristics such as beauty.

2. We will analyze *science as a form of knowledge* in its impact on human thought, rather than science as technology in its impact on human society. In other words, we will deal with "pure science" (scientific ideas, methods, theories, and ways of looking at the universe) rather than "applied science" (practical inventions, industrial processes, the instruments of war and peace). Applied science raises many important ethical and social issues, but these are not discussed here.[1]

3. We will consider *religion in the West*, primarily various forms of *Christianity*—and not, except incidentally, the religions of Asia. "Biblical religion" refers to the dominant viewpoint of the Bible, which has shaped the common assumptions of Judaism, Roman Catholicism, and Protestantism—such as the doctrine of creation or the idea of an active and purposeful God. The author's own perspective is that of liberal Protestantism, but the viewpoints of other Western traditions are frequently indicated.

4. In dealing with these problems we have two objectives: *to compare alternative positions* and *to suggest a consistent constructive position* in relation to these alternatives. Although one of these objectives or the other may be predominant in a given section, the intention to include both of them is a distinctive feature of this vol-

---

1. The relation of religion to applied science is discussed in Ian G. Barbour, *Christianity and the Scientist* (New York: Association Press, 1960). Among the problems considered are the motives for scientific research, ethical choices and the social responsibility of the scientist, public policy decisions involving the uses of science, and the impact of a technological orientation on human values.

ume. These goals are combined by employing a "dialectic" method in which aspects of several schools of thought are brought together into a constructive synthesis. The author's viewpoint, in other words, is defined within the context of recent discussion of these issues.

Within these limits, the book aims at *comprehensiveness* in three senses: (1) in including problems of history, of method, and of content; (2) in drawing from both the physical[2] and biological sciences on the one hand, and both theology and philosophy, on the other; and (3) in taking a comparative approach to alternative interpretations. It is designed to provide an over-all view of contemporary issues, and for this reason some sections are somewhat condensed and contain only summaries of arguments. It is not intended to substitute for more detailed treatments of more limited topics, but rather to direct the reader to such works (indicated in the footnotes[3]) and to help him in understanding and comparing them.

Some preliminary *distinctions among terms* may contribute to clarity. *Religion*, broadly defined, is total life-orientation in response to what is deemed worthy of ultimate concern and devotion (these concepts are discussed in Chapter 8). Like the term "science," it refers to a many-faceted phenomenon, expressed in a community of people embodying particular traditions and assumptions, a complex set of institutions and practices and beliefs. *Theology* is systematic reflection about the beliefs of a particular religious community. *Philosophy of religion* is the use of the critical methods of philosophy to clarify the assumptions and concepts of various religious traditions. (*Philosophy of science* serves a similar function for the

2. Theories of the origin of the universe (and their relation to the doctrine of creation) are presented in Chapter 12 below. Limitations of length prevented the inclusion of a separate chapter on astronomy, dealing with such additional problems as the second law of thermodynamics and the "heat death" of the sun (and the doctrine of eschatology or "last things"), the status of space and time in relativity (and the temporality of God), and the possibility of intelligent life on other planets (and the doctrines of man and Christ). I have discussed these problems briefly in a chapter in *New Frontiers of Christianity*, ed R. Raughley (New York: Association Press, 1962).

3. Full bibliographical information is given only in the first footnote in which a volume is mentioned (the page on which this footnote occurs can be found in the Index). The symbol "PB" indicates the availability of a *paperbound* edition—from the same publisher as the hard-cover edition unless otherwise stated; an asterisk indicates that all page references cited from that volume are from the paperbound edition.

sciences.) Among the areas of classical philosophy that bear on religion (and on science), *epistemology* deals with the nature of knowledge (methods of inquiry, criteria of truth, the role of the knower, the status of theories), and *metaphysics* deals with the most general categories for interpreting the structure of reality (time, causality, mind, matter, and so forth). Many authors today conceive the task of philosophy to be the *analysis of language* used in various areas of human life in terms of the functions it serves (see Chapter 9).

In these terms, a central concern of this volume is the relationship between *philosophy of religion* and *philosophy of science*, that is, comparative questions of epistemology, metaphysics, and language analysis in the two fields. Scientists and theologians have usually tried to relate science directly to religion, neglecting the contribution philosophy can make to the clarification of issues. On the other hand, professional philosophers have often had little contact with either the scientific or the religious community, and their abstract formulations sometimes bear little resemblance to what scientists and theologians are actually doing. The point of departure for philosophy of religion must be the worshiping community and its theological ideas; only then can philosophy serve a function both critical and relevant to religion. Similarly, philosophy of science must be based on the actual practice of scientific work.

Since we do not presuppose that our various readers will be familiar with the jargon of all three fields (science, religion, and philosophy), we have attempted to discuss current thought in these areas without using their respective technical terminology. One group to whom these chapters are addressed is composed of scientists and science students who are interested in the wider implications of their work and of its methods. A second consists of religious leaders, seminary students, and laymen concerned with intellectual problems raised by contemporary science. A number of universities and seminaries have in the last decade introduced courses in "Science and Religion" (or broader studies in "Religion and Culture" which deal with the relation of religion to science as well as to art, literature, psychology, and so forth); there is need for a comprehensive text for such courses. But the largest group we have had in mind includes those persons, whatever their professional field, who recognize the importance of scientific and religious ideas in the modern world and are concerned about the relation between them. Whitehead has called science and religion "the two strongest general forces which influence men." He wrote:

> When we consider what religion is for mankind and what science is, it is no exaggeration to say that the future course of history depends upon the decision of this generation as to the relations between them.[4]

4. Alfred N. Whitehead, *Science and the Modern World* (New York: The Macmillan Company, 1925; Cambridge: Cambridge University Press, 1925; Mentor PB°), p. 180.

PART ONE

Religion and the History of Science

2

Physics and Metaphysics
in the Seventeenth Century

The seventeenth century was a period of such crucial and rapid change in outlook that we may justifiably speak of the birth of modern science in this "century of genius." Two landmarks in the growth of the new science were Galileo's *Dialogues* (1632) and Newton's *Principia* (1687). The thought of these two men, whose lives span the century, illuminates the origins of the issues between science and religion which are our concern. It was in the physical sciences that the new intellectual climate first captured the imaginations of men and became the basis for a new world-view. To see the extent of the transition wrought, we will start by outlining briefly certain assumptions of the Middle Ages that were challenged in the seventeenth century. We will look successively at "The Medieval World-Drama," "Galileo's 'Two New Sciences,'" and "The Newtonian World-Machine." Two final sections summarize the positive contributions of religion to the new science and the major points of conflict.

Our objective is to analyze how views of God and man were altered during this century by the changing perspectives concerning *God's relation to nature* and *man's relation to nature*. Interpretations of these relationships were influenced by new ideas about the character of nature, and about ways of knowing nature and ways of knowing God. We will accordingly indicate briefly the approaches taken by medieval thought, by Galileo, and then by Newton, to the following topics: (1) methods in science, (2) the character of nature, (3) methods in theology, (4) God and his relation to nature, and (5) man and his relation to nature. We must ask why the new science and its methods had such an impact on religion in this crucial period. From physics men drew both metaphysical and epistemological conclusions that transformed their outlook and remolded their theology. We will find that Newton's view of God as the cosmic watchmaker was the correlate of his view of the world as a well-designed watch.

These chapters of *historical background* do not attempt to describe all the complex factors in the growth of modern thought. A few pivotal figures have been selected in order to sketch the origins of contemporary issues. In addition, the arbitrary choice of five topics involves an oversimplified schematism whose only excuse is the need for a brief introduction to problems of science and religion in the twentieth century. The section on the Middle Ages, which is included so that the novelty of seventeenth-century ideas will be apparent, contains only the barest outline. For thorough analyses of these historical developments the reader is referred to the studies listed in the footnotes.

I. The Medieval World-Drama

1. Methods in Science: Explanation by Purposes

For what type of explanation of an event should one search? What constitutes an adequate understanding of an occurrence? To what sort of questions about nature is it most important to seek answers? The Middle Ages sought explanations in terms of the true *form* or intelligible *essence* of an object and the *purpose* it fulfilled. The thirteenth-century recovery of Greek science, together with Thomas Aquinas' magnificent synthesis of Christian theology and Aristotelian philosophy, established in Christendom a distinctive approach to the explanation of nature that dominated Western thought until the seventeenth century.

Why do objects fall? For Aristotle and his followers, motion is explained by the tendency of each thing to seek its own natural resting-place. The "natural place" of fire is up, and that of earth is down. Heavier objects have a stronger tendency downward, so they must fall more rapidly. The *end* of the motion—in the sense both of "terminus" and of "purpose"—was of more interest than the intervening process. Why does an acorn grow? To become an oak. Why is there rain? To nourish crops. Causality is described by *future goals* ("final causes") and *innate tendencies* ("formal causes"), not just by the effects of past events ("efficient causes") acting on passive materials ("material causes"). The future goal need not be consciously entertained by an entity (for example, an acorn), but is built into its structure so that by its own nature it achieves the fulfillment of the end appropriate to its kind.

Attention was directed to the *final end* and not to the detailed process of change from moment to moment. The behavior of each creature follows from its essential nature, defined in terms of its function. If every creature realizes its potentialities, the illuminating questions to be asked concern the uses of things and what they can do. The central feature of all changes, in this view, is the transformation of *potentiality* into *actuality*. Logical connections, not simply temporal ones, must be traced. The categories of explanation are essence and potentiality, not mass and force connected by laws in space and time.[1]

This search for purposes was in part the result of conceiving every object as having a place in a cosmic hierarchy, the creation of *a purposeful God*. Suppose one asks: why does water boil at one temperature and not some other? The contemporary scientist will perhaps relate this temperature to other facts and laws and theories of molecular structure, but will eventually reach a point when he says: this is simply a brute fact, and it is meaningless to ask why it is thus. But the medieval tradition, going back to Plato and Aristotle, insisted that there must be a reason if the world is not irrational. God's purposes in creating things, though not always discernible, constitute the ultimate explanation of their behavior.

Because of this assumption of the rationality of the universe, both Greek and medieval science were primarily *deductive* (starting

1. See William C. Dampier, A *History of Science and Its Relations with Philosophy and Religion*, 4th ed. (Cambridge: Cambridge University Press, 1948), Chap. 2; also A. C. Crombie, *Medieval and Early Modern Science*, 2 vols. (Cambridge, Mass.: Harvard University Press, 1961; Doubleday PB); R. G. Collingwood, *The Idea of Nature* (Oxford: Clarendon Press, 1945; PB).

from general principles and reasoning to particular exemplifications of those principles) rather than inductive (starting from particular observations and generalizing from them). This dominance of deductive logic was closely related to the classical idea, particularly prominent in Plato, that knowledge is contemplation of *the perfect forms* of eternal truth, rather than observation of their imperfect embodiment in the changing world. The way a thing behaves was also linked with its status in the over-all scheme. The goal was not primarily, as in modern science, the description, prediction, and control of a limited phenomenon, but the understanding and contemplation of the meaning of the part in relation to the whole and, above all, to God. This does not mean that observation was totally absent from Aristotelian and medieval science. Many of their conclusions were in conformity with common experience. Aristotle had done considerable biological classification, which required careful observation. But the categories of teleology (purpose) did not in general lend themselves to *theories* that could be tested by further *experiment*. We shall see that Galileo deliberately set aside all questions of purpose and "final cause," and introduced a totally different kind of concept for the interpretation of nature.

2. Nature as a Hierarchy of Beings

Aristotelian cosmology and Christian theology were merged to form *the medieval picture of the universe*. Earth was the fixed central sphere surrounded by the concentric spheres of the heavens. The planets, in the Ptolemaic scheme, followed circles whose centers were attached to moving spheres; heavenly objects, being perfect and incorruptible, were said to make use only of the perfect form, the circle. The scheme was easily visualized and corresponded to the commonsense experience of the solidity of the earth. Here *position* and *destiny* coincided. Man was unique and central in both location and importance; the divine was more perfect and comprehensive, separated both geographically and metaphysically from the created order. Within this over-all pattern, every entity from greatest to least had its status and purpose in the graded *hierarchy of reality*. Everything was in its neatly arranged place in an integrated total plan. It was a "law-abiding world," but the laws were moral and not mechanical. This was the medieval view of the universe which the new science was to challenge.

There were, to be sure, various *attitudes toward nature* in tension during the Middle Ages. At times man's spiritual destiny seemed to so outweigh temporal relationships that the world was treated as a great allegory whose essential secret was its religious meaning, not its operation or its causes. Symbolic interpretations of nature were sometimes derived from ancient legends unrelated to any factual observations. At other times, particularly among the common people, nature seemed to be the seat of evil forces and demonic powers, as it had been to most of the Hellenistic world; it was to be a long struggle before science would be free from association with magic, sorcery, and astrology. To other men the sense of God's creation was overpowering; for St. Francis, for example, nature became a sacrament of the divine. Among the schoolmen, the conviction of God's rationality also encouraged an affirmative attitude toward nature which, we will suggest later, contributed indirectly to the rise of science.

Medieval thought was in general *realistic* in the sense that it held the world to be real as perceived, experienced, and understood. The rational powers of the intellect were believed to be capable of grasping the true essence of the world. Nature was immediately present to man and clearly intelligible to his mind. Color and warmth, love and purpose, were taken as integral characteristics of existing objects. The possibility of knowledge of the external world was never seriously questioned, as it has been in modern philosophy since Descartes. Note finally that nature was assumed to be essentially *static*, with all its species created in their present forms. It was a completed world in which there could be no fundamental novelty except as God acts in it. However, within the life of each creature there could be outward change and development as its God-given potentialities unfold. One might say that the organism provided the basic image of nature (rather than the machine, as in the Newtonian era); but the basic form of each organism was thought to be unchanging—an assumption that was not widely challenged until Darwin's day.

3. Methods in Theology: Reason and Revelation

To understand some of the subsequent conflicts of science and religion, we must briefly summarize the sources of authority in medieval theology. Scholastic thought was based on both *reason* and *revelation*, showing again the characteristic synthesis of elements from Greek philosophy and biblical faith. This double structure is found, for example, in ethics: there is the natural law of reason discoverable by examining man's built-in potentialities and ends, and there is the divine law given in God's direct commandments. The knowledge of God is likewise the subject of both *natural* and *revealed* theology. In each case the "natural" truths are open to all men, known by the unaided powers of human reason; the "revealed" truths include information, disclosed by God through Christ and the prophets, which has been transmitted through scripture and tradition as preserved by the church. Since all truth is from God, the two basic sources will be consistent with each other.

In Aquinas' system, *reason* is thus an important preamble to faith. It can establish some theological truths, including the existence of God.[2] The teleological argument leads from the evidence of design in nature to the idea of an intelligent Designer. The cosmological argument moves from the contingency of the world to its necessary ground, a First Cause of all effects. God has at least partially disclosed himself in the universe. But this natural theology remained secondary to revealed theology; it was not the main source of knowledge of God, as it was to become for many thinkers in the seventeenth and eighteenth centuries.

Revelation is necessary, according to Aquinas, because the most important theological truths are not accessible to reason. God's existence is rationally demonstrable, but not the trinity or the incarnation. The divine plan of salvation was made known by God himself, through the channels he chose to establish. Moreover not all men are philosophers; even those truths that can be proven philosophically have been made more readily available to the average man. *Faith* is thus primarily the acceptance of revealed truths on the authority of the church, rather than (as for the Reformers) an attitude of trust and commitment in direct personal relationship to God as known in Christ. In medieval thought the church is not only the channel of divine grace, mediated through Christ's death and the efficacy of the sacraments, but also the channel of divine truth, imparted through Christ's teaching and transmitted by the continuing community which is his chosen instrument.

The Bible was only one element in this total system of thought, and scripture was considered authoritative only as interpreted by

---

2. See St. Thomas Aquinas, *Summa Theologia*, Part I, Questions 2 and 12; Étienne Gilson, *The Christian Philosophy of Thomas Aquinas* (New York: Random House, 1956).

the church; moreover the doctrine of "levels of truth" allowed some flexibility for allegorical interpretation and poetic meaning. The conflict between science and scripture, when it arose, was thus not as acute for Catholicism as for the Protestant biblicism of the early seventeenth century. Instead, the new science represented for the Roman church a challenge to an integral intellectual scheme, the strength as well as the dangers of which lay in its synthesis of philosophical and biblical elements. The temptation was for the church to throw its authority behind this whole system of thought, including aspects that were dependent on Aristotelian assumptions.

4. God as the Supreme Good

In Aquinas' conception of God, Aristotle's *Unmoved Mover* and the Bible's *personal Father* had become one. The metaphysical First Cause of Greek philosophy was identified with the dynamic purposeful Creator of biblical theology. Though at times the more abstract philosophical attributes (omniscience, omnipotence, omnipresence, eternity) may seem to have predominated over more personalistic biblical images (Father, Judge, Saviour), Aquinas' writing clearly pictures a God who is concerned about man's redemption. We must here restrict ourselves to some comments on the Thomistic understanding of God's relation to nature.

The *cosmological argument* has sometimes been stated in terms of a causal chain: every event must have a cause, which in turn must be the effect of an earlier cause, and so forth, back to a First Cause. This conclusion could be escaped, however, if one postulated an infinite sequence of events. But as Aquinas presents the argument, the crucial feature of all events in the world—whether in a finite or an infinite series—is their contingency, the fact that they might not have occurred. Why is there anything, rather than nothing? Every entity in the world is dependent on other entities, and thus sharply distinguished from God, a necessary being whose existence is not dependent on the existence of other beings. Aquinas also gives the argument from design; but the argument did not exclusively determine his concept of God (as it did for many writers in the seventeenth and eighteenth centuries); for him the intelligent Designer was always the biblical Creator.

Moreover, in contrast with the Deism of the Enlightenment, Aquinas portrays God as *continuing ruler of nature*, and not just as its original creator. His governance is an active power sustaining and working through the natural order. God is the "prime cause" of every event, but there are also "secondary causes" through which he works. Aquinas believed that natural processes can be explained in relative independence of any direct acts of God, and yet their functioning depends on power not inherent in them, but provided by God's sustaining activity; divine *concurrence* is required for anything to happen. God is also the Supreme Good, the goal of nature. His activities as creator, ruler, and goal are not divided temporally as past, present, and future, for these functions interpenetrate each other. As the Supreme Good, he draws all things in the present toward their appointed ends; he is the divine harmony of all good, attracting each being toward perfection and toward himself. In this sense, Dante can say it is "love that moves the heavens and all the stars," for all things aspire to fulfill God's will.

God has *various ways of accomplishing his will*, beyond his action as Creator and Supreme Good. He works through natural causes. He governs the world through angels, and through the influence of celestial bodies. He acts directly through miracles to accomplish specific results and display his power. God's influence on nature is thus rich and complex, including a number of functions operating at various levels. The new concept of nature that developed with the emerging science was to influence drastically the interpretation of these relationships and the concept of God they imply.

5. Man as Center of the Cosmic Drama

If God was the supreme member of the hierarchy of being in medieval thought, man was *the center of the created order*. Nature was subordinate to man. The functions of creatures below him in the scale were explained mainly by their role in human purposes, for the world was designed to subserve man's interests. Nature was primarily the stage setting for the drama of God and man. World history was understood to follow the divine plan, whose epochs can be symbolized by five words: Creation, Covenant, Christ, Church, Consummation. The cosmic drama centers in God's redemptive act for the salvation of sinful man: the incarnation of Christ and his atoning death. Man's goal is union with God, and salvation lies in aligning his purposes with God's, making use of the means of grace God has appointed. Man is a union of mortal body and immortal soul. He is a free and rational being, whose duty and fulfillment lie in conforming at once to reason and to God's will. Everything else is to be scrutinized for its significance in man's pilgrimage and its purpose in the divine scheme leading ultimately up to God. Man, in this view, differs radically from all other creatures.

This was the total plan, the coherent pattern into which all things fitted and from which they derived their significance. It was a unified hierarchical order in which each thing played its part, striving to achieve its essential purpose. All nature served man, and man served God. Science, cosmology, history, and theology all expressed the same pattern of meaning. This, in briefest outline, was the medieval world-view, which in its main features was not greatly altered by the Reformation, but which was to be drastically transformed by the impact of modern science.

II. GALILEO'S "TWO NEW SCIENCES"

1. Methods in Science: Mathematics and Observation

How did the new science of the seventeenth century differ from that of the Middle Ages? The key feature was the new combination of mathematical reasoning and experimental observation. A century before Galileo, the importance of *mathematical simplicity* had already been defended by Copernicus.[3] The Ptolemaic scheme, in which the sun and planets were assumed to revolve around the earth, had required more and more amendments, by adding wheels within wheels, in order to agree with the astronomical data available; these additions were cumbersome and arbitrary. The Copernican model, in which the planets and the earth revolve around the sun, agreed with observations with comparable accuracy, and was much simpler mathematically. Copernicus extolled the beauty of a small number of concentric circles, much in the Pythagorean tradition of belief in the harmony of numbers. In the absence of any new data, the support he received was largely philosophical in character, for the revival of Platonism was beginning to challenge the dominance of Aristotle's authority.

In the writing of Kepler early in the seventeenth century, belief in *mathematical harmony* found even more rhapsodic expression. He was able to show that the accurate observational data he inherited from Tycho Brahe were consistent with a modification of

---

3. In addition to his *De Revolutionibus* (1543), see Thomas S. Kuhn, *The Copernican Revolution* (Cambridge, Mass.: Harvard University Press, 1957; Vintage PB); Arthur Koestler, *The Sleep Walkers* (New York: The Macmillan Co., 1959; Penguin PB).

the Copernican system, namely the assumption of elliptical rather than circular planetary orbits. Kepler saw "geometrical perfection" itself as the reason why the planets follow mathematically exact orbits. In his belief in "the mystery of number" and "the music of the spheres," as in his conviction that "God ever geometrizes," there were aesthetic and religious as well as scientific motives.[4] Yet in the process of stressing precise observations and the display of mathematical relationships, an important change was occurring: the universe was increasingly seen as a mathematical structure. The significant relationships were quantitative, not qualitative as for Aristotle. Without the achievements of mathematics neither the seventeenth-century scientific revolution nor the revolution in twentieth-century physics would have been possible.

It was in the work[5] of Galileo (1564–1642) that this mathematical approach was combined with an emphasis on experimentation. He has rightly been called the father of modern science, for in his work the distinctive features of the new methodology first found explicit formulation and fruitful practice. The combination of *theory* with *experiment* can of course be traced back to earlier centuries (scholars in northern Italy in the fifteenth century, Ockhamists at Oxford in the fourteenth century, and such figures as Archimedes in ancient Greece), but it became explicit in Galileo's careful investigations. Whitehead has described the new attitude:

> This new tinge to modern minds is a vehement and passionate interest in the relation of general principles to irreducible and stubborn facts. All the world over and at all times there have been practical men absorbed in "irreducible and stubborn facts"; all the world over and at all times there have been men of philosophic temperament who have been absorbed in the weaving of general principles. It is the union of passionate interest in the detailed facts with equal devotion to abstract generalization which forms the novelty.[6]

Galileo sometimes described "thought-experiments" that were apparently never actually carried out; in several passages he implies that experiments are needed only to convince his opponents of his mathematical conclusions. The rationalistic component of science

4. See Gerald Holton, "Johannes Kepler's Universe, Its Physics and Metaphysics," *American Journal of Physics*, Vol. 24 (1956), 340.

5. Galileo, *Dialogues* (1632), trans. T. Salusbury (Chicago: University of Chicago Press, 1953); see also Charles C. Gillispie, *The Edge of Objectivity* (Princeton, N.J.: Princeton University Press, 1960), Chap. 1.

6. Whitehead, *Science and the Modern World*, p. 3. Used by permission of The Macmillan Company and Cambridge University Press.

tended to predominate over the empirical component until later in the century. Yet Galileo did make extensive use of experiments. His description of the discovery of the equations of accelerated motion, using a ball rolling down an inclined plane, is a classic example of the combination of induction and deduction, reasoning back and forth between theory and experiment. He used concepts such as length, time, and velocity, which could be tied to measurements and expressed in mathematical symbols. He described how he considered a possible mathematical relationship between velocity and distance and then deduced the expected law this would yield—a deduction which turned out to be incompatible with experimental results. He tried other theoretical assumptions, calculated the equations deducible from them, and made experimental tests of these equations. Here were all the characteristics of the new science: *the distinctive type of concept, the combination of theory and experiment, and the goal of expressing laws of nature as mathematical relationships among measurable variables.*

The *experimental* side of the new science was indeed crucial. It received additional support from various sources, including the improved instruments produced in the growing trades, and the interest in practical problems fostered by developing technologies (such as metallurgy and military weaponry). But it is misleading to identify science with simple *empiricism*, as was done in Galileo's day by Bacon—and more recently by Hume and modern positivism. Bacon believed that science consists of the accumulation and classification of observations. He insisted that induction is the easy road to knowledge: make observations, summarize them, and generalize. Discovery can be a routine and automatic process, carried out, he said, "as by machinery"; only patience is needed, not difficult or abstract thought. The Baconian account leaves out the whole theoretical side of science, and above all it omits the role of creative imagination in the formation of new concepts.

As an example of *an imaginative new concept*, consider Galileo's idea of motion without air resistance (which was the key to the principle of inertia). His contribution here was no mere "careful observation," but a conception of the world as we do *not* experience it. He imagined observed motion to be the resultant of two abstractions, neither of which could be observed alone: a continuing uniform inertial motion and a frictional retarding force. Aristotle's view had been closer to everyday observations; a cart left to itself *does* come to rest if there is no horse to keep it moving. Galileo imagined an idealized frictionless case which, left to itself, would continue to move uniformly. Starting from such an "ideal case," he could argue that the cart comes to rest *not* because of any natural tendency to do so, but because friction hinders its natural (but unobservable) uniform motion.

As another example of the *change in conceptual categories*, consider the motion of a pendulum—say, a stone on a string swinging from a fixed support. To the Aristotelian, the important feature of the motion is the stone's final state—at rest in its lowest position; because it is constrained by the string, it takes several minutes to achieve this state by a diminishing back-and-forth motion. To Galileo, by contrast, the coming-to-rest of the pendulum is incidental and the interesting property is that it almost repeats its motion (that is, air friction is a secondary feature). The significant fact is that in a given swing the stone does not stop in the bottom position, but continues to move to the opposite extreme (because of its inertia). Galileo saw the pendulum's motion in a new way, and was led to ask a very different set of questions about it, and only then could he perform his distinctive set of experiments.

Teleological explanation, characteristic of earlier thought, had given way to *descriptive explanation*. Galileo asked not *why* objects fall, but *how* they fall. He was content to describe how phenomena progress, completely ignoring questions about the purposes they serve, which he saw as irrelevant to the problems in which he was interested. We cannot presume to know the ends of the Almighty, he suggested, but we can investigate the precise ways in which they are accomplished. The questions that were being asked of nature were fundamentally different from those the Middle Ages had asked. Interest was being directed not to final causes operating toward the future, nor to formal causes in the essence of the object, but to *efficient causes*. A limited area of phenomenal behavior was being described, apart from any all-embracing metaphysical system. In all these ways Galileo's work embodied the approach typical of modern science, and led to a new ideal of what it means to explain something.

2. Nature as Particles in Motion

Galileo's writing is notable not only for its exemplification of the methods of the new science but also for its preliminary formulation of a new picture of nature as *matter-in-motion*. The "corpuscular philosophy" of the seventeenth century was not yet the nineteenth-century "atomic theory" which, after Dalton, was supported by considerable empirical evidence. Yet it was more than a revival of the "atomism" of Democritus which had been entirely philosophical and speculative in character. What Galileo did was to extrapolate from his own work; he assumed that the ultimate constituents of nature were exhaustively describable *in the same categories* that he found to be so powerful in analyzing the motion of observable objects.

The categories of *mass, space,* and *time* were relatively unimportant to the scholastics, since temporal relations were considered accidental to the true character of an object. In Galileo's thought these categories were central because they could be treated mathematically. The world was taken to be composed of particles to which were ascribed only two properties: mass and velocity. Change no longer meant transition from potentiality to actuality, but the rearrangement of particles in time and space. During the seventeenth century the concepts with which the physicist could deal so successfully were gradually taken to characterize the real world without remainder. Galileo never elaborated a mechanistic view of nature, but some of the key assumptions of such a view are evident in his writings.

Galileo called mass and velocity *"primary qualities,"* characteristic of the objective world independent of the observer, and distinguished them from *"secondary qualities,"* such as color and temperature, which he believed to be purely subjective reactions of the senses to the world. Pain is in me, not in the pin which pricks me; so also heat and sound were said to reside in the mind, not in the object observed. Galileo concluded:

> I cannot believe that there exists in external bodies anything, other than their size, shape or motion (slow or rapid), which could excite in us our tastes, sounds, and odors. And indeed I should judge that, if ears, tongues, and noses be taken away, the number, shape, and motion of bodies would remain, but not their tastes, sounds, and odors. ... And I again judge that heat is altogether subjective.[7]

How did Galileo decide which qualities were to be considered "primary"? He said that his criterion was "permanence," but actu-

---

7. Galileo, *The Assayer*, trans. A. C. Danto for *Introduction to Contemporary Civilization in the West*, 2nd ed. (New York: Columbia University Press); reprinted in A. C. Danto and S. Morgenbesser, eds., *Philosophy of Science* (New York: Meridian PB, 1960), p. 30.

ally the determinative characteristic seems to have been measurability and reduction to mathematical representation. Ironically it is precisely these variables (mass and velocity) which in relativity theory turn out *not* to be independent of the observer.

It was Galileo's contemporary, Descartes, who gave the most complete philosophical exposition of this distinction between primary and secondary qualities, developed into a radical *dualism of matter and mind*. The external world is self-sufficient *matter* extended in space. Mathematics, which for Descartes was always the exemplar of the "clear and distinct ideas" of which one could be certain, was the key to understanding nature. Final causes were to be firmly excluded from explanations of the world. *Mind*, on the other hand, was unextended "thinking substance," defined in terms so dissimilar to those of matter that any possible interaction between such diverse entities is difficult to imagine. The whole range of life between mind and matter was put by Descartes on the side of matter; he claimed that all animals are automata, complex machines without intelligence or feeling. Even man's body was to be treated as a machine. Here was an engineer's view of nature that was to have profound impact on generations of scientists. Descartes allowed one exception, the mind of man: he postulated a gap in the chain of physical causes, wherein mental events (and the realm of religion) are located. To mind also were relegated all the qualities with which the new science could not deal, making it, in Randall's words, "a ready dumping ground for everything in experience which physics did not read in mechanical nature."[8]

The metaphysical chasm separating *observing mind* and the *observed world,* in the viewpoint set forth by Galileo and developed by Descartes, gave rise to the gamut of epistemological problems with which subsequent philosophy has wrestled. How can one be sure that the physical picture, so utterly different from our experience of the world, describes reality as it is in itself? How can the mind get outside itself to know nature? Does science describe the world as it is, or yield only a convenient ordering of our experience? We shall return later to some of the metaphysical and epistemological problems to which this mechanical view of nature gave rise.

8. John H. Randall, *The Making of the Modern Mind* (Boston: Houghton Mifflin, 1940), p. 268.

3. Methods in Theology: Aristotle, Scripture, and Nature

The scientific ideas of the early seventeenth century were taken to be challenges to the authority of both Aristotle and the Bible. *Aristotle's authority*, enshrined in the Thomistic synthesis, was of course vigorously defended in Roman Catholic circles. A Protestant scholasticism had developed in northern Europe; Luther's follower, Melanchthon, had introduced educational reforms that made extensive use of Aristotle. The metaphysical distinctions made by many Protestant theologians on the Continent late in the sixteenth century, and their practice of citing classical authorities, paralleled those of Catholic scholars. Thus much of the early opposition to science was a product of the respect in which Aristotle was held.

Because this Protestant scholasticism had developed a literalistic view of the Bible, the new scientific theories were also taken as a challenge to *the authority of scripture*. Luther, and even Calvin, had been somewhat flexible in biblical interpretation. For them, the locus of authority was not the verbal text itself, but the person of Christ to whom scripture pointed. Scripture was important as the witness to the redemptive events in which God's love and forgiveness in Christ had been mediated in their personal experience. To the early Reformers, the Living Word is confirmed in man's own experience by the Holy Spirit. But by the beginning of the seventeenth century the Bible was seen by many Protestants as a deposit of *inerrant information*, including information about scientific questions, which had been dictated by God. Rather than being a record of events in which God revealed himself, scripture was itself viewed as infallible knowledge in propositional form verbally imparted by God. Those holding this view opposed the Copernican theory as contrary to biblical passages which implied a geocentric universe.

Galileo himself was a devout Catholic and found *no conflict between his scientific and religious beliefs*. He upheld the importance of scripture but claimed that it reveals not scientific facts but spiritual knowledge for man's salvation, truths that are above reason and could not be discovered by observation. Theologians, he suggested, have no particular competence in astronomy; the Bible rarely touches on such matters, and even then it accommodates to the modes of understanding of its ancient readers, using "the popular manner of speaking" of its day. For scientific knowledge we must use scientific methods of observation. Sense-experience provides evidence which we cannot doubt, and since God is the author of nature as well as the author of scripture, the two sources of knowledge cannot conflict. In one of his letters Galileo wrote:

> I think that in discussions of physical problems we ought to begin not from the authority of scriptural passages but from sense-experiences and necessary demonstrations, for the holy Bible and the phenomena of nature proceed alike from the divine Word. . . . For that reason it appears that nothing physical which sense-experience sets before our eyes, or which necessary demonstrations prove to us, ought to be called in question (much less condemned) upon the testimony of biblical passages which may have some different meaning beneath their words. For the Bible is not chained in every expression to conditions as strict as those which govern all physical effects; nor is God any less excellently revealed in Nature's actions than in the sacred statements of the Bible.[9]

Nature, said Galileo, is the sole source of scientific knowledge; but it is also, along with scripture, a source of theological knowledge, *a way of knowing God.* Natural theology had for centuries been looked on as a preamble to revealed theology; Galileo put *nature* and *scripture* on the same level as avenues to God. His successors were to find in natural theology the primary basis for religious knowledge. Nature was to become the clue to history, not vice versa. The "unclear passages" of scripture were to be interpreted by the "clear results" of the new science.[10] Before long, this independent, natural basis of religion would replace the biblical understanding of revelation.

4. God as First Cause

With final causality dismissed, the idea of God as the Supreme Good toward which all things strive was replaced by God as *First Cause*, understood as the initial link in the chain of efficient causes. With Galileo there began the development whereby God was to become merely the original creator of the interacting atoms in which

---

9. Letter from Galileo to Castelli in 1613, from p. 182 of *Discoveries and Opinions of Galileo* by Stillman Drake. Copyright © 1957 by Stillman Drake. Reprinted by permission of Doubleday & Company, Inc.

10. See John Dillenberger, *Protestant Thought and Natural Science* (New York: Doubleday & Co., 1960), p. 89. See also Basil Willey, *The Seventeenth-Century Background* (London: Chatto & Windus, 1934; Doubleday PB).

resides all subsequent causality. Nature, once created, was considered to be independent and self-sufficient. In medieval as well as Reformation thought, God's concurrence had been a very direct and active relationship; the conviction that God works through natural forces was expressed in the idea that God is the primary cause of every event; secondary natural causes were held to be dependent on God's sustaining power. In the seventeenth century these doctrines were not so much denied as ignored. As attention focused on natural causes, God's role was gradually relegated to that of First Cause.

It is not surprising that some of Galileo's contemporaries feared that man's interest would be totally *diverted from God to nature.* For in the Christian tradition, history and human existence rather than nature have always been the main spheres of encounter with God. Even though in the seventeenth century it was still believed that God had designed the natural order, divine activity in the present was progressively minimized. The scientific enterprise was thus looked on by many spokesmen of the church as a distraction from the main purpose of living, and a diversion from questions of salvation and destiny. Some went further and said that unbridled curiosity would not only absorb man's interest but corrupt and seduce him into pride and self-sufficiency.

There were, even at this early stage, various attempts at the philosophical level to reconcile the picture of *a mechanical world* with *belief in God.* In Descartes' case, the extreme dualism of mind and matter provided a realm for the operation of both God and the human soul. Descartes was impressed by the mathematical rather than the experimental side of the new science. He was a thoroughgoing rationalist; only directly intuited "clear and distinct ideas" provide us with certainty, for sense-impressions are confused and unreliable. The mind apprehends *a priori* ideas which are not dependent on experience for their vindication. Man's idea of God is innate, a primordial apprehension of the divine; God's existence is implied by the idea of God when clearly understood. Thus for Descartes it is through the participation of man's mind in the realm of ideas that God is known. He did hold, however, that in addition to creating the world, God renews it in each instant; he maintained that time is discontinuous, and that but for God's continual re-creation the universe would collapse into nothingness. But the sequence of events in the world is determined by mechanical law and not divine action. The mechanical world of matter goes its own way in radical disjunction from the realms of God and the mind.

The solution proposed by Spinoza[11] went much further by rejecting the traditional concept of God. There is no cosmic purpose, he wrote, for all things occur in accordance with inflexible and objective laws of cause and effect. The world is a mechanical and mathematical order, not in any sense a personal and moral one. Spinoza was willing to use the term "God" to refer to the immutable structure of *the impersonal cosmic order*, but he specifically rejected any idea of God as a purposeful or intelligent being, saying that "neither intellect nor will appertain to God's nature." God is the "infinite substance" of which extension is one attribute, but it has no ethical properties since good and evil are entirely relative to human desires. The harmonious perfection of this world-system can itself be the supreme object of human devotion. True wisdom, he suggested, consists in resignation to the power of the universe; man must come to understand and accept the impartial necessity of inexorable law which governs his life. But Spinoza's response to the theological implications of a mechanical world involved too great a departure from prevalent ideas to be influential in his own century. Most men continued to affirm a traditional view of God along with an increasingly mechanical view of nature.

5. Man as Demoted Spectator

Until the time of Galileo there were no strong reasons for accepting *the Copernican theory*, and there were persuasive arguments against it (such as the apparent absence of stellar parallax). Although the full elaboration of a heliocentric system awaited the formulation of Newton's laws, Galileo found further evidence in its support. In 1610, using the newly invented telescope, he observed the mountains of the moon—clear indication that the moon is an irregular physical object and not a perfect "celestial sphere." Jupiter's moons showed that the earth was not the center of all motions, and the observed phases of Venus fitted perfectly with the Copernican scheme. But anyone accepting the new astronomy had to reorient his thought drastically in many areas. The older cosmology

11. Benedictus de Spinoza, *Ethics*, Part I.

set the eternal celestial realm in opposition to the terrestrial scene of change and decay; the graded "hierarchy of being" approached perfection as it approached the divine. The new cosmology obliterated this distinction between the corruptible and the incorruptible; it applied uniform natural categories to the whole universe. The identity of purpose and place was destroyed, and the total framework of significance was placed in jeopardy.

In particular, *man was demoted* from the center of the universe to a spinning, peripheral planet. Man's uniqueness and the idea of God's particular concern for him seemed in danger. Speculation about life on other planets is not a new phenomenon of the space age; the issue was raised by Galileo's opponents, and the implications of a "plurality of worlds" were extensively discussed during the ensuing century. Nicholas of Cusa and Giordano Bruno had already encountered vehement opposition to their ideas of the infinity of space. The new cosmology was resisted, then, not only because it challenged the authority of Aristotle and scripture, but because it threatened the whole Aristotelian scheme of purpose and meaning in which man's spatial location was correlated with his status in the cosmic hierarchy.

There were thus many factors which contributed to the unhappy page of history in which *Galileo was persecuted* by a defensive church. During the trial Cardinal Bellarmine made an interesting face-saving proposal: the heliocentric model could be used as a convenient calculating device for correlating observations and making predictions, provided it was not defended as a true representation of reality. (Osiander had made a similar proposal in a preface designed to make Copernicus' book more acceptable: "These hypotheses need not be true or even probable if they provide a calculation consistent with observations"; the suggestion resembles the ideas of recent positivists for whom theories are useful fictions for simplifying correlations among observations, rather than representations of reality.) Galileo at first accepted this formula for treating the Copernican theory as "hypothetical"; but in the *Dialogues* his own convictions were but thinly veiled, and in the trial of 1633 his views were condemned.[12]

Galileo's metaphysics left man a stranger in the universe of

---

12. See Giorgio De Santillana, *The Crime of Galileo* (Chicago: University of Chicago Press, 1955).

particles-in-motion which was increasingly taken to be the real world. Burtt suggests:

> We have the first stage in the reading of man quite out of the real and primary realm. His was a life of colors and sounds, of pleasures, of griefs, of passionate loves. Hence the real world must be the world outside of man. ... Man begins to appear for the first time in the history of thought as an irrelevant spectator and insignificant effect of the great mathematical system which is the substance of reality.[13]

Burtt perhaps tends to read back into Galileo's time a world-view that was neither systematically expressed nor widely held until a century later; but many of its constituent elements were already present. The mechanical view of nature Galileo had outlined was developed more fully during the second half of the seventeenth century by Newton and his followers.

III. THE NEWTONIAN WORLD-MACHINE

1. Methods in Science: Experiment and Theory

Sir Isaac Newton (1642–1727) brought to fulfillment the revolution in scientific outlook and the alliance of *mathematics* and *experimentation* which Galileo had pioneered. In his approach the empirical side was even stronger. Newton's invention of calculus was an important contribution, but he was also an ingenious experimenter in mechanics and optics. His method, insofar as he had one, involved the continual interaction of experiment and theory. But it should be underscored that there are no rules for discovering the *concepts* through which this may occur fruitfully. New concepts are the product, not of observation or of mathematical deduction alone, not even of the two together, but of creative imagination.

In the case of *the law of gravity*, his novel insight was the idea that the earth's gravitational pull might extend to the moon—in other words, that the moon might be continually falling toward the earth, as the apocryphal apple did. Newton had already realized from the laws of motion that what was required to keep the moon in orbit was a centripetal force (toward the earth) not a tangential force (pushing it along the orbit). He had shown that the force necessary for a planet to follow one of Kepler's ellipses would be

---

13. Edwin A. Burtt, *The Metaphysical Foundations of Modern Science*, rev. ed. (New York: Humanities Press, 1951; London: Routledge & Kegan Paul, Ltd.; Doubleday PB), pp. 89–90.

an attraction toward the sun, varying with the inverse square of the distance. Using the prevailing estimates of the distance to the moon, Newton calculated the period of the moon's revolution which would be expected if there were an inverse-square gravitational force toward the earth. The result disagreed by 12 per cent from the observed lunar period, and Newton dropped the problem. Later, when it was found that the estimates of the distance had been in error, he repeated the calculations with the new data and found excellent agreement. The whole incident provides an illuminating example of the interaction of *observation, theory, mathematical deduction,* and *an imaginative new concept.*

Newton was even more insistent than Galileo that the scientist's task is *descriptive,* and that premature speculation must be avoided. He was willing to investigate the behavior of objects influenced by gravity, while leaving unanswered the question of the nature of gravity; in the absence of experimental evidence, we must simply admit we don't know.[14] When he advanced speculations with less adequate empirical support, as in his corpuscular theory of light, he did so with considerable caution and tentativeness. "It is true that I argue the corporeity of light," he wrote, "but I do it without any positiveness, as the word 'perhaps' intimates, and make at most a very plausible consequence of the doctrine and not a fundamental supposition." He may not have been as free from metaphysical assumptions as he thought, but he did clearly recognize that a scientific theory could be useful even when it did not answer all the questions one might ask about a phenomenon. We mention in passing that in the Newtonian era scientific concepts were assumed to be literal representations of the world, reproductions of objective reality as it is in itself. We will find this "realism" challenged by Kant, and extensively debated by twentieth-century physicists and philosophers.

2. Nature as a Law-Abiding Machine

Newton's laws of motion and gravity seemed applicable to all objects from the smallest particle in the laboratory to the farthest planet. This was still a single harmonious order, as in the Middle Ages, but now it was a structure of forces and masses rather than a hierarchy of purposes. This magnificent synthesis was rightly ad-

---

14. See the Preface and General Scholium of Newton's *Principia,* trans. A. Motte (Berkeley: University of California Press, 1934).

mired, and the perfection of mathematical law made a great impact on Newton's contemporaries. It suggested an image of *the world as an intricate machine* following immutable laws, with every detail precisely predictable. Here was the basis for the philosophies of determinism and materialism which later generations were to develop. Newton himself believed that the world-machine was designed by an intelligent creator and expressed his purpose; to later interpreters, impersonal and blind forces appeared to be entirely self-contained, and all sense of meaning and purpose was lost.

The concepts of Newtonian physics, which had been so superbly successful in astronomy and mechanics, were increasingly adopted as an all-encompassing metaphysical scheme. Newton himself accepted Galileo's view that nature is exhaustively describable as *particles in motion*. The properties that could be treated mathematically—mass and velocity—were alone considered to be characteristics of the real world; other properties were taken to be purely subjective, having no existence outside the mind. Since efficient causes had replaced final causes, all causality was assumed to be reducible to forces between atoms, and all changes reducible to the rearrangement of atoms. John Locke wrote: "By the figure, bulk, texture, and motion of these small and insensible corpuscles all the phenomena of bodies may be explained." Burtt gives this summary:

> It was of the greatest consequence for succeeding thought that now the great Newton's authority was squarely behind the view of the cosmos which saw in man a puny, irrelevant spectator of the vast mathematical system whose regular motions according to mechanical principles constituted the world of nature. . . . The world that people had thought themselves living in—a world rich with color and sound, redolent with fragrance, filled with gladness, love, and beauty, speaking everywhere of purposive harmony and creative ideals—was crowded now into minute corners in the brains of scattered organic beings. The really important world outside was a world hard, cold, colorless, silent, and dead; a world of quantity, a world of mathematically computable motions in mechanical regularity. In Newton the Cartesian metaphysics, ambiguously interpreted and stripped of its distinctive claim for serious philosophical consideration, finally overthrew Aristotelianism and became the predominant world-view of modern times.[15]

A technique of investigation was on its way to becoming a total account of the world; a *method* was being turned into a *metaphysics*. Whitehead calls this "the fallacy of misplaced concrete-

---

15. Burtt, *Metaphysical Foundations*, p. 239. Used by permission of Humanities Press and Routledge & Kegan Paul, Ltd.

ness," which takes particular scientific abstractions as if they were concrete reality, and uses one mode of description as if it were the only one possible.[16] He is particularly critical of the Newtonian picture of nature as an instantaneous configuration of self-contained particles that are only externally related to each other; as we shall see, he attacks the assumption that all satisfactory explanations of a process must be given in terms of its smallest parts. In such a mechanical world, however, Newton himself still found room for both God and the human spirit.

3. Methods in Theology: "Natural Theology"

The "virtuosi," as the English scientists of the second half of the seventeenth century called themselves, were religious men, predominantly from Puritan backgrounds. The Charter of the Royal Society instructed its fellows to direct their studies "to the glory of God and the benefit of the human race." Robert Boyle said that science is a *religious task*, "the disclosure of the admirable workmanship which God displayed in the universe." Newton believed the universe bespeaks an all-powerful Creator. Sprat, the historian of the Royal Society, considered science a valuable aid to religion. The mood of these men is captured in Addison's hymn:

> The spacious firmament on high,
> With all the blue ethereal sky
> And spangled heavens a shining frame,
> Their great Original proclaim.

> The unwearied sun from day to day,
> Does his Creator's power display,
> And publishes to every land,
> The work of an Almighty hand.

The virtuosi not only identified themselves verbally with the Christian tradition in which they were nourished, but many of them seem to have experienced a personal response of *reverence* and *awe* in the marvels they beheld. Where the psalmist had written "The heavens declare the glory of God, and the firmament showeth his handiwork," the virtuosi felt they could appreciate this handiwork in ways not possible to any previous generation. Expressions of awed surprise and admiration at the skill of the Creator dot the pages of their writings. The sense of the grandeur and wis-

---

16. Whitehead, *Science and the Modern World*, Chap. 3.

dom of God was evidently a very positive experience for many of them, and not just an abstract intellectual formula.

Yet their approach to religion was departing increasingly from traditional Christianity. Many factors contributed to this shift. England had been torn by religious strife and civil war, and a need was felt for a minimum common basis of reasonable agreement. Contact with other cultures suggested the value of *religious universality*. A small but influential group of scholars known as the Cambridge Platonists had asserted that reason and revelation are not incompatible; they advocated a philosophical approach to theology (drawing particularly from Platonic idealism) and urged toleration rather than dogmatism. A growing confidence in human reason, a more optimistic view of man's capacities, and a desire to provide a rational defense of the essentials of religion are reflected in treatises such as Locke's *The Reasonableness of Christianity*. On the other hand, the virtuosi had a personal stake in defending themselves from the charge of irreligion, and went to great lengths to show that atomism does not lead to atheism. In particular, they had to reply to Hobbes' view that the universe is the product of the chance concourse of atoms; they wanted to establish that although they were atomists, they were not materialistic atomists.

The most common form taken by their writing about religion was some variation of *the argument from design*. This passage from Newton's *Optics* is typical:

> Whence is it that nature doth nothing in vain; and whence arises all that order and beauty which we see in the world? How came the bodies of animals to be contrived with so much art, and for what ends were their several parts? Was the eye contrived without skill in optics? ... Does it not appear from phenomena that there is a being incorporeal, living, intelligent ... ?[17]

The eye evoked particular admiration as a triumph of ingenuity and workmanship evidencing an intelligent Designer, but other illustrations were frequent. The rotation of the earth, the inclination of its axis, the proportions of land and sea, all seemed perfectly arranged—the day for work, the night for rest, the seasons for crops, and so forth. Boyle pointed out that lambs are born in the spring when there is fresh grass for them.

The virtuosi, like the medieval scholastics, found *a pattern of*

---

17. Isaac Newton, *Optics*, 3rd ed. (London, 1721), pp. 344f.

divine benevolence in the design of all things. Because they still saw man as a spiritual being and an exception to the mechanical pattern of the world, they often assumed that the purpose of the rest of nature was the convenience of man, as well as the glory of God to whose wisdom it witnessed. But unlike authors in the Middle Ages, they considered purposes to be entirely external to nature, and not immanent in their operation. Nature is a complete and functioning machine which is not itself striving toward any ends, and God is the original First Cause, not the Final Cause. Scientific explanations and descriptions of causal chains must be given strictly *without any reference to purposes.* Boyle, who detected purposes everywhere, was very critical of teleology as an explanation for present behavior. An answer to the ultimate question of "why" is no substitute for an answer to the immediate question of "how," which he said should be given in terms of the "bulk, shape, and motion" of constituent parts. A total explanation of things will go beyond mechanism, but this is not the object of experimental science. He maintained that there are levels of truth which must be carefully distinguished.[18]

The argument from design assumed, of course, that the world had been instantaneously created *in its present form.* The idea of evolution and change was simply absent from seventeenth-century thought about nature. If one assumed that the world came into existence fully developed, the argument for an intelligent Designer was persuasive; it was the only apparent alternative to the view that the world is the product of the chance concourse of atoms. The *problem of evil* and the existence of catastrophies and monsters in nature were dismissed by saying that over-all harmony outweighs occasional anomalies, or that God has higher purposes which mortal wisdom cannot penetrate, or that a few parts may have to suffer because of laws beneficial to the whole. More often the unpleasant aspects of nature were ignored and the facts selected to support the benevolent pattern that was assumed.

In addition to the argument from design, the areas of supposed consensus among the religions of the world were cited to support a *"reasonable and universal religious faith"* open to all men and not dependent on any particular historical revelation. This common core of belief was said to include three ideas: the existence of a

---

18. Robert Boyle, "The Christian Virtuoso," in *The Works of the Hon. Robert Boyle,* ed. T. Birch (London, 1772).

Supreme Being, the immortality of the soul, and the obligation to moral conduct. The virtuosi believed that this common core was also the essence of Christianity, which they thought they were defending; actually it represented a major departure from biblical faith. Religion became less a matter of living experience than of intellectual demonstration. Ethics were reduced to utilitarian prudence, and the ideal of spontaneous love was replaced by a minimum moral code. Nature, not history, was the clue to the knowledge of God. God as Creator, not God as Redeemer, was now the focus of interest. God's relation to the individual, and man's experience of forgiveness and reorientation, were seldom mentioned. Because scientific categories dominated religious thought, the idea of providence was discussed in relation to the physical world, but not in relation to history and human experience. In all these areas the virtuosi moved away from the Christ-centered orientation of the Middle Ages and Reformation.

"Rational religion" had been intended as a support for the essentials of Christianity, but by the next century it was to have become a substitute for them. In attempting to defend a "purified" gospel, basic modifications were made. Reason, originally a supplement to revelation, replaced it completely as the medium of knowledge of God. The change did not come about by open conflict, but by *the reinterpretation of Christianity from within*. Puritanism, far from opposing scientific endeavor, was on the whole favorable to it; the virtuosi's view of nature as God's handiwork supported their interest in research. Science and religion were here represented not by two opposing groups, but by changing interpretations by persons who were interested in both areas of thought.

4. God as Divine Clockmaker

Nowhere was the impact of scientific on religious thought greater than in the modification of views of the function of God in relation to nature. God became primarily the divine Architect, though various attempts were made to find a place for God's continuing activity within a mechanical natural order. Boyle's favorite analogy for the world was the famous clock at Strasbourg. The analogy served him well in arguing for the divine Clockmaker, for a clock is obviously not the work of chance but of skillful artifice by its original creator. But the analogy also makes clear the difficulties in finding any room for present divine activity, for a clock once started runs its own independent mechanical course.

Most of the virtuosi, as least until the end of the century, were willing to make an exception to the rule of law in the case of *biblical miracles*, which they felt to be part of their Christian heritage. God may intervene on rare occasions for special reasons since he is not bound by his creation. Some authors felt that miracles and the fulfillment of prophecies were evidence for the validity of revelation; they claimed that miracles were public events observable by the senses and attested by reliable witnesses. Other interpreters showed more ambivalent attitudes; having used the *regularity* of the world as their main argument for God, they did not want to make too much of the *irregularities*. Thus Boyle started by affirming God's freedom to rule his creatures, but ended by asserting that God's wisdom was displayed primarily in planning things so he would not have to intervene. God demonstrated his care for the welfare of his creatures in the perfection of the original creative act, which was itself the greatest miracle. Laws are the instruments through which he governs, and he violates them "very rarely." In discussing evil, Boyle explains that God does not intervene to save the individual from the effects of laws that are in general beneficial to the whole, even though they may cause suffering in a particular case. The unfailing rule of law, not miraculous intervention, is the chief evidence of God's wisdom.[19]

There were various attempts to preserve the doctrine of *providence*. Some writings simply affirmed a mechanical universe and a God who cares about each detail, without attempting to reconcile the two assertions. Others equated providence with God's prevision; foreseeing the chain of causes, he could adjust his agents in advance to secure his providential ends without violating the ensuing order. More commonly, providence received a very general interpretation. Not the particular events but *the total design* represented God's benevolence. He set things in motion in a harmonious way, planning the over-all structure and order of the world for the welfare of his creatures. Once started, the operation of nature would follow fixed laws, with material causes acting from their own necessity.

God's function in the present was thus reduced to the *preservation* of the cosmic order. God's *concurrence* had traditionally been

---

19. Boyle, *"The Usefulness of Experimental Philosophy," ibid.*

conceived as an active participation, and some of the virtuosi so interpreted it. Boyle, like Descartes, stated that if the Almighty were to discontinue his support of the universe it would collapse. Continuing divine involvement is necessary, he said, since a law is not a real power but only a pattern of regularity. But it was the clock analogy that provided the basic interpretive image of the world as a perfect machine, autonomous and self-sufficient, with natural causes acting in independence of God. "Divine preservation" started as active sustenance, became passive acquiescence, and was then forgotten. Frequent reference was made to God's dominion and governance, but the interpretation given to these terms made them applicable only to the original act of creation.

Perhaps partly because he did not want to see God's role limited to that of First Cause, and partly because his scientific data were inaccurate, Newton asserted that God has a continuing function in *adjusting the solar system.* He believed that there is no scientific explanation for the pattern of the planets, holding that coplanar orbits with velocities in the same direction cannot be accounted for by natural causes. There are also continuing irregularities in motion, he said, which would build up if God did not occasionally step in to correct them. In addition, God somehow prevents the stars from collapsing together under gravitational attraction. Newton also identified absolute space and time with God's omnipresence and eternity, but this was a purely passive role. God was represented primarily as the Maker external to what he has made; like the clockmaker, he could act only by intervening from outside. The traditional idea of divine immanence in nature was virtually lost until its recovery by eighteenth-century Romanticism and, in a different form, by Protestant liberalism in the light of evolution in the nineteenth century.

The *scientific inadequacy* of Newton's references to divine intervention became obvious in the next century; Laplace's nebular hypothesis was able to account for the coplanar character of the solar system, and the "irregularities" were shown to be due either to inaccurate observations or to perturbations that would eventually cancel each other out. Laplace was correct in saying of God's role in planetary motion, "I had no need of that hypothesis." The *theological inadequacy* of Newton's assertions was pointed out by Leibniz: a perfect God would not have created an imperfect mechanism requiring periodic correction. We might object further that

God the Cosmic Plumber, mending the leaks in his system, would be the Ultimate Conservative, concerned only to maintain the status quo. This was "the God of the gaps," introduced to explain areas of scientific ignorance, and destined to retreat in the light of new knowledge to become the Retired Architect, the inactive God of Deism.

Most of the virtuosi thus ended by reducing God's role to that of *First Cause*; the divine benevolence was expressed in his original act of creation and not in continuing fatherly care. But they defended this limited role with vigor, for they wanted to assert the primacy of spirit over matter without compromising the orderliness of the universe. Against Hobbes, they maintained that the universe is the product of intelligent purpose, not of blind chance. Against Leibniz, they maintained that creation was an act of God's will and freedom, not of rational necessity. Against Spinoza, they maintained that God is separate from the world and external to it, not identical with the nexus of inexorable law. Though the *function of God* was drastically reduced, the *conception of God* was still the traditional one of personal intelligence and will, not the pantheistic Absolute. Westfall observes:

> The ultimate result of the virtuosi's consideration of providence, as seen in Newton's statements on the subject, amounted to an implicit renunciation of particular providence, together with a strong reaffirmation of general providence. They asserted that the world is not an autonomous machine; they affirmed the predominance of spirit over matter in the creation.[20]

5. Man as Rational Mind

God and man were considered by the virtuosi to be the exceptions to the rule of mechanical law. The Newtonian universe was still a moral and purposeful order because it was designed by God, and man still had dignity because of his *reason*. Though man is quite alone within the vast and complex world-machine, he is not a complete alien because the rational order of nature is akin to human reason. Since nature is the product of divine reason, it is beneficent and is comprehensible by human reason. The traditional idea of soul is here identified with "rational spirit," and taken to guarantee man's unique status.

---

20. Richard S. Westfall, *Science and Religion in Seventeenth-Century England* (New Haven, Conn.: Yale University Press, 1958), p. 206.

John Locke and his successors hoped that the approach Newton had used so successfully to understand the natural order could be used to develop *a science of human nature and society.* These early attempts were, to be sure, modeled more after the rational-deductive elements of the new physics than after its experimental side. Criticisms of existing institutions in the light of what seemed "natural" and "reasonable" were strongly influenced by cultural traditions and class interests. Locke himself developed a concept of "natural rights" from which he could justify the Revolution of 1689; he was a powerful apologist for the great seventeenth-century struggles for civil liberties and religious toleration. In the next century there were to be many variations of the idea that Nature and Reason should be the guides of man and his institutions.

The distinctive *status of mind* was generally defended in this period, though without Descartes' theory of innate ideas. Hobbes' view that mind is reducible to the concourse of atoms was strenuously resisted. Man's mind, imprisoned in his brain, was believed to have only indirect contact with the world. Since there was no longer a metaphysical continuity in the universe, epistemology had become a problem for philosophy. But the triumph of Newtonian science had helped to increase confidence in human reason, and laid the groundwork for the Enlightenment view of man's inevitable progress. The mechanistic image was not yet applied to the whole of reality, as it was to be by the French *philosophes.* These further developments from the Newtonian world-view will occupy us in the next chapter.

IV. CONTRIBUTIONS OF RELIGION
TO THE RISE OF SCIENCE

Let us pause to ask some general questions about *the influence of religion on science* up to the time of Newton. From even our brief outline it is evident that at many points the growth of science was hindered by religious ideas and by the institutional church. Such instances of antagonism between religion and science were the theme of many historical accounts written in the aftermath of the Darwinian controversy.[21] More recent historians have recognized that the Western religious tradition also made important though

21. E.g., Andrew D. White, *A History of The Warfare of Science with Theology* (New York: D. Appleton & Company, 1896; Dover PB).

indirect positive contributions to science in its formative period. *The rise of modern science* was a complex social phenomenon covering several centuries and influenced by numerous factors.[22] There were economic forces, such as the growth of trade and commerce and the availability of wealth and leisure. Technological interest was encouraged by practical problems in metallurgy, navigation, the trades, and military weaponry. Skilled craftsmen and artisans were learning to make tools and instruments. The founding of such institutions as the Royal Society and the circulation of letters and journals aided the new enterprise. Our concern, however, lies with *the intellectual presuppositions* underlying the rise of science. Why was it in Western civilization alone, among all the cultures of the world, that science in its modern sense developed? Many historians contend that one important factor was the tacit attitude toward nature engendered by the unique combination of Greek and biblical ideas.

1. *Attitudes toward Nature and the Doctrine of Creation*

Interest in nature for its own sake had in previous centuries represented in part a reaction *against medieval thought*. Eschewing otherworldliness, men of the Renaissance had begun looking with new excitement to the potentialities of life in this world. At first, interest had been directed to the classical cultures of antiquity, to art and literature, to "secular" but nonscientific learning. But the creative genius of a Leonardo da Vinci was expressed in areas as varied as art, engineering, and anatomy. Exploration of geographical frontiers and natural phenomena increasingly challenged the curiosity of the adventurous. Again, the split between faith and reason in late medieval philosophy, and the rejection of the authority of the church in the Reformation, may have spurred *the search for knowledge* on which men could agree without appealing to ancient authorities. With the breakup of the medieval synthesis there was greater diversity of thought, a more widespread spirit of inquiry, and a more important role assigned to the individual in the pursuit of truth.

---

22. See Herbert Butterfield, *The Origins of Modern Science* (New York: The Macmillan Co., 1951; PB); R. S. Cohen, "Alternative Interpretations of The History of Science," *The Scientific Monthly*, Vol. 80 (1955), 111; reprinted in P. Frank, ed., *The Validation of Scientific Theories* (Boston: Beacon Press, 1954; Collier PB°); E. Zilsel, "Sociological Roots of Science," *American Journal of Sociology*, Vol. 47 (1942), 544.

But the medieval legacy also included implicit presuppositions about nature which were in many ways congenial to the scientific enterprise. First, the conviction of *the intelligibility of nature* contributed to what we have called the rational component of science. The medieval scholastics, like the Greek philosophers, did have great confidence in the rational powers of man. Moreover, they combined the Greek view of the orderliness and regularity of the universe with the biblical view of God as lawgiver. Monotheism implies the universality of order and coherence (though in the prescientific era this was not conceived primarily in terms of laws of cause and effect). Whitehead ends an extended discussion with these remarks:

> I do not think, however, that I have even yet brought out the greatest contribution of medievalism to the formation of the scientific movement. I mean the inexpungable belief that every detailed occurrence can be correlated with its antecedents in a perfectly definite manner, exemplifying general principles. . . . When we compare this tone of thought in Europe with the attitude of other civilizations when left to themselves, there seems but one source for its origin. It must have come from the medieval insistence on the rationality of God, conceived as with the personal energy of Jehovah and with the rationality of a Greek philosopher. . . . In Asia, the conceptions of God were of a being who was either too arbitrary or too impersonal for such ideas to have much effect on instinctive habits of mind. . . . My explanation is that the faith in the possibility of science, generated antecedently to the development of modern scientific theory, is an unconscious derivative from medieval theology.[23]

Second, the doctrine of creation implies that *the details of nature can be known only by observing them.* For if the world is the product of God's free act, he did not have to make it exactly as he did, and we can understand it only by actual observation.[24] The universe, in other words, is contingent on God's will, not a necessary consequence of first principles; the world is both orderly and contingent, for God is both rational and free. By contrast, Greek thought took a predominantly deductive approach; it held that, starting from general principles, one should be able to infer how

23. Whitehead, *Science and the Modern World*, pp. 13–14. Used by permission of The Macmillan Company and Cambridge University Press.
24. See M. B. Foster, "The Christian Doctrine of Creation and the Rise of Modern Natural Science," *Mind*, Vol. 43 (1934), 446; Vol. 44 (1935), 439; Vol. 45 (1936), 1; also John Baillie, *Natural Science and The Spiritual Life* (London: Oxford University Press, 1951).

all the details of the world are ordered. Every specific element of the cosmos, said Socrates, flows by necessity from God's nature. In addition, the Platonic tradition viewed matter as an inferior embodiment of pure rational forms; the eternal forms can be grasped in their essence by intuitive reason—not by examining finite objects that imperfectly illustrate them. It is perhaps not surprising that the rational side of Greek science (for example, mathematics and geometry) was stronger than its experimental side.[25]

Third, *an affirmative attitude toward nature* is dominant in the Bible. The goodness of the world is a corollary of the doctrine of creation. God's purposes involve the created order and the sphere of time and history. To be sure, there were world-denying themes in medieval thought (partly derived from the Hellenistic world), but the extremes of Gnosticism and Manichaeism, in which matter is inherently evil, were repudiated. Undoubtedly, considerable fear of the demonic in nature continued to haunt the popular imagination, and perhaps hindered the rise of science. But in men such as St. Benedict, St. Francis, and St. Thomas we can see the goodness of creation affirmed in several modes—practical, aesthetic, and intellectual. Yet biblical religion never deified natural forces or the vitalities of organic life; after the defeat of the "gods of nature," the world was not an object of worship and thus could become an object of study. In the Genesis account, man is explicitly given dominion over the rest of creation. By contrast, the views of nature in Asian religions (especially the Hindu doctrine of *Maya*, which asserts the essentially illusory character of the world of plurality and change) seem to have been on the whole less congenial to the development of a scientific interest in the natural order (see Chapter 12).

But if the biblical view of nature, along with the Greek emphasis on rationality, helped to foster science, why was *scientific development in the Middle Ages* relatively meager? Perhaps the answer lies partly in the weight of Aristotle's authority and the excessive rationalism of the scholastics, partly in the dominance of the institutional church against which both Renaissance and Reformation rebelled—and of course partly in social and economic factors. The scientific revolution happened only once in man's history, and one can but speculate as to why it did not occur at another time or

25. Cf. Mary B. Hesse, *Science and the Human Imagination* (London: SCM Press, 1954), pp. 38f.

place. Nevertheless many historians of science have acknowledged the importance of the Western religious tradition in molding unconscious assumptions about nature. Robert Cohen, who himself holds no brief for religion, asks:

> Could the recognition of statistical regularities and their mathematical expression have been reached by any other road than the theological one we actually traveled? The only test comparison with a developed civilization is that of nontheological China. As Needham and Northrop have remarked, theology in China had been so depersonalized, law made so ethical, humanistic, and particular, that the idea of a rational creator of all things was not formulated. Hence the idea that we lesser rational beings might, by virtue of that Godlike rationality, be able to decipher the laws of nature (in Galileo's phrase, we might read the mathematical language of the Book of Nature) never was accepted.[26]

2. The "Protestant Ethic" and the Pursuit of Science

Beyond the contribution of the biblical tradition in general, *Puritanism* in particular seems to have lent support to scientific endeavor. Without belittling advances that occurred elsewhere, one can say that seventeenth-century England was the turning point in the history of science, and that the Puritans were its chief agents. Seven out of ten members of the Royal Society were Puritans—a ratio far out of proportion to the population as a whole; most of the virtuosi were active churchmen, and many of the clergy encouraged or themselves took part in scientific pursuits. Puritan schools put science courses in their curricula. We have noted the conviction of Newton and others that the study of nature, the divine handiwork, redounds to God's glory. But the Puritan understanding of *vocation* seems to have provided additional motivation for scientific work.

The set of attitudes sometimes called *"the Protestant ethic"* (though it was not shared by all branches of Protestantism) was the development of a distinctive viewpoint toward daily work by seventeenth-century Calvinists, especially the Puritans in England. Calvin, like Luther, had rejected the idea that "religious" vocations are superior to "secular" ones; man should serve God not by withdrawing to a monastic life but by carrying out any honest and useful job with integrity and diligence. This enhancement of the

---

26. R. S. Cohen in Frank, ed., *Validation*, p. 206.

status of the layman (and of the dignity of labor) was a by-product of the Reformation doctrine that man is justified before God by divine grace—not by human works—yet he can respond to God's love by his life in the world. Calvinism was more activistic than Lutheranism in encouraging "this-worldly" enterprise, holding that work conducted in a rational and orderly way furthers the general welfare and is approved by God. The Christian should glorify God by working with honesty, sobriety, and thrift.

The correlation between this *"Protestant ethic"* and *the growth of capitalism* has been traced by Weber, Tawney, and others.[27] The virtues that it encouraged, hard work and thrift in particular, were precisely the characteristics needed for the new commercial under-takings. The Christian, knowing himself among the elect, was sup-posed to practice these virtues for their own sake; if he prospered in the process, this could be taken as a sign of God's favor. The idea of being able to serve God, one's fellow man, and oneself, all at the same time, was obviously subject to abuse; before long, men were pointing to their riches as evidence of being among the elect, thus rationalizing self-seeking individualism. But in the seventeenth century this distortion of the "vocational virtues" was kept in bounds by a strong sense of stewardship, that is, responsibility before God for the use of one's life and resources.

Now the "Protestant ethic" similarly endorsed *scientific work*; the study of nature was held to be at once intrinsically fascinating, beneficial to mankind, and divinely sanctioned, for it would both reveal God's handiwork and exemplify rational and orderly activity. Robert Merton states that "the formal organization of values con-stituted by Puritanism led to the largely unwitting furtherance of modern science."[28] Bernard Barber summarizes the relevance of Puritan beliefs for science:

> The Puritans held the view that man could understand God through understanding Nature, because God revealed himself in the workings

---

27. R. H. Tawney, *Religion and the Rise of Capitalism* (New York: Harcourt, Brace and Co., 1926; Mentor PB); critiques of the Weber-Tawney thesis are given in Kurt Samuellson, *Religion and Economic Action* (New York: Basic Books, 1961; Harper PB) and W. H. Hudson, "The Weber Thesis Re-examined," in S. A. Burrell, ed., *The Role of Religion in Modern European History* (New York: The Macmillan Co., 1964; PB).

28. Robert Merton, "Science and Technology in Seventeenth-Century England," *Osiris*, Vol. 4, Pt. 2 (1938); also his *Social Theory and Social Structure* (Glencoe, Ill.: The Free Press, 1949), Chaps. 18, 19.

of Nature. Therefore science was not antagonistic to religion but rather a firm basis for faith. They felt that since "good works" were a sign, if not a proof, of election to salvation, and that since one could glorify God through social utilitarianism, then science was good because it was an efficient instrument of good works and social improvement. And they valued reason highly because God had chosen man alone to possess it and because it restrained laziness and idolatry.[29]

It thus appears that both the biblical doctrine of creation and the vocational ethic of Puritanism contributed positively to the rise of science.

V. SUMMARY

In this chapter we have sketched five topics in their development from the medieval "World-Drama" to the Newtonian "World-Machine." From this account we now summarize the main *sources of conflict* between science and religion during this formative period, and attempt to distinguish the issues that were the product of short-lived circumstances from those that were of continuing importance.

1. METHODS IN SCIENCE. Considering in turn the Middle Ages, Galileo, and Newton, we moved from "Explanation by Purposes" to "Mathematics and Observation" and "Experiment and Theory." Preoccupation with purposes had for centuries diverted attention from mechanical causes and hindered the growth of the approach characteristic of modern science. In the seventeenth century, remarkable success was achieved by concentrating on descriptive explanation and "efficient" rather than "final" causes. Theory and experiment were linked by imaginative new concepts; these have remained the basic elements of scientific methodology. Theories were assumed to provide a literal representation of reality ("naive realism")—a viewpoint we will find challenged by many contemporary philosophers of science who, in the light of twentieth-century physics, stress the selective, abstractive, and symbolic character of scientific concepts, "models," and theories.

The virtuosi believed there were divine purposes in nature, but rightly held that these should play no role in the scientific account.

---

29. Reprinted with permission of The Free Press and George Allen & Unwin, Ltd., from p. 58 of *Science and the Social Order* by Bernard Barber. Copyright 1952 by the Free Press, a corporation. Collier PB.

Later generations were to conclude that mechanical explanation eliminates all theological meaning; the issue was to become acute again during the evolution controversy. We shall maintain, however, that when correctly expressed, analysis in theological terms is not displaced by analysis in scientific terms, since science and theology ask fundamentally different sorts of questions. In an age dominated by religion, it was necessary to assert the independence of science. Today, in an age dominated by science, it may be necessary to assert the independence of religion. The dominance of either science or religion, and the assumption that one must exclude the other, have been in part products of the failure to analyze adequately the characteristics of man's ways of knowing. The basic question is: what are the functions of differing types of explanations, and what is the structure of the knowing process? What are the strengths and limitations of the methods of science? These will be the subjects of Part Two.

2. THE CHARACTER OF NATURE. The natural world was viewed successively as "A Hierarchy of Beings," "Particles-in-Motion" and "A Law-Abiding Machine." We would argue that the mechanistic world-view of atomism should be evaluated as a philosophical interpretation rather than as a scientific conclusion. Burtt points to one of the motives behind the new view of nature:

> If we are right in judging that wishful thinking in the interest of religious salvation played a strong part in the construction of the medieval hierarchy of reality, is it not an equally plausible hypothesis to suppose that wishful thinking of another sort underlay this extreme doctrine of early modern physics—that because it was easier to get ahead in the reduction of nature to a system of mathematical equations by supposing that nothing existed outside of the human mind that was not so reducible, naturalists proceeded at once to make the convenient assumption?[30]

The conflict of religion at this point was not with science itself but with a metaphysics that identified one set of scientific concepts with the whole of reality. The mathematical ideal was used as the criterion for selecting from among the elements of experience those characteristics that would be attributed to the external world as "primary qualities." The success of the categories of physics produced the confidence that everything could be explained in terms

---

30. Burtt, *Metaphysical Foundations*, p. 305. Used by permission of Humanities Press and Routledge & Kegan Paul, Ltd.

of those categories. It was an essentially static view of nature, in which no fundamental novelty could occur.

During the ensuing century, the mechanistic interpretation of nature was to be developed further in the deterministic, materialistic, and atheistic philosophies of the French Enlightenment, before the Romantic reaction toward the close of the century reversed this trend. We shall see later that the revolution of twentieth-century physics casts doubt on some of the deterministic and mechanistic assumptions of the Newtonian world-view. A closely related problem is *reductionism*, the attributing of reality exclusively to the smallest constituents of the world, and the tendency to interpret higher levels of organization in terms of lower levels. To this problem we shall return in Part Three when we consider contemporary views of nature.

3. METHODS IN THEOLOGY. For the three periods considered we used the headings "Reason and Revelation," "Aristotle, Scripture, and Nature," and "Natural Theology." Biblical theology had been so merged with Aristotelianism in the Middle Ages that men reacted in the face of challenges to Aristotle's cosmology as if these were challenges to Christianity. This was perhaps the greatest source of conflict in Galileo's time, but by the end of the century was not a major issue. Yet it reflects a perennial problem: how can theology make use of and incorporate the best philosophy and science of its day, as Aquinas made use of Aristotle, and yet avoid distorting the essential Christian message by making an inflexible system that hinders response to new intellectual currents?

Biblical literalism contributed to the condemnation of Galileo by the Catholic church. Such literalism was also present in Protestant scholasticism, but was on the wane on the Continent by the middle of the seventeenth century, and it was never as dominant on the English scene. The same sort of conflict was to arise again, however, between fundamentalism and evolutionary theory. The basic issue here is whether or not biblical revelation is to be understood as infallible propositional information capable of dictating scientific conclusions. In a later chapter we will defend a view of revelation in historical events which attempts to avoid both appeal to a literal inerrant text, on the one hand, and the complete dismissal of revelation as a source of religious understanding, on the other.

Natural theology in the Middle Ages, as in subsequent Roman Catholicism, was a preamble to revealed theology. The arguments

for the existence of God were considered a valid intellectual defense of theism, but the most important religious truths were to be
found only in the tradition of the church. Among the Reformers
natural theology played a negligible part, for to them the basis of
religious knowledge was God's redemptive act in Christ, confirmed
in their personal experience of God's forgiveness. Galileo, however,
spoke of nature as a way of knowing God that was coordinate with
scripture. The English virtuosi, in turn, thought of natural theology
as a defense for Christianity, but in the process the traditional ideas
about Christ, redemption, and providence were ignored or modified.
The historic faith was increasingly reinterpreted so that attention
was confined to the affirmations it shared with other religions: belief in a Supreme Being, immortality, and moral conduct. It was
but one more step for the Deists of the next century to defend
natural theology and reject Christianity; some skeptics went further,
abandoning even these minimal assertions. That men had turned
from history and personal experience to nature as the chief clue to
knowledge of God reflected in part the new focus of interest. The
change was also influenced by new evaluations of the traditional
sources of religious authority and of the capacities of man's reason.
All of these questions remain crucial for us today.

It should be mentioned that the term *"natural theology"* is sometimes used (as by Aquinas) in a broad sense to refer to any theology not based on biblical revelation. In this volume we will use the
term in the narrower sense to refer to *theology derived from nature.*
(Thus we will consider "arguments from moral and religious experience" as a third category, separate from either natural or revealed
theology, rather than include them in natural theology as the
broader definition would require.) In any case, both definitions
include the three types of argument from nature that we have encountered in this chapter and will repeatedly meet again—namely,
arguments starting from (a) *particular gaps in the scientific account*, in which God is said to intervene (for example, Newton's
references to the readjustment of the planets, or among later
authors the idea of the special creation of man in evolutionary
history, or insistence on an unbridgeable line between matter and
life in the writings of some recent theologians; this type of reasoning seems particularly dubious, for it has often been undermined
when a "gap" was closed); (b) *the design of particular features of
organisms* (an argument that was widely used in the next century,

but one that had to be completely reformulated after Darwin); and
(c) *the orderliness, intelligibility, and contingency of nature* (general properties, not dependent on particular scientific discoveries).
Only the last of these arguments seems to be defensible today.

4. GOD'S RELATION TO NATURE. The central function of God in
nature changed from "The Supreme Good" to "The First Cause"
and "The Divine Clockmaker." The mechanical conception of nature thus influenced the dominant understanding of God. God's
role as Redeemer was for the most part ignored, and his activity
reduced in effect to that of Creator. Attempts to preserve a continuing function for God in the cosmic machine were inadequate. The
"God of the gaps," invoked to explain areas of scientific ignorance,
was unsatisfactory both scientifically and theologically.

Although the seventeenth-century virtuosi still considered themselves Christians, they ended with a concept of God that was indistinguishable from that of Deism: the God who started the
machine and left it to run by itself. But an active religion requires
a God related to man's life. In the Middle Ages, the sense of God's
reality pervaded all aspects of culture; philosophy and cosmology,
art and literature, the church and its sacraments, and belief in the
miraculous conspired to make God seem near at hand. For the
Reformers, God's presence in Christ and in the experience of forgiveness was always relevant to man's personal and corporate life.
Eighteenth-century Methodism and Pietism held that God works inwardly in human experience; nineteenth-century liberalism stressed
the idea of divine immanence in nature, with God actively involved
in the life of the world. But the God of Deism was too remote to
inspire religious commitment. Today we must still grapple with the
problem faced by the virtuosi: what are the modes of God's activity in relation to the natural order that science studies? How can
God act in a law-abiding world?

5. MAN'S RELATION TO NATURE. Man's changing status was traced
from "The Center of the Cosmic Drama" to "The Demoted Spectator" and "The Rational Mind." The displacement of man from a
central geographical position had been accepted by the end of the
century; after Newton it no longer remained a debatable issue. But
the reaction induced by Copernican astronomy was not unlike the
reaction to the status of man in evolution or to recent speculation
about intelligent life on other planets. In each case human uniqueness was cast in doubt; the neglected question was whether man's

cosmic significance was to be based on geographical or biological criteria. Yet the universe that science has been disclosing ever since Galileo has undoubtedly appeared less hospitable to human purposes than the hierarchical world of the Middle Ages.

In the seventeenth century, man's dignity seemed to rest in his power of reason. The realm of mind was taken to be the one exception to the rule of mechanical law. Man was not yet absorbed into nature, or metaphysically continuous with the natural process, as many nineteenth-century authors were to picture him. The status of mind and the relation of mind to matter appeared problematical, and have been central issues in philosophy ever since. The influence that new conceptions of man's place in nature have had upon changing views of human destiny and the goals of individual life will have to be traced in subsequent centuries.

Thus some of the causes of conflict between science and religion in this earliest phase were short-lived—for example, the respect in which Aristotle was held. Other problems remained acute in the following centuries but are perhaps less widespread today—for example, the tendency of theologians to make pronouncements about scientific theories, or of scientists to turn their technical concepts into all-inclusive metaphysical systems. The rise of science eventually had a number of beneficial results on religious thought, such as a clearer recognition of the distinction between scientific and religious questions, and the liberation of theological ideas from the prescientific cosmology with which they had been associated. Other issues from this early period continue to be of crucial importance today—how methods in theology are to be compared to methods in science, how God can act in a world of scientific law, and how man's distinctiveness and his participation in nature can be simultaneously portrayed.

3

Nature and God in the Eighteenth Century

None of the scientific discoveries of the eighteenth century had philosophical or theological repercussions comparable to those of Newton's work. In physics, the century saw the further development of mechanics by Lagrange, d'Alembert, Laplace, and others. The experiments of Priestley and Lavoisier with combustion and the identification of oxygen were the beginning of modern chemistry. In biology, Linnaeus formulated a comprehensive system of classification for plants, and Buffon performed a similar service for animal forms. By the end of the century the technological applications of physics were starting to have an impact on society, especially in the early phases of the Industrial Revolution in England. But the main change in the outlook of the age came not from any particular new discovery but from the spreading influence of the idea of science itself. This was a period of intellectual transition in which a characteristically modern temper emerged. We will again touch briefly on these climates of opinion, but only as they relate to the interaction of scientific and religious ideas.

Section I, "The Age of Reason," gives some examples of the movement to extend to other areas of thought the ideal of rationality that had been so impressively demonstrated in Newtonian physics. The new view of nature was deterministic and reductionistic. The dominant view of God was at first deist, but an increasing group of skeptics rejected all concepts of God and defended atheistic and materialistic philosophies. The new view of man was optimistic; the age was confident of human perfectibility through reason, and of inevitable social progress through science.

Section II, "The Romantic Reaction," indicates the reaction against these ideas, which occurred late in the century. Poets and novelists of the Romantic Movement defended man's freedom, imagination, and intuition; to them, nature was not an impersonal machine but a living companion to man, permeated by beauty, vitality, and an underlying spiritual reality. Such movements as Pietism and Methodism brought a revitalization of personal religion and a repudiation of the abstract rationalism of the Enlightenment.

Section III, "Philosophical Responses," outlines the understanding of science and religion set forth by two philosophers who greatly influenced subsequent thought. In Hume's writing, scientific empiricism and religious agnosticism were developed systematically. Kant, on the other hand, defended the role of religion and morality as realms sharply contrasting with the realm of science. His system of thought provided a new and distinctive way of reconciling the claims of science and religion.

I. The Age of Reason

The eighteenth century saw itself as the Age of Reason in which the ideal of rationality manifest in science would permeate all human activities. The Enlightenment, as the new intellectual movement was called, was a diverse phenomenon, varying among countries and among individual thinkers, yet it displayed typical attitudes that differed from those of any previous century. Its most articulate and extreme spokesmen were the French *philosophes* of the mid-century, but its spirit permeated Germany, England, and the American colonies and influenced the subsequent climate of thought throughout the modern world. From among the many ideas of the Enlightenment, we select three that are relevant to this volume. Nature was viewed as a self-sufficient deterministic mechanism whose operation could be explained by natural forces. God became a debatable hypothesis, defended by some as a reasonable assumption, rejected by others as a dubious dogma of a reactionary church.

Finally, the dominant mood was confidence in the perfectibility of man and the achievement of the ideal society by the application of reason to human affairs.

1. *Nature as a Deterministic Mechanism*

The generations following Newton held him in high esteem that approached adulation. Alexander Pope, whose precise literary style voiced the spirit of the new age, exulted:

> Nature and Nature's laws lay hid in night:
> God said, *Let* Newton *be!* and all was Light.[1]

Laplace wrote that Newton was not only the greatest genius that ever lived but the most fortunate, since there is only one universe and it can be the lot of but one man in history to be the interpreter of its laws. Newtonian mechanics became the "paradigm" or ideal example of scientific work; it supplied the guiding image of the kind of question that should be asked and the type of concept that should be used. Above all, the Newtonian paradigm established a new idea of what counts as a satisfactory explanation in science— and, by extrapolation, in any field.

Laplace himself carried further the mathematical analysis of *the mechanics of planetary motion*. He showed that the small irregularities caused by the mutual attraction of the planets, which Newton thought would be cumulative unless God stepped in to correct them, would instead automatically cancel each other out over a long timespan. His "nebular hypothesis," which proposed that the solar system was formed from the cooling and condensing of nebular gases, could account for the coplanar orbits of the planets without invoking God's intervention. Thus when Napoleon said to him, "M. Laplace, they tell me you have written this large book on the system of the universe, and have never even mentioned its Creator," Laplace could give his famous reply, "I had no need of that hypothesis."

Laplace was an articulate spokesman for the new view of nature as *a self-sufficient and impersonal mechanism*. The world was no longer seen as the purposeful divine drama of the Middle Ages or even as the continuing object of providential supervision, as for Newton, but as a set of interacting natural forces. If events are

---

1. Alexander Pope, "Epitaph on Newton," *The Works of Alexander Pope,* Elwin edition (London, 1882), Vol. 4, 390.

wholly governed by natural causes, any remaining gaps in the scientific account should be filled, not by introducing a *deus ex machina*, but by further search for physical explanations. Though many scientists continued to believe in the existence of God, no reference to such beliefs was considered appropriate within scientific treatises. The "secularization" of knowledge in science, as in other fields, meant that theological ideas, whatever their role elsewhere, were to be excluded from the study of the world.

Laplace also explicitly formulated the *determinism* implicit in the view of reality as matter-in-motion. The laws of mechanics, which were assumed to govern the motion of all objects from the smallest particle to the largest star, would in principle allow the prediction of the path of every particle from the forces acting on it:

> We ought then to regard the present state of the universe as the effect of its anterior state and as the cause of the one which is to follow. Given for one instant an intelligence which could comprehend all the forces by which nature is animated and the respective situation of the beings who compose it—an intelligence sufficiently vast to submit these data to analysis—it would embrace in the same foundation the movements of the greatest bodies of the universe and those of the lightest atom; for it, nothing would be uncertain and the future, as the past, would be present to its eyes[2]

Nature was here assumed to be a complete mechanical system of inflexible cause-and-effect, governed by exact and absolute laws, so that all future events are inexorably determined.

Moreover, Laplace's view was explicitly *reductionistic*. Epistemological reductionism was expressed in the conviction that all phenomena will ultimately be explained by physical laws; metaphysical reductionism is evident in his conviction that reality is constituted by its smallest components, matter-in-motion. One of the links between these two ideas was the belief that causal efficacy resides in the external impact of one particle on another, so that all explanations of cause and effect can ultimately be given in terms of mechanical forces between moving bodies. Diderot, along with many of the writers of the French *Encyclopédie*, defended a metaphysics of materialism, which claimed to account for all aspects of man. In *Man the Machine*, La Mettrie maintained that consciousness is an illusory by-product of atomic motions. It is perhaps

---

2. Pierre Simon Laplace, *A Philosophical Essay on Probabilities*, 6th ed., trans. F. W. Truscott and F. L. Emory, (New York: Dover, 1961), p. 4.

understandable that the concepts of mechanics, which had proved so fruitful, were deemed capable of giving an exhaustive analysis of all events. Dampier suggests that this was "a natural exaggeration of the power of the new knowledge which had impressed the minds of men with its range and scope, before they realized its necessary limits."[3]

2. God as a Debatable Hypothesis

There were of course many people in eighteenth-century Europe who continued to accept traditional religious ideas. But the distinctive new viewpoint characteristic of the intellectual leaders of the Enlightenment was the "rational religion" whose growth, dominance, and decline we may trace in three overlapping stages. In the first stage, which was a continuation of the views of the virtuosi described in the previous chapter, *rational religion* and *revelation* were regarded as alternative routes to the same basic truths. This common core of universal beliefs was said to include the ideas of God, moral conduct, and immortality. These three beliefs were also taken to be the essence of Christianity, which was "one form of the religion of reason whose principles are discoverable by all people in all ages." Matthew Tindal's *Christianity as Old as Creation*, published in 1730, stated that the Bible was a republication of these universal ideas and not a unique revelation. The argument from design was often used in this period. John Ray, the founder of modern botany, had written *The Wisdom of God Manifested in the Works of Creation* (1691), extolling the perfection of design in the world of plants and animals, and his book was widely quoted. Here was a supposedly clear path "through Nature to Nature's God."

The *existence of evil* in the world was minimized by these exponents of natural theology. A favorite argument employed to justify the presence of destructive animals or insects was the idea that God had not wanted to deny existence to any possible kind of being. It was asserted that there is an ascending ladder of creatures from worm to angel, "a great chain of being" with no links missing.[4] The advantages of creating a "full" universe, with all niches occupied, outweighed any disadvantages from the presence of less desirable types of being. The optimism of the age is seen in the assertion that

3. Dampier, *A History of Science*, p. 196.
4. A. O. Lovejoy, *The Great Chain of Being* (Cambridge, Mass.: Harvard University Press, 1936; Harper PB), Chaps. 6–8.

this is "the best of all possible worlds"; in Pope's words, "Whatever is, is right." The universe is complete and perfect, for the status quo is God's intention. Here was a "Cosmic Toryism"[5] which glorified things as they are and rejected the traditional conviction (which was linked to the doctrine of the Fall) that there is something radically wrong with the whole created world. Despite such modifications of tradition, the defenders of natural theology in this first stage were friendly to Christianity and believed that reason confirms its central tenets. But the greater reliance on human discovery, rather than God's self-disclosure, paved the way for more drastic changes.

The second stage, *the heyday of Deism*, saw natural theology used as a substitute for revelation.[6] The traditional concept of God had been considerably modified under the impact of the new science; as we have seen, the world-machine seemed to imply the divine Mechanic. The sufficiency of reason was confidently affirmed and scripture was assigned a subordinate role. Revealed theology was on the defensive, as in Bishop Butler's *Analogy of Religion, Natural and Revealed* (1736). It is symptomatic of his times that Butler tried to vindicate revelation by its analogy to natural theology (which he assumed was so widely accepted as not to need defense). The evidence from nature is by no means clear and simple, he suggested; it is not a realm of pure order and reason but of ambiguities and perplexities. Nor is scripture always obscure, as its critics claim. Instead we confront in both cases a mixture of clarity and obscurity; if nature is accepted as evidence of God, said Butler, then scripture should be equally acceptable. But the net effect of his argument was to cast doubt on natural theology rather than to strengthen the case for revelation.

The *waning of Deism* can be attributed primarily to its own inherent weaknesses. The Cosmic Designer, who started the world-machine and left it to run on its own, seemed impersonal and remote—not a God who cares for individuals and is actively related to man, or a Being to whom prayer would be appropriate. It is not surprising that such a do-nothing God, irrelevant to daily life, be-

---

5. Basil Willey, *Eighteenth-Century Background* (London: Chatto & Windus, 1940; Beacon PB), Chap. 3.
6. See Gerald R. Cragg, *Reason and Authority in the Eighteenth Century* (Cambridge: Cambridge University Press, 1964) and *The Church and the Age of Reason* (London: Penguin PB, 1960), Chaps. 5, 11, 15.

came a hypothesis for the origin of the world or a verbal formula which before long could be dispensed with completely. Deism was too abstract and rationalistic to capture the imagination of the average man. The Deists attacked the institutional church, and traditional Christianity was increasingly pictured as the enemy of the religion of reason. Miracles were rejected as primitive superstitions, and instances of cruelty and immorality in the biblical record were cited. Any creed, dogma, or ritual was suspect as out of keeping with the new temper. In England the attacks were moderate and restrained; in France they were often vehement and bitter, provoked by the church's unbending orthodoxy and repressive measures. Voltaire applied his wit to the ridicule of Christianity, though to his death he remained a Deist. Thomas Paine's *Age of Reason* found contradictions in the Bible and celebrated the victory of reason over superstition, but defended the idea of God and the moral law.

The Enlightened of the first generation supported both natural and revealed religion; those of the second adhered to natural religion but rejected revelation. By the third generation there were some skeptical voices calling for *the rejection of all forms of religion*. Holbach denied God, freedom, and immortality and proclaimed that matter is self-existent; Nature alone is worthy of worship: "O Nature! Sovereign of all beings! And you, her adorable daughters, virtue, reason, and truth! Be ever our only Divinities."[7] Diderot's materialistic philosophy became a more militant atheism when it was combined with the anticlericalism that was later to erupt so violently in the French Revolution. Hostility toward the church centered in its social conservatism, which was taken to be the enemy of all progress and freedom. Hume's *Dialogues on Natural Religion*, published in 1779, presented the case for skepticism in more philosophical terms, and gave to each of the arguments of natural religion a careful rebuttal which we will examine later in this chapter.

3. Man as Perfectible by Reason

The men of the Enlightenment were confident of *the power of reason* not only in science and in religion but in all human affairs.[8]

7. Baron d'Holbach, *Système de la Nature*, quoted in Franklin Baumer, *Religion and the Rise of Scepticism* (New York: Harcourt, Brace & Co., 1960), p. 64.
8. See Ernst Cassirer, *The Philosophy of the Enlightenment* (Princeton,

The Newton of the social sciences was expected momentarily; with the discovery of social laws it would soon be possible to understand society and regulate man's activities accordingly. As some interpreters saw it, once we know what is "natural" we can remove the artificial constraints imposed by governments; in economics, for example, the laws of supply and demand would automatically ensure the welfare of society. The "natural" was equated with the good and the rational. Here Nature [usually capitalized] was considered an ally of human progress; man still felt at home in an orderly and harmonious, if impersonal, world. Nature and Reason were to be the benign guides to mankind's ascent; and if their dictates seem to have varied considerably according to the liberal or conservative proclivities of particular authors, we must recall that "natural" and "reasonable" were at best rather vague concepts. Neither the detailed empirical data nor the systematic theoretical constructs of the later social sciences were yet present.

The *optimism about man* in many eighteenth-century writings was a major departure from the Christian tradition. Man is not born sinful, we read, but is born good and then corrupted by society. According to Rousseau, man is naturally virtuous, and evil arises from social institutions; we can protect the child's inherent goodness by allowing him to grow without external restraints. It was never quite clear why if nature is inherently good there is so much evil in the world, but it was agreed that evil somehow comes from the social environment and not from the attitudes of individuals. Many authors held that we must change the environment by establishing a rational society, for ignorance rather than sin limits human achievement; education and the spread of reason will accomplish the liberation of man. Condorcet wrote: "The result of my work will show by reasoning and facts that there is no limit set to the perfection of the powers of man, that human perfectibility is in reality indefinite."[9]

Expectations of human progress often knew no bounds. Awareness of the possibility of deliberate and far-reaching institutional change, which has been part of Western thought ever since the Enlightenment, was coupled with a utopian anticipation of the

---

N.J.: Princeton University Press, 1951; Beacon PB); Crane Brinton, *The Shaping of the Modern Mind* (New York: Mentor PB, 1953), Chap. 4.

9. Marquis de Condorcet, *The History of the Progress of the Human Spirit*, quoted in Randall, *Making of the Modern Mind*, p. 383.

perfection of society. It was assumed that science and material progress would automatically bring virtue and happiness. Heaven on earth would be man's achievement; the millennium was about to dawn. Soon war would be looked on as a crime. Here was a new philosophy of history in which a state of perfection would come in this life by man's efforts alone, and technology was to be the source of salvation. This was, as Carl Becker puts it, a "secular eschatology," a new vision of the heavenly city on earth.[10] Posterity, not God, would judge man's present endeavors. This was the future hope which made individual effort significant; the human race in its coming perfection was to be the object of devotion and loyalty.

Among many Enlightenment authors, especially in France, there was *great confidence in "social engineering"* and the technical control of society, with little recognition of the dangers that accompany power in the manipulation of men. Science was to be the great liberator—not the enslaver of man as in recent novels (for example, George Orwell's *1984*, Aldous Huxley's *Brave New World*). It was expected that man would rise to unprecedented heights, and all evils would vanish if individuals and societies would just follow the principles of reason. Far from being an age of skepticism, this was an age of great faith—in man and his capacities. Nature, God, and man were all approached in the same rationalistic spirit.

If some features of the Enlightenment deserve criticism, its *positive contributions* deserve acknowledgement also. It was one of the forces in the spread of religious toleration. There had been earlier voices on behalf of religious liberty—Baptists and Congregationalists upholding the principle of voluntary association, Quakers defending individual conscience, and so forth; the Enlightenment now added its defense of freedom of expression and its opposition to all forms of dogmatism and particularism. Again, the new outlook was a liberating force for human creativity, for the dignity of the individual, and for the legitimate autonomy of inquiry which is a valid aspect of secularization. At its best the eighteenth century showed a passion for social justice and humanitarian reform that can be admired even by those who do not share its utopian confidence in man's ability to engineer the ideal society. Finally, the rationalists, though antiorthodox, were seldom antireligious, and they lived in a culture that still reflected its Christian past.

---

10. Carl Becker, *The Heavenly City of the Eighteenth-Century Philosophers* (New Haven, Conn.: Yale University Press, 1932; PB), Chap. 4.

II. The Romantic Reaction

Romanticism was the rebellious child of the Enlightenment; it rejected a number of its parent's ideas, even while accepting without question many of the assumptions it inherited. The reaction against the Age of Reason is evident in many areas of thought during the last half of the eighteenth century (and continuing into the nineteenth), though the form it took and the date of its occurrence varied from country to country. In political theory there was a revival of conservatism and of concern for the values of earlier traditions—sometimes, as in the case of Edmund Burke, inspired in part by revulsion at the excesses of the French Revolution; there were new forms of nationalism and devotion to the fatherland and new philosophies of history as the unfolding of culture and spirit (for example, Hegel, Fichte, and others in Germany). We can note only two expressions of this protest that touch on science and religion. First, the Romantic Movement in literature asserted the limitations of science and attempted to deal with aspects of experience which had been neglected in the arid intellectualism of the Age of Reason. Imagination and intuition, it was now proclaimed, are as important as reason; the poet was said to respond to the beauty and inner life of nature which escape scientific analysis. Second, the Pietist and Methodist movements recovered the transforming power of personal religious experience, which had been lost among the abstract arguments of Deism.

1. Romanticism in Literature

The rejection of many of the ideals of the Enlightenment is both implicit and explicit in the literature of the Romantic Movement. The Age of Reason had concerned itself with a restricted range of human interests and experiences. "It was no accident," writes Randall, "that the scientific age of the Enlightenment produced little that can rank with the world's greatest art and poetry."[11] For it had neglected *man's emotional and imaginative life* in concentrating on his reason alone. The romantic protest turned to the richness, concreteness, and immediacy of living experience, which is not known through the artificial abstractions of scientific inquiry. The hero of

---

11. Randall, *Making of the Modern Mind*, p. 396.

Goethe's *Faust*, for example, had mastered all scientific knowledge but found it empty, and sought fulness of life by immersion in the vitality of experience. Such writers as Shelley and Byron celebrated the creative individual, the romantic hero in his struggles for love, friendship and fulfillment.

Romanticism exalted *freedom, individuality,* and *wholeness.* Against the determinism of the Enlightenment, man's freedom and creativity were proclaimed. Against preoccupation with unchanging laws in an essentially static world, there was new interest in growth and development, in the dynamic and historical—an orientation that helped to prepare the climate of thought in which the idea of the historicity of nature and its evolution could later be formulated. Against concern for the universal and the general, the new emphasis centered on uniqueness and individuality, the particular person in his self-expression. Against the abstractness of rational principles, the concreteness of human experience as lived was stressed. Against the atomism and reductionism of former decades, it was now said that organic wholes are more than the sum of their separate parts and must be grasped in their dynamic unity. And against the earlier expectation that technology and reason would bring human happiness, it now seemed that the human misery that accompanied the Industrial Revolution (and, in a very different form, the French Revolution) was evidence of the limitations of science and social engineering as sources of salvation.

A number of writers defended the importance of *feeling* and *imagination* in human understanding. Thus Coleridge suggested that the creative poet, by the fusion of metaphors and images into new wholes, communicates from the depth of his own experience and evokes the reader's response. We never know other persons by general concepts, but by acts of intuition and imagination which grasp their inner lives. Coleridge wrote extensively about existential questions of selfhood, remorse, and moral conscience. To him religious faith was not intellectual argumentation but fidelity, commitment, and decision. Man is a creature of feeling and emotion as well as reason, of heart and soul as well as mind.[12]

The *poet's vision of nature* portrayed much that the scientist had ignored. Romanticism carried on the Enlightenment's interest in

---

12. Samuel Taylor Coleridge, *Aids to Reflection* (New York: N. Tibbals and Son, 1872). See also Basil Willey, *Nineteenth-Century Studies* (London: Chatto & Windus, 1949), Chap. 1.

nature, but saw it in very different terms—not as an impersonal machine, but as a living companion, a source of warmth, vitality, and joy, of healing and restoring power. The poet's intuition can respond to the beauty of nature which eludes the cold abstractions of science. To Wordsworth a flower is far more than the botanist can study:

> Our meddling intellect
> Mis-shapes the beauteous forms of things
> We murder to dissect.[13]

> And I have felt
> A presence that disturbs me with the joy
> Of elevated thoughts, a sense sublime
> Of something far more deeply interfused,
> Whose dwelling is the light of setting suns,
> And the round ocean and the living air,
> And the blue sky and in the mind of man;
> A motion and a spirit that impels
> All thinking things, all objects of all thought,
> And rolls through all things.[14]

God is not the external creator of an impersonal machine, but a spirit pervading nature and known in man's own experience. The divine indwelling, God's immanence in the world and in the human soul, which had been lost in Deism, was reasserted by the romantic poets. Before long Tennyson would be writing that in fully understanding the flower in the crannied wall "I should know what God and man is." The beauty of nature, and its deeper spiritual reality, linking all beings together, are known in personal response, not in scientific analysis.

2. *Pietism and Methodism*

After the rationalism of the Deists and the formalism and indifference of the established churches, the upsurge of personal religion in the second half of the century was a powerful revitalization of traditional Christianity. The new evangelical fervor and recovery

---

13. William Wordsworth, "The Tables Turned," in H. F. Lowry and W. Thorp, *An Oxford Anthology of English Poetry* (New York: Oxford University Press, 1940), p. 589.
14. Wordsworth, "Tintern Abbey," in *ibid.*, p. 590.

of experiential religion occurred across national and denominational lines. In Germany, earlier in the century, *Pietism* was a reaction against Lutheran scholasticism. Spener and Francke led the movement to gather within the church small groups that could cultivate the devotional life and the inner experience of the soul. In other cases separate communities were formed, such as the Moravian Brethren who resolved to practice a more rigorous pattern of Christian life and morality. These groups spoke of the experience of the Holy Spirit and the new life in Christ, and urged a return to the simplicity of the gospel and its transforming power. Not dogmas or reasoned arguments but personal experience of God's presence and the regeneration of individual life were taken as primary. Kant, whom we shall consider shortly, acknowledged the influence of his pietistic upbringing and defended the importance of the realm of inner experience—especially man's moral conscience —as the basis of religion.

The Methodist movement brought a similar religious renewal to the British scene. John Wesley, in the decades following his "conversion" in 1738, preached a message of personal evangelical faith; in doctrine he did not depart substantially from the early Reformation, but in practice he stressed Christian commitment and conversion—"spiritual rebirth" in response to Christ as personal savior. Where the Enlightenment had seen ignorance as man's chief problem, and knowledge as its remedy, Wesley held that man's self-centeredness is overcome only in a more radical transformation and reorientation of the self. Love and ethical concern are fruits of the new life in Christ and the power of the Spirit in human experience. But Wesley also emphasized individual moral exertion and an ethic of pure living and Christian discipleship, at a time when moral laxity was widespread. He preached of man's freedom to strive for perfection; though sanctification occurs only with the help of God's grace, man is capable of growth in the Christian life. Only later did this ethical concern tend to become a legalistic moralism.

In America, the great *religious revivals* of the early nineteenth century swept westward with the frontier; the Deism which had been prominent at the time the nation was founded virtually disappeared. The message of repentance, acceptance of Christ, and practical morality was preached by camp-meeting orator, circuit rider, and rural pastor. From both Europe and America the expanding missionary movement took the gospel to the corners of the world. The theology of all these groups was traditional, and they justified their beliefs by quotations from the Bible. But because they emphasized personal religion rather than theological creeds, they helped to prepare the way for Protestant liberalism, which sought to justify beliefs as interpretations of religious experience. In the next chapter we will find Schleiermacher, the "father of liberal theology," making use of the romantic appeal to intuition and immediate awareness as well as the evangelical insistence on the primacy of religious experience, in a new attempt to reformulate theology on an experiential basis.

III. PHILOSOPHICAL RESPONSES

The two greatest philosophers of the eighteenth century were profoundly influenced by the growth of science, and both wrote extensively about religion, though they differed in their conclusions. Hume, emphasizing the empirical side of science, held that all knowledge is derived from sense-impressions; scientific theories and laws are summaries of observations. Judged by these standards, the evidence for religious beliefs appeared unconvincing, and Hume gave detailed replies to the arguments for a First Cause and an intelligent Designer. Kant's view of science, on the other hand, gave prominence to the role of man's mind in the interpretation of data. He defended the basis of religion in man's practical life and inner experience, especially in moral conscience. We will summarize the views of these two men on the relation of science and religion, since their theories of knowledge have had far-reaching influence on subsequent thought.

1. Scientific Empiricism and Religious Agnosticism (Hume)

Descartes, Leibniz, and Spinoza in the seventeenth century had been impressed by the rational, theoretical, mathematical side of the early physics. In line with the dominant Western philosophical tradition going back to Plato, they had maintained that true knowledge consists of the mind's grasp of innate ideas. For them, mathematics was the prototype of knowledge, for its reasoning is certain, universal, and a priori—that is, deducible from self-evident truths or the relationships among ideas without any resort to particular observations. Bacon, by contrast, had stressed the observational side of science, and Locke had given the first systematic formulation of

empiricism, which drew much of its inspiration from the importance of experiment and observation in Newtonian science. Locke
insisted that the mind, far from having any innate ideas, is a *tabula
rasa,* a blank tablet, on which the senses write. Ideas are empirical
in origin, built up from the particular impressions of the five senses.
The mind receives and rearranges physical sense-perceptions, not
universal forms or structures of thought.

Like Locke, David Hume (1711–1776) held that the only reliable
human knowledge is based on *sense-impressions* that are discrete,
fleeting, and fragmentary—patches of color, momentary sounds, and
the like. Ideas are memory-images of these perceptions, and their
validity must be tested by tracing them back to the sense-data from
which they arose. Any purported idea that is not derivable from the
senses is meaningless. Hume says that if an idea is ambiguous a
person should always "have recourse to the impressions which ren-
der it clear and precise":

> When we entertain, therefore, any suspicion that a philosophical term
> is employed without any meaning or idea (as is but too frequent),
> we need but to inquire, *from what impression is that supposed idea
> derived?* And if it be impossible to assign any, this will serve to con-
> firm our suspicion.[15]

Hume defends an "atomistic" view of experience as a succession of
separate and disconnected perceptions; he holds that we have no
knowledge of the relations between impressions. Moreover, the
human self is not a continuing entity with an enduring unity, but
a stream of such isolated impressions. The mind merely records,
rearranges, and compares sense-data. Hume is thus led to assert
that a scientific theory or law is simply a convenient summary
and correlation of individual observations—a view we will find
echoed by Hume's intellectual descendants, the logical positivists
of the twentieth century.

Among the concepts to which Hume applies this theory of knowledge is the idea of *causality.*[16] Traditionally causality had been
understood as necessary connection; if a cause occurs, then its effect
must occur. But, says Hume, we cannot observe necessary connec-

---

15. David Hume, *An Enquiry Concerning Human Understanding* (Chicago:
Open Court, 1927), p. 19.
16. See David Hume, *Treatise on Human Nature* (Oxford: Clarendon
Press, 1958), Book I Pt. 3; also *Enquiry Concerning Human Understanding,*
Secs. 4–7.

tion, or any kind of compulsion or power that one event has over another. We observe only repeated temporal succession among sense-impressions: A followed shortly by B on numerous occasions. This constant conjunction leads to a habit of association, so that when A occurs we come to expect B. But the connection is only psychological, an expectancy or anticipation formed in our minds by force of habit. The terms "cause" and "effect" do not correspond to any observable attributes, but only to our customary way of looking at events that repeatedly follow each other. Thus the so-called "laws of nature" are not prescriptions of what has to happen, and scientific knowledge is never universal or certain; laws are only probable expectations based on previous experience. Science does not require any absolute necessity in connections among occurrences, but only regularities in sequences of observations that lead us to assume they will be repeated.

If "causality" is only a habit of expectation, Hume argues, then *the argument for God as First Cause* is undermined.[17] For expectations can arise only from the repetition of sequences, and can never be justified from just one instance; moreover, a cause can never be known from its effect alone. We have indeed seen men making clocks, and thus when we find a clock we assume it was made by a clockmaker. But we have not observed a Creator creating other universes, and we cannot generalize from experience concerning the production of worlds. From similar effects we infer similar causes, but there are no analogies for the universe as a whole. Science asks only about limited sequences, not about the total process or the origin of the order and structure of events; any statement beyond science is speculation. Since every cause we have encountered was also an effect, it would be more reasonable (if we did speculate) to assume an infinite series of events in a self-sufficient universe, rather than an uncaused First Cause.

Hume also attacks the prevalent *argument from design*. Supposing that we were to accept the argument for a First Cause, he asks, what kind of cause would we infer? If there is order in the world, the organizing force might be within nature rather than external to it; the world appears less like a clock or machine than like a plant or animal with an internal principle of life. Why not stop with the assertion that there is some principle of order within the world, or

17. David Hume, *Dialogues Concerning Natural Religion* (New York: Social Science Publishers, 1948).

perhaps a generative force or a blind vitality? The phenomena of the universe are too varied for us to pick any one of its aspects as the basis for an analogy. There is also so much pain and suffering that we would have to assume either two world-powers, one working for good and the other for evil, or else a single morally neutral creator. From a finite world one could at best infer only a finite God; relative good in the world suggests only a relative goodness in its cause. We need postulate only a degree of power and intelligence sufficient to account for the properties of the effects, rather than ascribe infinite attributes and absolute perfections.

Hume thus *rejects the Enlightenment's confidence in the power of reason* in all areas of thought. He is skeptical of the possibility of demonstrable knowledge of the laws of nature. He shows that no universal laws can be derived from particular observations, and points to the circularity of all attempts to justify induction. He demonstrates that necessity can be attributed only to logical relations; all propositions about existent things are radically contingent, since "whatever is, might not be." But Hume says that when he steps out of his study he has to put aside his doubts (for example, about the existence of objects, selves, and causal connections), and fall back on "*common sense*" and "*natural belief*." Life would be impossible on the basis of "unmitigated skepticism."[18] He cannot avoid the conviction that events are caused; this is a "natural sentiment" based on feeling and instinct, even though it is not demonstrable on the basis of reason. Custom, common sense, and moral sentiment are reliable enough for practical purposes; but they do not lead to rationally justifiable knowledge.

There are some passages in Hume's writings in which he seems to allow for comparable "*natural beliefs*" *in religion*, or a kind of implicit faith that has its own validity quite apart from the dubious reasoning of natural theology. In the conclusion of the *Dialogues on Natural Religion*, Philo, the skeptic, confesses to "a deeper sense of religion impressed on the mind." He concedes that the presence of design strikes him "with irresistible force," even though the arguments for it are logically unconvincing, and he postulates a divine intelligence "bearing some remote analogy to the human mind." But he continues to doubt the idea of God's goodness, and the limited

18. David Hume, *Enquiry*, pp. 171f.

acknowledgment of "natural beliefs" in religion is at best rather vague and ambiguous. Other passages—such as his discussion of the insignificance of mind in the universe, or his suggestion that the principle of order is entirely internal to the world—seem to endorse a metaphysics of naturalism. But his most frequent assertions —which are supported by his own theory of knowledge—are neither theistic nor atheistic but *agnostic*: God's existence can be neither proved nor disproved, and in the absence of dependable evidence it is best to reserve judgment about such ultimate questions.[19]

Whatever his own positive beliefs may have been, Hume's main religious impact stemmed from his attack on Deism and natural theology. In future chapters we will scrutinize several presuppositions underlying his attack. We will find his *extreme empiricism* inadequate even as a description of science, for it neglects the crucial role of man's creative imagination in inventing concepts and theories by which the data are interpreted. We will reject his "atomistic" view of experience, and will stress the contextual character of knowledge, the apprehension of relations and wholes as well as parts. Again, the form of the teleological argument which he attacked assumed *the Newtonian world-machine* with an external Designer, analogous to clock and clockmaker. More recent reformulations of the argument are in certain respects less vulnerable to his critique, for they assume an evolutionary universe with immanent principles of order—more analogous to an organism than to a machine—and they ask about the ultimate basis of such built-in orderliness. Finally, we will find that many contemporary theologians agree with Hume in *rejecting natural theology*, but do so primarily on other grounds; they hold that religion is not based on rational argument but on historical revelation or on moral and religious experience. The use of moral experience as the point of departure for religious beliefs was proposed by Kant, who joined in undermining natural theology—but only "in order to make room for faith."

---

19. On the balance between an attenuated theism, an implicit naturalism and a philosophical agnosticism in his writings, see Stuart Hampshire in D. Pears, ed., *David Hume: A Symposium* (New York: St. Martin's Press, 1963); Antony Flew, *Hume's Philosophy of Belief* (London: Routledge & Kegan Paul, 1961), pp. 272–73; George Thomas, *Religious Philosophies of the West* (New York: Charles Scribner's Sons, 1965; PB), pp. 214–27; N. K. Smith, *The Philosophy of David Hume* (London: Macmillan, 1941).

2. Science and Religion as Separate Realms (Kant)

Immanuel Kant (1724–1804) provided a new approach to the reconciliation of science and religion. He was greatly impressed by Newtonian science with its dependence on empirical observation, but he held that there are limitations in the methods of science which leave room for religious beliefs. Let us examine first his analysis of science, in which elements of *empiricism* and *rationalism* are combined in a novel synthesis.[20] Kant agrees with Hume that there is no knowledge apart from experience. But he is convinced that the mind does not simply receive sense-data passively, but organizes them actively in accordance with its own interpretive principles. The mind brings to the confused flux of fragmentary impressions a distinctive way of structuring and relating them; the categories of human thought are imposed on the raw materials of the senses. But these forms of understanding are not, as the rationalists had assumed, innate *a priori* ideas known in themselves with certainty in independence of experience; they are instead ways of ordering experience, and are empty apart from their use on concrete data. Knowledge is thus the joint product of sensory material and the structure of consciousness which actively organizes and interprets by its own forms of understanding.

Among the *forms of sensibility* imposed by the mind are space and time. We organize experience, Kant says, by spatial and temporal relations, and we cannot imagine a world without them, even though space and time cannot be directly perceived. They are forms of thought which determine the way we both perceive and conceive of things. They specify the framework of possible experience, since they are part of our mode of apprehending relationships between events. Causality, in turn, is a *category of understanding* which is brought to the interpretation of sense-data rather than derived therefrom. The idea that "every event has a cause" is not an empirical observation or a generalization from experience, but an indispensable presupposition of human thought. Causality is a general form by means of which the mind unifies the chaos of discrete data. Man's mind provides all the most general categories for interpreting the relationships among impressions—notions such as whole and part, substance and attribute, cause and effect.

20. Immanuel Kant, *Critique of Pure Reason*, trans. N. K. Smith (New York: Humanities Press, 1950), pp. 41–62.

Scientific knowledge is thus limited to perceptual experience, the realm of *phenomena* or "appearances," according to Kant. We can know only how the world appears when seen through the forms of human understanding, the mental "spectacles" that influence not only perception but the very modes in which we can conceive of events. We can never know *"things-in-themselves"* apart from whatever distortions may be introduced by our mental processes. Science is valid within the sphere of phenomena but it is incapable of revealing what reality is like apart from our limited human modes of thought; science deals only with cause-effect, spatio-temporal relations. The world as it is in itself is forever inaccessible to us. Moreover, these limitations cannot be transcended by arguments for a First Cause, which Kant criticizes at length.[21] He agrees with Hume that the idea of causality can only be applied to perceptual experience (though he disagrees in ascribing its origin to man's built-in categories of understanding). We can have no experience of the-world-as-a-whole to which a causal interpretation might properly apply; the concept of cause can be used only for terms within a temporal series, not for the entire series. Hence neither the proof nor the disproof of God's existence is possible by the ordinary processes of human knowledge.

For Kant the starting point of religion lies in an entirely different realm, man's sense of *moral obligation*.[22] Not theoretical problems of metaphysics but practical problems of ethics require God as a postulate. Man experiences value as well as fact; he asks not only what is, but what ought to be, and above all, what he ought to do. Kant gives as one formulation of the moral law the injunction to act in such a fashion that the maxim of your action could be universally adopted by all men; that is, you should apply to yourself only the rules you would be willing for other men to apply. This leads to a second formulation, that "persons should always be treated as ends, never as means." These are "categorical imperatives," independent of particular circumstances or individual inclinations; they are universal obligations that are rationally justifiable for all human beings, and are not questions of a person's feelings or affections. Ethics for Kant consists in the duty to follow the universal law, the principle of unlimited generalization, which we

---

21. *Ibid.*, pp. 507ff.
22. *Kant's Critique of Practical Reason and other works on the Theory of Ethics*, trans. T. K. Abbott (London: Longmans Green, 1923), pp. 38ff.

know ought to be obeyed whether or not anyone else follows it. Kant goes on to suggest that *God is a postulate of the moral order.*[23] Religious beliefs are essentially assumptions required by our recognition of moral obligation. When we act from response to duty we implicitly affirm that the world is a moral order; the presence of moral law presupposes a lawgiver who is its source and guarantor. Moral endeavor requires some sort of correlation between virtue and ultimate happiness; we are led to postulate a Being who will bring about justice by ensuring that virtue is proportionately rewarded in the next life. Similarly, Kant holds that recognition of ethical imperatives implies the existence of *human freedom.* Determinism does indeed reign in the realm of phenomena studied by science, for causality is an inescapable category in the interpretation of all events in space and time, and science deals with patterns of causal law. But the acknowledgment of "ought" in practical life presupposes alternatives of choice. Hence practical reason affirms both God and freedom, even though theoretical reason cannot prove their existence.

Kant states that moral experience provides justification for thinking of God as real, *but does not provide the basis for claims of religious knowledge.* The certainty we have concerning God is practical rather than theoretical. We must act as if these beliefs were true, though we cannot prove their truth. Like Hume and the empiricists, Kant is suspicious of metaphysics and tries to avoid statements about reality or things-in-themselves; he insists on restricting theoretical reason to the interpretation of the phenomena of sense-experience. He resists using moral experience as the starting point for a new kind of theistic metaphysics.[24] To be sure, in some late passages Kant seems to hold that in moral obligation we experience God himself. He also finds in man's response to purpose and beauty in the world, which escape the scientist's analysis, significant evidence of a supraphenomenal order.[25] But even here he ends by admitting teleological explanation only as a "regulative principle" applicable solely to phenomena.

23. *Ibid.*, pp. 219f.
24. On the status of Kant's "postulate" of God, see Harald Hoffding, *A History of Modern Philosophy* (New York: Humanities Press, 1950), Chap. 7; F. E. England, *Kant's Conception of God* (London: Allen & Unwin, 1929); H. J. Paton, *The Categorical Imperative* (Chicago: University of Chicago Press, 1948).
25. Immanuel Kant, *Critique of Judgment*, trans. J. H. Bernard (New York: The Macmillan Company, 1931).

Kant's philosophy, then, was *a response to science and religion* of much greater epistemological complexity than the earlier response of Deism. "Two things," he wrote, "fill the mind with ever new and increasing admiration and awe, the oftener and more steadily we reflect on them: *the starry heavens above and the moral law within.*"[26] He had great respect for Newtonian science, and insisted that claims of knowledge must be restricted to empirically based relations among natural phenomena. Yet—in keeping with the biblical tradition and his own pietistic background—Kant attached great importance to moral choice, good and evil, sin and judgment; but he departed from that tradition in making ethics primary and central, and religion secondary and derivative. As a child of the Age of Reason, he interpreted ethics as obedience to universal rational principles; but he went beyond that Age in his recognition of the limitations of "theoretical reason" and in his use of "practical reason" as the basis of religion. To him, both the natural and the moral order were rational, but they constituted independent realms.

Kant thus provided *a new modus vivendi between science and religion.* Each has its own realm and function, and they do not compete with each other. Religion does not have to defend itself by pointing to the ever-diminishing gaps in the scientific account or to purported evidences of design. In the realm of phenomena, science is exhaustively competent and its laws are universally applicable. The function of religious beliefs is not to extend scientific explanations, but to clarify and support moral life by relating it to the character of ultimate reality.

> For Kant, science and religion occupy entirely different spheres and are given distinct functions which are so adjusted that they need never conflict. The realm of possible knowledge belongs to science, and science has complete freedom to explore that realm by its own method. The task of religion is to enlighten our moral devotion and give it cosmic serenity.[27]

Kant asserted that he had "found it necessary to deny knowledge in order to make room for faith."[28] Actually his critical writing—especially his skepticism of natural theology and metaphysics—had more immediate impact than his positive attempt to reconstruct theology on a moral foundation. Nevertheless, the influence of his

---

26. Kant, *Critique of Practical Reason*, p. 260.
27. E. A. Burtt, *Types of Religious Philosophy*, rev. ed. (New York: Harper and Brothers, 1951), p. 266.
28. Kant, *Critique of Pure Reason*, p. 29.

constructive ideas is evident in much of nineteenth-century philosophy and theology. In *philosophical idealism* (Hegel and his successors) the rationalist elements in Kant's thought were developed at the expense of his empiricist and antimetaphysical convictions; the structures of consciousness were taken to be the pattern of reality, and God was interpreted as Absolute Mind. In *Protestant liberalism*, Kant's moral interpretation of religion was combined with loyalty to the theological context of biblical ethics; man's value-experience was seen as the clue to the nature of reality, and the "moral argument" for the existence of God was set forth. Although *existentialism* (Kierkegaard and his successors) strongly rejected Kant's rationalism, later existentialists, starting from very different assumptions, have echoed Kant's contention that religion contributes to man's practical life and conduct rather than to metaphysical knowledge; they assert that man is a responsible agent before he is a knower, and that the context of religion is the activity of selves in decision, not abstract speculation. These schools of thought offered alternative analyses of the relations of science and religion, which we will encounter in the next chapter.

IV. SUMMARY

In this chapter we have briefly indicated the development during the eighteenth century of new patterns of thought concerning three of our topics:

1. GOD AND NATURE. Laplace's writing was taken as representative of the deterministic and reductionistic view of nature as a self-sufficient machine in which all future events are inexorably determined by the laws of matter-in-motion. (In later chapters we will suggest that such determinism is undermined today by the Heisenberg Principle, and that reductionism must be replaced by an organismic understanding of successive levels of organization in nature.) Concomitantly, God was portrayed as the remote and impersonal clockmaker, the cosmic architect of Deism—or omitted completely in the materialistic philosophies of the French Enlightenment. The Romantic Movement went to the opposite extreme, picturing nature as creative, spontaneous, and growing, permeated by beauty and an underlying spiritual reality. Here God's immanence in nature and in the soul of man was reasserted. Methodism, Pietism, and the evangelical revivals recovered the biblical view of a personal God actively related to man, but had little to say about God's relationship to nature.

2. METHODS IN SCIENCE. Many thinkers of the Enlightenment wanted to extend to all problems the methods of science, which they equated somewhat vaguely with the pursuit of the "natural" and the "reasonable"; neither the value of precise data, nor the role of human interpretive concepts, nor the distinctive problems arising in the social sciences were recognized in this initial enthusiasm for the omnicompetence of scientific methods. Hume dwelt on the empirical side of science and concluded that any idea that cannot be traced to sense-data is without significance; for him, as for recent positivists, empirical verification is the criterion for all knowledge. Kant, on the other hand, maintained that man's mind supplies crucial categories of interpretation. In Chapter 6 we will discuss in detail the relation betwen the empirical and the rational components of science.

3. METHODS IN THEOLOGY. There were three basic approaches to religious knowledge, and their relative strength varied greatly during the century. (a) *Revelation.* During the Enlightenment the idea of historical revelation came under increasing attack. But Methodism and Pietism later recovered the convictions of the Reformation concerning the centrality of Christ and scripture as sources of man's understanding of God. (b) *Natural Theology.* The early part of the century saw extensive use of the arguments for a First Cause and an intelligent Designer. But the influence of these arguments declined—in part because of specific criticisms, such as those of Hume and Kant, in part because of greater skepticism about the ability of reason to attain ultimate truth, and in part because the abstract approach of Deism did not capture the popular imagination. We will suggest later that the attitudes of natural theology bear little resemblance to those of the participants in actual religious communities. (c) *Moral and Religious Experience.* A third source of religious knowledge, distinct from both revealed and natural theology, came into prominence late in the century. The Romantic Movement defended intuition, imagination, and the immediacy of experience. The Methodist revival, though traditional in its doctrines, encouraged experiential religion and personal reorientation. Kant found the basis for religion in the experience of moral obligation. In each of these cases there was indicated a sphere for religion that did not compete with the sphere of science. These attempts to justify religious beliefs in terms of moral and religious experience were developed further in the nineteenth century and contributed to the formation of Protestant liberalism.

4

Biology and Theology
in the Nineteenth Century

The interaction of scientific and religious ideas in the nineteenth century was complex, for alongside new viewpoints there continued patterns of thought already firmly established in previous centuries. On the scientific side, physics expanded dramatically with theories about light, electricity, and thermodynamics; totally new types of scientific concepts were employed, such as interacting fields and statistical probabilities. Chemistry in its modern form grew, from its foundation in Dalton's atomic theory early in the century to Mendeleev's formulation of the periodic table and the rise of organic chemistry by its close. A flourishing practical technology based on these physical sciences was contributing to the industrial revolution, which changed the face of Western society and indirectly altered man's view of the world. Limitations of space restrict our discussion to biology, for it was in this area that the scientific development occurred which undoubtedly had the most far-reaching impact on human thought, constituting one of the major revolutions in intellectual history.

Darwin occupies a place in biology not unlike that of Newton in physics. Each man proposed a set of theoretical concepts which was able to encompass within a single unified scheme vast reaches of data from many types of phenomena—animate and inanimate, respectively. In both cases, scientific ideas greatly influenced other fields of thought. Each man's work served as the point of departure for the elaboration of a distinctive world-view—summed up in the image of nature as an intelligently designed machine, in Newton's case, and as a dynamic and progressive process, in Darwin's. The argument from design, so typical of the natural theology which merged Newtonian and deistic assumptions, was in turn one of the ideas most seriously challenged by the theory of evolution. In evaluating the views of Darwin, as of Newton, it is difficult to draw a line between scientific conclusions and philosophical or theological interpretations, but for the sake of clarity we must attempt to make such distinctions.

In the first section below, the contributions of Darwin and his forerunners at the scientific level are summarized. In Section II, "Theological Issues in Evolution," the central problems behind the ensuing controversy are analyzed: the challenge to purpose and design in the world, the threat to man's dignity, the character of the authority of the Bible, and the ambiguity of attempts to derive ethical norms from evolution. Section III, "Diverging Currents in Theology," considers some of the specific responses, from traditionalist to modernist, which occurred in Protestant and Catholic circles, and some varieties of evolutionary naturalism. Also indicated are additional factors in the rise of liberal theology, especially the new biblical scholarship and the appeal to religious experience as the basis of theological beliefs. A final section summarizes and evaluates these reactions to evolution.

I. DARWIN AND NATURAL SELECTION

The component elements of the theory of evolution had been separately proposed long before the publication of *Origin of Species* in 1859; it needed Darwin's genius and persistence to fit these ideas together into a unified theory and to collect an impressive array of evidence in its support. That this synthesis did not occur earlier may also be attributable, at least in part, to the prevalent assumptions which formed the mental climate of scientist and theologian alike; evolution involved a radically new way of looking at the history of nature. After brief mention of some of Darwin's forerunners in both geology and biology, we will outline his work as a scientist and suggest the view of nature implied by his theory.

1. *Forerunners of Darwin*

Charles Lyell's *Principles of Geology* (1830) marks the birth of modern geology. Up to this time, the prevailing geological theory had been *"catastrophism,"* which postulated a sequence of great cataclysms (Noah's flood being the most recent), between which God had created new species. Such a series of acts of divine creation bore some resemblance to the Genesis account, and yet could allow for the differing fossils discovered in successive rock strata. By 1801 Cuvier had reconstructed from fossil bones some twenty-three species now extinct, including the giant mastodon; but he held that such creatures were produced by divine intervention amid great world upheavals unlike any present-day events. As early as 1795 James Hutton had defended the opposing *"uniformitarian"* view, which assumed the operation of natural causes such as vulcanism, sedimentation, and erosion through great spans of time; Lyell carried uniformitarianism much further, and gave for a wide variety of geological phenomena the first detailed and systematic explanation which assumed that regular laws "within the existing order of nature" had acted throughout the past. Lyell's portrayal of the long, slow working of natural processes was acknowledged by Darwin as a formative influence on his own thought.

The new geology did not, however, alter the prevailing assumption of biologists concerning *the fixity of species.* In the previous century, Linnaeus had worked out the first comprehensive system of botanical classification; he held that the distinction of species depends on the existence of separate lineages which do not change. The usefulness of his classificatory scheme helped to perpetuate the conviction that there are permanent differences between species. To be sure, Buffon had pointed out the natural variability of species and suggested that the extinction of some types might be related to the struggle for survival. And in 1802 Lamarck had defended unlimited organic change, maintaining that an animal's organs develop through use and that these acquired modifications are inherited; for example, the short-necked ancestors of the giraffe would have gradually developed longer necks by reaching for leaves. But Lamarck's view found few supporters during his lifetime. The advocates of the stability of species prevailed—less because of opposition to science on the part of the church than because of ingrained habits of thought on the part of biologists themselves.[1] As the history of science often demonstrates, the scientist is part of a larger culture whose thought-patterns influence the questions he finds it important to ask, the categories by which he interprets his data, and the assumptions which govern the formulation of his theories.

Belief in *the stability of biological forms*, which for so long dominated Western thought, itself had several sources. It was in part a corollary of the conviction that each type of being was created by God in its present form, as depicted in Genesis. It was in some measure a product of the Aristotelian doctrine that all individual beings are embodiments of eternal forms or unchanging essences. Moreover, in "teleological explanation" the goals of each being and the "final causes" of its activity were taken as the primary explanation of the organism's structures, and the search for other types of explanation tended to be bypassed. Thus Darwin can be said to have given the deathblow to Aristotelian biology, as Newton did to Aristotelian physics. But until he did, the assumption of the fixity of the species was not seriously challenged.

In this period before Darwin, the rise of modern geology thus produced *no acute conflict between science and religion*. The issue of biblical authority caused little alarm. Uncritical biblical literalism had long since been questioned; the six days of Genesis were readily interpretable as "epochs," or taken as allegorical or figurative expressions. Moreover, none of the basic biblical affirmations had been challenged. The status of man was not yet threatened; if each species was endowed with its present form at the time it was created, and if man was a special creation by God, human uniqueness was protected. As Gillispie points out,[2] geology did not undermine the argument from design.

The argument from design in fact still enjoyed great popularity, despite the criticisms by Hume and Kant. Where Luther and Calvin had held that God's purposeful control of nature is not overtly

---

1. See Bentley Glass, ed., *Forerunners of Darwin* (Baltimore: Johns Hopkins Press, 1959); Gertrude Himmelfarb, *Darwin and the Darwinian Revolution* (New York: Doubleday & Co., 1959; PB).

2. Charles C. Gillispie, *Genesis and Geology* (Cambridge, Mass.: Harvard University Press, 1951; Harper PB).

visible to man, the "natural theologians" were by the early nineteenth century very confident in the power of man's reason to discover unambiguously within the biological order the beneficent plan of God's wisdom. Many volumes were written in this period tracing the providential adaptation of creatures to their goals; these works were aided by, and in turn even contributed to, the accumulation of careful anatomical observations. Paley's widely read *Natural Theology* (1802) gave many examples, such as the eye's complex structure coordinated to the one aim of vision. He argued that just as a person on a desert island, finding a watch whose parts are integrated in the accomplishment of a single purpose, must assume the existence of a watchmaker, so we, from the presence of design in natural organisms, must assume the existence of an intelligent Designer.

The *Bridgewater Treatises* popularized other biological discoveries "in which was displayed the benevolent contrivance of means to ends." There were books entitled *Physico-Theology, Insect-Theology,* and *Water-Theology,* extolling the workmanship and foresight of the Creator as revealed by new scientific findings. The reader was advised that if sometimes an organ looks superfluous or inefficient, either he does not understand it or he must conclude that a simpler construction would have failed to show God's ingenuity. The gradations of complexity among living forms, which were coming to light in great profusion, were understood not as clues to historical and developmental (phylogenetic) relationships, but as steps in the ordained hierarchy of life, the immutable "chain of being," of which man was the highest member and final end.[3] Usefulness to man, for whose benefit nature was contrived, was taken as a sufficient explanation for the existence of lower forms of life. Natural theology was here cast in a form that was to prove particularly vulnerable to the concept of evolution.

2. Darwin's Scientific Work

Serving as naturalist on the "Beagle" in 1832 as it started a five-year voyage around the world was the young Charles Darwin. The second volume of Lyell's book on geology reached him while he was observing flora and fauna in South America. The critical experience of the trip was his study of *slight variations among species,*

3. Loren Eiseley, *Darwin's Century* (New York: Doubleday & Co., 1958; PB°), Chap. 1.

especially those found between one island and the next in the remote Galapagos chain. For on each island a species could have developed in isolation from neighboring islands, and small differences could be preserved under similar environmental conditions. Six years later, reading Malthus on the role of human population pressure and competition, Darwin found the clue for a theory by which to interpret the data collected on the voyage. As he later records:

> . . . being well-prepared to appreciate the struggle for existence which everywhere goes on, from long-continued observation of the habits of animals and plants, it at once struck me that under these circumstances favorable variations would tend to be preserved and unfavorable ones to be destroyed. The result of this would be the formation of new species. Here, then, I had at last got a theory by which to work.[4]

His theory of natural selection combined several ideas: (a) *Random variations.* Darwin had ample evidence of the occurrence and the inheritability of minute and apparently spontaneous variations among the individual members of a species. He could only conjecture about the causes of these differences, but he recognized that his theory did not in itself require an explanation for them; all he needed to know was that variations do take place, whatever their cause. (b) *The struggle for survival.* In general, more young organisms are born than can survive to parenthood. Some variations confer a slight advantage in the intense competition for existence that occurs between members of a species and between different species in a given environment. (c) *The survival of the fittest.* The individuals having such an advantage will on the average live longer, have more progeny, and hence multiply slightly more rapidly. Over a long period of time this will result in the "natural selection" of such variations, and the corresponding reduction and finally elimination of other less favorable variations, so that the gradual transformation of the species occurs.

Darwin's work exhibits clearly the characteristic method of science, the fruitful interplay of *observation* and *theory.* No amount of data constitutes a scientific theory unless it is unified by the creative invention of an imaginative hypothesis; but no theory alone is of use in science unless it can be tested against individual observations

---

4. Francis Darwin, ed., *Life and Letters of Charles Darwin* (New York: D. Appleton & Co., 1887), Vol. I, 68.

and can guide the further collection of data. Before he finally published *Origin of Species* in 1859, Darwin had spent twenty-five years amassing from many fields an amazing array of facts on the variation of species. He studied in detail the breeding of domesticated animals, such as dogs, in which the owner selects from among a given species the variations he wants to favor, and thereby, after many generations of selection, produces new types never previously existing—from greyhound to St. Bernard to chihuahua. Here was evolution, with human choice replacing natural survival as the agent of selection among the small variations whose cumulative effects add up to major modifications. Darwin studied problems as diverse as hybridization of plants, comparative structures of embryos, "vestigial" or rudimentary organs, and the geographical distribution of animal and plant forms, both living and extinct. The sheer range and magnitude of the data he brought into correlation with his theory is staggering.

In his first book Darwin avoided mention of man, but a dozen years later he gave a thorough discussion of human origins in *The Descent of Man* (1871). He tried to show how all of man's characteristics might be accounted for in terms of the gradual modification of anthropoid ancestors by the process of natural selection. In the case of anatomical structure the close resemblance of man and gorilla had already been widely noted; Darwin indicated how upright posture, larger brain size, and other distinctive changes might have been produced. He insisted that human moral and mental faculties differ in degree rather than in kind from the capacities of animals, among which there are the rudiments of feeling and communication. Man's own existence, hitherto considered sacrosanct, was thus brought within the sphere of natural law and analyzed in the same categories applied to other forms of life.

3. Nature as Dynamic Process

Let us consider the impact of the theory of evolution on the prevailing view of nature. First, the *importance of change* had already been suggested in specific areas by earlier theories such as the nebular hypothesis in astronomy, uniformitarianism in geology, and the discovery of extinct species in paleontology, but it took Darwin's work to convince the scientific community that all of nature is in a state of flux. It is difficult for us today to imagine the revolution in thought which occurred when the world was no longer seen as an essentially static structure of immutable forms, but as characterized throughout by development and change. Stability had been only an illusion produced by man's limited time scale. There was introduced not only an almost inconceivably immense span of time but the concept that time itself—in nature and not just in the human drama—is irreversible and historical rather than cyclic or stationary. With the "unfreezing" of the patterns of life the world was transformed from a fixed hierarchical order into a dynamic process.

Second, nature became a complex of *interacting forces in organic interdependence*. The interaction of the individual with the environment assumed much greater significance. To be sure, the idea of struggle and the picture of "nature red in tooth and claw" seem in retrospect to have been carried to excess by Darwin's successors —perhaps in part because of the influence of the reigning social philosophy of competitive individualism. The concept was even extended to the "internal struggle" among the parts of an organism (for example, T. H. Huxley's references to competition among the molecules of the body, or Weismann's later postulation of natural selection among competing particles in the germ plasm). Today greater attention is given to the sources of coordination and organization within the body and the structures of internal stability and harmony, which were neglected in Darwin's day. Moreover, the cooperative aspects of nature, such as the social behavior of insects and animals, have been found to be as important as the competitive aspects. Nevertheless, the interactive character of "the web of life" and the importance of the environmental context have since Darwin been permanent features of our view of nature.

Third, evolution entailed the extension of *the rule of law* to new areas of nature. At first sight, the role of *chance* in Darwin's theory might seem to have constituted a limit to the domain of lawfulness. Variations arise accidentally, but they are preserved lawfully according to the advantage they confer. Though both law and chance thus contribute to change, attention was directed primarily to the lawlike aspects. The ratio of individuals surviving from variations with differing characteristics was taken to be in principle a quantitative question, calculable by the mathematics of probability; here was a new kind of law which incorporated chance, namely a statistical law. Moreover some of Darwin's defenders were advocates of determinism. T. H. Huxley, the most vocal British champion of evolution, held that chance is but the operation of natural laws not yet known, and argued that from primeval conditions all subsequent events could in principle have been predicted. Only at the close of the century was the role of chance emphasized, and welcomed as a release from the determinism of inexorable law; for Peirce, James, Bergson, and more recently Whitehead, chance was an indication of spontaneity, novelty, and creativity, a source of the genuinely new and unpredictable in the history of nature.

Fourth, nature was now understood to include *man and his culture*. To many observers the animal ancestry of man implied that human culture could also be analyzed in categories derived from biology. Some authors hoped to deduce from the principle of evolution the laws of every field, from astronomy to ethics. In other cases social scientists, eager to exploit the prestige of the new science, turned to biology for analogies, as in the previous century they had turned to physics. A society was said to be an organism, and social adaptation amid group struggle was the key to its survival. In more general terms, evolution stimulated the social scientist's interest in the processes of change and development. Critical methods of historical research were already in use, thanks largely to the Romantic Movement with its concern for origins and growth. These trends combined to encourage a historical and genetic approach, in which ideas, institutions, cultures, and religions were seen as evolving. There were many oversimplified schemes of the "stages" through which all societies pass; most later sociologists have repudiated this assumption that there is one uniform line of social development. The impact of evolution on the social sciences is beyond the scope of this volume, but we will find some parallel problems as we turn to the implications of evolution for theology.

II. THEOLOGICAL ISSUES IN EVOLUTION

In considering the debate that followed the publication of Darwin's *Origin*, it is not easy to disentangle the various issues involved, and in much of the controversy the levels of discussion were intermingled. Evolution as a biological theory was confused with evolutionary naturalism as an interpretive philosophy; some men supported both, others opposed both. An increasing group, however, accepted evolution but viewed it within a theistic context. We will postpone until the subsequent section a delineation of these patterns of interpretation—varieties of traditionalism, modernism, and naturalism—and try to list here some of the underlying issues raised by Darwin's work. Four problems that fall within the topics introduced in earlier chapters have been selected for comment: (1) God and Nature: The Challenge to Design; (2) Man and Nature: The Challenge to Human Dignity; (3) Methods in Science: The Challenge of Evolutionary Ethics; and (4) Methods in Theology: The Challenge to Scripture.

1. God and Nature: The Challenge to Design

The prevalent version of the argument from design was particularly vulnerable, for it had started from the observed *adaptation of organic structures to useful functions*. But such adaptation could be accounted for by natural selection without invoking any preconceived plan. Usefulness was an effect and not a cause; it was the end product of an impersonal process. The species in existence are present simply because they have survived while thousands of others lost out in the struggle for existence. Instead of marveling that a fish has an eye that can see under water, we should have reason to be surprised only if this were *not* the case. Moreover, some of the facts that had always created difficulties for the advocates of design—such as useless rudimentary organs and traces of long-vanished limbs—could now be readily explained.

In some of his writings Darwin expressed the view that the *laws* by which life evolved were created by God, though the particular species resulting were the product of *chance* rather than design:

> There seems no more design in the variability of organic beings and in the action of natural science than in the course which the wind blows. [Everything in nature is the result of fixed laws.] . . . On the other hand, I cannot anyhow be contented to view this wonderful universe, and especially the nature of man, and to conclude that everything is the result of brute force. I am inclined to look at everything as resulting from designed laws, with the details, whether good or bad, left to the working out of what we may call chance.[5]

Chance seemed to be the antithesis of design. Darwin assumed that organic change is the product of a very large number of random spontaneous variations occurring entirely independently of each

---

5. F. Darwin, *Life and Letters*, Vol. I, 279; Vol. II, 105. The sentence in brackets is found only in Nora Barlow, ed., *The Autobiography of Charles Darwin, 1809–1882, with Original Omissions Restored* (New York: Harcourt, Brace, 1959), p. 87.

other, so the final result is accidental and unpremeditated. But the element of lawfulness, which received greater emphasis than the idea of chance, was also understood in a way which denied design. To earlier generations, scientific laws expressed the wisdom and constancy of God and were instruments of his purposes. Now they were increasingly taken as the autonomous and mechanical operation of impersonal forces. Law as well as chance appeared to be blind and purposeless.

Darwin at one point indicated that lawfulness does not exclude the concept of *God as primary cause*; he even spoke of natural laws as the "secondary means" by which God created.[6] He came close to recognizing that the scientist studies the domain of secondary causes and cannot ask why nature works as it does. But the following passage suggests that his own epistemology was undermined by the admission of the lowly origins of man's mind, so that in his later years he took a more agnostic position. He maintains

> . . . the impossibility of conceiving this immense and wonderful universe, including man with his capacity for looking far backwards and far into futurity, as the result of blind chance or necessity. When thus reflecting I feel compelled to look to a First Cause having an intelligent mind in some degree analogous to that of man: and I deserve to be called a Theist. . . . But then arises the doubt, can the mind of man, which has, as I fully believe, been developed from a mind as low as that possessed by the lowest animals, be trusted when it draws such grand conclusions.[7]

Neither in the typical formulations of the design argument, such as Paley's, nor in the rejection of it by Darwin and others of his time, was the nature of divine causality discussed. Usually God's activity had simply been assumed to be like that of a workman; and evolution made this simple "maker" analogy untenable.

One way out of this dilemma was to *broaden the concept of design* by applying it not to specific organs or organisms but to the evolutionary process as a whole. Asa Gray, Harvard botanist and leading interpreter of scientific opinion to the American public, maintained that the over-all history of nature could be understood in purposeful terms, despite the occurrence of waste and struggle. "Emergence is design by wholesale, the direction of the process by

---

6. M. Mandelbaum, "Darwin's Religious Views," *Journal of The History of Ideas*, Vol. 19 (1958), 363; J. C. Greene, "Darwin and Religion," *Proceedings of American Philosophical Society*, Vol. 103 (1959), 715.

7. F. Darwin, ed., *Life and Letters*, Vol. I, 282.

which mind and moral personality arose, which are not explainable by matter in random motion." Gray defended the idea of a Creator working through evolution to produce a gradually unfolding design; he also argued that God providentially supplies the new variations in the right direction. Other scientists held that God does not intervene, but has built design into the very structure of the process through which higher forms of life and eventually man could come into being. The anthropologist Eiseley has recently written:

> Darwin did not destroy the argument from design. He destroyed only the watchmaker and the watch. . . . Darwin had delivered a death blow to a simple, a naively simple, form of the design argument, but as Huxley himself came to realize, it is still possible to argue for directivity in the process of life.[8]

2. Man and Nature: The Challenge to Human Dignity

In the Western tradition, *man was set apart* from all other creatures. Man alone was a rational being; human reason was considered totally different in kind from whatever intelligence animals have. Man alone possessed an immortal soul, which defined his true being and his relationship to God. Man's distinctiveness put him in many respects "outside" nature, despite his sharing with other creatures a common dependence on God and a common finitude and temporality. This uniqueness of status now appeared to be denied by the theory of evolution. Distinctions between human and animal characteristics were indeed minimized by Darwin and his followers. Surviving primitive tribes, as Darwin portrayed them, almost closed the gap between man and animal. Huxley claimed that there is less difference between man and the highest apes than between higher and lower apes. Man himself, absorbed into nature, seemed to be the product of accidental variations and the struggle for survival, a child of blind chance and law.

Man's moral sense had always been considered one of his most distinctive capacities, but Darwin claimed that it too had originated by selection. In the early history of mankind a tribe whose members had strong social instincts, such as fidelity and self-sacrifice for the common good, would have had an advantage over other

8. From p. 198 of *Darwin's Century* by Loren C. Eiseley. Copyright © 1958 by Loren C. Eiseley. Reprinted by permission of Doubleday & Company, Inc., and Victor Gollancz, Ltd.

tribes. If morality conferred survival value, standards of conscience would have tended to rise. In the extinction of savage races in conflict with more civilized ones Darwin saw further evidence of built-in ethical advance. In a similar fashion he traced each of man's emotional and intellectual characteristics back to origins in the earlier stages of human and subhuman development.

There were other biologists, however, who gave greater emphasis to the *distinctive characteristics of man.* A. R. Wallace, who had formulated the principle of natural selection independently of Darwin, recognized that the presence of the human brain radically altered the character of evolution; with the development of intellect, bodily specialization and changes in physical organs were outmoded. Wallace also recognized that the gap in intellect between man and ape was far greater than Darwin had acknowledged; nor could "primitive" tribes fill the gap, for their inherent mental capacities are actually as great as those of civilized peoples. Again, he saw the distinctiveness of language as symbolic communication, where Darwin had seen little difference between animal signals and human speech. At each of these points, subsequent investigation has tended to vindicate Wallace's contributions.

In his later writing, Wallace went further and claimed that natural selection cannot account for *man's higher faculties.* He pointed out that the brain size in very primitive tribes, which is comparable to that in highly civilized groups, actually provides a mental capacity far beyond the simple needs of their aboriginal patterns of life, for which a much smaller brain would have sufficed. "Natural selection could only have endowed savage man with a brain a little superior to that of an ape, whereas he actually possesses one very little inferior to that of a philosopher."[9] And how can one explain musical, artistic, or ethical capacities that contribute nothing to survival? Wallace felt that such "latent powers" possessed in advance of the need to employ them indicate that "some higher intelligence may have directed the process by which the human race was developed." More recent opinion has not supported Wallace's idea of "latent powers," but it has tended to agree with him in holding that man's evolution involved distinctive processes which Darwin's purely biological framework ignored.

It is perhaps understandable that Darwin overemphasized *the*

9. A. R. Wallace, *Contributions to the Theory of Natural Selection*, 2nd ed. (New York: The Macmillan Company, 1871), p. 356.

continuity of man and animal. The earlier tradition had portrayed such an absolute discontinuity that to establish man's rootedness in nature Darwin looked for all the ,similarities he could find, overlooking the differences. The tremendous scope of the theory of evolution had been amply demonstrated, and it was easy to assume that all human phenomena could be exhaustively interpreted in essentially biological terms. It is also understandable that there were both scientists and theologians who, in reaction to such claims, insisted that natural selection could not account for man. Today we can see that in the long history of the world, man's emergence marks a genuinely new chapter—one not disconnected from previous chapters, and yet involving factors not previously present. Something radically different takes place when culture rather than the genes becomes the principal means by which the past is transmitted to the future, and when conscious choice alters man's development.

Moreover, both opponents and proponents of evolution often seem to have made the implicit assumption that *man's descent determines his nature.* Much of the emotion accompanying the rejection of the idea that "we have apes in our family tree" can be traced to this notion that source fixes meaning. Belief in evolution was equated with belief that man is "nothing but an animal." Man's origins were too readily taken by both sides to be the chief clue to his significance; a subhuman past somehow came to imply a less than fully human present. This is a genetic or temporal form of "reductionism," which finds the significance of an entity not in its smallest parts, as with eighteenth-century materialism, but in its most primitive beginning; it is a philosophical assumption equally destructive to the dignity of man, and equally unwarranted as a conclusion from the data.

3. *Methods in Science: The Challenge of Evolutionary Ethics*

If Darwin and his defenders believed that the theory of evolution had undermined the argument from design and the traditional status of man, it might be expected that their attitudes toward the future would have been pessimistic. But amid the optimism of the late nineteenth-century the total evolutionary picture seemed to convey a hopeful message. In the climate of the Victorian era the idea of *evolutionary progress* became a secular substitute for providence; blind fate was transformed into beneficent cosmic process, which was taken to guarantee the final fruition of history and even the perfectibility of man. Faith in progress replaced the doctrines of creation and providence as assurance that the universe is not really purposeless. Neither uniform law nor accidental chance is any threat if it leads to inevitable advance and if nature is a coherent and intelligible system. The Harvard philosopher John Fiske wrote that man was reinstated because evolution "shows us distinctly, for the first time, how the creation and perfection of man is the goal toward which nature's work has been tending from the first." The Enlightenment faith in social progress had been expanded to confidence in a progressive universe.

Was this concept of progress a conclusion reached *by the methods of science?* Darwin himself was evidently aware of the ambiguity at this point. He recognized that in speaking of "the fittest to survive," a biologist is not rendering a moral judgment, but only referring to physical endurance. The "improvement" of a species means only an advantage in competition in a given environment; it might appear to be "retrogression" in a different environment or when viewed against the whole pattern of organic development. If Darwin and Spencer nevertheless often used "progress" in a way that implied a value judgment, they did so, says J. C. Greene,

> ... because in their heart of hearts they believed that the processes of nature operated, however slowly and sporadically, to produce ever higher forms of existence. As naturalists they tried to define "improvement," "fitness," "highness," and the like in biological terms, but their use of the terms was subtly colored by the indomitable optimism of their age. The nineteenth century believed in progress, but it was not very careful to define what it meant by progress.[10]

The problem of *the relation of ethical norms to evolution* becomes acute if man's free and conscious choice guides his own future evolution. In some passages, Darwin implied that anything man does is an expression of natural selection, and that if progress is inherent in the process no human decision can hinder it. In other passages, he urged man to choose deliberately the pattern which the rest of nature exemplifies. He warned that future progress would be hindered by sentimental policies which protect weaker individuals, such as the sick or maimed, who would be eliminated under more competitive conditions. "There should be

10. Quoted by permission from *The Death of Adam* by John C. Greene, © 1959 by the Iowa State University Press, p. 301. Mentor PB.

open competition for all men; and the most able should not be prevented by laws or customs from succeeding best and rearing the largest number of offspring." But Darwin was not altogether consistent, for there was "deep in his character a warm humanitarianism and a strong holdover of the Christian ethic in which he had been trained."[11] He recognized "a higher morality" which would encourage respect and love toward all men, including the weak; but such a morality would lessen the competitive struggle and thus undermine what he had taken to be the source of progress. He also pointed out that even among animals brute strength is often not the most important factor in survival.

The belief that *competition promotes progress* fitted in well, however, with the predominantly individualistic social philosophy common in this period. Biological and political ideas merged in what has been called *"social Darwinism."*[12] Even before he read Darwin, Herbert Spencer had tried to show that laissez faire private enterprise was in keeping with the stern disciplines of nature that produce biological improvement. He found in the evolutionary struggle as Darwin described it a justification for his claim that economic competition unhampered by government regulation fosters human welfare. The survival of the fittest was to be the instrument for the evolution of society also; here, too, rugged individualism would bring beneficial results. Competition between groups and the conflict of races had been valuable historically, "a continuous overrunning of the less powerful or less adapted by the more powerful or more adapted, a driving of inferior varieties into undesirable habitats, and, occasionally, an extermination of inferior varieties." But Spencer, like Darwin, faced difficulties in his attempt to derive ethical norms from evolution. Having made biological survival his criterion of progress, Spencer could provide no satisfactory basis for rejecting an appeal to arms, such as that of Prussian militarism which would try to prove a nation's fitness on the battlefield.

T. H. Huxley, taking issue with both Darwin and Spencer, held that valid *ethical norms cannot be derived from evolution.* Standards appropriate for human conduct simply cannot be obtained from examining natural selection or copying the law of the jungle:

11. *Ibid.*, p. 81.
12. See Richard Hofstadter, *Social Darwinism in American Thought*, rev. ed. (Boston: Beacon Press, 1955; PB).

"Let us understand, once for all, that the ethical progress of society depends not on imitating the cosmic process, still less in running away from it, but in combating it."[13] Huxley asserted:

> The practice of that which is ethically best—what we call goodness or virtue—involves a course of conduct which in all respects is opposed to that which leads to success in the cosmic struggle for existence. In place of ruthless self-assertion, it demands self-restraint; in place of thrusting aside or treading down all competitors, it requires that the individual shall not merely respect, but shall help his fellows; its influence is directed, not so much to the survival of the fittest, as to the fitting of as many as possible to survive. It repudiates the gladiatorial theory of existence.[14]

Having rejected both "evolutionary ethics" and revealed religion, Huxley fell back on a sort of moral intuitionism as the source of ethical norms—though the goals he actually defended seem principally to reflect his religious upbringing and surrounding culture. We will find this discussion of the relation between evolution, progress, and ethics continuing vigorously today, accompanied by a more careful analysis of the methodological distinctions between scientific and ethical questions.

4. Methods in Theology: The Challenge to Scripture

Long before Darwin, *biblical literalism* had been cast in doubt by scientific knowledge—from Copernican astronomy to the new geology. Moreover, the scholarly analysis of biblical texts—the historical and literary research known as "higher criticism"—had already on completely different grounds begun to call the inerrancy of scripture into question. It appears surprising therefore that part of the popular outcry against evolution centered on the challenge to biblical authority. One reason was that, for the first time, central biblical beliefs—the purposefulness of the world, the dignity of man, and the drama of man's creation and fall—seemed to be threatened. Many Christians knew only one way to defend these religious convictions, namely to reassert the doctrine of biblical infallibility that had been typical of the "scholastic" period of Protestant orthodoxy.

Besides, some of the leading scientists had linked evolution with

---

13. Thomas H. Huxley, *Evolution and Ethics* (New York: D. Appleton & Co., 1896), p. 83.
14. *Ibid.*, p. 81.

their own *atheistic viewpoints,* and conservative churchmen opposed both indiscriminately. Such a liaison between a scientific theory and a sweeping attack on religion had occurred previously among the French skeptics, but it was a less familiar phenomenon in England and America. Darwin himself was cautious in his criticism of religion, but some of his defenders—most notably Huxley—went on the offensive against Christianity in the name of the freedom of science. Again, a number of assumptions that had been part of the *intellectual milieu* of the West for centuries were closely associated with particular biblical passages, as we have seen; familiar patterns of thought were defended by appeals to scripture. For example, the traditional view of man's status seemed to many people inseparable from the biblical account of Adam's creation in a unique act of God.

For the biblical literalists, then, there could be *no compromise with evolution.* Genesis describes the once-for-all creation of species in their present form, and if Darwin maintained that species change he was simply mistaken. Philip Gosse proposed that God had put all those fossils in a plausibly misleading pattern in order to test man's faith. From the ages of Adam's descendants, Archbishop Ussher had calculated that creation must have occurred in 4004 B.C. Others pointed out that evolution is "only a theory, not a fact," and that "it has not been proved"—remarks that are valid but show an inadequate understanding of the character of scientific inquiry, for no scientific theory can ever be proved with certainty to be true or immune to future modification. There was abundant opportunity for appeal to prejudice—or to sentiment, as when Wilberforce asked Huxley whether he traced his descent from an ape on his grandfather's side or his grandmother's.

But there were many others whose view of scripture *allowed the acceptance of evolution.* The majority of Protestant authors distinguished between the religious ideas of Genesis and the ancient cosmology in which these ideas were expressed. They interpreted the biblical account as a symbolic and poetic rendition of affirmations about the dependence of the world on God—affirmations they found not incompatible with the picture of evolution as God's way of creating. The modernists went further; for them the Bible was a purely human document, a record of man's evolving religious insight. The evolutionary view of nature molded the modernist understanding of God; the divine was now an immanent force at work within the process, an indwelling spirit manifest in the creative advance of life to ever higher levels. Catholic thought avoided the extremes of both literalism and modernism. Though Rome was at first reluctant to accept evolution, a position was gradually defined which acknowledged man's physical derivation from animal ancestry but preserved his uniqueness as a spiritual being. Each of these responses must now be described.

III. DIVERGING CURRENTS IN THEOLOGY

We have seen that the theory of evolution raised questions about the argument from design, the status of man, the basis of ethics, and the authority of scripture. The reactions of particular religious groups varied from vehement repudiation of evolution to enthusiastic welcome.[15] We shall outline first some traditionalist interpretations, both on the part of conservative Protestants and in Roman Catholic circles. The modernist movement in Protestant thought is next discussed. Some of the additional factors in the rise of liberal theology are then indicated, especially historical research on biblical texts and the appeal to religious and moral experience. Finally, some examples of the attitudes toward evolution embodied in naturalistic philosophies are given.

1. Traditionalist Responses to Evolution

Reactions varied widely even within the traditional churches. Among *conservative Protestants* there was considerable reluctance to acknowledge either evolution or biblical scholarship, though most such groups eventually made at least some adjustment to both. One of the leading American conservatives was Charles Hodge of Princeton Seminary. His view of scripture would not in itself have prevented assent to evolution. He held that the truths which biblical authors "intended to teach"—in which they were inspired to act as infallible spokesmen for God—must be distin-

---

15. Among general treatments of the influence of evolution on nineteenth-century theology are: Gail Kennedy, ed., *Evolution and Religion* (Boston: D. C. Heath and Co., 1957; PB); John C. Greene, *Darwin and the Modern World-View* (Baton Rouge: Louisiana State University Press, 1961; Mentor PB); Stowe Persons, ed., *Evolutionary Thought in America* (New Haven, Conn.: Yale University Press, 1950); John Dillenberger, *Protestant Thought and Natural Science*, Chap. 8; H. Schneider, "The Influence of Darwin and Spencer on American Philosophical Theology," *Journal of the History of Ideas*, Vol. 6 (1945), 6.

guished from additional ideas which they "happened to believe"—in which they were often mistaken. This distinction allowed Hodge to defend Copernican astronomy, for the writers of the Bible "may have believed that the sun moves round the earth, but they do not so teach"; they shared with their countrymen "the views then prevalent as to the mechanism of the universe."[16] Hodge rejected the evolution of man, not in the name of scriptural inerrancy, but in the name of the biblical understanding of human nature and destiny. Although he granted that there may have been widespread changes in the past history of animals, he insisted that "man is not a developed ape." He also understood natural selection to imply the denial of God's design of the world and continuing relationship to it. Hodge ended by equating Darwinism with atheism.

There were other Protestants, however, who combined an *orthodox theology* with an *acceptance of evolution*. We have already noted some examples, such as Asa Gray, among the scientists. Among theologians, James McCosh, president of Princeton University and an influential Presbyterian, suggested that God not only established the initial design of the whole evolutionary process but continues to work through what appear to us as "spontaneous" changes. The "chance" variations, for which Darwin could give no explanation, may have been caused by "the supernatural choices of an intervening Designer," who directs apparently accidental variations to effect his purposes. Evolution was the way in which the creative activity of God was expressed in time. But in the case of human origins McCosh speculated that it might be necessary to assume some additional divine action if man's unique spiritual features are to be accounted for. As against the optimism of Spencer, he was keenly aware—as were both Calvin and Darwin—of the struggle and tragedy of existence. His views of man, God, and Christ were close to those of traditional Christianity, but he urged the churches to recognize the evidence for evolution.

Such conservative responses in the decades following Darwin should be distinguished from the particular combination of ideas known as *fundamentalism*, which was a later and more uncritical American movement. The name originated in a series of pamphlets

16. Charles Hodge, *Systematic Theology* (New York: Scribner, Armstrong & Co., 1872), p. 165; also Charles Hodge, *What is Darwinism?* (New York: Scribner, Armstrong & Co., 1874).

entitled *The Fundamentals,* starting in 1909, the movement was a conscious and defensive reaction against modernism which, it was felt, had sacrificed all distinctive Christian beliefs in accommodation to evolutionary philosophies. Fundamentalists, in contrast to conservatives, insisted on a literalistic version of biblical infallibility and emphasized Christ's atoning death, his second coming, and the sudden conversion of the believer in accepting Christ as personal saviour. The more extreme adherents attacked not only evolution but modern science and education in general, because of their atheistic and materialistic influence. The Scopes trial in Tennessee in 1925 was the last occasion on which this militant campaign against evolution received national prominence. Fundamentalist efforts to gain control of major seminaries and denominations were defeated by 1930, though the movement survives among smaller revivalistic sects. Conservative viewpoints, on the other hand, are still strongly represented within many of the large Protestant denominations.

For *Roman Catholicism* evolution was not in principle as disturbing as it was for Protestant conservatism. In Catholicism, revealed truth is to be sought not in scripture alone, but in scripture and tradition as interpreted by the living church. Moreover the doctrine that scripture is divinely inspired has not excluded considerable flexibility and diversity in biblical interpretation, and the concept of different "levels of truth" has always allowed allegorical rendition of problematic passages. Nevertheless, the first reaction of Rome was a strenuous repudiation of evolution, and books on the subject by Fathers Edward Leroy, John Zahn, and others were withdrawn. The Vatican Council of 1870 and subsequent encyclicals attacked the new trends in biblical scholarship, and the incipient modernist movement among Catholic intellectuals was specifically condemned in 1907.

Gradually, however, the new *biblical scholarship* was more favorably received by Rome, both during the pontificate of Leo XIII (1878–1903) and, more recently, under Pius XII (1939–1958). Whereas the Pontifical Biblical Commission in 1902 instructed that the "substantial authenticity" of the first five books of the Bible (the Pentateuch) must be taught, by 1948 it not only encouraged reexamination of scriptural problems but stated that the laws of the Pentateuch were the product of a long development in response to changing conditions. An encyclical in 1943 spoke of the Bible as "using the modes of expression of ancient peoples"; the modern interpreter must "go back wholly in spirit to those remote centuries and with the aid of history, archeology, ethnology, and other sciences, accurately determine what modes of writing . . . the authors did in fact use."[17] Under this more permissive policy Catholic scholars have made substantial contributions to recent biblical research.

There has also been cautious but increasing *Catholic acceptance of evolution.*[18] Since long before Darwin, some commentators had interpreted the six days of the creation story in metaphorical terms, or taken them to represent geological epochs. Others held that theological ideas, which were said to constitute the official teaching of Genesis, should be distinguished from the "unofficial," "incidental" and possibly erroneous scientific opinions of its authors; as with some of the conservative Protestants, divine inspiration was claimed only for the religious meaning the writer intended to convey. One point in the biblical account, however, has always been insisted upon as an actual historical event because of its theological significance: the special creation of Adam's soul. The doctrine of man's fall and his solidarity in the inheritance of original sin were understood to require a single individual from whom all mankind descended; and the special status of man's soul was taken to depend on its origination in a supernatural incursion into the natural order. In Chapter 12 we will present some recent versions of the Catholic teaching that the human body evolved organically from earlier animal forms, but that the human soul was introduced by God at one distinct point in time.

2. The Modernist Movement

Whereas traditionalists thus preserved classical doctrines with little modification, modernists departed from them extensively in accommodating to evolution. These were not external critics, but men within the church attempting to reformulate in the light of modern knowledge what they saw as the essence of Christianity. If parts of the older tradition had to be abandoned, other parts, they felt, could be liberated to support a more vital religious life.

17. Pius XII, *Divino Afflante Spiritu* (1943).
18. See Walter Ong, ed., *Darwin's Vision and Christian Perspectives* (New York: The Macmillan Company, 1960); see also references in Chapter 12 below.

They saw *scripture as a human record,* not of God's revelation to
man, but of man's search for God, the story of developing ideals
and growing religious insights. Biblical history is the progressive
evolution of religious awareness from primitive beginnings to its
culmination in ethical monotheism. The Bible, for these authors,
is not an inspired book, though it is an inspiring one, like other
great works which express profound ideas. The first chapters of
Genesis are to be read as a poetic expression of religious convictions concerning man's dependence on God and the orderliness
and the goodness of the world. But the modernists' central ideas
were derived not from historic revelation but from a new form of
natural theology.

The modernist view of God was dominated by the concept of
evolution. After Darwin, it was urged, divine creative activity must
be depicted not as external and once-for-all, but as within the
process and continuous in time. God's principal attribute is immanence in nature, rather than transcendence. For some of these
authors God became an impersonal Cosmic Force; but for most,
the traditional concept of a personal God was retained though his
mode of relationship to the world was modified. Any dualism of
natural and supernatural spheres was attacked, and the unity of
God, man, and nature was extolled; one divine spirit permeates the
universe. This monistic emphasis echoes themes familiar in Romanticism and philosophical idealism, modified by the evolutionary
view of nature. The modernists tended to deify the evolutionary
process, making it the means of grace and the source of progress.

The modernist view of man also differed markedly from the
classical doctrine. Not man's sinfulness and opposition to God, but
his moral progress and unity with God were set forth. Human
nature is itself essentially divine, for in man is the spark of God.
God is immanent in man as well as in nature, and human ideals
are the supreme product of God's spirit at work; hence human
aspiration and love are the key to understanding him. Religion is
rooted in human experience, and theological interpretations are
secondary; God is to be approached primarily through the soul of
man. Man's efforts, not some special divine action, will bring in the
Kingdom. Jesus was not the divine saviour, but the great teacher
of high ideals and the message of the fatherhood of God and the
brotherhood of man. Human salvation comes through increased
knowledge and noble goals, not through supernatural aid or any

basic reorientation of the self. Here, then, was a view of man that was in harmony with the optimistic faith so common in the late nineteenth century.

Henry Ward Beecher, American preacher and editor, was one of the first exponents of modernism to gain a wide hearing. Geological research, he wrote, has deciphered "the long-hidden record of God's revelation in the material world." The upward march of matter and mind shows us God's way of bringing about progress. "Of one thing I am certain, that whatever may have been the origin, it does not change either the destiny or the moral grandeur of man as he stands in the full light of civilization today." Beecher describes genuine religion in phrases like these:

> Simple religion is the unfolding of the best nature of man toward God; man has been hindered and embittered by the outrageous complexity of unbearable systems of theology. . . . Religion is that state of mind in which a man is related by his emotion, and through his emotions by his will and conduct, to God and to the proper performance of duty in this world.[19]

A systematic volume in the same vein is Lyman Abbott's *Theology of an Evolutionist.*[20] The Bible, as he saw it, represents the dawning of religious insight in men who were children of their times and apprehended truth only slowly and imperfectly. Abbott disagreed with the traditional notion of sin, holding that, since Darwin, an "immoral" act should be understood as simply a lapse into animality. The greatest modification of earlier tradition was his exposition of God's relation to nature. Classical theology, he wrote, pictures God apart from the universe, ruling over it like an emperor and intervening at various times—in creation, in revelation to a chosen people, in miracles. But in evolution we can see that God works from within by continuous growth, not by intervention or "manufacture" in which the agent is external to the product. All life is divine, for there is only one cosmic force, an "Infinite and Eternal Energy from which all things proceed."

Abbott seems to make God's action *an immanent force within nature.* There are no laws of nature that are not also laws of God's being; there is only one force, directed to intelligent ends, operat-

19. Henry Ward Beecher, "The Two Revelations," included in Kennedy, ed., *Evolution and Religion,* pp. 17, 19.

20. Lyman Abbott, *The Theology of an Evolutionist* (Boston: Houghton Mifflin Co., 1897).

ing within the world. As the human spirit dwells in the body, pervading and controlling it, so the Holy Spirit dwells within the universe and shapes it from within. The scientist can describe historical growth but he does not deal with its cause, which lies ultimately in God. Does this amount to pantheism? No, said Abbott, because while God's immanence is stressed his transcendence is not omitted. As the human spirit transcends its body, so God is not limited to nature, though he works through its vital processes as a "resident force."

Modernist views found a variety of other formulations. In Henry Drummond, the Scottish layman and scientist, they were combined with deep personal piety and devotion to Christ; man's continuing spiritual evolution was the theme of his book, *The Ascent of Man*. In John Fiske, who popularized evolution in America, modernism received more philosophical expression—closer to Spencer's position, but in a broadly theistic context; Fiske called it *Cosmic Philosophy*, a ringing affirmation of a progressing universe. The modernist movement in Roman Catholicism did not depart as radically from orthodox theology, but such men as Edward Leroy in France and George Tyrell in England defended evolution and the "higher criticism" of the Bible, and dwelt on the idea of divine immanence in nature; but the movement was not widespread, because it encountered official condemnation. Early in the twentieth century, views not unlike those of modernism were developed from philosophical but not specifically Christian premises in such books as Lloyd Morgan's *Emergent Evolution* and Henri Bergson's *Creative Evolution*, which will be discussed in a later chapter.

3. The Rise of Liberal Theology

The initial controversy over evolution tended to force theologians to the two extremes of traditionalism and modernism; each group, impressed by the deficiencies of the opposing position, defended its own convictions by theological methods which were increasingly unacceptable to the majority of churchmen. By the end of the century a *theological liberalism*, in many respects intermediate between traditionalism and modernism, was dominant in Protestant thought. It agreed with modernism in welcoming scientific knowledge of evolution, but held that modernism had departed too far from classical views of God and man. Its most distinctive feature was a new methodological approach, the appeal to human experience rather than to revealed or natural theology. Three significant developments, whose roots lie earlier in the century, contributed to the formation of liberal theology; we take time to describe them because of their importance for subsequent thought.

First, *the growth of biblical scholarship* engendered new attitudes toward revelation. In Germany and then in England, in universities and then in seminaries, objective methods of historical and literary research, similar to those applied to other ancient documents, were being used to analyze the biblical text.[21] In this light, the first five books of the Old Testament, traditionally ascribed to Moses, showed indications of multiple authorship. Careful examination of duplicated stories and of differences in style, vocabulary, and thought, gave evidence that these books in their present form are a compilation of several accounts of varying antiquity. Some sections, such as the details of priestly ritual in the Temple, were shown to have been codified in the exilic period, 800 years after Moses. Similar analysis of the Gospel of John, and its differences from the other gospels in both form and content, led scholars to view it as a theological essay about Christ's life written more than half a century after the crucifixion.

In *the new view of scripture*, attention was directed to the individual viewpoints and interests of the ancient authors, their purposes in writing, and the historical contexts in which they lived. They emerged as very human figures who shared the assumptions of their day and incorporated considerable legendary material in their writings. Archaeological evidence about other early cultures revealed not only many similarities but also characteristic differences, when compared to Hebrew thought. Greater familiarity with living religions around the world encouraged a "comparative" approach to their scriptures. Many of the modernists concluded that the Bible has little religious value; the liberals, on the other hand, granted the human character of the biblical record, but read it as a treasury of religious insights and teachings. Some of them, instead of rejecting the idea of revelation, reformulated it: God had revealed himself, not in the dictation of an infallible book,

---

21. For brief summaries, see S. Terrien, "History of the Interpretation of the Bible," in G. Buttrick, ed., *The Interpreter's Bible* (Nashville: Abingdon Press, 1951ff.); also Robert M. Grant, *A Short History of the Interpretation of the Bible* (New York: The Macmillan Co., 1963; PB).

but in his presence in the lives of Christ, the prophets, and the people of Israel. Scripture was then not revelation but a human witness to the human experience of revelation.

A second influence was *the appeal to religious experience* as the basis for justifying religious beliefs. This new point of departure was proposed early in the century by Friedrich Schleiermacher, often called "the father of liberal theology." He held that the basis of religion is not revealed doctrine as in traditionalism, nor cognitive reason as in natural theology, nor even ethical will as in Kant's system, but a distinctive religious awareness. Religion is a matter of living experience, not of formal beliefs; it is not reducible to practical ethics or speculative philosophy, but must be understood in its own terms. As did the authors of the Romantic Movement, Schleiermacher held that God is known by immediate apprehension rather than indirect inference. The element common to all religions he described as "a feeling of absolute dependence," a sense of finitude before the infinite, an awareness of unity with the whole.[22]

Schleiermacher held that theology should be derived from the *reflective interpretation of religious experience*. We should start not from "sin" as a theological concept, but from our consciousness of guilt and sense of alienation from God; not from a general scheme of "salvation," but from the experienced transformation of human life. If we are to dispense with all doctrines not derivable from our present experience, the traditional belief in miracles and the divinity of Christ will have to go. The Bible is valuable as the record of the religious experience of Israel, Christ, and the early church. Schleiermacher himself found the life of Christ an important source of religious understanding and believed that the Christian tradition has mediated the awareness of God which is the essence of religion; yet there was little place for historical revelation in the view of theological method that he espoused. Again, for Schleiermacher religion had an objective referent, for it was based on man's consciousness of God; but to some of his successors human consciousness was itself the object of inquiry, and a more man-centered and subjective emphasis resulted.

A third theme typical of liberal theology was *the primacy of the*

22. Friedrich Schleiermacher, *Speeches on Religion to Its Cultured Despisers* (London: K. Paul, Trench & Trübner, 1893; Harper PB).

ethical in religion. The legacy of Kant, evident in much of nineteenth-century Protestantism, was perpetuated in Albrecht Ritschl's "theology of moral values." Ritschl agreed with Kant that no knowledge of God can be achieved by "theoretical reason" or philosophical speculation; religion is a matter of "practical reason," inseparable from conscience and judgments of value. Ritschl, like Schleiermacher, looked to the experiential basis of religion, but he interpreted it primarily as man's ethical will. The central Christian experience is the transformation of an individual's life in response to the personality of Christ; Ritschl was therefore deeply interested in historical research concerning Christ's life. But personal religion, he wrote, goes beyond knowledge of the past, for it involves the experience of forgiveness and reconciliation in the present. Moreover it has a social dimension, the task of creating on earth the Kingdom of God in which love and service are expressed in human relationships.[23]

Ritschl pictured a sharp contrast between *the human sphere* and *the sphere of nature.* In part this was a continuation of the Kantian distinction between the objective realm which science investigates, and the realm of man's history and culture in which there is freedom and value. But it was also a reaction to the image of evolution as a process of conflict and struggle. The liberals were concerned to rescue man from nature; they did this not by denying evolution but by affirming the victory of spirit over nature. They defended man's free ethical personality from mechanical or materialistic interpretations. Religion could aid their cause by asserting the infinite value of the human soul and the spiritual supremacy of man over the impersonal natural order.

In the light of these three trends we can understand *liberal viewpoints concerning evolution.* The liberal conception of the Bible allowed unreserved assent to the scientific evidence for evolution. But this did not lead to drastic modification of religious beliefs, as it had for modernists, because here the basis of theology was sought elsewhere—in religious and moral experience, rather than in either revealed or natural theology. Liberals were in general able to take a more open and relaxed attitude toward evolution than either traditionalists or modernists, since less was at stake

23. Albrecht Ritschl, *The Christian Doctrine of Justification and Reconciliation* (Edinburgh: T. & T. Clark, 1902).

theologically. For the knowledge of God, as they saw it, comes primarily from man's religious and ethical consciousness, not from the Bible or the evolutionary process.

4. Naturalistic Philosophies of Evolution

The groups considered so far—traditionalists, modernists, and liberals—all defended theism, and all understood themselves to be within the Christian community, even though in varying degrees they modified classical doctrines. But there were other interpretations of evolution which involved *the total rejection of theism.* We have noticed the naturalistic perspectives of some of the early evolutionists. Darwin moved from a vague belief in a supreme power at the time he wrote the *Origin,* to the agnosticism and indifference to religious questions that marked his last years. T. H. Huxley went on the offensive against biblical authority and the argument from design; man is the product of impersonal and purposeless forces. But man's course should not imitate the brutal ways of the evolutionary past; civilization is a garden created by man in the midst of the jungle whose inroads he must continually combat. In Huxley's naturalism, man stands alone in a predominantly hostile nature.

Herbert Spencer made *evolutionary agnosticism* into a comprehensive system.[24] He did not deny the existence of some kind of God, but held that it can play no part in our understanding of the world. God was "the Unknowable," an incomprehensible absolute about which we can say nothing beyond the mere affirmation of its existence. But within the phenomenal world, evolution was for Spencer far more than a biological theory; it was the unifying key to all areas of knowledge. He asserted a single principle applicable to the growth of stars, organisms, and societies: the law of the integration of matter "from a relatively indefinite, incoherent homogeneity to a relatively definite coherent heterogeneity." The organs of animals—and the "organs" of societies—become more differentiated and specialized but also more integrated and coordinated. Spencer's attempts to derive ethics from evolution, his justification of competitive individualism by "social Darwinism," and his faith in automatic progress have already been mentioned.

An interesting *reply to Spencer* was given by Chauncey Wright

---

24. Herbert Spencer, *First Principles,* 6th ed. (Akron, Ohio: Werner, 1900).

of Harvard.[25] He pointed out that Spencer's general principle, "the movement of matter toward a relatively concentrated, multiform and determinate arrangement," was so vague that it could never be verified experimentally. He discussed in detail Spencer's failure to distinguish science from philosophy, and his lack of awareness of the methodological limitations of science. Belief in automatic progress, he suggested, is not derivable from the biological evidence, but arises from "the human need for some kind of moral faith." The positivistic temper of Wright's critique is evident in his insistence that no consequences can be drawn from evolution for cosmology, metaphysics, or religion. Evolution is a biological concept and not a universal explanatory principle.

A materialistic form of naturalism, sometimes called *evolutionary monism*, was defended by the German zoologist Ernst Haeckel. Natural selection and mechanical causality provide the solution to *The Riddle of the Universe*, as his best known book was entitled; matter and force are the only ultimate reality. Haeckel was in general a strict materialist, though he was not always consistent —he speculated at one point, for example, that the atom may have a simple soul or rudimentary psychic qualities. His confidence in the all-embracing explanatory power of the new biology is expressed in many passages:

> The cell consists of matter called protoplasm, composed chiefly of carbon with an admixture of hydrogen, nitrogen, and sulphur. These component parts properly united produce the soul and body of the animated world, and suitably nursed became man. With this single argument the mystery of the universe is explained, the Deity annulled, and a new era of infinite knowledge ushered in.[26]

The basic assertion of *materialism* is that whatever exists is of the same sort as matter. No really new kinds of entity can ever arise, for "every new phenomenon is the equivalent of a rearrangement of existing entities." Materialism as a metaphysical doctrine about the nature of reality was sometimes, as in the previous century, combined with the additional postulate of determinism. But determinism could be abandoned (because of the element of

25. Chauncey Wright, *Philosophical Discussions* (New York: Henry Holt & Co., 1878).

26. Ernst Haeckel, quoted on p. 346 of *Darwin's Century* by Loren C. Eiseley. Copyright © 1958 by Loren C. Eiseley. Reprinted by permission of Doubleday & Company, Inc., and Victor Gollancz, Ltd.

chance in random variations) without abandoning materialism, if the outcome of evolution was interpreted as the product of purely material factors.[27] In what we have called the genetic form of reductionism, life was said to be the chance product of matter and force, a "mere eddy in the primeval slime." Here was a more pessimistic outlook, contrasting with the confidence in nature which dominated the Victorian era. For this minority, nature was not man's benevolent parent or hospitable home, but an alien realm ruled by blind law and chance, operating on purposeless matter and indifferent to man's interests. In such a world man might lapse into despair or Stoic resignation, or he might fight back in Promethean defiance of the sort Bertrand Russell describes:

> Man is the product of causes which had no prevision of the end they were achieving; his origin, his growth, his hopes and fears, his loves and his beliefs, are but the outcome of accidental collocations of atoms. . . . Blind to good and evil, reckless of destruction, omnipotent matter rolls on its relentless way. . . . It is for Man, proudly defiant of the irresistible forces that tolerate for a moment his knowledge and his condemnation to sustain alone, a weary but unyielding Atlas, the world that his own ideals have fashioned despite the trampling march of unconscious power.[28]

We may conclude by mentioning briefly the role of evolution in *Friedrich Nietzsche's* thought, without stopping to describe other aspects of his complex writing or his tortured personality and lonely life. Nietzsche maintained that if evolution is taken seriously as a norm for man, our traditional values will have to be turned completely upside down.[29] In the fierce struggle for survival the qualities that are useful are not the Christian virtues, but self-assertion and the Will to Power. If good is that which survives, strength is the ultimate virtue. "What is good? All that heightens in man the feeling of power, the desire for power, power itself. What is bad? All that comes from weakness." Humility, love, and pity are a morality fit for slaves. A hero's morality consists in courage, vitality, ruthless egoism if need be, in the struggle for supremacy. The heroic individual must emancipate himself from

---

27. See F. A. Lange, *The History of Materialism* (Boston: J. R. Osgood & Co., 1877).
28. Bertrand Russell, *Mysticism and Logic* (New York: Doubleday PB, 1957), pp. 45, 54. Used by permission of George Allen & Unwin, Ltd.
29. Friedrich Nietzsche, *The Genealogy of Morals* (New York: Doubleday PB, 1956).

every moral scruple; he is above every law, and through his autonomous will must realize his own unique and creative individuality. We can acknowledge many profound insights in Nietzsche's attacks on conventionality and mass mediocrity, and in his unmasking of the hypocrisy and rationalization behind purported altruism. But when he called for the coming Superman, the new "mutation," discontinuous with the past, who would be master of the future, some of the seeds of Nazi ideology are evident. Nietzsche proposed a program of eugenics in which "inferior" strains will be eliminated so that there can come into being the race of heroes who will embody the Will to Power. Here evolution was used to justify ethical norms diametrically opposed to those of the Christian tradition.

IV. SUMMARY

By the close of the century, the fact of evolution was accepted by virtually all scientists, and by the vast majority of theologians. The causes of biological change were the subject of continuing discussion at both scientific and philosophical levels, and the broader interpretations of the evolutionary process varied widely. At one extreme, there were still many average Christians, especially in rural areas, who rejected evolution completely; but most of the leaders of even the more conservative churches realized that there was overwhelming evidence in its favor. At the opposite extreme, naturalistic philosophies had relatively little popular support. The liberal middle position between traditionalism and modernism was gaining in strength. Hofstadter writes that on the American scene by the 1880's

> ... evolution had made its way into the churches themselves, and there remained not a single figure of outstanding proportions in Protestant theology who still ventured to dispute it. But evolution had been translated into divine purpose, and in the hands of skillful preachers religion was livened and refreshed by the infusion of an authoritative idea from the field of science. The ranks of the old foes soon could hardly be distinguished as they merged in common hostility to pessimism or skepticism about the promise of American life.[30]

Let us, then, summarize the influence of evolutionary thought on the four problems that are the concern of this volume.

---

30. Hofstadter, *Social Darwinism in American Thought*, p. 30.

1. GOD AND NATURE. The "God of the gaps" was as unnecessary in biology after Darwin as in physics after Newton. Adaptive changes could be accounted for by random variation and natural selection without invoking divine intervention. We have Darwin to thank for finally making it clear that God is not a secondary cause operating on the same level as natural forces, or a means for filling gaps in the scientific account.

> The nineteenth-century definitely abandoned the belief in God as a scientific principle. The watchmaker Creator of the Enlightenment has vanished with the advance of rational scientific accounts of how the world came into being; and if religious men still believe in a Creator behind those long processes, they do it on religious rather than scientific grounds. To them, evolution is merely a more exact description of the way in which God's creative acts took place.[31]

Liberal theologians, and those traditionalists who accepted evolution, preserved the classical understanding of God, but now spoke of him as working continuously through the whole evolutionary process by means of secondary causes. Modernists, on the other hand, emphasized God's immanence, often to the virtual exclusion of transcendence, and God tended to become a force within a cosmic process which was itself divine. Two key issues, discussion of which has continued into the contemporary period, are the significance of the directionality of evolution, and the meaning of assertions that God works "in" or "through" natural causes. Some recent reformulations of the argument from design in the light of Darwin's work will also be examined (Chapter 12).

2. MAN AND NATURE. To support his case for man's rootedness in nature Darwin stressed the similarities between man and animal. As Eiseley puts it:

> Man, theologically, had for so long been accorded a special and supernatural place in creation that the evolutionists, in striving to carry their point that he was intimately related to the rest of life, sought to emphasize those characteristics which particularly revealed our humble origins.[32]

Largely because of this challenge to man's status, those traditionalists who did acknowledge the evolution of species admitted only grad-

---

31. Randall, *The Making of the Modern Mind*, p. 554. Used by permission of Houghton Mifflin Company.

32. From p. 238 of *Darwin's Century* by Loren C. Eiseley. Copyright © 1958 by Loren C. Eiseley. Reprinted by permission of Doubleday & Company, Inc., and Victor Gollancz, Ltd.

ually and often only partially its application to man; many of them defended human uniqueness by insisting on the creation of the soul in a special divine act. Modernists and liberals accepted man's subhuman beginnings but rescued human dignity by extolling the upward ascent of evolutionary progress, in which they saw a guarantee of human perfectibility and the victory of spirit over nature. Dillenberger suggests that in trying to prove that man is more than brute, they, too, overstated their case:

> One could almost suggest that the pathos of liberal theology was its having to rescue man from animality for the sake of theology, and that its occasional attempt to make man divine was itself a desperate gambit to rescue him from nature understood in respect to blind forces or animality.[33]

More recent biologists have given greater attention to man's distinctiveness—his rational powers, capacity for symbolic communication, freedom of choice, and cultural evolution; while among theologians today a more sober estimate of human limitations prevails than among most of their nineteenth-century counterparts.

3. THE METHODS OF SCIENCE. In itself, Darwin's work was a brilliant exemplification of empirical observation and theoretical hypothesis in fruitful interplay. But could the methods of science also deal with the wider implications of evolution for cosmology, historical progress, and human ethics? The very fact that support from science was claimed for such divergent world-views should give us pause. A biological concept was variously converted into naturalism, cosmic evolutionism, or an argument for theism—each of which, we would submit, must be defended as a philosophical interpretation rather than as a scientific conclusion. Greene writes:

> Every great scientific synthesis stimulates efforts to view the whole of reality in its terms, and Darwin's theory of natural selection was no exception. But the views of reality that originate in this way are not in themselves scientific, nor are they subject to scientific verification.[34]

Similarly, considerable ambiguity attended the attempts to derive ethical norms and to justify doctrines of historical progress on the basis of evolutionary evidence alone. Today the relation of evolu-

---

33. John Dillenberger, "Man and The World," copyright 1959 Christian Century Foundation. Reprinted by permission from the June 3, 1959, issue of *The Christian Century*, Vol. 76, 667.

34. Greene, *Darwin and the Modern World-View*, p. 132. Used by permission of Louisiana State University Press.

tion to ethics continues to be of lively interest, but there is greater awareness of the difference between a scientific theory and its extension into a universal explanatory scheme or an all-embracing world-view. The nineteenth century has taught us the dangers when theologians too readily interfere in scientific questions, or when scientists too readily adjudicate theological questions.

4. METHODS IN THEOLOGY. (a) *Revelation.* Among reactions to both evolution and biblical scholarship the extreme positions were at first most prominent: insistence on biblical literalism by some conservatives, and rejection of all forms of revelation by some modernists. In the emerging liberal view, the Bible was valued as the fallible human record of man's religious experience—and also as witness to revelation, understood not as the dictation of a guaranteed text but as God's presence and activity in the life of Israel, the prophets, and Christ. (b) *Natural theology.* The argument from design, in the form Paley had popularized, was permanently undermined by the theory of evolution. In a reformulated version, which was never as widely used, purposeful design was to be seen in the laws and structures through which life and mind had emerged, and in the directionality of the total process. (c) *Religious and moral experience.* The distinctive new element that became dominant in nineteenth-century theological method was the appeal to human experience as the basis for theology. Schleiermacher looked to man's religious awareness and consciousness of God, and Ritschl and his successors emphasized moral experience. All three of these basic approaches continue into the twentieth century, with reinterpretations of revelation and experience gaining new currency; even natural theology still has occasional defenders.

5

Science and Religion in the Twentieth Century

Since the remainder of the volume deals with the twentieth century, this short chapter is included with only a limited objective in mind. It carries further just *one* of the topics we have been tracing historically: *methods in religion* as influenced by modern science. It is intended for the reader unfamiliar with recent developments in *philosophy* (positivism, linguistic analysis, existentialism, process philosophy) and in *theology* (neo-orthodoxy, liberalism). Each of these viewpoints leads to a distinctive way of looking at the relations of science and religion, which we will simply describe briefly here. Discussion and criticism of these schools of thought will occur throughout subsequent chapters in the analysis of particular problems. Any scheme for classifying these contemporary viewpoints is somewhat arbitrary, but for convenience we group them in three sections: "Contrasts of Theology and Science," "Parallels of Theology and Science," and "Derivations of Theology from Science."

I. Contrasts of Theology and Science

We present first some variations on the theme that *the methods of science and religion are radically different.* The two enterprises, according to these authors, should be completely separate and

115

independent. Not only do their content and subject matter have
nothing in common, but their ways of knowing are so dissimilar
that there are no points of fruitful comparison or analogy. The
defense of religion from attack by science is accomplished by
totally separating them; no conflicts are possible because any issue
is assigned to one field or the other, but never both, on jurisdic-
tional grounds. But by the same token neither can contribute
positively to the other. What is of interest to theology is not of
interest to science nor accessible to it, and vice versa. They occupy, as it were, watertight compartments in human thought. Past
"conflicts" are attributed to failures in recognizing these distinctions.

Varying accounts are given of the reasons for the discontinuity
between theological and scientific understanding. In *neo-orthodoxy*,
it is the uniqueness of revelation that distinguishes theology from
all human discovery. In *existentialism*, the dichotomy between personal existence and impersonal objects is the ground of the contrast. For *linguistic analysis*, the difference in the functions of
religious and scientific language is the basis of the distinction.
But the three interpretations unite, not only in contrasting theology
and science, but in expressing reservations about the competency
of reason in reaching religious understanding. They also agree on
the absence of metaphysical implications in scientific theories. They
join in asserting that science yields only technical knowledge of
predictable regularities in nature and should not be expected to
provide the basis for a philosophy of life or a set of ethical norms.
These authors all decline the services of metaphysics as a bridge
between science and religion, and they attack attempts by theists
and atheists alike to use science in the support of theological and
philosophical positions. Scientist and theologian, it is said, should
each tend to his own business and not meddle in the affairs of the
other.

1. God's Self-Revelation versus Man's Discovery (Neo-Orthodoxy)

No single man has had greater influence on twentieth-century
Protestant thought than Karl Barth.[1] Writing after the first war,
when worldwide conflicts had shaken optimism about man and

---

1. A good introduction to Barth's thought is his *Dogmatics in Outline* (London: SCM Press, 1949; Harper PB); brief summaries are given in William
Hordern, *A Layman's Guide to Protestant Theology* (New York: The Macmil-

his abilities, he reacted sharply *against the nineteenth-century liberalism* in which he had been trained. Barth claimed that in the hands of the liberals Christianity had lost its distinctive message: God had become an immanent force within the cosmic process, Christ was reduced to an example of human goodness, man's sinfulness was ignored in the assumption of inevitable progress and—most important of all—divine revelation had been replaced by human attempts to discover God through philosophical reflection, moral conscience, or religious experience.

Against such views, Barth insisted that God is always the "wholly other," the transcendent Lord, who can be known only *when he chooses to reveal himself*, as he did preeminently in Jesus Christ. This sovereign and holy God is radically distinct from the world, separated from sinful man by a gulf which could be crossed only from the divine, not the human side. God's self-disclosure to man, not man's search for God, must be the starting point of theology. In each comparison in which liberalism had pictured continuity and similarity, Barth found *discontinuity and dissimilarity* predominant: discontinuity between revelation and natural reason, between God and the world, between Christ and other men, between Christianity and other religions. Theology must be radically theocentric and Christocentric, looking to God and his act in Christ, not to human ideas and capacities. Faith is not reasoned argument, but God's gift and man's obedience in personal response to God's initiative.

Barth maintains that the primary revelation was *the person of Christ*, the Word made flesh. Scripture is a purely human record witnessing to this revelatory event. God acted in Christ, not in the dictation of an infallible book; hence we can accept everything that historical criticism and documentary analysis discover about the human limitations of the writers of the Bible and the cultural influences on their thought. Moreover, God acts in present encounter with man, addressing particular persons through this record of past events, revealing himself as Judge and Redeemer today, especially through the preaching of the Word. For the content of revelation is not a set of propositions about God, but God himself present in judgment and forgiveness.

Barthian theology received widespread response in Europe be-

lan Co., 1955; PB), Chap. 6, and H. R. Mackintosh, *Types of Modern Theology* (London: Nisbet, 1937), Chap. 8.

tween the wars. It had recovered the Reformation conviction of the sovereignty of God, the centrality of Christ, the power of sin and grace, and the distinctiveness of revelation, all of which had been lost by modernists and by many liberals; yet Barthians did not reject the historical analysis of biblical documents, as fundamentalists and many conservatives had done. Here was a reformulation of the concept of revelation that could take biblical criticism into account. This new orthodoxy, or "neo-orthodoxy" as it came to be called, influenced religious thought throughout the West, and apeared in modified form in the writings of Emil Brunner, Reinhold Niebuhr, and others. It is still common among Protestant theologians on the Continent and is strongly represented in America (though since World War II many of its adherents have moved closer to the more sober liberalism of recent decades; as in politics, the progressive conservative may end up very near the chastened liberal).

The distinction between the methods of theology and science, according to neo-orthodoxy, derives from the difference between their objects of knowledge. Theology deals with the transcendent and mysterious God, who is so radically unlike the world which science studies that the same methods cannot be expected to be used in both disciplines. God is known only because he has revealed himself in Christ; science advances by human discovery and contributes nothing to a religious faith which depends entirely on divine initiative. Neo-orthodox authors are very critical of any natural theology which argues from evidences of design in nature. God is not known through his creation apart from Christ, for sin blinds human reason to the vision of the world as God's handiwork. The gap between man and God cannot be bridged from the human side. There are no points of contact between the ideas of science and those of theology.

Science can thus *neither contribute to nor conflict with* theology. In fundamentalism the possibility of conflict existed, for scientific theories and infallible biblical passages might both claim to be literal descriptions of the same events. But according to neo-orthodoxy, scripture tells us nothing authoritative about scientific questions; the "scientific" ideas of the biblical authors were the erroneous speculations of ancient times. As Niebuhr puts it, we should take the Bible "seriously but not literally." We shall see, for example, that most contemporary biblical scholars represent the Genesis story as a symbolic portrayal of the basic relation of man and the world to God; its message concerns man's creatureliness and dependence on God, and the goodness of the natural order. These religious meanings can be separated from the ancient cosmology in which they were expressed. Adam is taken not as a historical individual but as a symbol of Everyman in his movement from innocence to responsibility, sin and guilt. Such insights have nothing to do with scientific accounts of origins. Thus the scientist is free to carry out his work without interference from the theologian, and vice versa, for their methods and their subject matter are totally dissimilar.[2]

2. *Subjective Involvement versus Objective Detachment (Existentialism)*

In existentialism the divergence between methods in theology and science arises primarily from the contrast between the sphere of *personal selfhood* and the sphere of *impersonal objects*. Existentialism is not a system of ideas but an attitude or orientation finding very diverse expression among theistic and atheistic authors.[3] Kierkegaard, the intense Danish theologian of the early nineteenth century, was the seminal influence, though his writings went almost unnoticed until the present century. Many existentialist themes were powerfully set forth in the literature of postwar Europe, especially in the plays and novels of Sartre and Camus. In Heidegger and Jaspers these themes appeared in philosophical form, and theologians as different as Buber and Bultmann have given them expression within particular religious traditions.

Existentialism in all its forms asserts that we can know authentic human existence *only by being personally involved* as concrete individuals making free decisions—not by formulating abstract general concepts or universal laws about man. Each of us is a unique creative subject who must resist being treated as an object in a system of ideas or in the machinations of a mass society. A

---

2. Examples of a neo-orthodox perspective on science and religion are W. A. Whitehouse, *Christian Faith and the Scientific Attitude* (New York: Philosophical Library, 1952), and Aldert van der Ziel, *The Natural Sciences and the Christian Message* (Minneapolis: Denison, 1960). See also Chapter 12, Section II, and Chapter 13, Section I, below.

3. See James Collins, *The Existentialists* (Chicago: Henry Regnery, 1952; PB); David Roberts, *Existentialism and Religious Belief* (New York: Oxford University Press, 1957; PB).

few existentialists have criticized scientists for treating man deterministically as an object to be manipulated and controlled, or for contributing to the depersonalization which technology has inflicted on human culture. But most existentialist authors have granted the usefulness of scientific knowledge, claiming only that the central events in the life of personal selfhood are beyond its scope.[4] They have maintained that the most significant facets of *human existence* are understood only by decision, commitment, and involvement in life, and never in the detached, rationalistic attitude of the scientist. Of the many themes of existentialism—anxiety, despair, guilt, death, freedom, creativity, decision—our concern here is only its epistemology, namely a subject-centered approach to knowledge. Here the basic antithesis is between *personal subjectivity* and *impersonal objectivity.*

The Jewish philosopher Martin Buber has given a widely quoted account[5] of the difference between the way a person is related to an object and the way he is related to another person. The first, which Buber calls *I-It*, is the detached analysis and manipulative control of impersonal things. *I-Thou* relationships, by contrast, are characterized by total involvement and participation of the whole self, directness and immediacy of apprehension, and concern for the other person as an end in himself. Such encounter occurs in the reciprocal interaction and openness of true dialogue, and in the awareness, sensitivity, and availability of genuine love. The I-Thou encounter can be entered into, but it cannot be reduced to concepts from the world of "It," the realm of space and time and causality. For Buber, man's confrontation with God always has the immediacy and involvement of an I-Thou relationship, whereas scientific inquiry occurs in the domain of the I-It.

Rudolph Bultmann[6] has developed a distinctive and influential form of *Christian existentialism.* One of his central theses is that the Bible erroneously speaks of God's activity as though it could be described in the language of space and time. Any such "objective" terminology, used to represent the divine which transcends

———————
4. E.g., Carl Michalson, *The Rationality of Faith* (New York: Charles Scribner's Sons, 1963).
5. Martin Buber, *I and Thou*, trans. R. G. Smith (Edinburgh: T. & T. Clark, 1937; Scribner PB).
6. A simple presentation is Rudolph Bultmann, *Jesus Christ and Mythology* (New York: Charles Scribner's Sons, 1958; PB). See also Schubert Ogden, *Christ without Myth* (New York: Harper and Brothers, 1961).

space and time, Bultmann calls "*mythical.*" Today, he insists, we
know from science that spatiotemporal events are governed by
rigorous causal laws, and we know from theological reflection
that the transcendent God and his acts cannot be "objectified" as
if they were on the same plane as natural occurrences. But instead of dismissing mythical language as simply false (as nineteenth-century liberalism did), Bultmann wants to preserve what
he takes to be its original existential meaning in human experience,
translating it into the language of man's self-understanding, his
hopes and fears, decisions and actions. The key question is always:
what does the mythical imagery say about *my personal existence*
and about *my relationship to God*? The Christian message always
refers to new possibilities for my life—decision, rebirth, the realization of my true being—and not to observable occurrences in the
external world apart from my involvement. For example, he holds
that the Resurrection was not a physical event of the sort that
might have been photographed, but rather an occurrence in the
experience of the early church, the return of faith in Christ—which
is repeated in the life of the believer today when the salvation-
event transforms his own existence. Similarly, the doctrine of creation is not a statement about cosmological origins, but a confession
that I am totally dependent on God. Thus the Christian message
refers not to objective happenings in the world, but to *the new
understanding of ourselves* that is given by God amid the anxieties
and hopes of our personal life histories. Theology, dealing with
the realms of selfhood and transcendence, has no points of contact
with science, which investigates impersonal objects in the external
world without the personal involvement of the subject.[7]

3. *The Variety of Uses of Language (Linguistic Analysis)*

In addition to the neo-orthodox emphasis on revelation, and the
existentialist insistence on personal involvement, a third development in twentieth-century thought has contributed to the sharp
differentiation of science from religion: the rise of linguistic analysis, which is today the dominant viewpoint among British and

7. An existentialist analysis of science and religion is given by M. Holmes
Hartshorne, *The Promise of Science and the Power of Faith* (Philadelphia:
Westminster Press, 1958). See also the first half of Karl Heim, *Christian Faith
and Natural Science* (New York: Harper and Brothers, 1953; PB). Both Bultmann and Heim are discussed at length in Chapter 13 below.

American philosophers. We must start by describing its precursor, the *logical positivist* movement of the 1930's. Logical positivism was in part a revival of *the empiricist tradition*. It returned to Hume's argument that all one can know of reality are fleeting fragments of separate sense-data. We recall Hume's contention that what we call causality is simply a habit of associating certain items of sense-data because of their past conjunction. According to the positivist, a scientific theory is not a representation of the world, but a short-hand calculational device for summarizing sense-data; it provides for economy of thought in organizing observations and making predictions. We will examine these assertions in the next chapter.

Another influence in the formation of logical positivism was *the revolution in physics* in the early twentieth century. In relativity theory, the length of an object and the time between two events are not absolute properties of objects in themselves; they are the results of particular measuring processes and vary according to the frame of reference of the observer. Length and time are not attributes of things in the world, but relationships defined by specifying experimental procedures. The positivists concluded that the scientist should use only concepts for which he can give "operational definitions" in terms of observations. Moreover, in quantum physics an electron does not have position and velocity; its wave function is an abstract symbolism from which certain correlations among observable quantities can be derived. These somewhat technical developments, which need not detain us now, cast doubt on the commonsense "realist" view that a scientific theory is a picture or replica of the real world as it exists apart from the observer, and gave some support to the view that a theory is simply a scheme for correlating experimental data.

A third aspect of logical positivism was the new interest in *the logical structure of language*. In the writings of the "Vienna Circle" in the 1930's, and in A. J. Ayer's popularization,[8] the logic of scientific discourse was taken as the norm for all propositions. In the notorious *"verification principle"* it was asserted that only empirical statements verifiable by sense-experience have meaning (formal definitions or tautologies are also meaningful but convey no factual information). Most traditional sentences in philosophy, and all those in metaphysics, ethics, and theology, were said to be neither

8. A. J. Ayer, *Language, Truth and Logic*, 2nd. ed. (London: Victor Gollancz, Ltd., 1946; Dover PB°).

true nor false, but meaningless (that is, "vacuous pseudostatements" devoid of any literal significance); having no factual content, they state nothing and merely express the speaker's emotions or feelings. Logical positivism held that the task of the philosopher is not to assert anything about the world (which only the scientist can do) but to clarify the language and the concepts used in the various sciences.

The difficulties in the logical positivist position and its development into *linguistic analysis* are the main topics of Chapter 9, and will not be recounted here. Suffice it to say that where the logical positivists saw sentences as doing only one legitimate job (reporting empirical facts), the linguistic analysts are impressed by the variety of functions which language serves.[9] The viewpoint now prevalent in British philosophy is indicated by the slogan: "Don't ask about the meaning of a statement; ask about its use." What are people doing in using it? Since various types of sentences reflect differing interests—artistic, moral, scientific, religious, and so forth —each area of discourse must use the categories and the logic it finds most appropriate for its purposes. In the case of science, analysts often adopt an "instrumental" view in which theories are said to be "useful" rather than true; the main function of scientific language is said to be prediction and control.

A variety of *functions of religious language* have been delineated.[10] The broadest function is the provision of a total life orientation in terms of an object of ultimate concern and devotion. Some authors emphasize the ethical aspects and take religious language to be a recommendation of a way of life and an acknowledgment of allegiance to a set of moral principles. Again, religious statements are said to propose a distinctive self-understanding, engendering characteristic attitudes toward human existence. Other

---

9. See, e.g., J. O. Urmson, *Philosophical Analysis* (London: Oxford University Press, 1956).

10. References on this varied literature will be found in Chapter 9 below. A useful summary is given by Frederick Ferré, *Language, Logic and God* (New York: Harper and Brothers, 1961). A recent treatment of science and religion from the standpoint of linguistic analysis is T. R. Miles, *Religion and the Scientific Outlook* (London: George Allen & Unwin, Ltd., 1959). See also Chapter 12, Section II, below. Two volumes which make considerable use of the idea of alternative languages are Albert N. Wells, *The Christian Message in a Scientific Age* (Richmond, Va.: John Knox Press, 1962), and John Habgood, *Truths in Tension* (New York: Holt, Rinehart & Winston, 1965; British edition entitled *Religion and Science*).

statements serve primarily to express and evoke commitment and worship; religious language, it is urged, must always be examined in the context of its use, that is, in the worshiping community. These functions, which are very different from those served by scientific language, were excluded from meaningful discourse by the logical poistivists but are now topics extensively discussed by philosophers. Linguistic analysts agree with logical positivists, however, in insisting that scientific language itself has a limited and essentially technical function which is always closely tied to its own distinctive type of observations. We will call this a *"positivistic" view of science*, the view that scientific inquiry does not yield any metaphysical generalizations about the nature of reality. For example, we shall find that the British philosopher Toulmin is critical of attempts to derive either a theistic or a naturalistic metaphysics from evolution—which he insists is a theory applicable only by the biologist within his strictly scientific work, not in his off-hours speculations. Scientific theories are useful tools for summarizing data, making predictions, or controlling processes; they are not representations of reality. Science deals with regularities among phenomena, and it has no wider metaphysical or theological implications.

It is not uncommon today for *neo-orthodox* or *existentialist theology* to be combined with *a positivistic view of science*.[11] In such a combination, the separation of the spheres of science and religion is enforced from both sides. The metaphysical disclaimers of many scientists and philosophers today are welcomed by these men, for they help to "clear the field" for religion by undermining rival naturalistic faiths which once claimed the support of science. Neo-orthodox writers even welcome positivistic attacks on natural theology. Moreover, if science leads only to technical knowledge of regularities in phenomena, and if in addition philosophy is confined to the analysis of language, then religious faith is outside the scope of possible scientific or philosophical attack. The independence of the two fields is guaranteed from both sides if each is restricted to its own domain. Such total isolation of science and religion repre-

---

11. E.g., Alasdair MacIntyre's essay in A. MacIntyre, ed., *Metaphysical Beliefs* (London: SCM Press, 1957); or Paul Holmer, *Theology and the Scientific Study of Religion* (Minneapolis: Denison, 1961); or John A. Hutchison, *Language and Faith* (Philadelphia: Westminster Press, 1963).

sents the dominant attitude in recent decades, but in Part Two we shall find a number of reasons for calling it into question.

II. PARALLELS OF THEOLOGY AND SCIENCE

The authors in the first group—advocates of neo-orthodoxy, existentialism, and linguistic analysis—conceive of theology as contrasting strongly with science. They interpret science positivistically as an undertaking that yields useful technical knowledge but not wider philosophical or theological conclusions. They view theology, on the other hand, as an autonomous enterprise with its own starting point in revelation, its own relevance for human existence, and its own distinctive use of language. The group we now consider finds *methodological parallels* between the two fields; the word "parallel" is taken to imply considerable independence of content with significant similarities in structure. These authors do not attempt (as do those in the third group below) to derive theological conclusions directly from scientific discoveries. But they do find points of comparison among methods of inquiry, and they hold that many of the rational and empirical attitudes of the scientist can be shared by the theologian. These men try to see both science and religion within a unified view of the world. *Liberal theology* is interested in attitudes of inquiry; it claims that a man's religious beliefs should be a reasonable interpretation of all areas of human experience, employing critical reflection not unlike that which the scientist applies in his work. *Process philosophy* elaborates a metaphysical system applicable to all aspects of reality including God and events in the world. These thinkers are usually critical of the positivistic view of science, and their writings show at least limited interaction between scientific and theological ideas.

1. Similar Attitudes in Science and Religion (Liberal Theology)

We traced the rise of *liberal theology* in the nineteenth century in Schleiermacher's view of theology as the interpretation of religious experience and in the concentration on moral experience among the followers of Kant. The movement continued in the twentieth century and assumed a wide variety of forms. Partly because of the influence of neo-orthodoxy, the more traditional wing of liberalism has grown at the expense of the modernist wing (which had virtually lost all sense of identification with historic Christianity). Common themes of liberal theology have been its stress on the immanence rather than the transcendence of God, the example of Christ's life rather than the effects of his atoning death, and the possibilities of man's moral improvement rather than his sinfulness. In each of the pairs of terms between which neo-orthodoxy emphasizes discontinuity, liberalism finds *continuity*: continuity between revelation and reason, between faith and human experience, between God and the world, between Christ and other men, between Christianity and other religions. There are no radical gaps here—there are differences in degree, but not in kind.

According to most liberals, *attitudes similar to those of the scientist are appropriate in religious inquiry*.[12] Theology, it is said, should be broadly empirical and rational; it should provide a consistent and comprehensive world-view based on the critical interpretation of all human experience. Religious beliefs are pragmatically vindicated by their consequences in human life and their ability to fill man's deepest needs. The spirit of openness and tentativeness which the scientist exemplifies should be adopted by the theologian too; religious and moral experience are among the most significant evidence to be considered. Liberals do not usually eliminate the concept of revelation, but they reinterpret it in two ways. First, they tend to minimize the uniqueness of biblical revelation. God reveals himself through many channels: through the structures of the created order, through man's moral conscience, and through the various religious traditions of the world—and preeminently, but by no means exclusively, in Christ. Second, it is asserted that revelation must always be received and interpreted by men and is distorted by limited human comprehension. Thus liberals talk about man's discovery of God, as well as God's initiative toward man. The Bible is viewed as the record of a people's progressive search for God and response to him.

Charles Raven has expressed many of the characteristic themes of liberalism. He advocates *a broadly empirical attitude toward religious experience*. Concerning methods of inquiry, he writes that "the main process is the same whether we are investigating the

---

12. Liberal theology is clearly presented in Harold DeWolf, *The Case for Theology in Liberal Perspective* (Philadelphia: Westminster Press, 1959), or his longer *A Theology of the Living Church* (New York: Harper and Brothers, 1953).

structure of an atom or a problem in animal evolution, a period of history or the religious experience of a saint."[13] The primary data of theology are "the lives and experience of the saints through whom God most fully reveals himself to us." Man responds to the infinite in awe and penitence, but he must then interpret this encounter rationally. The resulting religious beliefs can be tested pragmatically by their fruits, especially in creative human relations of love and service. Raven shares the liberal's distrust of all dichotomies, including the sharp division of the natural from the supernatural. Our account of things must "tell a single tale which shall treat the whole universe as one and indivisible."

To take another example, the Oxford physicist, C. A. Coulson, holds that *the methods of science and religion have much in common.* The scientist's experience as a human being goes beyond his laboratory data and may include a sense of reverence and humility, an awareness of beauty and order, and a reflective contemplation of the world. The unity of nature and the harmony of its laws may take one as far as belief in a cosmic mind, but man's religious experience points to the personal character of ultimate reality. For some people the power of a renewed life or the vision of Christ as a summary of the spiritual quality of the universe will be a further step. "For we live among our fellows, and we can make sense of our relationship to them, and of their human needs, only in terms of a God—partly seen in science, and in art and history and philosophy, partly experienced in wholly personal terms in the 'living present' and verified in the power of a transformed life."[14]

In addition to the assertion that enlightened religion uses methods basically similar to those in science, it is claimed that, conversely, *science involves presuppositions and moral commitments* not unlike those in religion. The gulf between science and religion is here narrowed, as it were, from both sides. Thus Coulson argues that science has presuppositions—for example, that the world is lawful and intelligible; the scientist has an unprovable faith in the orderliness of the universe. Moreover the moral attitudes required by science are similar to the religious virtues: humility, cooperation, universality, and integrity. In contrast to the positivist view, prom-

13. Charles E. Raven, *Natural Religion and Christian Theology* (Cambridge: Cambridge University Press, 1953), Vol. 2, 10.
14. C. A. Coulson, *Science and Christian Belief* (Chapel Hill: University of North Carolina Press, 1955), p. 117. See also his *Science and the Idea of God* (Cambridge: Cambridge University Press, 1958).

inence is given to the role of human factors in science, such as the
scientist's personal judgment, commitment to truth, and participation in a community of inquiry.[15] This interpretation presents many
features of science that resemble those of religion, and vice versa.

2. An Inclusive Metaphysical System (Process Philosophy)

An impressive attempt to include science and religion within a
unified view of reality is the "process philosophy" of Alfred North
Whitehead, which perhaps represents the only new systematic
metaphysics developed in the twentieth century. Whitehead made
important contributions to mathematics and philosophy of science
before he turned to the construction of "a system of ideas which
bring aesthetic, moral and religious interests into relation with
those concepts of the world which have their origin in natural
science."[16] Whitehead defines *metaphysics* as the study of the most
general characteristics of events. By imaginative generalization from
immediate experience, he seeks the development of an inclusive
conceptual scheme whose categories will be sufficiently universal to
be exemplified by all entities in the world, a set of ideas in terms
of which every element in experience can be interpreted. Metaphysics must be *coherent*, Whitehead maintains; that is, its concepts
not only should be logically consistent but should be part of a
unified system of interrelated ideas that presuppose each other. But
it also should have empirical relevance, for it must be *applicable
to experience*; one should be able to interpret all types of events in
terms of its fundamental ideas. Whitehead recognizes that the discrimination of elements in experience is itself influenced by one's
interpretive categories, which provide a new way of looking at the
world. Nevertheless he holds that the justification of any system of

---

15. Two interesting volumes emphasizing the human element in science are
Michael Polanyi, *Personal Knowledge* (Chicago: University of Chicago Press,
1958; Harper PB); and Harold K. Schilling, *Science and Religion* (New York:
Charles Scribner's Sons, 1962).

16. Alfred N. Whitehead, *Process and Reality* (New York: The Macmillan
Co., 1929; Harper PB°), p. vi. His most readable books are *Science and the
Modern World* and *Religion in the Making* (New York: The Macmillan Co.,
1926; Meridian PB°). Excellent expositions of his metaphysics are given by
William Christian, *An Interpretation of Whitehead's Metaphysics* (New Haven,
Conn.: Yale University Press, 1959) and Ivor Leclerc, *Whitehead's Metaphys-
ics* (New York: The Macmillan Co., 1958). A summary is available in A. H.
Johnson, *Whitehead's Theory of Reality* (Boston: Beacon Press, 1952; Dover
PB).

thought lies in its ability to organize and elucidate immediate experience.

Among the data that metaphysics must consider, Whitehead suggests, are both religious and scientific experience. He maintains that *religion* "contributes its own independent evidence, which metaphysics must take account of in framing its description."

> Religion claims that its concepts, though derived primarily from special experiences, are yet of universal validity, to be applied by faith to the ordering of all experience. Rational religion appeals to the direct intuition of special occasions, and to the elucidatory power of its concepts for all occasions. . . . The dogmas of religion are the attempts to formulate in precise terms the truths disclosed in the religious experience of mankind. In exactly the same way the dogmas of physical science are the attempts to formulate in precise terms the truths disclosed in the sense perception of mankind.[17]

However, in his systematic writing Whitehead's concept of God is derived less from consideration of religious experience than from the requirements of his total system; God is primarily understood as the ground of order and novelty in the world. In Chapter 13 we will investigate his view of God's role in the process by which every event comes into being.

The *science* of the twentieth century, with which Whitehead was thoroughly familiar, had considerable influence on his thinking; he was not, of course, attempting to invent a new scientific theory, but to suggest ways in which our most general concepts about the nature of reality should take the new science into account. Let us summarize some of *the basic ideas of process philosophy*:

1. *The primacy of time.* The world is a process of becoming, a flux of events. Transition and activity are more fundamental than permanence and substance. Whitehead reacted against the idea, which had dominated philosophy since Aristotle, that every entity consists of an unchanging substance with changing attributes, a permanent substratum sustaining variable qualities. He pictures the basic components of reality as interrelated dynamic events, not self-sufficient static substances. He also rejects the atomist's view of reality as unchanging particles that are merely externally rearranged. If we start with permanence, change can only be an appearance; but if we start with change, we can account for permanence and

---

17. Whitehead, *Religion in the Making*, pp. 31, 57. Used by permission of The Macmillan Company and Cambridge University Press.

self-identity as the repetition of relatively enduring patterns of activity. Whitehead was also influenced by the new role of time in science: genuine transition and novelty in evolution, the developmental approach in biology, and the replacement of material particles by vibratory patterns in quantum physics. (A vibration must have time as well as space to exist at all; like a musical note, it requires a temporal span to be defined.) The future is to some extent open and indeterminate; reality exhibits creativity, spontaneity, and emergence. There are genuine alternative possibilities, that is, potentialities which may or may not be actualized.

2. *The interfusion of events.* The world is a web of interconnected events, a network of mutual influences. Events are interdependent; every event has essential reference to other times and places. An entity is actually constituted by its relationships (for example, a person is who he is precisely in his various interpersonal roles). Nothing exists except by participation. Each occurrence in turn exerts an influence which enters into the very being of other occurrences. Whitehead points again to the new physics: formerly men imagined independent, localized, self-contained particles bumping into each other externally and passively without themselves undergoing alteration; today we talk about interpenetrating fields that extend throughout space. But the principle is a general one: reality is an interwoven network of relationships, a field of mutual influences.

3. *Reality as organic process.* The word "process" implies temporal change and interconnected activity. Whitehead also calls his metaphysics "the philosophy of organism"; the basic analogy for interpreting the world is not a machine but an organism, which is a highly integrated and dynamic pattern of interdependent events. The parts contribute to and are also modified by the unified activity of the whole. Each level of organization—atom, molecule, cell, organ, organism, community—receives from and in turn influences the patterns of activity at other levels. Every event occurs in a context which affects it. Perhaps this may best be called a *"social view of reality,"*[18] for in a society there is unity and interaction without loss of the individuality of the members; Whitehead defends a pluralism in which the integrity of each event is preserved.

4. *The self-creation of each event.* Although Whitehead emphasizes the interdependence of events he does not end with a monism

---

18. Cf. Charles Hartshorne, *Reality as Social Process* (Glencoe, Ill.: The Free Press, 1953).

in which the parts are swallowed up in the whole. An event is not just the intersection of lines of interaction; it is an entity in its own right with its own individuality. He maintains a genuine pluralism in which every event is a unique synthesis of the influences on it, a new unity formed from an initial diversity. It takes account of other events and reacts and responds to them. During the moment when each event is occurring it is on its own, closed to further influences, and free to appropriate and integrate its relationships in its own way. Each event is a center of spontaneity and self-creation, contributing distinctively to the world. Whitehead wants us to look at the world from the viewpoint of the entity itself, imagining it as an experiencing subject. Reality thus consists of an interacting plurality of individual acts of experience.

These four ideas indicate merely the general character of process philosophy. Their usefulness can be judged only as the system is further developed and applied to the interpretation of particular areas of experience; examples of their application to the behavior of organisms are given in Chapter 11, and to theological problems in Chapter 13. For our immediate purposes what is important is the method used, namely, the development of an inclusive metaphysical system that is held to be relevant to both science and religion. It differs from the metaphysics of atomistic materialism in the eighteenth century and evolutionary naturalism in the nineteenth, both in its more complex and dynamic view of nature and in its attempt to do justice to a wide range of human experience—aesthetic, moral, and religious; Whitehead recognizes the abstractive, partial, and symbolic character of scientific concepts.

III. Derivations of Theology from Science

The group of authors we first considered (Section I) holds that the methods of science and theology are radically different, and that scientific discoveries have no theological implications. The second group finds parallels in the methods of the two fields; liberal theology encourages in religious inquiry attitudes similar to those in scientific inquiry, and process philosophy seeks metaphysical categories applicable to all aspects of reality including God and nature. A third group draws theological conclusions more directly from science, claiming that the existence of God can be inferred either from general features of nature, such as design and order, or from specific findings, such as the directedness of evolution, the increase of entropy, or the mathematical character of modern physics. These are the modern exponents of the tradition we have traced through the centuries as "natural theology" (defined as a theology derived from nature). They are mentioned only briefly here because they are contingent upon scientific theories that will be discussed later in Part Three.

1. Arguments from Design and Order

These very general characteristics of nature do not refer to any particular findings of science. They are often invoked in liberal theology and play an important part in process philosophy, and thus could have been included in the previous section. We list them separately only because they are frequently presented as independent arguments, usually with explicit reference to scientific findings. The older form of teleology, based on the "design" of particular organs (the eye, for instance), was of course undermined by Darwin. The *reformulated teleological argument*, however, finds evidence of design built into the structure of a world in which evolution can occur, in the total system of laws and conditions whereby life and intelligence and personality were brought forth, and in the interconnectedness, coordination and harmonization of different levels of existence.[19] Such reasoning yields no irrefutable proof of a Designer, but it is claimed that there is considerable evidence for which theism is the most plausible assumption.

Among the features cited are the congruence between the human mind and the rational structure of the world, the ubiquity of beauty, and the fitness of the world to produce and sustain moral personality (for example, the presence of both stability and plasticity in the environment). Even at the chemical level, life depends on the intricate dovetailing of many complex properties, and higher levels require the cooperative interaction of many apparently independent features. Again, the presence of conditions for the realization of such human values as love, friendship, and justice seem to point to dimensions of reality beyond chemical and biological laws. A number of scientists see orderliness, in one or another of these forms, as evidence for the existence of an intelligent Designer.[20]

---

19. See F. R. Tennant, *Philosophical Theology*, Vol. 2 (Cambridge: Cambridge University Press, 1930); L. J. Henderson, *The Fitness of the Environment* (New York: The Macmillan Co., 1913; Beacon PB); Peter Bertocci, *An Introduction to the Philosophy of Religion* (New York: Prentice-Hall, Inc., 1951). These authors are discussed in Chapter 12 below.
20. Arthur Compton, *The Human Meaning of Science* (Chapel Hill: Uni-

2. *Arguments from Physics and Biology*

A number of more specific scientific discoveries have been interpreted as evidence for theism. These are not usually "gaps" within the scientific account of the sort exploited for theological purposes in previous centuries; but they are claimed to represent limits to scientific explanation, or clues to the nature of reality, to which science itself witnesses. Since each of these arguments will be analyzed—and, in general, criticized—in later chapters, we simply list some examples here:

1. Astronomical evidence for *the "instantaneous creation" theory*, or physical evidence for *the Second Law of Thermodynamics* (increasing entropy), is said to indicate a finite timespan for the universe, and thus to support the idea of God as Creator.[21]

2. *The Heisenberg Uncertainty Principle*, understood as evidence of indeterminacy at the atomic level, is said to provide a scientific basis for the defense of the idea of human freedom.[22]

3. *The abstract, mathematical character of twentieth-century physics*, in which atoms are the wave patterns of differential equations rather than billiard-ball particles, is taken to support philosophical idealism, the thesis that reality is basically mental.[23]

4. *The directional advance of evolution* is taken as evidence of a creative force in nature, a guidance toward higher forms.[24] In arguments of this kind particular scientific findings are taken to have important theological implications, and we will have to examine each of them in detail.

---

versity of North Carolina Press, 1940); or Kirtley Mather's essay in H. Shapley, ed., *Science Ponders Religion* (New York: Appleton-Century-Crofts, 1960).

21. William Pollard, *The Cosmic Drama* (New York: National Council of the Episcopal Church, 1955); Pius XII, allocution to the Pontifical Academy of Sciences (1951), trans. by P. J. McLaughlin as *Modern Science and God* (Dublin: Clonmore & Reynolds, 1952).

22. Arthur Compton, *The Freedom of Man* (New Haven, Conn.: Yale University Press, 1935); Arthur Eddington, *The Nature of the Physical World* (Cambridge: Cambridge University Press, 1928; Ann Arbor PB*).

23. Eddington, *ibid.*; also Arthur Eddington, *Science and the Unseen World* (London: G. Allen and Unwin Ltd., 1929); James Jeans, *The Mysterious Universe* (Cambridge: Cambridge University Press, 1930; Dutton PB).

24. C. Lloyd Morgan, *Emergent Evolution* (London: William & Norgate, 1923); Samuel Alexander, *Space, Time and Deity* (New York: The Macmillan Co., 1920), Henri Bergson, *Creative Evolution*, trans. A. Mitchell (New York: Henry Holt & Co., 1911). We will suggest in Chapter 12 that Pierre Teilhard de Chardin, *The Phenomenon of Man*, trans. B. Wall (New York: Harper & Brothers, 1959; PB), although similar in many ways to these earlier works, is basically not a new version of natural theology.

This chapter has not attempted a survey of all contemporary schools of thought. (We have, for instance, made no mention of Neo-Thomist[25] or Neo-Kantian[26] writings.) Our only objective has been the description of major trends in twentieth-century philosophy and theology which have influenced attitudes toward the relation of science and religion. Some of these views represented the further development of ideas mentioned in previous chapters, and others were radically new ideas. Among "Contrasts of Theology and Science," *neo-orthodoxy* recovered the classical conviction of the centrality of Christ, but reinterpreted the idea of revelation so that it conflicted neither with science nor with biblical scholarship. Totally new types of distinction were introduced, both in the claim of *existentialism* that "all religious statements refer to the realm of personal existence," and in the assertion of *linguistic analysis* that "the function of religious language is the expression and evocation of self-commitment to a way of life." In "Parallels of Theology and Science," the focus of *liberalism* on moral and religious experience was not unlike the approach of late nineteenth-century Protestant thought. *Process philosophy*, on the other hand, worked out a distinctive new metaphysics considerably influenced by twentieth-century science. Finally, "Derivations of Theology from Science" included reformulations of older ideas in the tradition of natural theology—such as new versions of the design argument—and also put forward distinctive arguments based on more recent scientific discoveries.

These schools of thought were merely summarized in this chapter without discussion or criticism. They will be discussed and analyzed throughout Part Two, which is devoted to a point-by-point comparison of *the methods of science* with *the methods of religion*. This will leave for Part Three the exploration of two issues whose history was traced in earlier chapters: *man's relation to nature* and *God's relation to nature*.

---

25. Neo-Thomist views of science and religion include Henry J. Koren, ed., *Readings in the Philosophy of Nature* (Westminster, Md.: The Newman Press, 1959; PB); E. F. Caldin, *The Power and Limits of Science* (London: Chapman & Hall, 1956); Brother Benignus Gerrity, *Nature, Knowledge and God* (Milwaukee: Bruce Publishing Co., 1947). An excellent discussion of contemporary science from a neo-Thomist viewpoint is by an Anglican, E. L. Mascall, *Christian Theology and Natural Science* (New York: Ronald Press, 1956). Recent Catholic thought is discussed in Chapters 12 and 13 below.
26. Varying forms of neo-Kantianism are reflected in C. F. von Weizsäcker, *The World View of Modern Physics* (Chicago: University of Chicago Press, 1952) and in the writings of Cassirer, Margenau, and others (see Chapter 6).

PART TWO

Religion and

the Methods

of Science

6

The Methods of Science

For many people today the challenge to religious belief arises not from any conflict of content between science and religion but from the assumption that the scientific method is the only road to knowledge. Thus the concern for methodological issues, found among both scientists and theologians, has far-reaching implications for the outlook of modern man. Examination of present-day interpretations of the methods of science will provide a basis for comparison in subsequent chapters with the methods of religion, about which there has also been significant recent thought. Illuminating similarities as well as striking differences in the epistemological approaches of the two fields will be evident. But any such comparison must rest on a clear understanding of the character of the scientific enterprise itself, to which we devote this chapter. We will then be in a better position to assess the strengths and limitations of science, and the roles of the subject (knower) and the object (known) in scientific knowledge.

In Section I, "Experience and Interpretation in Science," the interaction of experiment and theory and the criteria used in evaluating theories are examined. The place of deduction, induction, and creative imagination is discussed. Section II, "The Scientific Community and its Language," stresses the corporate context of research and the use of analogies and models in scientific thought. The symbolic character of modern physical concepts, which cannot be considered literal descriptions of reality, is noted. Section III, "The Relation of Scientific Concepts to Reality," summarizes the debate among philosophers whether a theory is to be viewed as a summary of data (positivism), a useful tool for control and prediction (instrumentalism), a mental structure (idealism), or a representation of the world (realism). The concluding section defends a critical realism which holds that the goal of science is to understand nature, not simply to control it or make predictions.

I. EXPERIENCE AND INTERPRETATION IN SCIENCE

At the outset it should be stated that there is no "*scientific method*," no formula with five easy steps guaranteed to lead to discoveries. There are many methods, used at different stages of inquiry, in widely varying circumstances. The clear, systematic schemes of the logicians or of the science teacher's lectures may be far removed from the *ad hoc* procedures and circuitous adventures of the man on the frontier of research. But we can at least note certain broad features characteristic of scientific thought. Since the author is a physicist, illustrations will be drawn largely from his own field.

In the work of Galileo, Newton, and Darwin we have seen the distinctive combination of experiential and interpretive elements. The experiential component is comprised of observations and data, the products of the *experimental* side of science. The interpretive component includes the concepts, laws, and theories that constitute its *theoretical* side. A highly idealized procedure would start with observations, from which tentative hypotheses would be formulated, whose implications could be tested experimentally. These experiments would lead to the construction of a more complete theory, which in turn would suggest new experiments resulting in modifications and extensions of the theory. In practice, however, the two components cannot be so clearly separated nor the logical steps so neatly distinguished.

1. The Interaction of Experiment and Theory

The popular stereotype portrays science as consisting of *precise observation*. The scientist, in this image, deals with "pure facts" that yield "indubitable knowledge." In positivism, which was perhaps the dominant school in the philosophy of science a generation ago, theories were said to be summaries of data, shorthand resumés of experience, convenient ways of classifying facts. But many recent philosophers of science have challenged this empiricist emphasis on the experimental side and have pointed to the crucial role of theoretical concepts in scientific progress.

For one thing, *there are no uninterpreted facts.* Even in the act of perception itself, the irreducible "data" given are not, as Hume claimed, isolated patches of color or other fragmentary sensations, but total patterns in which interpretation has already entered. We organize our experience in the light of particular interests, and we attend to selected features. So, too, scientific activity never consists in simply "collecting all the facts"; significant experimentation requires a selection of relevant variables and a purposeful experimental design dependent on the questions that are considered fruitful and the problems that have been formulated. "Observations" are always abstractions from our total experience, and they are expressed in terms of conceptual structures. The processes of measurement, as well as the language in which results are reported, are influenced by prior theories. Each stage of investigation presupposes many principles that for the moment are taken for granted. Thus all "data" are, as Hanson puts it, already "theory-laden."[1]

Though the data of science are never "bare facts," they are always based on *data of the public world.* In some cases they may be obtained from observation and description, and in others from controlled experimentation and exact quantitative measurement. They are "publicly verifiable"—not because "anyone" could verify them, but because they represent the common experience of the scientific community at a given time. For there is always an interpretive component present. A doctor sees an X-ray plate differently from someone without medical training. Galileo saw a pendulum as an object with inertia which almost repeats its oscillating motion, whereas his predecessors had seen it as a constrained falling object which slowly attains its final state of rest. The line between "observation" and "theory," then, is not sharp; the distinction is pragmatic and shifts with the advance of science and with differing immediate purposes in inquiry.

The theoretical component of science consists of laws and theories whose separate terms we will call *concepts.* "Mass," "acceleration,"

---

1. Norwood R. Hanson, *Patterns of Discovery* (Cambridge: Cambridge University Press, 1958), Chap. 1.

and "pressure" are not directly observable, and they are not given to us by nature. They are mental constructs used to interpret observations; they are symbols that help us to organize experience. The links between theoretical concepts and experimental observations have been termed "rules of correspondence,"[2] "epistemic correlations,"[3] or "coordinating definitions."[4] For some concepts these *rules of correspondence* may be very direct and simple, as for example the association of "length" with the result of a particular measuring operation. For other concepts, such as "energy" or "neutron," rules of correspondence may be more complex. For some concepts, such as the "wave-function" of quantum mechanics, there are only very indirect relationships to other concepts, which in turn correspond to observable events.

Laws are correlations between two or more concepts that are closely related to observables. They represent the systematic ordering of experience, the attempt to describe observations in terms of regular patterns. These may be put in the form of graphs, equations, or verbal expressions of interrelations between concepts, and they have varying degrees of generality and abstraction. Kepler's Laws of planetary motion and Galileo's equations of motion relating time, distance, and acceleration may be considered prototypes of such laws. Another example is Boyle's Law, which states that for a given quantity of gas (such as the air trapped in a bicycle tire pump) the pressure is inversely proportional to the volume (for example, if the volume is reduced by a factor of 2, the pressure doubles). Associated with laws are statements about their limiting conditions and scope (in Boyle's Law, the temperature must be constant and the pressure not so great that the gas is near liquefaction).

Laws may or may not imply relationships which could be spoken of as *causal*. Many laws (including the examples above) express concurrent variation or functional dependence with no implication that changes in one variable are the "cause" of changes in another. Some laws are statistical in character. Because laws are correlations

2. Henry Margenau, *The Nature of Physical Reality* (New York: McGraw-Hill Book Co., 1950; PB); Ernest Nagel, *The Structure of Science* (New York: Harcourt, Brace and World, 1961).

3. Filmer S. C. Northrop, *The Logic of the Sciences and Humanities* (New York: The Macmillan Co., 1947; Meridian PB).

4. Hans Reichenbach, *The Rise of Scientific Philosophy* (Berkeley: University of California Press, 1951; PB).

between concepts which are closely associated with observables, they are often called "experimental laws"; but it should be remembered that they always go beyond the experimental data. A law formulates a universal relation, which allows the derivation of values not given in the original data. Moreover, it is *not* expressed directly in terms of sense-data, though it is based on observation. As Nagel states:

> None of the customary examples of experimental laws are in fact about sense data, since they employ notions and involve assumptions that go far beyond anything directly given to sense. . . . Reports of what are commonly regarded as experimental observations are frequently couched in the language of what is admittedly some theory.[5]

Finally, *theories* are unified and generalized conceptual schemes from which laws can be derived. Compared to laws, theories are further from direct observation and are more comprehensive, connecting greater ranges of phenomena with higher generality. Because coherent structures of concepts usually involve new ways of looking at phenomena, their development reflects greater creativity and originality. A theory is constructed in such a way that previously known laws can be deduced from it, but it is never simply a restatement of those laws, and often a theory leads to the discovery of new laws. Thus from Newton's theory of gravitation, Kepler's Laws could be deduced, but the former has much greater generality since it applied also to the moon and to objects on the earth. In order to account for Boyle's Law and other laws relating the pressure, volume, temperature, and combining ratios of gases, the kinetic theory was later developed, in which gases were assumed to consist of colliding elastic particles (the so-called "billiard-ball model"). But the kinetic theory also accounted for other laws and led to unanticipated discoveries concerning viscosity, diffusion, heat conduction, and so forth. Among theories of great generality which we shall describe later are the quantum theory and the theory of evolution.

2. The Formation of Theories

How are theories formed? The *inductive ideal*, for which Bacon, Hume, and Mill were spokesmen, depicts science as generalizing from particular experimental sequences to universal patterns. Recur-

---

5. Nagel, *The Structure of Science*, pp. 81–82. Used by permission of Harcourt, Brace and World, Inc., and Routledge & Kegan Paul, Ltd.

rent uniformities in oft-repeated experiments, followed by "simple enumeration" and comparison (for example, "concomitant variation"), are supposed to lead directly to general laws. We will neglect for the moment the problem of how such generalizations can be justified as a basis for predicting the future, and whether induction depends on philosophical assumptions about "the uniformity of nature." Viewed simply as a description of what scientists do, this account seems unsatisfactory. The mere amassing of data or cataloguing of facts does not produce a scientific theory. But new concepts and abstract interpretive constructions do enable us to see coherent patterns of relationship among the data. Often the introduction of new assumptions, idealizations ("frictionless planes") or concepts (Galileo's "acceleration") permit novel ways of representing phenomena. Theoretical terms are *mental constructs* which may be suggested by the data but are never given to us directly by nature. They have a status logically different from that of the data, and hence offer a type of explanation that no mere summary of the data could achieve. The empiricist tradition has never adequately represented the role of concepts and theories in science.

The deductive ideal[6] emphasizes the process of reasoning in the opposite direction, namely the derivation of verifiable observation-statements from general theories (taken with rules of correspondence). This approach has the virtue of recognizing the difference in logical status between theories and observations, which is overlooked in the inductive approach. The deductive pattern is, as we shall see, a plausible portrayal of the way theories are tested, but it throws little light on the process with which the inductive pattern at least tries to deal: the initial formation of a theory. As Hanson says: "Physicists do not start from hypotheses; they start from data. By the time a law has been fixed into a hypothetical-deductive system, really original physical thinking is over."[7]

Although inductive and deductive ideals accurately portray certain aspects of scientific activity, they omit from their accounts the leap of *creative imagination*. There is a logic for testing theories but no logic for creating them; there are no recipes for making

6. See Karl R. Popper, *The Logic of Scientific Discovery* (New York: Basic Books, 1959; Science Editions PB); Richard B. Braithwaite, *Scientific Explanation* (Cambridge: Cambridge University Press, 1953; Harper PB).
7. Hanson, *Patterns of Discovery*, p. 70.

original discoveries. Even attempts to identify scientific creativity in terms of specific abilities or character traits have had limited success.[8] But one can at least look at important discoveries in the past, though their circumstances were highly diverse. Many creative ideas have occurred unexpectedly in an intuitive flash, as in the case when Archimedes shouted "Eureka" in his bath. Darwin had read Malthus on human population pressure, but was preoccupied with other things when it suddenly struck him that a similar concept would provide the key to evolution; the idea of natural selection was born. "I can remember," he recalls, "the very spot in the road, whilst in my carriage, when to my joy the solution occurred to me." Poincaré's classic essay describes how several crucial ideas came to him "spontaneously" during periods of relaxation when he had temporarily abandoned a problem.[9] We must remember that for each of these men there had been long periods of previous preparation, discipline, and reflection on the problem; and of course such sudden inspirations must subsequently be tested, since many "flashes of insight" turn out to be wrong. But the actual origin of the novel idea in these instances was sudden and unexpected, and appears to have been the product of the subconscious mind—in which there is a remarkable fluidity of image combinations and freedom to break from established schemes.

New theories have often arisen from *novel combinations of ideas* previously entertained in isolation. Koestler and Ghiselin[10] suggest that creative imagination in both science and literature is frequently associated with the interplay between two conceptual frameworks. It involves the synthesis of a new whole, the reordering of old elements into a fresh configuration. Often it arises from the perception of an analogy between apparently unrelated situations. Newton connected two very familiar facts—the fall of an apple and the

---

8. See, e.g., the papers and extensive bibliography in C. W. Taylor and F. Barron, eds., *Scientific Creativity: Its Recognition and Development* (New York: John Wiley and Sons, 1963).

9. Henri Poincaré, "Mathematical Creation," in his *Foundations of Science*, trans. G. Bruce Halsted (New York: The Science Press, 1913). See also Jacques Hadamard, *Essay on the Psychology of Invention in the Mathematical Field* (Princeton, N.J.: Princeton University Press, 1945; Dover PB); W. I. B. Beveridge, *The Art of Scientific Investigation* (New York: W. W. Norton & Co., 1950; Modern Library PB), Chap. 6.

10. Arthur Koestler, *The Act of Creation* (New York: The Macmillan Co., 1964); Brewster Ghiselin, ed., *The Creative Process* (Berkeley: University of California Press, 1952; Mentor PB).

revolution of the moon. Darwin saw an analogy between population pressure and the survival of animal species. We will analyze
in the next section the systematic function of analogies and models
in science. Here we point out the parallel between scientific and
artistic creativity. A metaphor in poetry arises from a new connection between previously separated areas of experience, a "transaction between two contexts" in which one element influences the
way a second is seen.[11] In the work of both artist and scientist,
Bronowski suggests, there is an aesthetic delight in the coherence
of form and structure in experience, and an enjoyment of pattern
in diversity.[12] Campbell has written:

> For it has been admitted that though discovery of laws depends ulti-
> mately not on fixed rules but on the imagination of highly gifted in-
> dividuals, this imaginative and personal element is much more prom-
> inent in the development of theories; the neglect of theories leads
> directly to the neglect of the imaginative and personal element in
> science. It leads to an utterly false contrast between "materialistic"
> science and the "humanistic" studies of literature, history, and art. . . .
> What I want to impress on the reader is how purely personal was
> Newton's idea. His theory of universal gravitation, suggested to him
> by the trivial fall of an apple, was a product of his individual mind,
> just as much as the Fifth Symphony (said to have been suggested by
> another trivial incident, the knocking at a door) was a product of
> Beethoven's.[13]

The *diversity of mental operations* in scientific inquiry thus cannot be reduced to any single "ideal type." In the derivation of simple "empirical" laws, induction predominates, but even here the
scientist does more than merely summarize the data. In the formation of new theories, creative imagination transcends any process
of strictly logical reasoning. In the testing of theories, deduction is
prominent; but in place of any simple "empirical verification" we
will defend the relevance of a variety of criteria.

3. Criteria for Evaluating Theories

There are three criteria by which a theory may be evaluated: its
agreement with observations, the internal relations among its con-

11. Jerome Bruner, *On Knowing: Essays for the Left Hand* (Cambridge:
Harvard University Press, 1963; Athenaeum PB); Max Black, *Models and
Metaphors* (Ithaca, N.Y.: Cornell University Press, 1962).
12. J. Bronowski, *Science and Human Values* (New York: Julian Messner,
Inc., 1956; Harper PB), Chap. 1.
13. Norman Campbell, *What is Science?* (London: Methuen & Co., 1921;
Dover PB*), pp. 97, 102.

cepts, and its comprehensiveness. The first criterion is *relation to data* that are reproducible within the scientific community. Empirical agreement is a crucial property of any acceptable theory. Toulmin[14] refers to a theory as an "inference ticket," a technique for inferring observable relationships, which can then be tested. From a theory alone it is possible to deduce laws; from laws *plus* given initial conditions (together with rules of correspondence) it is possible to deduce relations among observables, which can be compared to data obtained in the past or expected in the future. For example, from the laws of planetary motion *plus* data about the present positions of sun and moon one can calculate the expected time of the next eclipse, and the prediction can then be checked by observation.

The second criterion refers to the relations among theoretical concepts. *Consistency* and *coherence* mean respectively the absence of logical contradictions and the presence of what Margenau calls "multiple connections" among concepts within the internal structure of a particular theory, or with those of other theories believed to be valid. *Simplicity* signifies the smallest number of independent assumptions (for example, the Copernican theory was simpler than the Ptolemaic in requiring fewer assumptions which were *ad hoc*— that is, not derivable from the fundamental structure of the theory). But simplicity has other nuances which are notoriously difficult to define; Cohen and Nagel say it includes "an incalculable aesthetic element,"[15] and many scientists speak of the "elegance" of a theory. Coherence, order, symmetry, and simplicity of formal structure are sought. In the origins of Einstein's theory of relativity, new experiments (including those of Michelson and Morley) did not play the determinative part most accounts have pictured; his quest was rather for the symmetry of frames of reference in electromagnetism, and he used only experimental facts that had been known for fifty years.[16] Again, the dissatisfaction expressed by physicists concerning the large number of apparently unrelated "elementary particles" discovered during the 1950's, and the search for some systematic order among them, is testimony to the rationalistic ideal

14. Stephen Toulmin, *The Philosophy of Science* (London: Hutchison University Library, 1953; Harper PB).
15. Morris Cohen and Ernest Nagel, *An Introduction to Logic and Scientific Method* (New York: Harcourt, Brace & Co., 1934), p. 215.
16. P. Schillp, ed., *Albert Einstein: Philosopher-Scientist* (Evanston, Ill.: Library of Living Philosophers, 1949), p. 53.

among scientists, along with their empirical ideal. These "internal" criteria applied within a theoretical system are of course never adequate alone, since a set of concepts may be self-consistent but unrelated to the world.

A third group of criteria deals with the *comprehensiveness* of a theory. This includes its initial *generality*, or ability to show underlying unity in apparently diverse phenomena. *Fruitfulness* or fertility—the value of a theory for suggesting new hypotheses, laws, concepts, or experiments—is close to Margenau's "extensibility" and Toulmin's "deployability." Usually such extension arises from the refinement or development of a theory. For example, the early kinetic theory of gases assumed elastic particles of negligible size, and it was a simple modification to make allowance for the finite size of the particles and to assume forces between them; thereby the discrepancies between the behavior of gases at high pressures and the predictions obtained from Boyle's Law could be accounted for.

It should be emphasized that the comparison of theory with experiment is often very indirect. A whole *network of ideas* is always tested at once. Margenau speaks of "circuits of verification" because it is often necessary to reason from a set of observations through a matrix of interlocking concepts—some of them far removed from anything observable—before one is able to draw any inferences tied in again to observations. Moreover, as Copi points out,[17] it is never possible to test an individual hypothesis in a "crucial experiment." Only a group of hypotheses and assumptions can serve as premises for a deduction; and if the deduction is not confirmed experimentally, one can never be sure which of the hypotheses and assumptions is in error. (One can defend a hypothesis in the face of any given experimental result by rejecting some other assumption in the group—though beyond a certain point one may have to introduce so many special *ad hoc* assumptions that simplicity suffers.) In practice one usually works in the framework of "accepted" theories, and throws all the doubt on one new hypothesis at a time. But even this can yield no "crucial experiment" in any absolute sense, since well-accepted theories have been overthrown, and the hidden assumptions may be just the ones that should have been

17. Irving M. Copi, "Crucial Experiments," in E. H. Madden, ed., *The Structure of Science* (Boston: Houghton Mifflin Co., 1960).

questioned. "The structure of science grows in an organic fashion; . . . the notion that scientific hypotheses, theories or laws are wholly discrete and independent is a naive and outdated view."[18] The process of testing is contextual and involves constellations of concepts and theories.

No theory can be proven to be true. The most that can be said for a theory is that it is in better agreement with the known data and is more coherent and comprehensive than alternative theories available at the moment. There may be other theories which will in the future meet those criteria as well or better. All formulations are tentative and subject to revision; certainty is never achieved. The chemist Arrhenius received the Nobel prize for his electrolytic theory of dissociation; the same prize was given later to Debye for showing the inadequacies of Arrhenius' theory. The concept of parity (spin symmetry), long accepted as a fundamental principle of nuclear structure, was undermined in 1956. On logical grounds, one can say that at least one hypothesis of a group is *false* if from the group one can deduce conclusions that *disagree* with experiment; but one *cannot* say they are *true* if the deduced conclusions *agree* with experiment, for another group of hypotheses might lead to the same conclusions.[19] One can seldom show that a theory has the unique capacity to account for the data—though one can sometimes on mathematical or theoretical grounds limit the number of possible rival theories (another indication of the importance of theoretical as well as experimental considerations in science). Yet obviously in many cases we can have considerable confidence that a theory is a reasonably good approximation. After all, predictions from nuclear theory, that under certain conditions a rapid chain reaction would occur, were confirmed; in the New Mexico desert, the bomb went off.

Some philosophers who recognize the impossibility of any final "empirical verification" have developed *modified forms of empiricism.* Carnap and Reichenbach[20] advocated calculating the *probability* that a theory is valid—that is, the ratio of the confirmed deductions from the theory to the total number of possible de-

---

18. *Ibid.*, p. 33.
19. See Northrop, *The Logic of the Sciences and Humanities*, pp. 146f.
20. Rudolf Carnap, *Logical Foundations of Probability* (Chicago: University of Chicago Press, 1950); Reichenbach, *The Rise of Scientific Philosophy*, Chap. 14.

ductions from it. But in practice the latter can never be specified because a theory has an indefinite range of consequences. Popper[21] proposed that even though theories are never verifiable, they must in principle be *falsifiable*. In choosing between two theories, he said that the scientist should use the one yielding the greatest number of deductions that could conceivably be proved false experimentally; for if such a theory survives empirical testing, he can have greater confidence in it. However, we would reply that in practice an experimental discrepancy, even though it always "counts against" a theory, does not have this absolute power to overthrow it, particularly if there are no alternative theories available. Observations discordant with an accepted theory are more likely to be dismissed as "anomalies" or unexplained deviations, or set aside for later study, rather than be taken to "falsify" the theory.[22]

Even such a modified empiricism, then, fails to include the variety of criteria that influence the scientist's outlook. We must simply acknowledge that, particularly in comparing alternative theories of wide generality, the criteria we have listed *may not yield any clearcut conclusion*. Frank states:

> We have learned by a great many examples that the general principles of science are not unambiguously determined by the observed facts. If we add requirements of simplicity and agreement with common sense, the determination becomes narrower, but it does not become unique. . . . There is never only one theory that is in complete agreement with all observed facts, but several theories that are in partial agreement. We have to select the final theory by a compromise. The final theory has to be in fair agreement with observed fact and must also be fairly simple. If we consider this point it is obvious that such a "final" theory cannot be "The Truth". . . . After application of all these criteria, there remains often a choice among several theories.[23]

The element of personal judgment enters in the evaluation of the data, the estimation of simplicity and generality, and the relative importance ascribed to different criteria. Such assessment occurs not explicitly in abstract discussion but implicitly in practice, especially in the face of new and controversial hypotheses.

21. Popper, *The Logic of Scientific Discovery*; also Karl R. Popper, *Conjectures and Refutations* (New York: Basic Books, 1962).
22. Some examples are given in Polanyi, *Personal Knowledge*, pp. 148–58.
23. Philipp Frank, *Philosophy of Science* (Englewood Cliffs, N.J.: Prentice-Hall, Inc., 1957; PB), pp. 355, 359.

4. Understanding as the Goal of Science

We will urge, finally, that the goal of science is to understand nature, and that the *empirical confirmation of predictions* is only one element in the testing of theories. By contrast, some empiricists assign a central role to prediction; coherence and comprehensiveness are then justified only because they contribute to the attainment of agreement with observations. If prediction is the goal, these other criteria are at best practical maxims introduced for the sake of ease of manipulation or economy of thought. But if understanding is the goal—intellectual control rather than practical control—then coherence and comprehensiveness are integral to the aims of inquiry.

Let us consider the claim that *explanation* is logically equivalent to *prediction*. Hempel[24] says that the scientist's goal is to show that an event (whether past or future) is an instance of a general law (that is, that the event can be deduced from the law plus information about previous conditions). Explaining a past event, he writes, is always equivalent to showing that it could have been predicted from its antecedents. This view has been challenged on a number of grounds. For example, Scriven[25] points out that the theory of natural selection is an accepted scientific explanation, yet few people would claim that from it one could have predicted the course of evolution. On the other hand, one might from past experience make a reliable prediction (for example, that radio disturbances will follow a solar flare) which would not count as an explanation, since no intelligible reasons for the occurrence of the predicted events are offered.[26] The law "red sky in the morning, rain by evening" would, even if always valid, provide no explanation of rain. A scientist would have no greater interest than other men in a crystal ball which predicts all events; such an inscrutable but accurate prognosticator would have great practical but no scientific value.

---

24. Carl G. Hempel and Paul Oppenheim, "The Logic of Explanation," in H. Feigl and M. Brodbeck, eds., *Readings in the Philosophy of Science* (New York: Appleton-Century-Crofts, 1953).

25. Michael Scriven, "Explanation and Prediction in Evolutionary Theory," *Science*, Vol. 130 (1959), 477.

26. See also Israel Scheffler, *The Anatomy of Inquiry* (New York: Alfred A. Knopf, 1963), pp. 43f. Several papers representative of the current discussion, and a good bibliography, can be found in B. Baumrin, ed., *Philosophy of Science: The Delaware Seminar* (New York: Interscience Publishers, 1963), Vols. 1 and 2.

Even though laws allow predictions to be made, it is *theories* that have explanatory force because of the intelligibility they yield. They provide a type of explanation or understanding that even the most complicated prediction-formula lacks. Theories display an extensibility to new types of phenomena which is not found among laws. Moreover, the scientist is not satisfied with predictive laws until he gains insight into theoretical structures that can account for their success. The intellectual satisfaction that theories provide is a product of rational as well as empirical components. Toulmin points out that the Babylonians could make very precise predictions in astronomy from mathematical time-series tables, worked out by trial and error with no theoretical basis; they "acquired great forecasting-power, but they conspicuously lacked understanding," for the explanatory power of a theory lies in the *ideas* which make patterns of relationships intelligible:

> The central aims of science lie in the field of intellectual creation; other activities—diagnostic, classificatory, industrial, or predictive—are properly called "scientific" from their connection with the explanatory ideas and ideals which are the heart of natural science. . . . The central aims of science are, rather, concerned with a search for understanding—a desire to make the course of Nature not just predictable but intelligible—and this has meant looking for rational patterns of connections in terms of which we can make sense of the flux of events.[27]

In a similar vein, Hanson describes science as *a search for pattern*: "Physics is a search for intelligibility. Only secondarily is it a search for new objects and facts."[28]

In summary, scientific inquiry is a complex process, with experimental and theoretical components inextricably interwoven. The formation of theories depends on the logical process of inductive generalization and on the creative originality of human imagination. In evaluating theories, both the empirical criterion of agreement with observations and the rational criteria of coherence and comprehensiveness are present. The primary goal of science is intellectual understanding; control is a secondary consideration. This is the broad structure of scientific methodology, whose distinctive characteristics we must now scrutinize.

---

27. Stephen Toulmin, *Foresight and Understanding* (Bloomington: Indiana University Press, 1961; Harper PB°), pp. 38, 99.
28. Hanson, *Patterns of Discovery*, p. 18.

II. THE SCIENTIFIC COMMUNITY AND ITS LANGUAGE

To understand the structure of science more clearly we must look at *science-in-the-making*, the actual work of scientists. Philosophers of science are interested in the logical structure of scientific propositions. Science teachers also give more attention to "the logic of the discovered" than to the process of discovery. To some extent this is inevitable, for a teacher wants to present principles in a systematic way; but often students gain little understanding of the scientific enterprise. Even the occasional historical references tend to encourage a view of science as a succession of "great geniuses"; little comprehension of the social fabric of scientific endeavor is gained. Preoccupation with the logic of science, and desire to present science as a "success story," obscure insight into the slow and often tortuous way it has actually grown, the many false starts, plausible but fruitless hypotheses and frustrating impasses that are part of its life. Neglect of the dynamics of science in operation produces a distorted image of its methods. Science should be treated not as a noun but as a verb, a form of human activity.

Some of these neglected features have been pointed out in recent studies in the history of science and the sociology of science. Others are evident in the writings of scientists themselves. It will be apparent below that *science is a very human enterprise* and shares many characteristics with other activities in which men engage. We will consider the role of the scientific community, the symbolic language it employs, and the models and analogies by which it interprets the world. This will provide the basis for a comparison in a later chapter with the role of the religious community and its models and analogies.

1. The Scientific Community and Its Paradigms

The *corporate character of inquiry* is reflected in the indispensability of interaction between scientists: the dependence of each man on his predecessors, the necessity of having one's results checked by others, the reliance of experimentalist on theoretician and vice versa, the value of knowledge from other fields, the fruitfulness of discussion and mutual criticism, and the stimulus of peers who alone can competently evaluate one's work. The respect of fellow scientists is surely one of the chief motives in research. The variety of types of scientist needs to be recognized: the Nobel-prize genius and the routine investigator, the technician and the administrator, the individual inventor and the member of a large research team. Science is a social enterprise, a cooperative venture.

The presence of this community has always been essential to the progress of science. The Royal Society and the French Academy were important factors in the rise of science. *Communicability* is one of the attributes of scientific knowledge, and the imposition of secrecy, whether by government or industry, is antithetical to its growth. Communication is today achieved primarily through journals and professional meetings which are the main channels for the reporting of results and the stimulation of new work. The organization of science is highly complex, enmeshed in the structures of government, industry, and education. It has its own chains of command and hierarchies of power that interlock with those of other institutions.

The scientific community, like any group in society, has *a set of attitudes* which are influenced by but not identical with those of the culture at large. Schilling gives a vivid portrayal:

> It has its own ideals and characteristic way of life; its own standards, mores, conventions, signs and symbols, language and jargon, professional ethics, sanctions and controls, authority, institutions and organizations, publications; its own creeds and beliefs, orthodoxies and heresies—and effective ways of dealing with the latter. This community is affected, as are other communities, by the usual vagaries, adequacies, and shortcomings of human beings. It has its politics, its pulling and hauling, its pressure groups; its differing schools of thought, its divisions and schisms; its personal loyalties and animosities, jealousies, hatreds, and rallying cries; its fads and fashions.[29]

"Unorthodox" views may be rejected by the scientific community (as hypnotism was for many years) or ignored (as the question of extrasensory perception is today by most psychologists) or tolerated with disapproval (as osteopathy has been by the medical profession).

It is this set of attitudes and traditions that *holds the scientific community together*. "Its members," writes Polanyi, "recognize the same set of persons as their masters and derive from this allegiance a common tradition, of which each carries on a particular strand."[30]

29. Harold K. Schilling, "A Human Enterprise," *Science*, Vol. 127 (1958), 1324. See also his *Science and Religion*, Chap. 4.
30. Polanyi, *Personal Knowledge*, p. 163.

Joint acceptance of these beliefs, and the presence of common loyalties and commitments, make self-government possible, so that the
authority of the community's consensus and of particular preroga-
tives, such as those of a journal editor, are voluntarily acknowledged
rather than externally imposed. Conant[31] points out that coordination of individual research activities takes place for the most part
informally through the interaction of the individual and the community. Preparation for a career in science involves not just memo-
rizing information and acquiring skills, but coming to share attitudes by participating in the life of a particular community. This
absorption of standards and presuppositions is one result of the
research apprenticeship every doctoral candidate undergoes.

In addition, the scientists in a given field share *patterns of expectation* and *conceptions of regularity and intelligibility* that govern
their work. We noted earlier that as "standard cases" for discussing
motion, Aristotle took familiar objects for which there is considerable resistance (for example, a cart pulled by a horse). By contrast,
Galileo and Newton used idealized frictionless motion as the standard in terms of which to analyze actual situations; they saw continued uniform motion, rather than coming to rest, as natural and
self-explanatory (needing no further explanation). Toulmin shows
that such *"explanatory paradigms"* determine what we take to be
"problems," what we see as "facts," and what we consider to be
satisfactory explanations:

> Science progresses, not by recognizing the truth of new observations
> alone, but by making sense of them. To this task of interpretation we
> bring principles of regularity, conceptions of natural order, paradigms,
> ideals, or what-you-will: intellectual patterns which define the range
> of things we can accept (in Copernicus' phrase) as "sufficiently abso-
> lute and pleasing to the mind."[32]

According to Toulmin, these changing explanatory ideals are empirical in only a very broad way, since they cannot be directly
confronted with the results of observations. They prove their worth
over a longer period of time, and serve rather as "preconceived
notions" for the individual scientist in most of his work.

T. S. Kuhn has given historical documentation to a similar thesis

---

31. James B. Conant, *On Understanding Science* (New Haven, Conn.: Yale
University Press, 1947), Chap. 1.
32. Toulmin, *Foresight and Understanding*, p. 81. Used by permission of
Indiana University Press.

that *the authority of a scientific community* supports a particular set of assumptions by means of its *paradigms.*[33] Paradigms are "standard examples" of past scientific work which are accepted by a given group of scientists at a given time. These are the prevailing examples used in textbooks, and by learning them students acquire concurrently the theoretical concepts, experimental methods, and norms of the field. Paradigms also guide the group's research, for they implicitly define what sorts of question may legitimately be asked, what techniques are fruitful, what types of solution are admissible. Most scientific endeavor is carried on within the framework of such a "received tradition" which defines the kinds of explanation to be sought (thus when Newton's laws were a paradigm, explanations were sought in terms of forces and corpuscular motions). The tradition influences the concepts through which the scientist sees the world, the expectations by which his work is governed, and the language he uses.

Kuhn suggests that the rare occurrence of *a major change of paradigms* produces such far-reaching effects that it can be called a scientific revolution. (Among his examples are Copernican astronomy, Newtonian physics, Lavoisier's discovery of oxygen, and Einstein's relativity.) A new paradigm requires the overthrow of the old, not just an addition to previous theories. The familiar data are seen in an entirely new way and the old terms acquire altered meanings. Kuhn compares these changes with the shift in a visual gestalt (for example, when a sketch of the outside of a box viewed from below is suddenly seen as the inside of a box viewed from above). For a brief period, adherents of two different paradigms may be competing for the allegiance of their colleagues; Kuhn claims that the choice between them is not determined by the criteria of ordinary research:

> Though each may hope to convert the other to his way of seeing his science and its problems, neither may hope to prove his case. The competition between paradigms is not the sort of battle that can be resolved by proofs. . . . Before they can hope to communicate fully, one group or the other must experience the conversion that we have been calling a paradigm shift. Just because it is a transition between incommensurables, the transition between competing paradigms cannot be made a step at a time, forced by logic and neutral experience. Like

33. Thomas S. Kuhn, *The Structure of Scientific Revolutions* (Chicago: University of Chicago Press, 1962; PB); for a reply to Kuhn's thesis, see Dudley Shapere in *Philosophical Review*, Vol. 73 (1964), 383.

a gestalt switch it must occur all at once (though not necessarily in an instant) or not at all.[34]

There is no higher authority than *the scientific community* for making such decisions between paradigms, Kuhn concludes. Of course the ordinary criteria (empirical fit, intellectual beauty, and so forth) contribute to the choice; but they do not determine it unequivocally, especially in the early stages when the new paradigm has not been developed or applied extensively. Often the new conceptual structure entails an altered estimation as to what kinds of problems are significant, and this cannot be settled by logic alone. Scientists legitimately resist revolutions, since their previous commitments have permeated their thinking. Sometimes a new view is completely accepted only when the older generation has died off or has been "converted" to it. Thus the choice between competing paradigms is neither totally arbitrary and subjective, on the one hand, nor completely determined by systematic rules, on the other. It is a choice which ultimately only the scientific community itself can make. Hence the corporate context of scientific inquiry is not just a fact of interest to sociologists and historians, but a feature that should be taken into account in the analysis of methodology.

It would be easy to dismiss Kuhn's thesis as applicable only to the past history of science; are not *theories today* on firmer ground, and unlikely to be replaced by new ones? Kuhn would reply that to each generation a set of paradigms seems securely established, and only in retrospect are its limitations evident. Again, one may object, does not the new set of concepts in a scientific revolution incorporate all that was valid in the old; does it not account for all the previous evidence, and more besides? Does not the new and more inclusive theory often treat the old as a special limiting case, as the equations of Einstein's relativity reduce to Newton's Laws for objects moving at low velocities? But, says Kuhn, revolutions entail the rejection of the old, not simply the addition of the new; the concepts used by Einstein and by Newton (mass, velocity, and so forth) do not have the same meaning.

Now we would suggest that Kuhn has overemphasized *the arbi-*

---

34. Kuhn, *The Structure of Scientific Revolutions*, pp. 147, 149. Copyright 1962 by the University of Chicago Press. See also his essay, "The Function of Dogma in Scientific Research," in A. C. Crombie, ed., *Scientific Change* (New York: Basic Books, 1963).

trary character of paradigm shifts. A paradigm may in practice function in a unitary way to guide a research tradition; but in reflecting about it we must try to differentiate its various components, for they are evaluated in varying ways. For example, Newtonian mechanics, as the paradigm of classical physics, included a group of specific concepts and theories (which are subject to the criteria previously discussed); it also expressed assumptions as to what constitutes a satisfactory explanation or a promising research method (the fruitfulness of these assumptions throughout physics—indeed, throughout the sciences—is relevant here); in addition it indirectly transmitted certain very general presuppositions about nature (lawfulness, regularity, intelligibility—which we will consider in the next chapter). Although Kuhn legitimately attacks the view that science is strictly cumulative, he fails to indicate that even in a "revolution" many features of previous tradition are retained after the shift. Most of the data obtained and many of the prevailing methods and assumptions are carried over. For there is continuity, especially in any relatively mature science, and there is progress, though seldom in a straight line. Kuhn's writing (like that of Hanson, Toulmin, and Polanyi) represents a salutary reaction against the positivism that formerly dominated the philosophy of science, but he perhaps gives undue weight to the subjective, relativistic and communal features which earlier accounts ignored.

2. *The Symbolic Character of Scientific Language*

All language is learned and used in interpersonal situations; it is a means of communication and *a function of community.* Similarly, specialized languages of discourse for particular purposes are products of specialized communities. Each of these communities has its own symbolic language in terms of which it interprets certain aspects of its experience. The types of concepts that are used and the patterns of thought the language embodies are determined by the assumptions and interests of the community. Symbols are used "expressively" to articulate a state of the subject, and "referentially" to designate a state of an object. These functions are never completely separable, but clearly in science the referential function predominates. A subject uses a symbol to refer to an object, but the referent is represented in only an indirect and partial way. Benjamin asserts:

> Every symbol aims to represent its referent, but no symbol is able to portray *all* of the features of the referent; hence, it is obliged to omit

one or more of them. Given any symbol, therefore, one may infer the referent, since the symbol resembles it, but not all of the referent, since the symbol is an abstraction. . . . Since the human mind is incapable of grasping any event in all of its configurations, certain of its relations are more or less arbitrarily neglected and are not included in the resulting symbol. As a consequence, every symbol is abstract in its representations of nature; it loses some of nature and hence is not strictly adequate as a representative.[35]

Thus the language of every community of inquiry is *abstractive and selective* and replaces complex experiences by symbolic constructs and diagrammatic sketches of those aspects in which it is interested. In physics problems an elephant on a slippery river bank becomes a mass with a coefficient of friction, and a Beethoven symphony becomes a set of molecular vibrations. When a field of study can thus abstract single factors for investigation, it can be more exact; but its schematic representation of limited aspects is further from the total situation of life, and from the immediacy and variety of human experience with all its levels of meaning. The purposes in inquiry determine the kind of symbolic scheme developed.

In previous centuries this symbolic character of scientific language was overlooked; science was assumed to provide *a literal description* of an objective world. Its concepts were thought of as exact and complete replicas of nature as it is in itself—a view we now call "naive realism." There was assumed to be a one-to-one isomorphic correspondence between every feature of a theory and a matching feature of the entity it reproduced or "mirrored." Today concepts are considered to be *symbols* that deal with only certain aspects of the phenomena in order to achieve particular and limited purposes. The contribution of man's mind in inventing concepts, and the role of imagination and creativity in the formation of new theories, are widely acknowledged. Concepts are not given to us ready-made by nature; they are terms in human symbol-systems.

In the case of *atomic physics* the relation of the scientific symbolism to the reality represented is extraordinarily indirect. Here abstract mathematical equations give only the probability that particular experimental results will occur when given operations are performed on an atom; no visualizable picture of what the atom might be like in itself is provided. The *abandonment of picturability* is one of the striking features of modern physics. Micro-nature

35. A. Cornelius Benjamin, *Introduction to the Philosophy of Science* (New York: The Macmillan Co., 1937), pp. 69, 449.

seems to be a different kind of reality from the world of everyday experience; our usual categories are apparently not applicable, so we must use a highly abstract symbolism. The atomic world is not only inaccessible to direct observation, and inexpressible in terms of the senses; we are unable even to imagine it. There is a radical disjunction between the way things behave and every way in which we try to visualize them, as we shall see in Chapter 10. For example, in some experiments we may picture electrons as waves and in others as particles, but there seems no consistent way of imagining what an electron is like in itself.

3. The Use of Analogies and Models

In discussing creativity we indicated that scientific concepts have often arisen from the exploitation of analogies. Let us define an *analogy* as an observed or postulated similarity between two situations. (Two entities are defined as similar if some of their characteristics are the same and others are different; the similarity may be one of form, function, or property.) As an aid to inquiry, analogy is the extension of patterns of relationship drawn from one area of experience to coordinate other types of experience. To the chemist Kekulé, an analogy of geometrical form, drawn from an unexpected visual image, suggested the shape of the molecule of benzene, with which he had been working. In a dream he saw a snake grasp its tail in its mouth; when he awoke he realized that a ring-shaped molecular structure would account for the properties of benzene— a hypothesis which further experimentation supported.

A *model* in science is a systematic analogy postulated between a phenomenon whose laws are already known and one under investigation. In the case of a "mathematical model," there is a formal similarity in the equations representing the two phenomena, but there may be no similarities between the observed phenomena themselves (for example, the same differential equation describes the vibration of an elliptical membrane and the motion of an acrobat). In a "mechanical model," the analogue is a system of objects whose motion is describable by the laws of classical mechanics (such as the "billiard-ball model" on which the kinetic theory of gases was based). In general, it is assumed that the new phenomenon has some, but not all, of the properties of the analogue (for example, gas molecules have mass and collide elastically like billiard balls, but they need not have color). In the "Bohr model" of the atom, electrons are pictured revolving in orbits around the nucleus like a miniature solar system. From models are derived theoretical relationships, often expressed mathematically, which can be evaluated by the empirical and rational criteria discussed earlier.

Analogies and models have unquestionably been *a fruitful source of scientific theories.*[36] The wave theory of light was developed largely by analogy with the wave properties of sound. Mechanical models were common in nineteenth-century science; Lord Kelvin asserted that a person does not really understand something until he has a mechanical model of it. But the dangers in the use of models also became evident, particularly the tendency to "overextend" them by assuming that all characters of the analogue will be present in the new situation. Thus the analogy of light waves with sound waves, which was so useful at one stage, led to the fruitless search for the "ether," the assumed medium of propagation; two systems manifesting a resemblance in many properties were erroneously believed to share another property. Moreover, since theories were held to be literal descriptions of reality it was assumed that the object under study was just like the model. It was forgotten that (1) analogies are only similarities in some but not all characters, (2) models only suggest possible hypotheses, which must then be tested experimentally, and (3) theories are symbolic and selective representations.

The dangers in the use of models led some authors to view them as only *temporary psychological aids in the formation of theories.* Duhem[37] urged that models should be used with caution and discarded as soon as possible. The ideal theory, he said, would be a mathematical formalism without any interpretation by a model. This position was associated with the positivist assertion that theories are summaries of data and not representations of reality. When the abstract probability functions of quantum theory replaced the Bohr model of the atom, there seemed added evidence that one should try to get along without visualizable models. If

---

36. E. Farber, "Chemical Discoveries by Means of Analogies," *Isis*, Vol. 41 (1950), 20; M. B. Hesse, "Models in Physics," *British Journal of Philosophy of Science*, Vol. 4 (1953), 198.

37. Pierre Duhem, *The Aim and Structure of Physical Theory*, trans. P. Wigner (Princeton, N.J.: Princeton University Press, 1954), Pt. I, Chap. 4.

sets of equations can correlate observations and permit predictions to be made, why keep models from which misleading conclusions might be derived? But there have also been vigorous *defenders of the use of models.* Campbell,[38] replying to Duhem, affirmed that a model goes beyond a formula both in providing an intellectually satisfying interpretation and in suggesting new ways in which a theory might be extended. Max Black[39] points out that models use language drawn from a domain which is already familiar; also a model is vivid and grasped as a whole, whereas a set of formulas is too complex and abstract to provide this immediacy and unity of comprehension. Moreover, models are often extensible; no one can say in advance when a model may still serve a useful function or be developed further. We noticed that the kinetic theory of gases, based on the billiard-ball model, could account for Boyle's Law. From the fact that Boyle's Law does not hold at high pressures one might have argued that the model was limited and should be discarded. Instead it was an extension of the model which was fruitful; consideration of the finite size of the assumed particles, and the forces between them, allowed the derivation of Van der Waal's equation for the behavior of gases at high pressures. And it was the model, not the formalism, which enabled additional phenomena (gas viscosity, heat conduction) to be explained.

In a careful discussion of models,[40] Hesse maintains that in general an analogue has some features which at any given time have been shown to be similar to the phenomenon, some which are dissimilar, and a third group of characteristics whose possible similarity is uncertain; the latter often give *clues for new hypotheses to be tested.* Moreover, observed similarities may indicate possible ways of interpreting previously uninterpreted terms in a formalism. When the wave theory of light was being developed, it was not evident with which observable characteristics the amplitude and the frequency of the assumed light wave should be associated. But the analogy between *brightness* of light and *loudness* of sound (which was already known to correspond to amplitude)

---

38. N. R. Campbell, *Physics, the Elements* (Cambridge: Cambridge University Press, 1920; Dover PB entitled *Foundations of Science*), Chap. 4.

39. Black, *Models and Metaphors*, Chap. 13.

40. Mary B. Hesse, *Analogies and Models in Science* (New York: Sheed and Ward, 1963), Chap. 2.

and between *color* and *pitch* (which corresponds to frequency) suggested interpretations which further data supported. Toulmin writes: "It is in fact a great virtue of a good model that it does suggest further questions, taking us beyond the phenomena from which we began, and tempts us to formulate hypotheses which turn out to be experimentally fertile."[41] Nagel defends not only the pragmatic value of models, but the contribution they make to the unity of science through emphasis on similarities between areas of inquiry:

> It would be a mistake to conclude, however, that once the new theory has been formulated the model has played its part and has no further function in the use made of a theory. . . . It may lead to suggestions concerning directions to be followed in fresh areas of experimental inquiry, and for clues as to how the formulations of experimental laws need to be modified so as to enlarge the scope of their valid application. . . . From this perspective an analogy between an old and a new theory is not simply an aid in exploiting the latter but a desideratum many scientists seek to achieve in the construction of explanatory systems.[42]

The lesson to be learned from the mistakes of nineteenth-century physics is not that models must be discarded, but that they *must not be interpreted literally*. We will see that some of the confusion about the "wave-particle dualism" arose from failure to note the analogical use of the terms "wave" and "particle" in describing the behavior of electrons. An analogy is never a total identity or a comprehensive description, but only a simplified comparison of limited aspects. The particular type of analogy that formerly dominated science, namely mechanical and visualizable models, has proven inadequate. Quantum physics represents the atom by wave-functions that cannot be visualized; but even such abstract symbolic systems involve the use of analogies (for example, Heisenberg's matrix mechanics was analogous to the Fourier analysis of the harmonics of waves), but their concepts are only indirectly related to experimental data and to the categories of everyday experience.

We must now discuss more explicitly how this symbolic and analogical language used by the scientific community is related

---

41. Toulmin, *Philosophy of Science*, p. 37.
42. Nagel, *Structure of Science*, pp. 112, 114. Used by permission of Harcourt, Brace & World, Inc., and Routledge & Kegan Paul, Ltd.

to the world and to the experimental data on which it is based. We consider several current viewpoints before attempting to show how an understanding of the symbolic character of language might allow us to combine what is valid in these various schools of thought.

III. THE RELATION OF SCIENTIFIC CONCEPTS TO REALITY

What is the status of scientific laws, theories, and concepts? How is the language of science related to the subject who uses it and the object it purports to represent? We have indicated that until this century most scientists assumed a simple realism in which theories were conceived as exact replicas of the world; by contrast, some of the concepts of twentieth-century physics are only very indirectly related to observations, and cannot be considered literal representations of objects as they are in themselves. It will be instructive to examine carefully four philosophical interpretations; the difference between them may seem to be a somewhat technical matter, but one's conclusions will influence one's view of science and its relation to religion. In positivism, a theory is viewed as a summary of data; in instrumentalism, a theory is a useful tool; in idealism, a theory is a mental structure; and in realism, it is a representation of the world.

1. Theories as Summaries of Data (Positivism)

The empiricist tradition, going back to Bacon, Hume, and Mill, has placed emphasis on the observational side of science. Mach, Russell (at one stage), Pearson, and Bridgman are among those who have seen concepts and theories as summaries of data, labor-saving *mental devices for classifying observations.* "Atoms," "electrons," and "molecules" are merely convenient categories for summarizing and simplifying laboratory data; theoretical concepts are formulae for giving *resumés* of experience. They lead to economy of thought, but since they do not themselves designate anything capable of direct observation they are not to be considered real. Karl Pearson wrote:

> Either the atom is real, that is, capable of being a direct sense impression, or else it is ideal, that is, a purely mental conception by the aid of which we are enabled to formulate natural laws. . . . To no con-

cept, however invaluable it may be as a means of describing the routine of perceptions, ought phenomenal existence to be ascribed until its perceptual equivalent has actually been disclosed.[43]

There have been two main variants of positivism. To *phenomenalists*, data mean sense-data, and all verifiable propositions must be translatable into statements about sense-impressions. Russell (prior to 1927) tried to develop ways of reducing all scientific propositions to statements about sensory awareness; if the term "atom" is a function of sense-data, it should be replaceable by the latter whenever it occurs. The *physicalist* version (for example, in Neurath and the early Carnap) requires the translation of all conceptual statements into "thing-language," that is, statements about events in the public world or direct experimental results. For Bridgman, all concepts must be operationally defined and measured by specifiable laboratory procedures. Impressed by the way relativity theory had undermined commonsense ideas of length and time, he urged the identification of concepts with performable experimental operations: "The concept is synonymous with the corresponding set of operations."[44]

Elsewhere we will criticize the way positivism (as an interpretation of science) was extended into logical positivism (as a philosophy stressing the "verification principle" and the rejection of metaphysics, ethics, and theology). Here it can be noted that even the attempt to translate all scientific sentences into *sense-data language* was never successfully carried out, and partial attempts produced unmanageable systems.[45] We have maintained, in any case, that man starts not from bare, separate sense-data but from patterns of experienced relationships in which interpretation is already present. We have suggested that reports of scientific "data" are always "theory-laden," for there are no uninterpreted facts, and all language is selective, abstractive, and symbolic. There is no "neutral observation language" devoid of interpretation. We have already had occasion to criticize the view that theories origi-

43. Karl Pearson, *The Grammar of Science*, 3rd ed. (New York: The Macmillan Co., 1911; Meridian PB), pp. 96, 212.
44. Percy Bridgman, *The Logic of Modern Physics* (New York: The Macmillan Co., 1927; PB), p. 5.
45. See C. G. Hempel, "Problems and Changes in the Empiricist Criterion of Meaning," *Revue Internationale de Philosophie*, Vol. 4 (1950), reprinted in A. J. Ayer, *Logical Positivism* (Glencoe, Ill.: Free Press, 1959).

nate in a process of induction or "summarization of data"; this portrayal simply does not correspond to the thought-processes of the creative scientist.

The attempt to *eliminate all conceptual terms* was as difficult to defend in principle as to carry out in practice. For a concept-statement is related to indefinite numbers and types of possible object-statements. From a theory it may be possible to deduce experimental laws applying to phenomena quite different from the original data, as we saw with the kinetic theory of gases. Toulmin points out that a concept (such as "gas molecule") differs logically from an observation (such as "gas volume"). As he puts it, theoretical physics is not a type of "natural history" or collection of classified facts. The whole point of a theory is that it introduces new types of terms. A theory is taken as an explanation of the phenomena precisely because it makes use of ideas of a different logical level and has greater comprehensiveness and generality than the phenomena themselves. Like earlier forms of empiricism, positivism fails to represent the crucial role of concepts and theories in the history of science.

2. Theories as Useful Tools (Instrumentalism)

In Chapter 5 (and at greater length in Chapter 9) the development of British philosophy from logical positivism into *linguistic analysis* is described. Analysis does not consist of any one set of conclusions, but of the attempt to clarify various types of language and the functions they serve in man's life. Applied to the language of science, it has usually produced an *instrumentalist* view of scientific theories, which is perhaps the most prevalent interpretation among philosophers of science today. Toulmin[46] (along with F. P. Ramsey, Ryle, and others) holds that laws are "maxims or directions for the investigator to find his way about," whereas theories are "techniques for drawing inferences," useful primarily for making predictions.

Instrumentalists give a larger role than positivists to the activity of the knower in the imaginative creation of conceptual schemes. The knower does more than record and organize; he abstracts, idealizes, constructs, and invents. Theories are spoken of as *regulative maxims, principles of procedure,* or *techniques to be employed*

---

46. Toulmin, *The Philosophy of Science.* (However, his more recent writings stress the contribution of theories to "understanding" rather than "prediction.")

for accomplishing desired purposes in scientific investigation. They are fictions in the sense of being human inventions for coordinating or generating observation-statements. Attention is directed to the way a theory is used, its function as a means of inquiry. Theories are thus conceived as (a) calculating devices for making accurate predictions, (b) organizing guides for directing further experimentation, and (c) practical tools for achieving technical control. They are to be judged by their usefulness in achieving these goals, not by their truth or falsity.

In this view, scientific concepts are functionally related to observations but *need not themselves be reducible to observations.* The instrumentalist believes that the positivist attempt to translate all concepts into a set of equivalent data-statements can never succeed because the fruitfulness of a concept includes its future employment with phenomena at present unknown; such a translation, even if it could be achieved, would hinder rather than advance its value as a mental tool. It is pointed out that scientists employ "limiting concepts" (such as frictionless planes) or concepts without direct rules of correspondence (such as atomic wave-functions), which refer neither to observations nor to real objects in the world. Similarly, the retention of models, which positivists usually condemn, is defended by instrumentalists on pragmatic grounds.

In contrast to positivists, instrumentalists do not require that concepts should correspond to observables, and they make no effort to eliminate theoretical terms; in contrast to realists, however, they do *not* insist that there are *real entities* corresponding to concepts. Laws and theories are invented, not discovered. "Do electrons exist?" is not a useful question to ask, says Toulmin; in scientific language the term is not employed referentially. "It is a mistake to put questions about the reality or existence of theoretical entities too much in the center of the picture. . . ."[47] A theory organizes the behavior of nature by what Toulmin calls "as-it-were" reference to hypothetical models, but does not attempt to describe nature "as it is." In similar fashion, Braithwaite proposes that the question of the existence of electrons should be bypassed completely in favor of asking how the word "electron" occurs in the structures of theories.

Instrumentalism, with its breadth, flexibility, and interest in

47. *Ibid.*, p. 138.

the uses of language, is less subject to criticism than was positivism for failing to describe what scientists actually do, The difficulties here concern *the status of theories.* Contemporary exponents do not hold that theories are completely arbitrary, nor do they concur with idealists that concepts originate in the mind's structure imposed on experience. But they seldom give a clear answer to the question: why do some theories work, whereas others do not? Nagel criticizes instrumentalism by suggesting that "a theory is an effective tool of inquiry only if things and events *are actually so related* that the conclusions the theory enables us to infer from given experimental data are in good agreement with further matters of observed fact."[48] The usefulness of theories is dependent on objective features of the experimental situation and not on personal whims. Nagel points out that most scientists see statements of theories as premises which might be shown to be *false,* since when taken with initial conditions they imply statements about observable facts which might be found to be false. To say that a theory is "unsatisfactory" as a rule for inference-drawing, or as a leading principle for further inquiry, amounts to saying that it is false. Scientists talk about evidence for or against the validity of a theory, not just for or against its use. Finally, instrumentalism can offer no objection to the adoption of two contradictory theories if both are useful; yet such a practice is not followed by scientists, and new discoveries have arisen from attempts to resolve conflicting ideas.

3. Theories as Mental Structures (Idealism)

Idealism goes even further than instrumentalism in accentuating the contribution of the knower; here the structures of theory are entirely *imposed by the mind* on the chaos of sense-data. The philosophical idealism exemplified by Eddington, Jeans, and Milne finds few supporters today, but a modified neo-Kantianism is found in Cassirer, Margenau, and in a somewhat different form among continental physicists such as von Weizsäcker.

Eddington uses vivid imagery to convey the determinative influence he assigns to *man's mind* in all knowledge. He pictures us following footsteps in the sand, only to discover that the tracks are our own:

---

48. Nagel, *Structure of Science,* p. 134 (italics added).

The mind has by its selective power fitted the processes of Nature into a frame of law of a pattern largely of its own choosing; and in the discovery of this system of law the mind may be regarded as regaining from Nature that which the mind has put into Nature.[49]

Eddington has attempted to derive both the fundamental laws of physics and the "constants of nature" from *a priori* considerations without utilizing any experimental results. He holds that the characteristics which we think we find in nature are manufactured by ourselves in the acts by which we observe and measure. By "subjective selection" we have molded the world into a form we can understand:

The fundamental laws and constants of physics are wholly subjective . . . for we could not have this kind of *a priori* knowledge of laws governing an objective universe. The subjective laws are a consequence of the conceptual frame of thought into which our observational knowledge is forced by our method of formulating it.[50]

Eddington's treatise is complex and difficult to follow. According to his critics, his reasoning makes implicit use of many assumptions which came indirectly *from experimental findings,* either as specific methods which have been found successful or as postulates of a very general character (for example, in quantum mechanics and relativity). Whittaker states that "in effect the epistemological principles were by no means independent of knowledge derived from sense-perception";[51] qualitative results and the forms of empirical laws were introduced into the system. Similar criticisms apply to Milne's *a priori* approach using the principle of communicability among observers as the starting point.[52] As compared with the actual practice of the scientific community, the views of Eddington and Milne neglect the experimental side, just as positivism neglects the theoretical side.

Margenau also gives prominence to *the activity of the mind* in imposing a structure on the uninterpreted data. His scheme gives greater recognition than Eddington's to the role of observa-

49. Eddington, *The Nature of the Physical World*, p. 244. Used by permission of Cambridge University Press.

50. Arthur Eddington, *The Philosophy of Physical Science* (Cambridge: Cambridge University Press, 1949; Ann Arbor PB*), p. 105.

51. E. Whittaker, *From Euclid to Eddington* (Cambridge: Cambridge University Press, 1949), p. 185.

52. E. A. Milne, *Modern Cosmology and the Christian Idea of God* (London: Oxford University Press, 1952).

tions, but it concurs with the Kantian assertion that chaotic sense-data have no knowable structure apart from the activity of the mind which organizes them by its conceptual constructs. Like the instrumentalists, Margenau acknowledges the predominant role of the subject in scientific knowledge; but instead of speaking of theoretical concepts as useful fictions, he asserts that *"the construct is reality."* Since constructs change as our knowledge grows, this means that reality changes. He asserts that the neutron did not exist and was not real prior to its "invention" in 1932. Margenau states his conclusion thus:

> Science defines a dynamic kind of reality, one that grows and changes as our understanding grows and changes. . . . I am perfectly willing to admit that reality does change as discovery proceeds. I can see nothing basically wrong with a real world which undergoes modifications along with the flux of experience. . . . It is easy to succumb to the temptation of distinguishing at the outset between the permanence of physical entities and the permanence of theories about them, saying for example that the entities are not affected by the vicissitudes of theories. . . . Our indoctrination with principles of being and our historic concern over immutables make us want to say that our *knowledge of* reality changes when discoveries are made.[53]

Margenau would reject Eddington's rationalistic attempt to derive theories *a priori* from the necessary structures of thought itself apart from experience; "circuits of empirical verification" have an essential place in his presentation. But it is not clear why, on his view, there should be agreement between empirical observations and some mental constructs but not others. The realist answers that such concepts correspond more closely to the structures of actual events in the world; our concepts may change but physical reality does not.

4. Theories as Representations of the World (Realism)

Against the positivist, the realist asserts that the real is not the observable. Against the instrumentalist, he affirms that valid concepts are true as well as useful. Against the idealist, he maintains that concepts represent the structure of events in the world. The patterns in the data are not imposed by us, but originate at least in part in *objective relationships in nature*. The object, not the subject,

---

53. Margenau, *The Nature of Physical Reality*, pp. 288, 295, 459. Used by permission of the McGraw-Hill Book Company.

makes the predominant contribution to knowledge. Hence science is discovery and exploration, not just construction and invention. Atoms are as real as tables, though their modes of behavior are quite different. Among those who have supported some form of realism—though with differing views as to what constitutes reality —have been Planck, Einstein, Campbell, Werkmeister, process philosophers (following Whitehead), naturalists (such as Nagel), and neo-Thomists.[54]

Realists insist that *being is prior to knowing*. Despite the fact that descriptions of the world are in part our creation, the world is such as to bear description in some ways and not in others. Thus neither the positivist's restriction of attention to sense-data nor the idealist's identification of reality with changing mental constructs is considered satisfactory. Some realists argue that the postulation of a world transcending both constructs and data is necessary in order to explain the "convergence" of scientific findings. Others hold that an awareness of encounter with nature is present in immediate experience.

The realist challenges the positivist doctrine that the real is the perceptible. He notes that many scientific entities today, especially in the domain of the very small, are inevitably *not directly apprehensible*. Nagel points out that it would be irrelevant even if we could perceive molecules:

> Nevertheless, molecular theory would still continue to formulate the traits of molecules in *relational* terms—in terms of relations of molecules to other molecules and to other things—not in terms of any of their qualities that might be directly apprehended through our organs of sense. For the *raison d'être* of molecular theory is not to supply information about the sensory qualities of molecules but to enable us to understand (and predict) the occurrence of events and the relations of their interdependence in terms of pervasive structural patterns into which they enter.[55]

Nagel recommends that, for what it designates to be considered *real*, a concept (other than a purely logical term) must enter at

54. Some of the linguistic analysts have moved toward a realist position, e.g., J. J. C. Smart, *Philosophic and Scientific Realism* (London: Routledge & Kegan Paul, 1963); P. K. Feyerabend, "Materialism and the Mind-Body Problem," *Review of Metaphysics*, Vol. 17 (1963), 49; or "Attempt at a Realistic Interpretation of Experience," *Proceedings of the Aristotelian Society*, Vol. 58 (1958), 143.
55. Nagel, *Structure of Science*, p. 146. Used by permission of Harcourt, Brace & World, Inc., and Routledge & Kegan Paul, Ltd.

least one experimental law other than that by which it is defined. With such a definition he can say that atoms and electrons are real. This criterion underscores the relational character of scientific terms; earlier we spoke of the contextual testing of networks of interdependent ideas rather than separate concepts. To say that "*atoms exist*" would then be equivalent to saying that there is satisfactory evidence for the atomic theory. As Nagel puts it:

> Since in testing a theory we test the totality of assumptions it makes, so the rejoinder continues, if a theory is regarded as well established on the available evidence, all its component assumptions must also be so regarded. . . . In short, to assert that in this sense atoms exist is to claim that available evidence is sufficient to establish the adequacy of the theory as a leading principle for an extensive domain of inquiry. But as has already been noted, this is in effect only verbally different from saying that the theory is so well confirmed by the evidence that the theory can be tentatively accepted as true.[56]

For many realists, *intelligibility* rather than observability is the hallmark of the real. It is precisely the organizing power of theoretical structures which shows that they correspond to the structure of the world. Thus Campbell writes:

> A molecule is real, and real in the same way, as the gases the laws of which it explains. It is an idea essential to the intelligibility of the world, not to one mind, but to all. . . . And if anything is real that renders the world intelligible, then surely the ideas of theories—molecules and extinct animals and all the rest—have just as much claim to reality as the ideas of laws.[57]

Whitehead develops a *realist epistemology*, both in his discussion of perception and his treatment of science. He rejects the starting point of positivism, Hume's thesis that knowledge originates in a flux of fragmentary and disconnected sense-experiences; he is equally critical of the starting point of idealism, Kant's thesis that mental categories are imposed on chaotic sense-experience. For Whitehead, the raw material of experience already has a unity, apprehended integrally by all our faculties; and this experience includes an awareness of our mutual interaction with our environment. Only on analysis can we abstract "sense-data" from the totalities we perceive. We experience colored objects, not colors. We attend to reactions and responses, not to isolated mental states.

56. *Ibid.*, pp. 142, 151.
57. Campbell, *What is Science?* pp. 106, 108. Used by permission of Methuen & Co., Ltd., and Dover Publications, Inc.

Our primitive awareness is of being in a world, not of constructing one. Whitehead speaks of "a consciousness of ourselves as arising out of rapport, interconnection and participation in processes reaching beyond ourselves."[58]

Whitehead affirms "the ontological principle" that the world is to be understood only by reference to *existent beings* in and for themselves. The basic constituents of the real world he takes to be events united in processes rather than separate substances with qualities. Scientific concepts represent only certain abstract aspects of this network of events influencing each other; it is "misplaced concreteness" to mistake such abstractions for the total reality of temporal process. Thus Whitehead's realism gives prominence to the object rather than the subject in knowledge, but the role of the subject is by no means omitted, since (a) reality consists not of things but of events occurring in networks of relations which include both the knower and the known; (b) knowledge arises not from either subject or object alone but from a situation of mutual interaction, and (c) scientific language is symbolic, deriving from the subject's selective abstraction from the total situation.

IV. CONCLUSIONS: ON KNOWING IN SCIENCE

We must now draw together some of the comments in the preceding sections, starting with the foregoing debate concerning the status of theories. We note first that *scientists usually assume realism* in their work. Astronomers, geologists, biologists, and chemists almost always take theories to represent events in the world. Dinosaurs are held to be creatures that actually roamed the earth, not useful fictions with which we organize the fossil data. Presumably there is no change in status as one considers smaller entities; there is no point at which one could draw any sharp line as one moved from amoeba to virus to molecule to electron. A virus is assumed to be both "object-like" and real; an electron does not at all resemble everyday objects, but this does not mean that it is any less real. Even the physicists, who more than others have been forced to examine the status of their concepts, still speak of the *discovery* (rather than the *invention*) of the electron. Although scientists are usually philosophically unreflective, we must nevertheless take seri-

---

58. A. N. Whitehead, *Symbolism* (Cambridge: Cambridge University Press, 1928; Capricorn PB), p. 65.

ously the assumptions embodied in the language of the scientific community. Most scientists understand themselves to be dealing with the structure of events in the world and not with summaries of data, useful fictions, or mental constructs. They see science as a path to understanding, not just as a tool for manipulation, prediction, and control. Moreover, their reluctance to adopt two useful but contradictory theories, and their interest in unifying the concepts of the separate sciences, seem to presuppose not only the value of economy of thought but some reference to a world under investigation.

At the same time we must recognize the *difficulties in any naive realism* which overlooks the role of man's mind in the creation of theories. The creativity of human imagination in the formation of theories was stressed earlier in the chapter. Theories are not given to us ready-made by nature; there is no simple access to the world as it exists in itself independently of being known, and mental constructs influence the interpretation of all experience. These are factors that the instrumentalist rightly emphasizes (though we have argued that he draws the wrong conclusion from them). A *"critical realism"* must acknowledge both the creativity of man's mind, and the existence of patterns in events that are not created by man's mind. It was suggested (Section II) that scientific language does not provide a replica of nature but a symbolic system that is abstract and selective and deals with limited aspects of the situation for particular purposes.

Critical realism acknowledges the indirectness of reference *and* the realistic intent of language as used in the scientific community. It can point to both the extraordinarily abstract character of theoretical. physics *and* the necessity of experimental observation which distinguishes it from pure mathematics. It recognizes that no theory is an exact description of the world, *and* that the world is such as to bear interpretation in some ways and not in others. It affirms the role of mental construction and imaginative activity in the formation of theories, *and* it asserts that some constructs agree with observations better than others only because events have an objective pattern.

The only tests of the adequacy of a concept or theory in representing the world are the combination of *empirical and rational criteria* discussed in Section I. If the goal of science is to *understand nature,* we can unify the concern for empirical testing found in positivism with the concern for intellectual coherence found in idealism, while avoiding the exclusive preoccupation of either. The extraordinarily indirect relationship between theory and experiment in modern physics perhaps seemed to encourage the two extremes. Positivists were impressed by the unobservability of the entities designated by theoretical concepts, and they ended by treating only the experimental side as real. But they failed to note that all data are theory-laden, and that only networks of theory and experiment can be tested together. Idealists, on the other hand, were impressed that theoretical physics is a self-consistent formal mathematical system, and they asserted that the true nature of reality is mental. But they failed to stress the empirical basis of modern science, which differentiates it from the "self-evident principles" of medieval science and the "*a priori* thought-forms" of neo-Kantianism. Overemphasis on either empirical or rational criteria distorts the character of scientific activity.

The real is *the intelligible, not the observable.* As Nagel puts it, "the *raison d'être* of molecular theory is not to supply information about the sensory qualities of molecules." The particular type of intelligible pattern sought is indeed always related to empirical evidence, but a valid concept need not designate something observable or even describable in everyday language; neither visualizable models nor commonsense categories are used in modern physics. Hesse suggests that we need to broaden our view of the character of the real:

> When the entities of physics refused to conform to the ordinary conditions for the existence of physical objects—determinate position in space, continuing existence through time, possession of the ordinary properties of matter, and so on—the natural reaction was to deny "real existence" to physical entities, and to call them "merely logical terms in conceptual formulas of calculation." But if we abandon such a restricted conception of existence (a conception which has been shown to be untenable, not only by modern physics, but also by all the philosophical critics of naive realism, from Berkeley and Hume onwards) we leave the way open for an interpretation of experience which asserts the real existence of all patterns in nature which are expressed by scientific concepts correctly used.[59]

The scientific enterprise, in summary, is a *many-faceted phenomenon.* Its genius has been precisely the interaction of components

---

59. Hesse, *Science and Human Imagination*, p. 151. Used by permission of SCM Press.

which oversimplified accounts have portrayed in isolation. It involves both experiment and theory, neither of which taken alone constitutes science. It requires both logical processes and a creative imagination transcending logic. Its theories are evaluated at once by empirical agreement, rational coherence, and comprehensiveness. Individual activity and originality are significant but occur within the tradition of a scientific community and under the influence of its paradigms. Scientific language does refer to the world, but only symbolically and partially, sometimes using analogies or models of limited scope.

The resulting theories are not guaranteed to be the final truth; any of them may in the future be amended, modified, or in rare cases, overthrown in a major "revolution." Yet scientific theories do have a *reliability*, and the scientific community does eventually achieve a *consensus*, seldom found in other types of inquiry. Although some aspects of scientific knowledge change, many aspects are preserved, contributing to an over-all cumulative advance that differs from that of other disciplines. In the next chapter we will examine science further and compare it with inquiry in other fields.

7

From the Sciences
to the Humanities

Instead of going directly from problems of method in science to those in religion, we will in this chapter point to two general methodological issues as they occur in other academic disciplines. No systematic analysis of the social sciences or humanities is here attempted. Our goal is simply to note in other areas the presence of two problems that will be important when we come to religion: the personal involvement of the subject, and the claim of the uniqueness of particular events.

According to the common image, the sciences are *"objective,"* which is taken to mean that they are determined by their objects of inquiry, whereas the humanities are *"subjective,"* that is, largely the product of the individual subject. C. P. Snow[1] suggests that this stereotype is a prime cause of the gap between the "two cul-

1. C. P. Snow, *The Two Cultures and the Scientific Revolution* (Cambridge: Cambridge University Press, 1961; Mentor PB), Chap. 1. Among recent volumes devoted to the problem of the "two cultures" are Bronowski, *Science and Human Values*; Harcourt Brown, ed., *Science and the Creative Spirit* (Toronto: University of Toronto Press, 1958); Moody E. Prior, *Science and the Humanities* (Evanston, Ill.: Northwestern University Press, 1962); Harold G. Cassidy, *The Sciences and the Arts* (New York: Harper and Brothers, 1962).

tures" today. Men in the scientific culture accuse men in the literary and humanistic culture of wallowing in private subjectivity; the humanists in turn accuse the scientists of attempting to impose a detached and impersonal objectivity which distorts authentic human existence. Again, the scientist is said to deal with lawful and repeatable events, the humanist with unique and particular ones.

We will argue, however, that both subject and object play important parts in all inquiry, that personal involvement is present in all fields, and that no simple contrast of lawful versus unique events can be defended. Science is indeed a distinctive discipline, but it is not as sharply set off from other fields as is sometimes assumed. Moreover, a "third culture," namely the social sciences, on which we will briefly comment, serves as a bridge between the sciences and the humanities. Instead of a sharp dichotomy, we have rather a spectrum with varying degrees and types of personal involvement, and varying types of interest in the lawfulness and uniqueness which are characteristics shared by all events. These issues will recur in the subsequent discussion of religion.

Section I, "Objectivity and Personal Involvement in Science," considers the influence of the knower on scientific data, and the points at which the personal judgment of the scientist cannot be replaced by formal rules. In Section II, "Objectivity and Personal Involvement in the Social Sciences," the contribution of the knower's introspective awareness and interpretive presuppositions in the understanding of other persons is briefly discussed. Section III, "Lawfulness and Uniqueness in History," maintains that the historian's concern for unique and unrepeatable events does not exclude his use of implicit lawlike generalizations.

I. OBJECTIVITY AND PERSONAL INVOLVEMENT IN SCIENCE

In the popular stereotype, scientific inquiry is said to be objective because it is determined by the object of knowledge, not by the subject who knows. In the light of actual scientific work, however, this view of objectivity must be modified to allow for *the contribution of the scientist* as experimental agent, as creative thinker, and as personal self. The object of study cannot be known in its existence "independent of the observer," for it is influenced by the observer in the very process of measurement. The assessment of theories is made not by the application of "formal rules," but by the personal judgment of the scientist. We will submit that the idea of objectivity should not be discarded but rather reformulated to include the contribution of the subject; we will reinterpret objectivity as *intersubjective testability* and *commitment to universality*.

1. The Influence of the Observer on the Data

Scientific data are said to be objective because they derive from external objects in the public world. In this respect the astronomer seems to be the exemplar of objectivity, for it appears that events which happened thousands of years ago on stars billions of miles away could not be disturbed by the process of studying them. "Data" means "the given," that which is *independent* of the subject's volition, confronting him in a uniform and stable way, and accessible to other observers. Because science attempts to deal with external objects, results are stated with as little reference to the observer as possible. Every science teacher has had to impress this *impersonality* on students learning to write lab reports. The English department might welcome the sentence: "Even though I had a headache that afternoon, I put the test tubes on the scales and I saw . . ."; in the Chemistry department the first person must be left out: "The test tube weighed. . . ." Statements about experiments refer to events in the public world.

The ideal of studying the world as it is in itself must, however, be qualified by recognition of *the influence of the measuring process* on the measurement obtained. In modern physics no clear separation of an independent object and a passive observer is possible. We shall see in Chapter 10 that the indeterminacy of the Heisenberg Principle can, at least in some situations, be attributed to "the disturbance of the system" by the measuring process. In order for the position of an electron to be known it must interact with another particle or wave of light, which disturbs the electron's position unpredictably. In relativity the mass, size, and time scale of an object are not constant properties of the body alone, but depend on the frame of reference of the observer. This "involvement of the observer" refers to the effects of a measuring process *as a physical operation*—the experiment might be performed by automatic equipment and the results recorded by camera with no scientist present. It is the process of experimentation, not the scientist as a person or a mind, which must be taken into account (hence modern physics provides no justification for metaphysical idealism). The point is rather that there is no simple separation of observer and observed because one deals always with *relationships* and *interactions* rather than objects in themselves. Objectivity thus cannot mean "the study of an independent object," for a strictly independent object can never be known.

Though the data arise from the interaction of object and subject, are not scientific phenomena at least *"publicly observable"*? It is true that scientists use observation procedures that are, so far as possible, reproducible; they standardize instruments and specify measuring operations not subject to individual idiosyncrasies. There is also a necessary distinction between what Holton calls "private science" (the actual work of the scientist) and "public science" (the aspects of his work selected to report to the scientific community).[2] It is an amazing process of refinement by which the very human activity that goes on in the laboratory—broken test tubes, blind alleys, discussions with colleagues, personal motivations—ends as a single impersonal sentence in a journal: "The reaction is aided by the addition of 3% NaOH." Only the reproducible results are reported.

Despite this ideal of public observability, there are *no completely uninterpreted data* in science. In the previous chapter it was suggested that all data are to some extent "theory-laden." The processes of measurement and the language in which results are reported are influenced by the assumptions and concepts of the investigator. The totally neutral observation language which the positivist sought seems unattainable. For "data" are always a selection from experience in terms of one's purposes and expectations. What the scientist looks for, and to some extent what he sees, is influenced by the traditions and paradigms of the scientific community. Attitudes change as to what problems are worth investigating, what kinds of questions are fruitful, and what types of concepts are likely to be promising. By the objectivity of the data, then, we can mean only its *reproducibility* within a scientific community sharing a common set of assumptions and concepts. This provides the basis for communication and agreement; but it does not imply that the data are independent of either the observer's experimental operations or his interpretive categories.

2. Gerald Holton, *Introduction to Concepts and Theories in Physical Science* (Cambridge, Mass.: Addison-Wesley Press, 1952), Chap. 13.

2. The Personal Judgment of the Scientist

The formation of theories was discussed in the previous chapter (creative imagination, origination of new concepts, use of analogies and models); we hardly need reemphasize the role of the subject therein. It seems unlikely that a computer will ever produce a new concept. Again, in regard to the testing of theories we rejected any simple notion of objectivity as "empirical verification," since there is never conclusive "verification," and criteria are never merely "empirical." But, granted that a variety of empirical and rational criteria are relevant, is not the process of evaluating theories an objective one, in the sense that it follows formal rules? Could not the criteria be specified so that a choice between theories would not require anything as subjective as the personal judgment of the scientist? Logical processes are impersonal and could be carried out by a computer. Some aspects of science are indeed of this character, particularly data-recording, data-processing, classifying and calculating manipulations.

But it appears that many aspects of the evaluation of theories cannot be expressed in formal rules. Even in determining "agreement with observations," the assessment of evidence requires personal judgment. The estimation of errors and of the reliability of an experiment cannot be completely reduced to formulae. Let us suppose there is disagreement between a theoretical prediction and an experimental value; should this difference be considered significant, or should it be ascribed to a chance variation, or attributed to an unidentified experimental error, or ignored as an "anomaly" for which it is hoped that some explanation will eventually be found? The amount of evidence one will require for a conclusion depends on many considerations. In some situations a correlation between two variables is considered significant if the probability is less than 5 per cent that the correlation found could have been due to chance. But in cases where other reasons, often only vaguely articulated, lead us to believe that the presence of a functional relationship is "very unlikely," we may dismiss as "merely chance" the occurrence of correlations against which the statistical odds are very much higher.

Judgments as to what kinds of connections are plausible thus influence one's interpretation of data. Consider "Bode's Law," which correlates the radii of successive planetary orbits in the solar system with the succession of terms in a particular mathematical series. At one point scientists were impressed by the fact that agreement between the data and the formula was fairly good. Subsequently, when there seemed to be no conceivable explanation for such a law, the agreement was dismissed as a coincidence. But more recently there has been renewed interest in the significance of Bode's Law, in the light of new hypotheses concerning the origin of the solar system. To take another example, many critics dismiss J. B. Rhine's data on Extra-Sensory Perception, even in cases where they can find no fault with his experimental design or data analysis. They are so convinced that mental telepathy is implausible that even when, against fantastically high odds, one person correctly guesses the cards in the hand of a person in another room, they aver it must be "luck," or "there must be some other explanation." This reluctance to accept ESP is of course the product of many factors: the presuppositions dominant in contemporary psychology, the many previous fraudulent claims of "mental telepathy," the difficulty in obtaining reproducible data, and above all the absence of any theory to account for the ESP data or any conceptual framework by which it could be related to other data. Whether the critics' conclusions are legitimate or not, the case illustrates the point that many considerations enter a person's assessment of data.

Evaluation of theories themselves also cannot be reduced to a formal process. Attempts to calculate the "probability of the validity of a hypothesis" have not been convincing (for example, Reichenbach's suggestion that we measure the validity of a theory by dividing the number of observable facts that can logically be derived from it by the number of such facts that have been confirmed experimentally). Frank seems justified in rejecting this view: "The reasons for which scientists accept a certain theory are very little connected with the 'probability' of the theory."[3] Even if we could program a machine to choose between theories, a person would still have to decide on the criteria it would use and would have to accept or reject its choice. Especially in regard to theories that are of wide generality or are still controversial, there are always many factors involved. If a computer could give some evaluation of "intellectual beauty" or "simplicity," which seems unlikely, how much weight should it assign to such considerations? The judgments of individual scientists vary, and the predominant views of the scien-

3. Frank, *Philosophy of Science*, p. 325.

tific community have changed; in precisely the controversial cases on which we might welcome help from a computer, no unambiguous verdict would be forthcoming. And in the choice between competing paradigms the usual criteria are not even applicable in any direct way.

The *personal judgment* of a scientist in such cases may be compared to that of a judge weighing evidence in the light of ambiguous precedents, or that of a doctor deciding on a difficult diagnosis in a serious case. For all three men objectivity is not the absence of personal judgment but, as Polanyi puts it, the presence of *universal intent*.[4] It is commitment to universality and rationality, not an attempt at impersonal detachment, which prevents such decisions from being purely subjective. The judge does not choose from private whim; he accepts the responsibility of justice even when justice cannot be reduced to formal rules. The editors of scientific journals and the committees making grants for proposed research must have considerable discretionary power in their decisions (particularly concerning very original and creative projects) because such evaluation cannot be proven by exact formal criteria, but require the personal judgment of the evaluators.

We may note finally some of the *presuppositions* of the scientific enterprise. There are, of course, certain very broad attitudes required for fruitful inquiry in any field, such as curiosity, imagination, honesty, and freedom of thought and communication. More specifically, the scientist has an ingrained conviction concerning the intelligibility, orderliness, and dependability of the world. He does not ask, "Does this disease have a cause?"; he asks, "What is the cause of this disease?"—that is, he assumes an answer to the first question without ever asking it, and without any formal premise (such as "Same cause, same effect"). The status of this assumption of *"the uniformity of nature"* has been extensively debated.[5] It has sometimes been justified (for example, by Mill) as an empirical generalization from observations. More common today is the instrumentalist view that the idea of uniformity is a procedural maxim or policy for inquiry, a directive to search for regularities. It is said to be a useful methodological recommendation ("Look for recurrent patterns"), rather than an absolute metaphysical claim about

4. Polanyi, *Personal Knowledge*, pp. 64f.
5. E.g., Nagel, *Structure of Science*, pp. 316–24; Schilling, *Science and Religion*, pp. 205–12; Toulmin, *Philosophy of Science*, pp. 140–54; Caldin, *The Power and Limits of Science*, pp. 60–63; A. Pap, "Does Science Have Metaphysical Presuppositions?" in Feigl and Brodbeck, eds., *Readings*.

reality ("Nature is always lawful"). We would reply, however, that it is not simply an arbitrary maxim; the policy it recommends is fruitful only because the world is indeed orderly. Confidence in a procedural policy reflects tacit metaphysical assumptions. We would suggest that the orderliness of nature is *an implicit assumption* of science. Clearly it is not a formal presupposition or a logical premise, and it is never mentioned in scientific research itself; it is simply taken for granted in the scientific community and in the culture of which it is a part. But it is no less influential for being unrecognized; and although it does not enter the logical structure of scientific reasoning, it should not be dismissed as "merely psychological," for it is essential to the scientific enterprise. We explored in Chapter 2 the Greek and biblical roots of attitudes toward nature—especially the doctrine of creation—which encouraged the growth of science. The success of early science in turn helped to direct attention to certain kinds of order and intelligibility (causal sequences, quantitative laws, and the like) at the expense of types of order in which other cultures have a predominant interest (the aesthetic enjoyment of nature, for instance). Current cultural assumptions have been molded by science itself, and confidence in the lawfulness and intelligibility of the universe is deeply ingrained in our consciousness (though we shall see that modern physics calls into question the idea of absolute lawfulness and causality, and indicates limits to the intelligibility which commonsense concepts and picturable models can yield). Yet even today there are alternative world-views under which science would not flourish. There would be little support for scientific activity in a culture radically permeated by the outlook of atheistic existentialism—for which the world is an irrational chaos, a meaningless stage for the drama of personal existence. Again, adherents of a strongly otherworldly religion would lack any strong interest in the material order. Images of nature and outlooks on the world strongly affect scientific motivation, even though their role in the day-to-day work of the scientist is less evident than that of the other nonempirical factors we have been considering.

3. Objectivity as Intersubjective Testability

We have examined several aspects of objectivity, and in each case found that the subject as well as the object contributes to scientific inquiry. The data are not "independent of the observer," for the situation is disturbed by the scientist *as experimental agent.* Concepts are not provided ready-made by nature, but constructed by the scientist *as creative thinker.* Theories are not "empirically verified," but evaluated by empirical and rational criteria conjointly; such an evaluation cannot be carried out by "formal rules," but only by the judgment of the scientist *as a responsible person.* Science is a human enterprise and not a mechanical process. We have attacked inadequate views of objectivity which omit the role of the subject. Now we must show why, despite these contributions of the subject, science does not end in private subjectivity.

The first aspect of a reformulated idea of objectivity is *intersubjective testability.* Because the scientific community is the context of all research, the activity of the subject does not lead to arbitrary and private caprice. For the subject's involvement in a community transcending idiosyncratic differences carries inquiry beyond any individual interests. If the goal of science is to understand nature, universality is based in part on the conviction that the same structure of nature is open to investigation by other scientists. Science is thus *personal but not private.* We will use the term "personal involvement" to refer to the activity of the subject, because the word "subjectivity" has come to stand for that which is purely private, individual, and unreliable. It is *personal involvement in community,* not lack of involvement, which here preserves a valid aspect of objectivity.

We can now reinterpret *"public observability"* and *"empirical verifiability"* not as the elimination of the contribution of the subject but as *agreement within the scientific community.* (The "public," in any case, cannot mean the man on the street, who would be totally lost in a modern laboratory.) The scientific community is international in scope, but its members share a common tradition. Despite the fact that data are always interpreted in conceptual categories (which may change drastically in a "revolution"), they have a high degree of reliability and reproducibility. In addition, an impressive agreement exists within the scientific community concerning theories, especially in a relatively mature science. And though at any given time there may be competing schools of thought, a convergence toward consensus does seem in general to occur.

The second valid aspect of the ideal of objectivity is *universality.* The scientist focuses on aspects of experience that are universal.

Here is a self-transcendence in deliberately reaching beyond individuality, and a self-discipline in being willing to be led by the evidence regardless of one's own personal preferences. No private interests obscure openness to new ideas in the pursuit of truth. Intellectual integrity characterizes all genuine inquiry; the scholar must acknowledge the evidence he finds even if it casts doubt on a theory he himself has formulated. The *empirical and rational criteria* discussed earlier are the hallmarks of such universality, though they cannot be specified by exact rules. On this view the rational criteria, just as much as agreement with observations, are a test of universality.

The scientist's *commitment to universality* does not exclude, but in fact requires, a particular kind of personal involvement. It is, in Polanyi's phrase, the "universal intent" of the commitment that enables personal involvement to contribute to the pursuit of truth rather than hinder it. It is sometimes said that the objectivity of scientific inquiry consists in its "disinterestedness." If this is taken to refer to the desire to look beyond purely private "interests," the term may be applied here. But if "disinterested" implies a detached attitude without personal involvement, it hardly characterizes the scientist. For the scientist may be passionately dedicated to the values of science; he may be intensely "interested" in his work, and far from indifferent to its outcome, completely absorbed in an exciting and adventurous discovery.

As we move from the natural sciences to the social sciences and thence to the humanities, we will find that *the personal involvement of the knower* influences the process of inquiry in more and more determinative ways. The subject exercises greater personal judgment in selecting, evaluating, and interpreting the data, and his presuppositions and values affect his theoretical constructions more strongly. The scientist is able to confine his scientific role as a person to relatively limited areas of his personality. To be sure, for some men science is the main source of meaning in life; but the significance of human existence and destiny do not depend on particular scientific theories, as they do depend on particular religious beliefs. Studying science does not necessarily implicate all areas of life; by contrast, understanding a work of art or drama, or the experience of worship, demands a more total participation. The extent and range of the involvement of the knower varies with the nature of the reality known.

We can thus picture *a spectrum with varying forms of personal involvement.* We would deny the claim that there is an absolute dichotomy between a purely impersonal "objective" science, on the one hand, and a "subjective" sphere of personal selfhood, on the other. Such a claim is made by both the existentialist and the positivist, who agree on a sharp division into two realms (though they disagree concerning the status of the knowledge which the realm of selfhood yields). But such a dichotomy neglects the role of the subject in science. Within a spectrum there are no such absolute differences, though significant variations in the role of personal involvement can be recognized.

II. OBJECTIVITY AND PERSONAL INVOLVEMENT IN THE SOCIAL SCIENCES

Most of the foregoing remarks about the role of the subject in the natural sciences would apply with even greater force in the social sciences. The influence of observation processes on the data is stronger—for example, polls predicting an election may change the election outcome. Social data, too, are already theory-laden, interpreted and reported in conceptual categories—for example, judgments in classifying social phenomena depend on the differences that are regarded as relevant. Lately there has been considerable discussion about concept-formation and the role of models in the social sciences. Any general discussion of such methodological problems is beyond the scope of this volume.[6] Our purpose is simply to give two examples of recent debates in the social sciences which support our thesis that science and religion may be placed in a spectrum of personal involvement. The first concerns the contribution of the observer's own subjective experience to his understanding of the subjective life of the persons he is studying. The second concerns the influence of individual and cultural presuppositions on the social scientist's objectivity.

---

6. See, e.g., Felix Kaufmann, *Methodology of the Social Sciences* (New York: The Humanities Press, 1958); Llewellyn Gross, ed., *Symposium on Sociological Theory* (Evanston, Ill.: Row Peterson, 1959); Quentin Gibson, *The Logic of Social Inquiry* (London: Routledge & Kegan Paul, 1960); Robert Brown, *Explanation in Social Science* (London: Routledge & Kegan Paul, 1963); Nagel, *Structure of Science*, Chaps. 13 and 14; Arnold Rose, *Theory and Method in the Social Sciences* (Minneapolis: University of Minnesota Press, 1954).

1. Personal Involvement and the Study of Man

Let us look initially at the status of the subjective experience of the persons who are the objects of study, before considering the role of the observer's own introspective experience. First, is it legitimate to use concepts referring to *the subjective states of the persons being studied?* Some social scientists have asserted that their goal is the establishment of uniform laws among *directly observable phenomena.*[7] Social regularities, like economic laws, exist quite apart from what the participants think about them, and can be discovered from the correlations among publicly observable events. In psychology, the positivist's injunction to use only observable variables was rigorously adopted in early *behaviorism;* correlations between input stimuli and output responses from the human organism were to be investigated without postulating any unobservable internal realm. "In a rigorous scientific vocabulary private effects are practically eliminated," wrote B. F. Skinner.[8] But it was increasingly recognized that the organism's verbal reports about its own experience are a characteristic aspect of its behavior. (We may be suspicious of the story of the resolute behaviorist who wanted to rely only on observations and greeted his friend: "You feel fine today. How do I feel?") Constructs referring to internal states are now generally accepted, and it is acknowledged that such states are not equivalent to any specifiable overt behavior.[9]

Most sociologists today similarly recognize the importance of *the ideas held by people*—the attitudes, concepts, and self-understanding of the participants. Not all would go as far as Max Weber's assertion that cultural phenomena are significant only as they are related to the meanings and value-orientations of persons.[10] The economist Hayek claims that "the relations between men and all

7. E.g., Emile Durkheim, *Suicide*, trans. J. A. Spaulding & G. Simpson (Glencoe, Ill.: The Free Press, 1951); Vilfredo Pareto, *The Mind and Society*, trans. A. Bongiorno & A. Livingston (New York: Harcourt, Brace and Co., 1935).

8. B. F. Skinner, "The Operational Analysis of Psychological Terms," in Feigl and Brodbeck, eds., *Readings*, p. 588.

9. See, e.g., Sigmund Koch, ed., *Psychology: A Study of a Science* (New York: McGraw-Hill Book Co., 1959), Vol. 3. Koch's "Epilogue" summarizes the conclusions of the contributors to Vols. 1–3.

10. Max Weber, *The Methodology of the Social Sciences*, trans. Shils and Finch (Glencoe, Ill.: The Free Press, 1949).

their social institutions can be understood only in terms of what men think about them."[11] A more cautious appraisal by Winch points out that "the social relations between men, and the ideas which men's actions embody, are really the same thing considered from different points of view."[12] For example, people interpret the round pieces of metal they hand each other as "money," and their action reflects a network of assumptions about government, banks, and economic values. "Casting a vote" expresses a particular configuration of political ideas, and so forth.

But note that such ideas are not "subjective" in the sense of "private" or "individual." *The social context of thought and language* has been a recurrent theme of linguistic analysis.[13] The "rules" governing the use of language and the symbolic meaning of acts are products of society. To exhibit "motives" or "reasons" for an act is to make it intelligible in relation to the expectations and familiar patterns of ideas of that society. This is something quite different from establishing correlations between observed behaviors. Winch suggests that "we might well be able to make predictions of great accuracy and still not be able to claim any real understanding of what the people involved were doing."[14] The social scientist, then, must study the significance of acts to the participants, and he can do so without neglecting their unconscious drives or the impersonal social forces of which they are not aware.

The importance of *the ideas of the participants* has been vehemently defended by historians. To understand the past we must know about the states of mind of the men involved, and not simply about external mechanical causes; to explain a human action means to account for it in terms of the ideas and choices of the actors.[15] The query "Why did Brutus kill Caesar?" calls for the study of his dispositions and loyalties, his conscious and unconscious motives. Sometimes the centrality of such human ideas in the field of history is used as an argument for classifying it with the humanities (or their supposed absence from sociology and psychology is taken as

11. Friedrich Hayek, *The Counter-revolution of Science* (Glencoe, Ill.: The Free Press, 1952), p. 33.

12. Peter Winch, *The Idea of a Social Science* (London: Routledge & Kegan Paul, 1958), p. 121.

13. E.g., Ludwig Wittgenstein, *Philosophical Investigations*, trans. G. E. M. Anscombe (New York: The Macmillan Co., 1953), Pt. I, pp. 215ff.

14. Winch, *The Idea of a Social Science*, p. 115.

15. R. G. Collingwood, *The Idea of History* (London: Oxford University Press, 1946; PB), Pt. V.

grounds for identifying the latter with the natural sciences). We find no such sharp line that would justify the division of *academia* into two opposing camps, but rather a "spectrum" within which the role of man's subjective life varies greatly.

But how can the unobservable experience of the participants be known? This brings us to our second question: Does *the observer's own subjective experience* contribute to his understanding of the persons he is studying? A widely discussed tradition has argued that: (a) genuine understanding (*"verstehen"* in German) of another person requires sympathetic imagination or *empathy*, and (b) empathy is possible only because of *introspection*—that is, our self-knowledge provides the basis for our understanding of other persons. Human action, so the argument runs, can be interpreted in terms of unobservable motives, dispositions, and values only because we have immediate knowledge of their operation in our own lives.

As might be expected, historians have been prominent defenders of this tradition. Collingwood maintains that only by *imaginative identification* with men in the past can the scholar enter into the meanings and intentions which governed their actions; only by reliving their lives, as it were, can he reconstruct them. The writing of history is essentially sympathetic reenactment. Butterfield speaks for many of his colleagues:

> Historical writing . . . has refused to be satisfied with any merely causal or stand-offish attitude toward the personalities of the past. It does not treat them as mere things, or just measure such features of them as the scientist might measure; and it does not content itself with merely reporting about them in the way an external observer would do. It insists that the story cannot be told correctly unless we see the personalities from the inside, feeling with them as an actor might feel the part he is playing—thinking their thoughts over again and sitting in the position not of the observer but of the doer of the action.[16]

Social scientists have often advocated a similar position. Parsons believes that *empathy* is required to get at "the point of view of the actors" and their "normative ends and mental processes," which are for him the focus of sociological interest.[17] MacIver has made

---

16. Herbert Butterfield, *History and Human Relations* (New York: The Macmillan Co., 1952; London: William Collins, Sons & Co., Ltd.), p. 145.

17. Talcott Parsons, *The Structure of Social Action* (New York: McGraw-Hill Book Co., 1937).

a strong case for "imaginative reconstruction," based on the observer's experience, as the method by which one can study causal
relations among the actions of persons.[18] Allport discusses at length
the value of empathy in psychology, "the imaginative transposing
of oneself into the thinking, feeling and acting of another."[19]

Now we would grant the importance of trying to see things from
the point of view of the person being studied. But we would deny
the claim of some proponents of empathy that such an understanding is achieved by an act of *uninterpreted immediate knowledge* whereby the experience of another person is, in Collingwood's
words, "directly comprehended in a single act of intuitive insight."
We would maintain, on the contrary, that all knowledge of other
persons involves *interpretive concepts* that must be *tested* by the
same criteria as concepts in the natural sciences. Understanding
someone else's intentions depends on obtaining evidence, not on
undisciplined speculation, direct intuition, or "imagining how I
would have felt." After all, the subjective life of persons in another culture may follow patterns quite unlike those in one's own
experience; the "obvious" interpretation of an act may be totally
erroneous, and introspection may only be misleading. Moreover,
even the observer's own subjective awareness is interpreted in
terms of concepts learned from others, a socially acquired language, a pattern of expectations, and so forth. Thus he must direct
his attention to publicly established meanings and not simply to
the "private experiences" of either himself or his object of study.

What role, then, does *introspection* play? Obviously the investigator's own experience helps him to decide what sort of evidence
to look for, and gives clues to the interpretation of the evidence
he finds. Empathy makes a contribution, not by providing immediate and direct knowledge, nor simply by giving hunches about
correlating purely external behavior, but by suggesting possible
internal connections; the observer's own experience is a fruitful
source of interpretive hypotheses concerning motives and intentions, but hypotheses must always be tested against evidence.

From what source do we derive our understanding of *the nature
of personal existence*? It is an oversimplification to say that I know

18. Robert MacIver, *Social Causation* (New York: Ginn and Company,
1942; Harper PB).
19. Gordon Allport, *Pattern and Growth in Personality* (New York: Holt,
Rinehart and Winston, 1961), p. 533. See also his *Personality* (New York:
Henry Holt, 1937), Chap. 19.

what a "person" is in myself first, and then infer or project personal existence in other people; it is equally dubious to say that I directly intuit the subjective life of those I confront. *Concepts of selfhood* arise in *interpersonal* relations, so that awareness of myself and of other persons develop together. Elaboration of such an intersubjective or "social" conception of selfhood, which we cannot undertake here, would require modification of most "introspectionist" accounts. There do appear to be basic structures of relationship among motives and ideas which are common to all personal existence. Yet actions must ultimately be related, not to the patterns of the observer's experience, but to the patterns of the actor's experience; the observer's experience provides invaluable analogies and possible parallels, which are not substitutes for evidence but clues to obtaining evidence. His own involvement as a person does contribute to his inquiry, but not in a way that makes intersubjective testability unnecessary.

An extreme but illuminating case of such personal involvement is that of the *psychotherapist* attempting to understand a client. Carl Rogers has graphically described his function as *both observer and participant*, and the tension between the two roles.[20] As scientist he seeks objective knowledge and predictability; as therapist he is in a personal relationship and his own selfhood is involved. Sympathetic imagination is necessary, yet effectiveness as therapist depends on the use of scientific generalizations. H. S. Sullivan terms this role "participant observer." A similar picture is drawn by Redfield in discussing the interplay between the "outside view" and the "inside view" when a sociologist participates in a community or a culture.[21] If such sympathetic imagination aids inquiry, we may conclude that the social scientist is sometimes far more deeply involved as a person than is the natural scientist.

2. Subjectivity and Objectivity in the Social Sciences

A specific point of controversy concerning the influence of personal involvement on objectivity centers in *the values and presuppositions* of the social scientist.[22] (We are not here considering his

---

20. Carl Rogers, *On Becoming a Person* (Boston: Houghton Mifflin Co., 1961), Chap. 10.
21. Robert Redfield, *The Little Community* (Chicago: University of Chicago Press, 1955).
22. See Gunnar Myrdal, *Value in Social Theory* (New York: Harper and Brothers, 1958); Howard Becker, *Through Values to Social Interpretation* (Durham, N.C.: Duke University Press, 1950); William Kolb, "The Changing

role as policy adviser and social critic, nor his research about social values, nor the ethical problems arising from the manipulation of persons, but only the effects of his own commitments on the interpretation of social data.) Here the assumptions brought to inquiry affect the problems selected for study, the sorts of questions asked, the types of data sought, and the concepts in which theories are developed. Since Marx and Freud, it has been recognized that rationalization of self-interest and unconscious motives do distort man's perception of the social world, and bias his conclusions about it. Karl Mannheim maintained that the social process

> penetrates even into the "perspective of thought," that is, the manner in which one views an object, what one perceives in it and how one construes it in thinking. . . . The very principles in the light of which knowledge is to be criticized are themselves found to be socially and historically conditioned.[23]

Because of cultural presuppositions and ideological commitments which color all thought, the social sciences can yield only "perspectival views" which are historically relative, according to these interpreters.

Many historians have been even more emphatic in *denying the possibility of objectivity*. The motives and interests of an author influence the type of factor he considers relevant. Facts do not proclaim their own meaning; if history is more than the chronicle of disconnected events, then selection and interpretation are inescapable. Carl Becker has repeatedly underscored the contribution of the knower:

> The history of any event is never precisely the same to two different persons; and it is well known that every generation writes the same history in a new way, and puts upon it a new construction . . . influenced by present purposes, desires, prepossessions, and prejudices, all of which enter the process of knowing. The actual event contributes something to the imagined picture; but the mind that holds the imagined picture always contributes something too.[24]

Prominence of Values in Modern Sociological Theory," in Becker and Boskoff, eds., *Modern Sociological Theory* (New York: The Dryden Press, 1957); H. Schoeck and J. W. Wiggins, eds., *Scientism and Values* (Princeton, N.J.: D. Van Nostrand, 1960); L. Gross, ed., *Symposium*, Pt. VII.

23. Karl Mannheim, *Ideology and Utopia* (New York: Harcourt, Brace and Co., 1936; London: Routledge & Kegan Paul, Ltd.; Harcourt PB), pp. 259, 262.

24. Carl Becker, "What Are Historical Facts?" *Western Political Quarterly*, Vol. 8, No. 3 (1955); reprinted in H. Meyerhoff, ed., *The Philosophy of History in Our Time* (New York: Doubleday PB, 1959), p. 132; see also Charles Beard's essay in the same volume.

Now we must grant that such forms of *personal involvement* constitute a far more serious problem in the social than in the natural sciences. We cannot accept the claim that "the fact that the social scientist has always been part of a social structure is no more of a handicap to its objective study than the fact that he is also part of the physical universe he studies."[25] Nevertheless we would argue that a *properly understood objectivity is a legitimate ideal* which should not be discarded even though it is never completely attainable. Although no theory is simply given to us by the data, the testing of theories does require an openness to reality and a willingness to let the material speak to us as directly as possible. Fidelity to evidence, openmindedness, modesty in one's claims, self-criticism, and readiness to learn from other interpreters are demands of scholarly inquiry in any field.

Explicitly stated assumptions may be less dangerous than hidden ones. Perhaps, as Myrdal urges,[26] an author of a major work should try to formulate and state his presuppositions for two reasons: to become more aware of them himself and to allow his readers to take them into account. Moreover, the idea of objectivity as *intersubjective testability* points to the usefulness of mutual exchange in revealing individual biases; some personal limitations can be corrected by comparing conclusions with other interpreters. Differing "perspectival views" sometimes supplement each other and can be combined to give a synthesis more complete than that from any single viewpoint; in other instances a "common denominator" can be found in disparate interpretations. Intersubjective testability always implies an appeal to common standards that go beyond private judgment. The historian is held responsible by his colleagues to justify his conclusions and to indicate the warrants for his inferences, even though his final verdict may be woven of many diverse strands.

One cannot escape the fact, however, that the standards and criteria of testing in any community of inquiry reflect *cultural presuppositions.* Methodological assumptions are themselves subject to historical variation. The adequacy of a particular criterion cannot be proved by the criterion itself; assessments of what constitutes sound social analysis can be expected to change. A person's

25. George A. Lundberg, *Can Science Save Us?* (New York: Longmans, Green and Co., 1947; PB), p. 23.
26. Gunnar Myrdal, *An American Dilemma* (New York: Harper and Brothers, 1944), Preface; also his *Value in Social Theory*, pp. 120f.

evaluation of contemporary theories of personality will depend in part on his estimation of the relative importance of various criteria (comprehensiveness, relevance to significant life problems, fruitfulness in stimulating reproducible experiments, and so forth). Finally, it is not always possible to find a "common denominator" among differing interpretive categories reflecting social perspectives which rest on widely divergent basic assumptions and images of man—for example, Marxist, Christian, and Hindu views.

At this basic level, then, it appears that *the images of man* used in social and historical interpretation are not simply derived from the data, but reflect philosophical presuppositions. Walsh comments on conceptions of the nature of man in the writing of history:

> I cannot escape, if I am to make any sense of my material, making some general judgments about human nature, and in these I shall find my own views constantly cropping up. . . . Whilst a large part of the content of our conception is drawn from human experience, and alters as our experience is added to, it remains true that there is hard core in it which is not come by in the same way. This hard core I connect with our moral and metaphysical beliefs. . . . We could not even begin to understand unless we presupposed some propositions about human nature, unless we applied some notion of what is reasonable and normal in human behavior.[27]

Are such questions as human freedom (versus determinism), or the historical efficacy of social ideals (versus economic forces), subject to "intersubjective testability"? Fundamental conceptions of *the nature of man* are in part based on previous experience, and are indirectly tested by their ability to order the data and to do justice to the full range of human experience.[28] But this is a very broad and not unambiguous process of evaluation; there is no "crucial experiment" which would be totally inexplicable in one framework and perfectly intelligible in another. Particular images of man are embedded in over-all philosophical positions which are interpretations of the totality of human experience—moral, religious, social,

27. W. H. Walsh, *An Introduction to the Philosophy of History* (London: Hutchinson & Co., Ltd., 1961; Harper PB), pp. 221, 223.
28. See William L. Kolb, "Images of Man and the Sociology of Religion," *Journal for the Scientific Study of Religion* (October 1961), p. 5; Reinhard Bendix, "The Image of Man in the Social Sciences," in Lipset and Smelser, eds., *Sociology: The Progress of a Decade* (Englewood Cliffs, N.J.: Prentice-Hall, 1961); C. Wright Mills, *The Sociological Imagination* (New York: Oxford University Press, 1959); Talcott Parsons and Edward A. Shils, eds., *Toward a General Theory of Action* (Cambridge, Mass.: Harvard University Press, 1951).

and scientific. Such commitments, which we will examine in the
next chapter, seem to be even less susceptible to direct testing
than the paradigms of the natural sciences or the implicit assumptions about the orderliness of nature.

III. Lawfulness and Uniqueness in History

In addition to the assertion that the sciences are "objective" and
the humanities "subjective," the statement is sometimes made that
the sciences deal with "lawful" events and the humanities with
"unique" ones. An historical event, a human person, or a work of
art is said to be particular and unrepeatable; it cannot be approached by the methods the scientist uses to study lawful and
repeatable phenomena. We will choose as a case study the field of
history, and will try to show that there are not two classes of
events, "unique" and "lawful," but rather that any event can be
considered either in its particularity *or* in the patterns it exhibits.
We will suggest that the historian does use implicit generalizations in understanding individual configurations. Once again we
find among fields of inquiry not a sharp dichotomy but a spectrum
of differing kinds of interests.

1. The Uniqueness of Historical Events

The term *idiographic* (from *idios*, individual) has been used to
designate the portrayal of unique and unrepeatable events.[29] It has
been alleged that history deals with the singular particularity of individual occurrences, and hence must use methods radically different from those of the scientist's *nomothetic* approach (from *nomos*,
law) to lawfully recurring phenomena. Among historians early in
this century[30] such a sharp distinction between history and science
had a variety of motives, including an emphasis on the unsystem-
atic variety and irreducibility of concrete facts (which had been
lost in the sweeping "philosophies of history" of Hegel and Marx),
a defense of human freedom and individuality (which were threatened by the assumption of deterministic laws), and a loyalty to the
Kantian tradition of disjunction between man and nature.

29. See discussion of Windelband and Rickert in Collingwood, *The Idea of
History*, pp. 165–71.
30. See essays by Benedetto Croce, R. G. Collingwood, and Wilhelm Dilthey
in Patrick Gardiner, ed., *Theories of History* (Glencoe, Ill.: The Free Press,
1959).

It has been argued more recently on logical grounds that *singular statements about particulars* are a distinctive feature of the historical mode of inquiry.[31] A historian does not explain the Reformation by showing it to be a case of reformations-in-general, nor is he interested in formulating such laws. Generalizations about revolutions throw little light on the American, French, or Russian Revolutions; it is precisely the peculiarities of the Russian Revolution—the role of Lenin, let us say—that are of interest. Even if the historian does propose general hypotheses, he is reluctant to detach them from the particulars in which they are embodied; the meaning is conveyed by the pattern of details, not extracted and presented independently.

Such allegations of uniqueness have been strenuously opposed by a number of philosophers who urge that *historical inquiry should conform to the pattern of science.* Any valid explanation, they insist, consists of subsumption under general laws; that is, the event to be explained must be shown to be deducible from a "covering law," together with statements about antecedent conditions. Explaining an event is said to be equivalent to showing that it could have been predicted. In an influential article Hempel states:

> General laws have quite analogous functions in history and in the natural sciences. In view of the structural equality of explanation and prediction, it may be said that an explanation is not complete unless it might as well have functioned as a prediction. If the final event can be derived from the initial conditions and universal hypotheses stated in the explanation, then it might as well have been predicted before it actually happened.[32]

Other philosophers, including Popper, Hook, and White,[33] have also urged that history be made more scientific by deliberate adoption of *the "covering-law" ideal.* As Hume showed, examination of two events alone can never establish a causal connection between

31. E.g., William Dray, *Laws and Explanation in History* (London: Oxford University Press, 1957), pp. 44f.; also his *Philosophy of History* (Englewood Cliffs, N.J.: Prentice-Hall PB, 1964). The issue is extensively discussed in Gardiner, ed., *Theories of History*, and Sidney Hook, ed., *Philosophy and History* (New York: New York University Press, 1963).

32. C. G. Hempel, "The Function of General Laws in History," *Journal of Philosophy*, Vol. 39 (1942); reprinted in H. Feigl and W. Sellars, eds., *Readings in Philosophical Analysis* (New York: Appleton-Century-Crofts, 1949), pp. 459, 462.

33. Karl Popper, *The Poverty of Historicism* (London: Routledge & Kegan Paul, 1957); Sidney Hook and Morton White essays in Meyerhoff, ed., *The Philosophy of History*.

them; causal imputation can be justified only by appeal to general laws, which should be made explicit. The historian, like the scientist, must be concerned about regular structures.

What are we to make of this continuing debate between defenders of uniqueness and of lawfulness? Let us start by examining the meaning of "uniqueness." Clearly *every event is unique in some respects*; no occurrence—even in the physics lab—is ever exactly duplicated in all its inexhaustible detail. But this does not exclude the presence of regular and repeatable features. Grünbaum comments:

> Every insignificant tick of my watch is a unique event, for no two ticks can be simultaneous with a third event. . . . Since the cause-effect relation is a relation between kinds of events, it is never necessary that all the features of a given cause be duplicated in order to produce the same kind of effects.[34]

Neither scientific nor historical explanations ever account for everything in a given situation, but this does not invalidate the analysis of the lawful properties that are chosen for study. On the other hand, *no event is absolutely unique*, even in history. The use of language presupposes common characteristics, such as those reflected in the words "nation," "revolution," "battle," and the like. Nothing could be said about an event if it were completely *sui generis*.

Every event is thus unique if one adopts a minimal definition (unique = dissimilar in *some* respect from all other events). *No* event is unique if one adopts a maximal definition (unique = dissimilar in *all* respects from all other events). Let us instead say that an event will be treated as unique insofar as it is *uninformative to classify it with other events*. Uniqueness in this sense will be variable in degree and will be *relative to the purposes of inquiry*, rather than an absolute metaphysical characteristic of events in themselves. Rescher[35] suggests that for the historian the assassination of Archduke Ferdinand before the outbreak of World War I is not illuminated by classifying it with "shootings," or "political assassinations"; its most interesting aspects are not related to their

34. A. Grünbaum, "Causality and the Science of Human Behavior," *American Scientist*, Vol. 40 (1952); reprinted in Feigl and Brodbeck, *Readings*, p. 769.

35. N. Rescher, "On the Probability of Nonrecurring Events," in H. Feigl and G. Maxwell, eds., *Current Issues in the Philosophy of Science* (New York: Holt, Rinehart and Winston, 1961).

membership in identifiable groups of events. In contrast, by the act of classifying a patient's symptoms under "pneumonia" a doctor knows more about the probable relations among present and future events and possible courses of action.

There are thus not two different kinds of events, lawful and unique. There are simply different kinds of interest in events which can be considered *both as lawful and as unique*. The sequence of events confronting a scientist may have occurred only once, and may even be unrepeatable in practice and perhaps in principle— for example, the origins of the astronomical universe, the earth's geological history, the evolution of man, the genetic combination in an individual's heredity. But certain aspects of these sequences can be studied in other contexts in which lawful and repeatable regularities are evident. The same selectivity is present in all scientific work. The individuality of the exact pattern of weeds in the botanist's garden this morning is trivial; he selects only the repeatable features which can contribute to scientific understanding. But the individuality of a great historical figure is interesting and important to us.

Turning to the role of laws, it is clear in the first place that in practice *historians do not have as their goal the establishment of universal laws*. Toynbee's sweeping generalities are almost invariably described as "not part of history proper," though they may be praised as magnificent excursions into the more speculative realms of "philosophy of history," or, insofar as they are empirically based, as contributions to a sociology of culture. Joynt and Rescher[36] suggest that although historical writing does not aim at the formulation of such universal laws, it does search for *lawlike generalizations* of limited scope, applicable within particular epochs or conditions. (For example, statements about the value of certain military tactics with given weapons imply that the same tactics would prove effective again under similar conditions.) It may be questioned, however, whether the formulation of even such "restricted generalizations" is the aim of the historian, for they usually remain embodied in and conveyed by particular cases.

Secondly, *historians do seek to establish connections between particular events*, despite their misgivings about the status of causal statements. The view that the historian's business is simply to de-

36. C. B. Joynt and N. Rescher, "On Explanation in History," *Mind*, Vol. 68 (1959), 388.

scribe rather than to explain would be difficult to maintain in the light of the frequent use of "because," "thus," and other "explanatory" words and answers to "why-questions." The bare recital of sequences of independent events would be a disconnected chronicle. Most historical writing attempts to establish patterns among events, to assess the significance of various influences, and to trace the consequences of actions. If he is not to be hopelessly bogged down in a welter of particulars, an author must select relevant factors and show how a given situation grew out of a previous situation.

Thirdly, the tracing of such connections between events *does require the implicit use of generalizations.* These generalizations are of many types: descriptive terms and concepts implying classifications; patterns relating motives and reasons to actions; commonsense observations about human behavior; and parallels with other historical situations. Walsh[37] is impressed by "the subtlety and depth of insight into the possibilities of human nature shown by the great historians"; he discusses the use of nontechnical knowledge in tracing relationships among events. Gardiner and Watkins[38] have attempted to find a place for uniqueness within such generalizations; they see the goal of historical explanation as the deduction of particular actions from the dispositional characteristics of individual agents. By subsuming actions under "lawlike statements" (though not strict laws) they preserve the "covering-law" ideal while making room for the purposive motives of particular personalities.

2. The Logic of Historical Explanation

If the foregoing analysis is correct, it appears that the historian is not interested in formulating general laws, but he nevertheless *uses laws to understand particular events.* Nagel, Popper, and others[39] suggest that the historian uses generalities to understand particulars, whereas the scientist uses particulars to establish generalities. In science, concrete data are instrumental means to the end of discovering laws, making predictions, and eventually con-

37. Walsh, *An Introduction to the Philosophy of History,* Chap. 3.
38. Patrick Gardiner, *The Nature of Historical Explanation* (London: Oxford University Press, 1952); J. N. Watkins, "Ideal Types and Historical Explanation," in Feigl and Brodbeck, *Readings.*
39. Nagel, *Structure of Science,* pp. 550f; Popper, *Poverty of Historicism,* Chap. 4.

trolling processes; individual events are of interest only as instances of universal laws. The historian's goal, on the other hand, is to understand the particular events of the past for their own sake. In order to help trace specific interrelations among occurrences he often borrows generalizations from fields such as sociology and psychology. He is a "consumer" rather than a "producer" of laws; he applies them but does not discover them.

> Whether an event is selected for treatment as a unique, concrete particular, or treated as the non-unique examplar of a class of events, is essentially a matter of human interest and perspective. . . . History does not collect facts to establish laws; rather it seeks to exploit laws to explain facts.[40]

More commonly the historian uses commonsense generalizations rather than explicit laws. His goal is understanding, which involves selecting relevant facts and tracing connections and seeing patterns with which he is familiar from other contexts. He does not simply stand in awe in front of an isolated event, nor chronicle a succession of unrelated happenings. The role of these "lawlike" patterns is often overlooked by the advocates of pure "uniqueness."

But the enthusiasts of the "covering-law" model, for their part, give a drastically oversimplified picture of the kinds of regularity which the historian implicitly acknowledges. The purported equivalence of *explanation* and *prediction* does not hold, we have argued, even in the work of the scientist. Both in science and history one might be able to show that a past event was predictable from its antecedents, and yet not understand the reasons for its occurrence. To tell someone "that's what always happens under these circumstances" does not constitute an explanation, even if the statement is a valid law. In science, theories rather than empirical laws have explanatory force because of the intelligibility they provide in terms of detailed subpatterns, structures, or modes of operation. What the historian seeks is more like the understanding provided by theories than like the predictive power provided by laws.

There are, of course, special *difficulties in the idea of prediction in history*. At the practical level, prediction is prevented by the historical contingencies that introduce new "givens" entering as "brute facts" from outside the framework of analysis—the stray bullet that killed Stonewall Jackson, the microbe that brought

---

40. C. B. Joynt and N. Rescher, "The Problem of Uniqueness in History," *History and Theory*, Vol. 1 (1961), 151, 154.

Alexander the Great to an untimely death, the birth of a girl instead of a boy to Henry VIII, the storm that contributed to Cornwallis' defeat at Yorktown. In more philosophical terms, the presence of human freedom is incompatible with determinism and "historical inevitability," which prediction and lawfulness presuppose.[41] To predict the Gettysburg address or a Beethoven Symphony or Newton's *Principia* would mean that one could have written these works before their authors did. Even when a historian refers to the causes of an event, he does not give the total set of "sufficient conditions" from which it could have been predicted. He gives only a few of the contributing factors, singled out because of the particular interests of his inquiry; he may be concerned about "precipitating incidents" and crucial decisions, or about "underlying causes" and background situations.

Moreover, references to *the reasons of agents* occur in many historical narratives. Dray indicates the form of intelligibility introduced when the agent's standpoint, rather than the spectator's, is taken:

> When we subsume an action under a law, our approach is that of a spectator of action; we look for a pattern or regularity in it. But when we give an explanation in terms of the purpose which guided the action, the problem it was intended to resolve, the principle which it applied, etc., we adopt the standpoint from which the action was done: the standpoint of an agent. . . . There is a sense of "explain" in which an action is only explained when it is seen in a context of rational deliberation, when it is seen from the point of view of an agent.[42]

Although such explanations sometimes make use of psychological laws, they more often involve setting an action in the context of the disposition and behavior of a particular person; they usually require explication of a structure of thought, motives, or goals.

There is in the historian's work a final feature to which there seems to be greater sensitivity in the "idiographic" than in the "nomothetic" school, namely the extent to which *consideration of the total context* influences conclusions about the relation between any two particular events. It is for this reason that a historian,

---

41. See Herbert Butterfield, *Christianity and History* (New York: Charles Scribner's Sons, 1949; PB); Reinhold Niebuhr, *Faith and History* (New York: Charles Scribner's Sons, 1949).

42. Dray, *Laws and Explanation in History*, pp. 140, 150. Used by permission of Oxford University Press.

when challenged, will usually defend a thesis not by citing general laws but by filling in further details, by interpolating intermediate developments, and by giving more information about particulars. He appeals to his opponent's judgment about the individual case (though always, we have suggested, making implicit use of generalizations). Historical explanation involves *configurational understanding*, the attempt to see the relation of the parts in a particular whole. Good historical writing is judged both by fidelity to evidence and by the way in which the details are fitted together into a total pattern. The historian tries to establish an *intelligible context* for an event, rather than to deduce it from laws. This task is not unlike that of the dramatist. The first half of a play does not permit you to predict the second half, yet it helps you to understand the latter; subsequent events are dependent on earlier ones, and if you arrive late at the theater, you do not understand what is going on.

We suggested earlier that *all knowledge is contextual,* so that history is in this respect distinguished from science in degree rather than in kind. We have emphasized the epistemological context—e.g., interpretation of data depends on a framework of theory, and concepts are tested in networks not in isolation. (In Part Three we will discuss the metaphysical context—for example, the activity of the "part" depends on that of the "whole," on relationships rather than entities in isolation.) Kenneth Boulding has shown[43] that in various domains of knowledge our identification of data is controlled by "images of wholes." Knowledge is not built up "atomistically" from parts to wholes, he says; our partial understanding of wholes influences our interpretation of parts, right from the start. The interpretation of the relation between two historical events is a function of both the theoretical context in which it is viewed and the historical context in which the events occurred; but similar statements could be made about other fields of inquiry.

Thus a legitimate concern for uniqueness is expressed in the historian's recognition that he must consider *the particular total configuration* in which an event is found. But let us acknowledge that the historian does not, as sometimes claimed, "comprehend the whole situation in its entirety"; he, too, is selective, paying attention to certain patterns and ignoring others. His account never

43. Kenneth Boulding, *The Image* (Ann Arbor: University of Michigan Press, 1956; PB).

reproduces the full particularity and multileveled richness of human experience as lived. Our conclusion is that events cannot be
separated into two classes, "unique" and "lawful," but that history
and science do represent differing kinds of interest within the
spectrum of human inquiry. The idea of "particular contexts"
allows us to reinterpret what is valid in both "idiographic" and
"nomothetic" traditions.

If space allowed, we could trace precisely the same debate about
lawfulness and uniqueness among *clinical psychologists.* Meehl, for
instance, upholds a nomothetic approach, and claims that the most
reliable basis for prediction is the quantitative analysis of the
results of comparative test scores.[44] Allport, by contrast, defends
idiographic understanding of "the unique individual who is more
than just the intersection of a number of quantitative variables."[45]
Any given "personality trait" modifies other traits and functions
distinctively in a particular combination; therefore the total person
must be studied as an organized and integrated system, a coherent
whole. The total pattern or configuration, Allport asserts, is grasped
as a unity, not as a sum of parts atomistically examined; a sensitive
counselor must be able to understand a personality complex unlike
any he has encountered before.

The viewpoint we have developed would lead us to acknowledge
the importance of *the total context of personality,* but also to insist
that the understanding of particular patterns always *makes use of
generalizations.* There are orderly and stable regularities in the
life of an individual over a period of time, and there are statistical
generalizations in the comparison of persons. (If there were no
such similarities, there would be only a psychology of John Smith,
but no general study of personality; if you could learn nothing
from his case which might be applicable elsewhere, you might as
well burn his file when he dies.) And any generalization is of
course an abstraction from the particularity and wholeness of concrete individuals. Such an analysis would again lead to the conclusion that uniqueness and lawfulness are not mutually exclusive.

----
44. Paul Meehl, *Statistical Versus Clinical Prediction* (Minneapolis: University of Minnesota Press, 1954), pp. 132f; cf. A. Roy Eckardt, "The Contribution of Nomothesis in the Science of Man," *American Scientist,* Vol. 49
(1961), 76.
45. Allport, *Pattern and Growth,* Chaps. 1, 21; also his *The Use of Personal
Documents in Psychological Science* (New York: Social Science Research
Council, 1942), Chap. 4; cf. Samuel J. Beck, "The Science of Personality:
Nomothetic or Idiographic?" *Psychological Review* (November 1953), p. 353.

IV. Conclusions: On Subject and Object

The first theme of this chapter has been *the participation of the knower* in all inquiry. The interpretation of experience requires mental construction and personal judgment; the contributions of subject and object are never completely separable. We have pictured a spectrum of varying degrees and types of personal involvement. In the social sciences, cultural perspectives and individual values and images of man inevitably condition the selection and interpretation of data and the creation of concepts and theories. It was suggested that introspective experience contributes indirectly to the understanding of other persons, and that the attempt to see events from both the agent's and the spectator's frame of reference is desirable. We defended the ideal of *objectivity* construed as intersubjective testability and commitment to universality.

If we were to extend this spectrum to *the humanities*, we would find a degree of *personal involvement* considerably greater than in the social sciences. Some comments have already been made about history, which is often included among the humanities. The appreciation of art and music requires active personal participation; analysis of aesthetic form is no substitute for immersion in and total response to a work of art. Literature and drama similarly demand engagement and identification; assumption of the agent's viewpoint rather than the spectator's is a prerequisite of comprehension. But a discussion of literature might also show that the element of universal intent is not totally lacking, for cognitive understanding as well as emotional response is elicited. The dramatist is concerned to say something about reality, not just about his own private feelings. The poet starts from his response to the world, yet he hopes to evoke a similar response in others; his symbols are at least partially referential and not, as positivists claimed, entirely expressive. The poet gives only oblique hints about the nature of reality, and his affirmations are often indirect and subtle, but they are not purely private and subjective.[46]

The second theme of this chapter has been *the concept of uniqueness*. It was suggested that though every event is in some respects

---

46. See, e.g., Philip Wheelwright, *The Burning Fountain* (Bloomington: Indiana University Press, 1954) and *Metaphor and Reality* (Bloomington: Indiana University Press, 1962).

unique, scientific procedures attempt to establish laws and theories by selecting regular and repeatable patterns among events. The historian and the psychologist, however, give greater attention to particularity, though not without making use of generalizations. If we were to discuss the humanities, such concern for uniqueness would be even more evident. A work of art or music exemplifies general formal structures, but its distinctive individuality is the object of interest. Any expression of artistic creativity and any literary or dramatic masterpiece is original and unrepeatable. The poet attempts to convey the novelty of a concrete experience by fresh juxtapositions of images. It is only by confronting the reader with particular situations that the artist expresses any implicit generalizations, and these are not abstracted from their particular embodiments.

In connection with uniqueness we touched on an idea that will recur in future chapters: *configurational understanding* of total patterns. In dealing with history or personality, one tries to see in a particular context *the relationships among the parts of a whole*. Such configurational understanding seems to be characteristic of the humanities. A work of art, music, poetry, or drama must be appreciated as a totality; examination of the parts "out of context" is not precluded, but the final judgment about the parts rests upon their contribution to the integral pattern of the whole. We cannot digress to explore these two themes in the humanities in general, but will consider their relevance for religion in the next chapter. (The arts, in any case, involve somewhat special features, distinct from history, philosophy, and religion.)

As a way of summarizing the position we have taken on (1) objectivity versus personal involvement and (2) lawfulness versus uniqueness, let us assert that we have attempted to avoid the mistakes made by positivism on the one side, and existentialism on the other. A condensed (and hence oversimplified) version of the *positivist* view of these two issues might run like this: (1) *Objectivity*, understood to mean the exclusion of personal and subjective factors, characterizes all valid knowledge in any field. The spectator's viewpoint, rather than the actor's, alone provides trustworthy data. Prediction and empirical verification are taken to be the hallmarks of science. (2) *Nomothetic* knowledge formulated in lawful regularities alone constitutes genuine explanation. The "unique" is but the intersection of many regularities; complex systems will eventually be reduced to repeatable elements. The positivist prefers to start from *parts* rather than wholes. He sees the value of cautious and limited research, dealing with small fragments of a situation, in which reproducible results can be obtained. His approach tends to be reductionistic and atomistic; he assumes determinism at least as a methodological postulate.

Existentialism takes the opposite stand on both issues: (1) *Personal involvement* alone enables a person to understand the most important aspects of reality. The actor's standpoint, not the spectator's, has access to authentic existence. Participation in life and commitment in action are dominant in this subject-centered approach to knowledge. Most existentialists do not of course dismiss scientific knowledge, but they see its scope as severely limited, especially in understanding man. (2) The existentialist stresses *uniqueness*, individuality, and freedom rather than lawful regularity. Life cannot be captured by systematic abstractions; it is known only by immersion in concrete existence, and it is expressed in particularity rather than in universal principles. A person is not an instance of a general "human nature"; in decision each man creates himself and makes his own possibilities and values. The concrete *whole* rather than the part is significant, configurational understanding rather than analysis of components. The existentialist views literature as the vehicle par excellence for conveying the nature of human existence, since it allows for personal involvement, uniqueness, configurational understanding, and freedom.

Now if one sees science as the positivists do, and the humanities as the existentialists do, one does indeed have "two cultures" of opposite characteristics. "Intermediate" fields would have to choose one camp or the other. But we have suggested that the dichotomy is unsound. Science is a more human enterprise, and the humanities have more universal intent than these images suggest, and the "third culture" (the social sciences) has much in common with both; we have a spectrum of fields, not two opposing camps. As we have reinterpreted two pairs of disputed concepts, they no longer represent mutually exclusive alternatives: *objectivity* as intersubjective testability does not exclude *personal involvement,* and *uniqueness* as concern for particular configurations does not exclude recognition of *lawful patterns*. Both subject and object contribute to knowledge in all fields, and all events can be treated as unique or as lawful.

Among twentieth-century philosophical schools, *process philosophy* has a more balanced outlook than either positivism or existentialism concerning these two themes. Whitehead's critical realism allows for the role of both subject and object in knowledge. Uniqueness and lawfulness are both important concepts in his thought; he sees reality as genuinely pluralistic, even though every entity is constituted by its relationships. Each entity is distinct and individual, on its own in creating itself in each fragment of time. Yet this spontaneity and novelty occurs within structures of regularity; the scientist can abstract and select these lawful patterns from the concrete situations of the world, and construct symbolic systems to represent them. Again, process philosophy gives prominence to wholes, but does not ignore analysis into parts, as we shall see when we examine Whitehead's metaphysics in Part Three.

8

The Methods of Religion

In this chapter and in the one following, the methods of religion will be compared with the methods of science. In Section I, "Experience and Interpretation in Religion," some similarities between science and religion are explored, including the interaction of experience and interpretation, the role of the community and its paradigms, and the use of symbols, analogies, and models. The starting point for the discussion in Section II, "Personal Involvement and Religious Faith," is the existentialist assertion that religion contrasts sharply with science because it is concerned with the realm of personal selfhood. The distinctive nature of "ultimate concern" and "religious commitment," and their differences from the more speculative stance of natural theology, are set forth. Nevertheless it is suggested that faith and reason are not mutually exclusive and that cognitive assent to particular beliefs is an important aspect of religion.

Section III, "Revelation and Uniqueness," considers the dependence of biblical religion on particular historical events; in this respect religion seems very unlike science. We will maintain, however, that there is no uninterpreted revelation, and that the revelatory power of past events is known in their ability to illuminate present experience. The relation of particularity and universality for the theologian, the scientist, and the historian are compared. A final contrast, based on the differing functions of scientific and religious language as described by linguistic analysis, is the topic of the subsequent chapter; the key issue therein is whether anything akin to the "empirical verification" of religious propositions is possible.

I. Experience and Interpretation in Religion

We start by considering possible parallels between science and religion. First, there is an interaction between experience and interpretation in religion which in some ways resembles that occurring in science; here, too, there is no uninterpreted experience. As previously, our discussion must rest on concrete examples, which will be taken from the religious traditions of the West. Next, the role of the religious community and its paradigms is described. Finally, it is shown that the use of analogies and models in religious language is in many ways similar to their use in science.

1. Religious Experience and Theological Interpretation

Let us ask to what extent the basic structure of *experience* and *interpretation* in religion might be taken to parallel that in science. The statement by Whitehead quoted earlier may serve as a point of departure:

> The dogmas of religion are the attempts to formulate in precise terms the truths disclosed in the religious experience of mankind. In exactly the same way the dogmas of physical science are the attempts to formulate in precise terms the truths disclosed in the sense-perception of mankind.[1]

Consider also the following sentence from William James:

> We may now lay it down as certain that in the distinctively religious sphere of experience, many persons (how many we cannot tell) possess the objects of their belief, not in the form of mere conceptions which their intellects accept as true, but rather in the form of quasi-sensible realities directly apprehended.[2]

Or again, John Baillie writes:

> The witness of all true religion is that there is no reality which more directly confronts us than the reality of God. No other reality is nearer to us than he. The realities of sense are more obvious, but his is the

---

1. Whitehead, *Religion in the Making*, p. 57. Used by permission of the Macmillan Company and Cambridge University Press.

2. William James, *Varieties of Religious Experience* (New York: Random House, n.d.; Mentor PB), p. 63. Used by permission of Paul R. Reynolds, Inc.

more intimate, touching us as it does so much nearer to the core of our being.[3]

When we examine this experiential component in religion, we recognize at once that since it does not derive from sense-experience there will be crucial problems of intersubjective testability to which we will have to return.

One of the distinctive elements in man's *religious experience* is awe and reverence before what is holy and sacred to him. This is closely associated with the awareness of dependence, finitude, and contingency of which Schleiermacher wrote. Rudolf Otto's classic study[4] deals with the experience of the "numinous," in which mystery, fascination, and wonder are combined. Other common features in biblical religion are an acknowledgment of moral obligation and a sense of guilt in falling short thereof. The association of the four elements of (1) awe and reverence, (2) humility and guilt, (3) the acceptance of forgiveness, and (4) responsibility for action in society, is typical of the experience of the Hebrew prophets. All four are present in Isaiah's vision in the temple:

"Holy, holy, holy is the Lord of hosts; the whole earth is full of his glory." And the foundations of the thresholds shook at the voice of him who called, and the house was filled with smoke. And I said: "Woe is me! For I am lost; for I am a man of unclean lips and I dwell in the midst of a people of unclean lips; for my eyes have seen the King, the Lord of hosts." Then flew one of the seraphim to me, having in his hand a burning coal which he had taken with tongs from the altar. And he touched my mouth, and said: "Behold, this has touched your lips; your guilt is taken away, and your sin forgiven." And I heard the voice of the Lord saying "Whom shall I send, and who will go for us?" Then I said "Here I am! Send me." And he said, "Go, and say to this people. . . ."[5]

The *experiential character of biblical religion* is evident not only in the centrality of worship but also in concern about life in the present. The prophetic message often included, as in Isaiah's case, the interpretation of current situations in the light of what was understood to be God's purposes in concrete historical events and human communities. The corporate experience of Israel was the

3. John Baillie, *Our Knowledge of God* (New York: Charles Scribner's Sons, 1939; London: Oxford University Press; Scribner's PB), p. 155.

4. Rudolf Otto, *The Idea of the Holy*, trans. J. W. Harvey (London: Oxford University Press, 1923; PB).

5. Isaiah 6:3–9 (all biblical quotations are from the Revised Standard Version of the Bible, copyrighted 1946 and 1952).

210   RELIGION AND THE METHODS OF SCIENCE

context in which God was encountered. So too the authors of the
New Testament were writing of what had happened to them and
attempting to interpret their own experience, the transformation
that had occurred in their lives, and their common response to the
person of Christ. Their primary witness was the recital of events,
not philosophical arguments. The early church was not speculating
about theological ideas in the abstract; it was trying to understand
what had occurred in its life. The experience of individuals in
community is thus the starting point of theological interpretation.

No sharp separation can be made, however, between *experience*
and *interpretation*. We recall that even scientific data are "theory-
laden," and data in the social sciences are seen from the perspective
of observers who are historically and culturally conditioned. In
religion also there is *no uninterpreted experience*. Here, too, man
is a creative and active constructor of symbols. There is a continual
two-way interaction between experience and interpretation by
which each influences the other. Jonathan Edwards, in discussing
the influence of prevailing theological ideas on the experience of
conversion, wrote:

> Very often their experience at first appears like a confused chaos, but
> then those parts are selected which bear the nearest resemblance to
> such particular steps as are insisted on; and these are dwelt upon in
> their thoughts, and spoken of from time to time, till they grow more
> and more conspicuous in their view, and other parts which are ne-
> glected grow more and more obscure. Thus what they have experi-
> enced is insensibly strained so as to bring it into an exact conformity
> to the scheme already established in their minds.[6]

Theology as the systematic analysis of religion interprets the experience of the worshiping community, but theological ideas in turn
affect the life of this community; beliefs have implications for worship, ethics, and all aspects of corporate and individual life, and
thereby influence the data.

If there is no uninterpreted experience, then there can be *no
direct religious knowledge* which is immediate and certain. For
when human interpretation is present, there is always the possibility of misinterpretation, especially through wishful thinking,
which reads into experience more than is warranted. Moreover,

6. Jonathan Edwards, *Treatise on Religious Affections*, quoted in William
James, *Varieties of Religious Experience*, p. 197.

any verbal communication requires the use of symbolic language and conceptual structures that are culturally conditioned. The mystic's vision can never itself certify the reality of its object; it must be considered as interpreted experience rather than as immediate knowledge. The sense of "confrontation," "encounter," "meeting," and "otherness," as well as the element of unexpectedness which seems to point to an activity independent of our control, are no guarantee of the validity of our understanding of these events. All theology is subject to the process of criticism and testing which will be examined later. The finitude and relativity of our viewpoint and the inevitability of historical influences in our interpretive perspectives must be recognized from the outset.

2. The Christian Experience of Reconciliation

We will take time to describe in detail one of the areas of experience which has been important in Christian thought. Men and women down through the ages have spoken of the *reorientation of their lives* in what they understood to be a new relationship to God.[7] Let us refer to this change, not in traditional terminology, but in contemporary concepts depicting human existence. Paul Tillich calls it the transition from *estrangement* to *reconciliation*,[8] and we may use his terms as headings under which to try to spell out for ourselves what occurs. The initial condition of estrangement is threefold:

1. *Estrangement from others.* Because we are insecure and self-centered, we are isolated from other persons. We hide our real feelings, and we wear "masks" and play "roles" to bolster our egos. We are anxious about the impression we are making, so we put on fronts to build up our status; these false fronts are barriers that cut us off from each other. Lovelessness and loneliness go together. Corporate pride and self-interest contribute similarly to alienation among groups and nations.

2. *Estrangement from our true selves.* We are divided persons, pulled in various directions by conflicting goals. We feel guilty,

7. See Harold DeWolf, *A Theology for the Living Church*, Chap. 34; David E. Roberts, *Psychotherapy and a Christian View of Man* (New York: Charles Scribner's Sons, 1950; PB), Chap. 9.

8. Paul Tillich, *Systematic Theology* (Chicago: University of Chicago Press, 1957), Vol. 2.

unable to accept ourselves as we are with our particular potentialities and limitations, and we do not understand ourselves. Our situation is described in the tragic epitaph of *The Death of a Salesman*: "He never knew who he was."

3. *Estrangement from God, the ground of meaning.* The ultimate insecurity is the threat that life might be meaningless. Modern man often experiences emptiness and purposelessness, sometimes anxiety and futility, and occasionally despair. Writes W. H. Auden: "We are afraid of pain, but more afraid of silence; for no nightmare of hostile objects could be as terrible as this void."

The central experience of the Christian faith may be described as the transformation of these three forms of estrangement by a new reconciliation with other persons, with ourselves, and with God:

1. *Reconciliation with God.* Basic to this reorientation is the recognition that God accepts us as we are, not because we have earned his love or worked our way into his favor. The center of the New Testament is the conviction that God's love and forgiveness overcomes our separation from him. The Reformers referred to this restoration of relationship as "justification by faith" rather than by works. Tillich describes the experience of grace in these words:

> Sometimes a wave of light breaks into our darkness, and it is as though a voice were saying: "You are accepted. You are accepted by that which is greater than you, and the name of which you do not know. Do not ask for that name now; perhaps you will find it later. Do not try to do anything now; perhaps later you will do much. Do not seek for anything; do not perform anything. Simply accept the fact that you are accepted!" When that happens to us, we experience grace, and reconciliation bridges the gulf of estrangement.[9]

Anxiety about the threat of meaninglessness is overcome; here is a new possibility of trust and a center of meaning. In this reorientation there are new purposes for living and motives for action.

2. *Reconciliation with our true selves.* In the security of being accepted by God, we are free to look at ourselves more honestly; because God accepts us, we can accept ourselves. In the presence of God we can drop our masks, and we can let go of some of our defense mechanisms and pretenses. In the experience of repentance and forgiveness we can be released from guilt and self-hatred on

---

9. Paul Tillich, *The Shaking of the Foundations* (New York: Charles Scribner's Sons, 1948; PB), p. 162.

the one hand, and from pride and self-righteousness on the other. Self-understanding and internal integration can replace conflicting ideals and internal divisions. In this direction lies true fulfillment.

3. *Reconciliation with others.* The new relationship to God can enable us to love others. Only when a person is liberated from excessive self-concern can he forget about himself for a while; he can accept other persons as they are because he has known God's acceptance of himself as he is. He can have a freedom in his relation to other people which the person who is self-centered and anxious about his own status can never know. He can bring sensitivity, tenderness, and forgiveness into human relationships, seeing the redemptive possibilities in the life of communities, and working for reconciliation between man and man.

Now these descriptions of estrangement and reconciliation are *interpretations of experience.* They are not pure uninterpreted experience yielding immediate knowledge; nor, at the opposite extreme, are they abstract doctrinal statements unrelated to experience. The terms employed above are intended to maintain the experiential reference which for many people is no longer suggested by the theological concepts of "sin" and "salvation." Usually any such steps toward reconciliation are gradual and partial rather than sudden and total. This reorientation must never be claimed as a completed accomplishment, but as *a new possibility—the* genuinely creative possibility for one's life, a pattern of existence of which one sees glimpses in one's own life and the life of others. St. Paul spoke of "joy, peace, and love" as the fruits of the Spirit, but even for him there was continued struggle, repentance, and dependence on God. If we encounter a God of justice and righteousness as well as of love, we are both comforted and disturbed; we worship him not to make ourselves secure, but because he evokes our reverence, humility, and obedience. Moreover, the vision of this possibility is not our own accomplishment but a gift mediated to us through a community.

3. The Role of the Religious Community

The *social character of knowledge* has already been stressed. The child learns a language embodying concepts that affect the way he organizes experience. If a child grows up in isolation from other persons, his self-awareness and awareness of the world appear to be hardly "human"; the self and what it knows is in large measure constituted by the community. We noted earlier the role of the scientific community in research. Schilling points out that just as there is no "one-man physics," so there is no "one-man religion."[10] Here also inquiry occurs in the context of a community which shares common purposes, attitudes, hopes, and loyalties. There is a social fabric of mutual interaction, trust, aid, and criticism. For religion as for science the corporate life transmits a structure of ideals, standards, presuppositions, and patterns of behavior. Becoming a physicist or becoming a Christian, says Pollard, is a process of acquiring distinctive attitudes by becoming incorporated into a community.[11] The religious community, too, has its "paradigms," key examples from the past that influence all its activities.

The religious community, like the scientific, has its own symbolic language in terms of which it *describes its common experience.* Here also the language conveys little to persons who have not participated in the life of the community. Once again, the interaction of the individual with the group is a crucial aspect of the knowledge-situation. In the Judeo-Christian tradition, worship is primarily corporate, and the church or synagogue is also necessary for the tasks of service to others, witness to the world in word and deed, and self-understanding and self-criticism in theological discussion. This is a community of forgiveness, mutual support, and common memory; in living recollection, the individual becomes a participant in a history of redemptive events.

Participation in a corporate history is a striking feature of the practices of both Judaism and Christianity. Many aspects of congregational worship throughout the year are historical commemorations which portray the present life of individual and group in the light of their past. These communities are constituted not by isolated visions or mystical moments, but by a shared life in response to historical events. God is referred to not by metaphysical attributes but by historical relationships; he is "the God of Abraham," "the Lord who delivered us from bondage in Egypt," and "the God and Father of our Lord Jesus Christ." The chief forms of confession and creed are the recital of events rather than of general principles. The Bible itself, which a generation ago was often pictured as a succession of "great personalities," is now taken

---

10. Schilling, *Science and Religion*, Chap. 4.
11. William Pollard, *Physicist and Christian* (Greenwich, Conn.: Seabury Press, 1961; Collier PB), pp. 3ff.

to be the drama of God's dealings with a people, inseparable from the history of a community.[12]

The covenant at Sinai is the central event in Israel's memory. It marked the creation of a personal bond, not just a formal contract; it inaugurated a shared life, freely entered by both parties. God's purposes required the formation of a people, "a holy nation," for only a community can embody patterns of worship and justice. The covenant is a living relationship in every present, the enduring center of the covenant community. The intense religious experience of the prophets was, as in Isaiah's case, always related to the ongoing life of the community. Moreover, a recall to the covenant was a recall to the distinctive feature of ethical monotheism: a God with moral purposes in history, who takes the initiative in judging and redeeming the life of a people, and who is concerned with the total life of man because his purposes can be fulfilled only in the fabric of communal life. In all these respects there was a strong contrast with the polytheistic religions of surrounding cultures whose deities were associated with nature, which was considered to be cyclic, nonhistorical and basically amoral. Thus Israel's recollection of her formation and history as a community has at the same time continued to preserve her distinctive religious beliefs.[13]

The center of the memory of *the Christian community* is of course the person of Christ. The disciples came to see Christ as both the fulfillment and the transformation of Israel's expectations. Here, too, it was through response to events in history, not to theological principles, that the community came into being, and recollection of these events serves to preserve its distinctive beliefs. Once again, God was understood to be at work not simply in the lives of individuals, but in the life of a group; the Holy Spirit was God's activity *in the church*, not in solitary religious experience. So great was the sense of mutual participation and the dependence of each person on the life of the whole, that St. Paul could compare the church to a single organism.[14] It is the continuing community which remembers that in Christ's life estrangement was overcome

---

12. E.g., Bernard Anderson, *Understanding the Old Testament,* and Howard Kee and Franklin Young, *Understanding the New Testament* (both Englewood Cliffs, N.J.: Prentice-Hall, Inc., 1957).

13. See Abraham Heschel, *God in Search of Man* (New York: Farrar, Straus and Cudahy, Inc., 1955; Meridian PB), Pt. II; H. H. Rowley, *The Faith of Israel* (Philadelphia: Westminster Press, 1957).

14. I Corinthians 12:14f.

by reconciliation; the community mediates to the individual the threefold possibility of reconciliation. There are, to be sure, great dangers inherent in any institution: it can become an end in itself, a static organization pursuing its own self-interest and bound so tightly to its past that it is unable to meet new challenges. Nevertheless, *the church as a living community* is always the context of Christian life and thought.

4. Analogies and Models in Religious Language

Symbolism has been of interest to philosophers[15] as well as anthropologists. In each area of discourse it is held that some aspect of experience is interpreted symbolically by man's creative imagination. There has been extensive discussion of particular forms of *religious symbolism*.[16] For example, *ritual* is symbolic action, which may express and celebrate a community's religious convictions, often by symbolic participation in significant events in its memory (for example, the Lord's Supper in Christian worship). Religious *myths* are stories that suggest life-orientations by placing the human situation in a cosmic setting, "integrating man, the cosmos, and the sacred";[17] their common themes are primordial beginnings, life and death in man and nature, the goals and destinies of individuals and groups. We must bypass discussion of these special types of symbolism in order to look at the general structure of religious language.

Analogies are one source of interpretive symbols in religion[18] as in science. We stated that an analogy is the extension of patterns of relationship drawn from one area of experience to coordinate other types of experience. Such analogical language is frequently found in man's interpretation of religious experience and in his symbols for deity. Perhaps the common character of such responses accounts for the frequency of analogies such as king, rock, or

---

15. Ernst Cassirer, *An Essay on Man* (New Haven, Conn.: Yale University Press, 1944; Doubleday PB); Suzanne Langer, *Philosophy in a New Key* (Cambridge, Mass.: Harvard University Press, 1942; Mentor PB).

16. See Sidney Hook, ed., *Religious Experience and Truth* (New York: New York University Press, 1961), Pt. I; F. Ernest Johnson, ed., *Religious Symbolism* (New York: Harper and Brothers, 1955).

17. Mircea Eliade and Joseph Kitagawa, eds., *The History of Religions* (Chicago: University of Chicago Press, 1959), p. 103.

18. See E. L. Mascall, *Existence and Analogy* (New York: Longmans, Green and Co., 1949).

tower; the symbols of light and height are perhaps even more common. Dorothy Emmet suggests that the awe and sublimity experienced in looking up at a height is taken as an appropriate analogy to man's response to God.[19] Even the terms used to express transcendence, such as "above" and "beyond," whose purpose is precisely to point to the limitations of all analogies, are themselves spatial analogies. Another form of analogy is the parable, a vivid story about everyday life. A parable usually has one central point of similarity between the narrated incident and some aspect of the relation between man and God; it does not, like an allegory, have many symbolic elements each representing something. Instead of being formally defined, God is compared to a father who forgives a prodigal son, or a shepherd who seeks a lost sheep.

A *model*, it will be recalled, is a systematic set of analogies drawn from a single more familiar situation, e.g., the "billiard-ball model" of a gas. In biblical theology the central model for God is a human person. One must immediately ask which aspects of any model are taken to be relevant, and which, like the color of the billiard balls, are held to be irrelevant and inapplicable. Does the personal model imply that God has hands and feet? An early passage speaks of God as "walking in the garden in the cool of the day,"[20] but the Bible generally avoids predication of physical attributes. Does God have intelligence and purpose? These are taken to be essential aspects without which one could not speak of personality. The ascription of human emotions stands on the border, and is subject to increasing refinement and qualification. Moreover, particular kinds of person are specified as models: a sovereign ruler, a just judge, and finally a loving father. But for the Christian there is one supreme model for God: the person of Christ. Theological discussions of the status of Christ (for example, the "Christological controversies" of the fourth and fifth centuries) may be understood as attempts to define which aspects of this model are relevant.[21]

Many of *the dangers in the use of models* in science are present

---

19. Dorothy Emmet, *The Nature of Metaphysical Thinking* (London: Macmillan & Co., Ltd., 1949), Chap. 5.

20. Genesis 3:8.

21. See Frederick Ferré, "Mapping the Logic of Models in Science and Theology," *The Christian Scholar*, Vol. 46 (1963), p. 9; also Ian Ramsey, *Models and Mystery* (London: Oxford University Press, 1964); and John McIntyre, *The Shape of Christology* (London: SCM Press, 1966).

in religion also. One may expect too much from a model and identify it with reality, as literalism does, forgetting that even those aspects of a model which are relevant do not provide an exhaustive representation. Again, we have noted the *abandonment of picturability* in physics. The biblical tradition, though it has often used visual images, has been aware of their limitations. The biblical prohibition against any "graven image" or "likeness" reflects not only a warning against idolatry but also a conviction that God cannot be captured in any visual form. Perhaps one reason for the frequency of auditory symbols (the "voice of the Lord," the "word of God") is that the spoken word allows a communication of meaning without pictorial representation. Moreover, God is always beyond human comprehension and "his ways are not our ways." He may be "like unto a father" but he is also "beyond our farthest thoughts," a mystery which eludes all our attempts to imagine him. The Bible shows considerable reticence about trying to describe God. The man at worship, like the man in the laboratory, uses language with realistic intent, and yet he recognizes that his symbols are not a replica of reality.

Scientific models, we said, provide a *vividness, immediacy*, and *unity* of mental grasp not found in a multiplicity of abstract formulae. Models in religion have an even greater vividness and dramatic force which make them powerful vehicles for conveying the patterns of meaning by which men orient their lives. Often they are associated with mental images which come to have a strong emotional influence. Religious models are evocative of personal response; they serve to remind the hearer of elements in his own experience. A model in either field is extensible, serving to coordinate experience beyond the situation in which it first arose. Finally, models in religion lead to *conceptual* and *propositional* formulations (corresponding in some ways to theories in science); we will suggest at a later point that the evaluation of such conceptual schemes is one of the tasks of theology.

II. Personal Involvement and Religious Faith

Some parallels have been traced between science and religion regarding experience and interpretation, the significance of the community, and the use of models. But does not the extent of personal involvement in religion constitute a difference that outweighs any similarities? Such considerations lead existentialists to assert that the two fields use essentially dissimilar approaches to understanding. We can agree that religion is a matter of "ultimate concern"; in biblical theology the knower is indeed a participant agent rather than a detached spectator. But we will propose that these are differences in degree and manner of involvement, rather than any absolute dichotomy between science and religion. Moreover, there are aspects of religion which share the universal intent of science, namely cognitive assent to beliefs that are held to be true. Faith and reason, in short, are not mutually exclusive.

1. Personal Participation and "Ultimate Concern"

Tillich[22] has said that religion, in its broadest terms, always deals with questions of "ultimate concern," which have three characteristics. First, to have an ultimate concern is to have *unreserved commitment*, allegiance, and loyalty. It is a matter of life-and-death seriousness, since the meaning of one's existence is at stake; one bets his life in response to implicit promises of fulfillment or destruction. Second, an ultimate concern provides a *supreme value* in terms of which other values are justified and ordered. It is the top priority for which other achievements would be sacrificed, the final ground on which one's structure of values depends; often a person's decisions in crises reveal his actual value hierarchies. Third, an ultimate concern entails an *inclusive perspective* or a life-orientation, for it relates to all areas of life and it involves the whole person. It is thus both the center of a world-view and the center of integration of personality.

Personal involvement is inescapable here precisely because the central religious question is about *the objects of one's devotion and loyalty*. There can be detached and analytical language *about* religion (for example, research in the psychology of religion or sociology of religion); but the language *of* religion cannot be disinterested, neutral, and dispassionate, for what is acknowledged in any religion is a center of loyalty and commitment. Existential decision and personal response are defining characteristics of religion as "total life-orientation in response to what is deemed worthy of ultimate concern and devotion."

Apart from these characteristics of religion in general, there are

---

22. Paul Tillich, *The Dynamics of Faith* (New York: Harper and Brothers, 1957; PB), Chap. 1.

220   RELIGION AND THE METHODS OF SCIENCE

particular features of Judaism and Christianity that require the
involvement of the subject by *participation in the living memory of
a community.* H. Richard Niebuhr distinguishes "internal history,"
which deals with selves in community, from "external history," the
impersonal report of events from the viewpoint of the impartial
spectator. He compares the memory of the founding of our nation
embodied in the Gettysburg address ("Our fathers brought forth
upon this continent . . . ") with the external description of those
same events in the *Cambridge Modern History.* Niebuhr continues:

> The inspiration of Christianity has been derived from history, it is
> true, but not from history as seen by a spectator; the constant ref-
> erence is to subjective events, that is, to events in the lives of subjects.
> What distinguishes such historic recall from the private histories of
> mystics is that it refers to communal events, remembered by a com-
> munity and in a community. Subjectivity here is not equivalent to
> isolation, nonverifiability, and ineffability; our history can be com-
> municated and persons can refresh as well as criticize each other's
> memories of what has happened to them in the common life. . . . One
> must look with them and not at them to verify their visions, partici-
> pate in their history rather than regard it if one would apprehend
> what they apprehended. The history of the inner life can only be
> confessed by selves who speak of what happened to them in the com-
> munity of other selves.[23]

The necessity of involvement in biblical religion is also associated
with the idea of *a personal God.* We have previously referred to
Buber's characterization of the difference between knowing things
and knowing persons. In human relationships, an *I-Thou* situation
is one of directness and immediacy, responsiveness, and sensitivity,
in which one "makes oneself available to the other person." One is
concerned about the other as an end in himself, not as a means
which can be manipulated and utilized for one's own ends. In
genuine dialogue there is openness, awareness, responsibility, and
the reciprocity of true encounter and communication from being
to being; there is confrontation and meeting in the immediacy of
the present. So, too, in confronting God, man is in an *I-Thou* relationship of total participation and availability.

Finally, in its biblical meaning *faith* is not the acceptance of
doctrines on authority but an attitude of trust and commitment:

23. H. Richard Niebuhr, *The Meaning of Revelation* (New York: The Macmillan Co., 1941; PB), p. 73.

To understand the biblical use of the word it is essential to realize that it contains no suggestion of an apprehension in some way inferior to reasoned knowledge, believing where we cannot prove. It goes back to the Hebrew use, where the core of the concept is reliability, steadfastness, confidence—usually with respect to a person, rather than a statement. It is personal trust arising in a personal relationship.[24]

Faith in God is an aspect of a personal relationship, resembling in some ways faith in a friend or in one's doctor, or a husband's faith in his wife. None of these is "blind faith," for each is related to experience and is a response which is evoked. Marriage is a "venture of faith," not simply because its success is not predictable, but because it requires decision, self-commitment, and trust. In the biblical view, religious faith similarly means loyalty and fidelity; it includes a measure of courage and confidence despite the risks— in many New Testament passages faith is contrasted with fear and anxiety. It is an orientation of will, more like "believing *in*" a person than "believing *that*" a proposition is valid. This trust is a response evoked by God's "trustworthiness"—his forgiveness and grace; it is at the same time a human act of "entrustment," for in relying on God man renounces self-sufficiency. Turning to God implies turning away from previous objects of trust. Faith implies "faithfulness"—dependence, allegiance, and obedience.[25]

Just as understanding another person at the deepest level demands personal involvement rather than detached analysis, so in religion the purely analytical spectator cuts himself off from the very experiences that are most significant. Here a condition of knowing is willingness to act on the basis of one's commitments. When a person falls in love, he has a new center of loyalty, devotion, and concern, and a new focus of interests, values, and purposes in living. Faith in God likewise involves new attitudes toward oneself and others; we have spoken of these new attitudes as *reorientation*, the overcoming of estrangement by reconciliation. One looks in a new direction because of a new relationship to God. This is not just a new idea or a new ideal but a new experience in which, at least in part, self-centeredness is broken by forgiveness; this is a restructuring of one's life-pattern, a transformation more

24. Alan Richardson, ed., *A Theological Word Book of the Bible* (New York: The Macmillan Co., 1951; PB), p. 76.
25. See H. Richard Niebuhr, *Radical Monotheism and Western Culture* (New York: Harper and Brothers, 1960), Chap. 1.

fundamental than acquiring new information. Biblical religion is
thus intimately related to all aspects of personality, not to intellect
alone.

2. Biblical Theology versus Natural Theology

In contrast to biblical theology, *natural theology* (both in the
narrower sense of arguments from nature, and in the broader sense
of arguments from characteristics of existence) has usually encouraged the more rationalistic attitudes of analytical detachment
and philosophical speculation. For Aristotle, the existence of God
was an inference from the world: the First Cause, the Unmoved
Mover, the Cosmic Designer. We saw these ideas taken up by
Aquinas, though only as a preamble to revealed theology; with the
growth of Deism in the eighteenth century, this approach was often
used by itself, and we will later examine contemporary versions of
it. In these arguments an attitude is adopted which minimizes personal involvement; their goal is intellectual assent to the proposition "God exists." In the jargon of linguistic analysis, natural
theology uses "spectator-language," whereas biblical theology uses
"actor-language."

But writers of the Bible seem to have been much more concerned with the worship and service of God than with the development of "proofs of his existence." *Biblical faith* is never equated
with the conclusion of a philosophical argument. Moreover, such
arguments have seldom been the path by which men have actually
reached their religious beliefs; those who expound them are usually already committed to a theistic viewpoint. The choice is not
between "faith" and "no faith," but only "faith in what?" For man's
ultimate loyalties and objects of devotion are not established by
reason alone.[26]

The limitations of the approach used in natural theology are also
evident if it is acknowledged that there are *moral as well as intellectual conditions* for knowledge of God. There are such conditions even for knowledge of oneself or one's neighbor. We sup-
press the truth about ourselves with rationalizations and pretenses;
the self-righteousness of a group, a class, or a nation warps its
self-perception. Similarly, egocentricity and lack of sensitivity distort our judgment of our fellowman. So also man's self-sufficiency

---

26. See John Hutchison, *Faith, Reason and Existence* (New York: Oxford
University Press, 1956), Chaps. 4 and 5.

and sin have traditionally been considered barriers to knowing God. What a man loves, said St. Augustine, influences what he knows. Contrast the Enlightenment conviction that the chief cause of man's troubles is ignorance, with St. Paul's confession: "For I do not do the good I want, but the evil I do not want is what I do." The biblical tradition has always asserted that man's basic problem lies in his will: his self-centered orientation and idolatrous loyalties. The reorientation of the self involves more than philosophical arguments. Moreover, the power of psychological forces which influence man's processes of reasoning has been amply demonstrated by evidence of the sway of the unconscious over all of man's thought. The very word "rationalization" points to the curious fact that what appears to be rationality can be the distortion of reason.

Among *neo-orthodox* writers natural theology is viewed as insufficient primarily because it is held that God has revealed himself unambiguously only in key events in history (Section III below); but other reasons are also offered. Reinhold Niebuhr[27] maintains that the partial knowledge deducible from nature "objectifies God" and becomes for us "an item of impersonal information." Only in revelation does God disclose himself as a subject, and we respond as persons. Emil Brunner[28] says that the greater the degree of personal involvement in knowledge, the greater is the distortion of human reason by sin; in science such distortion is minimal, but in religion it prevents natural theology from yielding any "saving knowledge of God."

All these statements make it clear that biblical religion does manifest *a type of personal involvement* not present in science, or even in natural theology. Nevertheless it appears to the present author that existentialists have taken a genuine difference in emphasis and made it into an absolute dichotomy. For on the one hand it was proposed in the previous chapter that in science the knower does participate significantly in the knowing process; it was suggested that when other fields of inquiry are taken into account there is *a spectrum of various degrees and types of personal involvement*, rather than a sharp division of supposed "objectivity" and "subjectivity." And on the other hand, religion has

27. Reinhold Niebuhr, *The Nature and Destiny of Man* (New York: Charles Scribner's Sons, 1941; PB), Vol. 2, 64f.
28. Emil Brunner, *Revelation and Reason* (Philadelphia: Westminster Press, 1946), pp. 368f.

important features that bear a closer resemblance to scientific inquiry than those we have been considering.

3. The Interaction of Faith and Reason

Is there anything in religion that corresponds to the ideal of *objectivity* in science? Objectivity when construed as the absence of personal involvement is clearly incompatible with religious faith. It appears to be against such a misconception of objectivity that existentialists have reacted so violently. Kierkegaard's statement that in religion "truth is subjectivity" was a way of insisting that faith is radically inward and must be personally appropriated; religious truth must be lived in concrete particularity and not just stated in universal doctrines or creedal systems. But we may reply that such a concept of pure *subjectivity* offers no safeguard against arbitrariness and individual caprice. And if objectivity is understood as intersubjective testability and universal intent, as we have urged, there is at least the possibility that personal involvement can be acknowledged without reducing religious beliefs to private preferences. Truth is not determined merely by our choice, however much its appropriation may depend on us. Religious symbols are intended referentially and not simply expressively.

We can grant, then, that religion does not consist primarily in cognitive assent to a set of propositions, and yet insist that it does have an important *cognitive component*. Religious beliefs are held to be true, not just useful; their assertions about reality are universal in intent. Although the questions raised by religion are not those raised by science (and hence any natural theology built on scientific findings is dubious), in both fields statements are made which are held to be valid not just for one knower but potentially for all. Unless a person can give reasons for his beliefs they become matters of personal taste. This dedication to universal truth rather than private preference is in fact a demand made by biblical religion itself, not something imposed from outside. Our task at this point is not to elaborate this cognitive component but to show that it is compatible with the personal involvement described above.

Religious faith itself has cognitive implications, for it gives rise to *a new perspective* for viewing the world and new insights that illuminate subsequent experience. Alan Richardson points to the close linkage between faith-commitments and key interpretive categories:

> To have some faith or other is the condition of understanding, since faith supplies the key-category by means of which access to a unified view of things is gained. . . . The philosopher himself must select his own categories of interpretation; he must seize upon a "key-feature" or find a "clue" to the making of a unity out of the many. Every philosopher who attempts to build a metaphysic is ultimately dependent upon some "faith-principle," whether he is a Christian or a non-Christian, religious or antireligious. . . . The adequacy of any particular "faith-principle" must be judged by its ability to order the whole range of data supplied by the empirical sciences (including theology) in a rational and coherent philosophy of life and the world.[29]

Among the *tasks of reason* in religion are: (1) The *systematic interpretation* of religious experience and revelatory events in history. This includes analysis of the theological concepts in terms of which faith is understood. (2) The *testing* of these interpretations. We will consider shortly the use of such criteria as consistency, comprehensiveness, and adequacy to the full range of human experience, as well as pragmatic evaluation of results in life. Intellectual integrity also requires confrontation with other interpretive perspectives. (3) Investigation of the *implications* of religious beliefs. Unless the relationship of theology to culture, its application to new areas of individual and social life, and its interaction with other areas of thought are rationally explored, religion remains irrelevant to most of man's daily life. (4) *Communication* with other persons. All language, including that of religion, incorporates rational structures. Even though symbol and analogy are prominent in religion, theology must express beliefs in conceptual ideas, which always express metaphysical categories.

It is *not* implied here that personal reorientation is a product of reason alone, nor that Christian beliefs are to be derived by rational inference from objective facts, as in natural theology. There is a givenness to both religious experience and revelation; we start with Christ and our response to him, which we could not have deduced from universal principles. We interpret what we take to be God's confrontation in our lives; our task is to understand what has happened to us as individuals and as a community. This is

---

29. Alan Richardson, *Christian Apologetics* (New York: Harper and Brothers, 1947), pp. 136, 230.

not "reason seeking faith" but rather, as Anselm put it, *"faith seeking understanding."*[30] Our theological interpretations can be tested against the continuing experience of ourselves and others. Do they increase our self-understanding and shed light on the ever-changing situations we face? How does the world appear when it is seen from a theistic point of view? Personal involvement, then, does not exclude rational analysis; faith and reason must always be in interaction.

4. Religious Commitment and Reflective Inquiry

But is there not a tension between the *commitment* religion requires and the *tentativeness* that inquiry in any field demands? The scientist tentatively accepts a hypothesis and acts on the basis of its assumed truth in order to test it; but in religion, testing means living in accordance with a choice in which not just a theory but the man himself and the significance of his life are at stake. If a person's philosophy of life is an interpretation of his experience, too tentative and detached an attitude may cut him off from the very sorts of experience which are most crucial in understanding religion. God is not worshiped as a "tentative hypothesis." As in art and literature, the sensitivity and response of the participant influence the range and depth of his experience. The testing of religion must occur in life, for its central questions are about the objects of a man's trust, his responsible action, and the challenge of a possible pattern of life. The theologian, moreover, always stands in a particular historical community which he attempts to understand, interpret, and criticize. He must participate in its life and in the experiences from which the images and analogies of the language of worship arise; and yet he must also reflect on the conceptual structures in which theological interpretations are developed.

We would venture the suggestion that, despite the tension between them, a combination of *personal involvement and reflective inquiry* is required. One can understand another person more adequately if there is a relationship of personal involvement as well as critical reflection on that relationship. The life of a community needs to be understood from within, in its "internal his-

---

30. See Roger Hazelton, *Renewing the Mind* (New York: The Macmillan Co., 1949).

tory," and from without, in its "external history." Dorothy Emmet
speaks of the difficulty a person will have in "keeping a sufficient
detachment from the world to be able to develop his power of
sustained thought and reflection, and being sufficiently in it for
his reflection not to become unreal."[31] Commitment alone, without
inquiry, tends to become fanaticism or narrow dogmatism; inquiry
alone, without commitment, tends to end as skepticism or trivial
speculation irrelevant to real life. Sometimes it may be necessary
to alternate between personal involvement and reflection on that
involvement, for worship and critical reflection at their most significant levels do not occur simultaneously. It is by no means easy
to hold beliefs for which you would be willing to die, and yet to
remain open to new insights; but it is precisely such a combination
of commitment and inquiry that constitutes religious maturity.

Perhaps the same point can be made suggesting that *faith* does
not exclude *doubt*. For doubt is an ingredient of all inquiry, a
challenge to the neat schemes in which we think we have everything wrapped up. Often it is an expression of man's integrity,
and a product of his dedication to truth. Tennyson asserted: "There
is more faith in honest doubt than in half our creeds." Now if
faith were the acceptance of revealed propositions, it would be
incompatible with doubt. But if faith means trust and commitment,
it is compatible with considerable doubt about our theological
interpretations. Faith as we have described it does not automatically turn uncertainties into certainties. What it does is take us beyond the detached speculative attitude which prevents the most
significant sorts of experience; it enables us to live and act amid
the uncertainties of life without pretensions of intellectual or moral
infallibility. But it does not give us wisdom or virtue transcending
the limitations of human existence.

One of the functions of doubt in religious inquiry is *to destroy
the inadequate pictures of God* which we have fashioned—often
in our own image. Doubt frees us from illusions of having captured
God's glory in a creed. It calls into question every symbol through
which we point to the living God who cannot be imprisoned in
either models or conceptual systems. We are dislodged from all the
attempted securities on which we rely, including certainties of

---

31. Dorothy Emmet, *Philosophy and Faith* (London: SCM Press, 1936),
p. 63.

belief. Religious faith, like every creative venture, entails risk. Just as involvement in the world's suffering makes us vulnerable to its pain, so involvement in the world's intellectual life makes us vulnerable to its ideas.

Recognition of the continual need for *the corrective of self-criticism* has been called "the Protestant principle," though it is a principle often honored in the breach. No church or book or creed is infallible and no formulation is irrevocable. God, not our theology, is the object of our trust. The claim of any human institution or theological system to finality must be questioned, for there is always the danger of absolutizing the relative. The prophets of all ages have been willing to criticize their own religious community; they have never assumed, as we often do today, that religion is automatically a good thing. All too often our beliefs are distorted by wishful thinking or by the defense of group interests—for example, the use of God to support human purposes such as "the American way of life." Sometimes when this self-criticism was lacking within the church it had to be expressed by those outside, as in Marx's judgment on the class biases of a clergy insensitive to social problems, or Freud's condemnation of the escapism of sentimental religiosity. At other times the voice of self-criticism has been strong within the church, representing a combination of faith and doubt.[32]

Our *conclusions* in this section might run as follows. Personal involvement is indeed, as the existentialists assert, a central feature both of religion as "ultimate concern" and of the biblical understanding of "faith" as trust and commitment. But since personal involvement is not absent in science, we find religion and science to differ in the degree and form of involvement, not in any absolute contrast. Moreover, religion makes cognitive claims whose intent is universal, and in this respect it parallels science. Reason interacts with faith, and although there is tension between the attitudes of inquiry and commitment, or of doubt and faith, they are not mutually exclusive. This cognitive component of religion is the topic of the next chapter; our purpose here has been to suggest that it need not conflict with the necessity of personal involvement.

---

32. See, e.g., M. Holmes Hartshorne, *The Faith to Doubt* (Englewood Cliffs, N.J.: Prentice-Hall PB, 1963).

III. REVELATION AND UNIQUENESS

Another distinctive feature of the Western religious tradition is its dependence on unique revelatory events in history; God is believed to have revealed himself at particular times and places. Neo-orthodoxy has asserted that religious knowledge is made possible only by God's initiative in disclosing himself to man; such a source of knowledge obviously has no parallel in science. We will submit, however, that all revelatory events involve both God and man, and therefore there is no uninterpreted revelation. Moreover, revelation is recognized precisely by its ability to illuminate present experience. The God who acted at specific times is the same God who created the general structures of life and who is encountered in the present. The relation of the particular to the general for the theologian differs from that for either the scientist or the historian, but common elements are present.

1. Revelation and Interpretation

In earlier chapters the centrality of revelation in the Middle Ages and Reformation, and its virtual abandonment in the Enlightenment and nineteenth-century modernism, was traced. We outlined Karl Barth's attempt to recover the primacy of revelation without denying the results of critical biblical scholarship. In liberalism, on the other hand, the human element in the reception and interpretation of revelation received stress. A number of recent authors have presented a concept of revelation that combines insights from both neo-orthodoxy and liberalism, representing a position somewhere between the Barthians and the liberals of the 1930's, along the following lines.

Revelation occurred in *historic events involving both God and man.* On the human side, these events represent man's experience of God at crucial points in his history. On the divine side, they represent God's action in revealing himself to man, taking the initiative in the life of individuals and communities. Human experience and divine self-disclosure are then two sides of the same event. In the history of Israel, God was revealed in events and in the prophetic interpretation of them in the light of the prophet's religious experience—for example, a military victory or defeat was

seen in relation to God's purposes. The Christian community finds
God revealed in the career and person of Christ, in which again
divine *and* human activity were combined. Revelation, says Archbishop Temple, occurs in events together with their interpretation.[33]

In this view the locus of God's action was not the dictation of
an inerrant book, or the transmission of infallible doctrines, but
events in the lives of individuals and communities. The Bible
itself is a purely human record about these revelatory events. The
opinions of its authors were sometimes partial and limited, influenced by the thought-forms of their day. Divine revelation and
human response were always interwoven; the God-given encounter
was experienced, interpreted, and reported by fallible men. If
scripture is part of human history, it can be examined by all the
methods of historical and literary scholarship; but if it is also a
record of events in which God acted, it can be an instrument of
God's continuing purposes. For confrontation with the Bible encourages *our present experience of God*; God speaks to us through
it, since we are part of the same continuing drama. If revelation
means God's self-disclosure, he can be known as the living God
only in the present. Revelation is fulfilled in the activity of God
in present experience, which has traditionally been represented
by the concept of the Holy Spirit.

Because revelation leads to a new relationship to God, it is
inseparable from the *reorientation* and *reconciliation* referred to
earlier. In confrontation with Christ, man comes to a new understanding of God and also of himself and what is required of him.
Man accepts not a body of information but God's love and forgiveness as well as judgment; there can be no knowledge of God unless
we ourselves are involved. Revelation is not a system of divine
propositions, a package of doctrines which man could possess
apart from his own experience of God. "The transfer of faith from
the dimension of personal encounter into the dimension of factual
instruction," writes Brunner, "is the great tragedy in the history
of Christianity."[34]

---

33. William Temple, *Nature, Man and God* (London: Macmillan and Co.,
Ltd., 1934), pp. 313f. On contemporary interpretations of revelation, see Daniel Williams, *What Present-Day Theologians are Thinking* (New York: Harper
and Brothers, 1952), Chap. 2; John Baillie, *The Idea of Revelation in Recent
Thought* (New York: Columbia University Press, 1956, PB).

34. Emil Brunner, *The Christian Doctrine of God* (Philadelphia: Westminster Press, 1950), p. 54.

Revelation also helps man to *understand his life today*. In general, the facts of experience do not simply organize themselves; one needs categories of interpretation and crucial ideas in terms of which they can be organized. A nation interprets its present experience in terms of key events in its past; America sees the meaning of its contemporary decisions in the light of the Declaration of Independence. In an individual relationship to a friend, a crisis may provide clues in terms of which other actions can be understood. For the Christian community, the life of Christ is such a key event which illuminates the rest of experience and helps us understand ourselves and what has happened to us. Here is H. Richard Niebuhr's definition of revelation:

> Revelation means for us that part of our inner history which illuminates the rest of it and which is itself intelligible. Sometimes when we read a difficult book, seeking to follow a complicated argument, we come across a luminous sentence from which we can go forward and backward and so attain some understanding of the whole. Revelation is like that. . . . The special occasion to which we appeal in the Christian church is called Jesus Christ in whom we see the righteousness of God, his power and his wisdom. But from that special occasion we derive the concepts which make possible the elucidation of all the events in our history. Revelation means this intelligible event which makes all other events intelligible.[35]

The view of revelation we have presented has two distinctive features. First, in all aspects of revelation both God and man are involved; there is *no uninterpreted revelation*. Even the crucial historical events of the past, which might seem to constitute the "objective" aspect of revelation, cannot be divorced from human interpretation, past and present. The contribution of the knower cannot be ignored here, any more than in other areas of inquiry. This leads directly to the second point: any discussion of revelation must refer to *both past and present*. Though the revelatory events are in the past, they can be considered only in relation to the knower in the present, that is, to problems of historical interpretation, religious experience, and self-understanding today.

2. *Revelation and Human Experience*

We thus agree with neo-orthodoxy on the importance of revelation, but we diverge by holding that we cannot avoid viewing it

---

35. Niebuhr, *The Meaning of Revelation*, p. 93. Used by permission of The Macmillan Company.

from the standpoint of *man's contemporary experience.* A past
event is accepted as revelatory in part because it illuminates man's
present individual and communal existence. The God who reveals
himself in history is also the God who created the structures of the
world and is active in man's present experience, and he is self-
consistent. In theological terms, the same God is Redeemer and
Creator; grace is the fulfillment of the natural rather than its
destruction. Temple puts it thus:

> Unless all existence is a medium of revelation, no particular revelation
> is possible. . . . It is necessary to stress with all possible emphasis this
> universal quality of revelation in general before going on to discuss
> the various modes of particular revelation; for the latter, if detached
> from the former, loses its root in the rational coherence of the world
> and consequently becomes itself a superstition and a fruitful source of
> superstitions.[36]

One of the earliest theological formulations of this close link
between revelation and general experience was the affirmation
that the principle and purpose embodied in Christ was also the
principle and purpose of the universe, the *Logos* (as in the opening verse of the Gospel of John, usually translated: "In the beginning was the *Word*"). The God revealed in Christ is at the same
time the Lord of all things; there is no discontinuity in his operations. The cross reveals God's *universal* love, everywhere expressed
though not everywhere recognized. The power of reconciliation in
Christ's life is the power of reconciliation in all human life. The
special event enables us to see what is universally present.

Is the relationship of the *particular* to the *general* in theology
at all similar to that in either history or science? It must be said
first that the theologian is not interested in unique events for their
own sake (as the historian is), nor as instances of lawful patterns
(as the scientist is), but rather as situations in which God revealed
himself. But because he looks at particular events the theologian
faces problems not unlike those of the historian. In the last chapter
it was concluded that the historian uses many resources, including
implicit generalizations concerning human nature and behavior,
though these are not stated apart from particular narratives. We
would propose that the theologian, attempting to portray human
and divine activity, perhaps follows a somewhat similar procedure,

36. Temple, *Nature, Man and God,* p. 306. Used by permission of The
Macmillan Company.

that is, he focuses on the particular but implicitly draws from the general—the knowledge of God from religious experience and the structure of creation, the lives of saints and prophets, and so forth. And in both cases the particular event is seen *as part of a configuration*; the interpretive context and the historical context are all-important. The significance of an event—for example, Israel's defeat by Assyria—was understood by the prophets in relation to the previous history of the covenant community as well as the prophets' own experience of God. Or again, would Christ have been accepted as Messiah by his disciples if there had not been present beforehand a context of historical expectations and interpretive categories, and if afterward Pentecost and the continuing experience of the Holy Spirit had not transformed their lives? A particular event is not revelatory as an isolated occurrence but as part of a pattern, a revelatory gestalt.

It might be argued that the total revelatory configuration is *absolutely unique*. The historian, after all, is studying human actions which, if not recurrent, are at least similar to other human actions; but the theologian, some would say, is dealing with events for which there are no precedents at all. In reply we would submit that an absolutely unique event could not be spoken of in human language, and no analogies or models could be used. A purely "idiographic" approach would be as limited in theology as it was found to be in history. Furthermore, it appears that in interpreting revelatory events the theologian inevitably draws from a wider range of experience and history. This does not mean that he forgets about particular events, as occurs in natural theology (which takes, as it were, a more "nomothetic" approach). It is the interaction of the particular and the general, the idiographic and the nomothetic, which we are defending.

Though it starts from specific events, theology has a *concern for universality* which is in some respects more reminiscent of science than of history.[37] The theologian does not stop with the particular, as the historian does, for what he finds revealed is a God who is Lord of all. It is precisely the universal import of the unique that is significant for him. Revelation is the decisive key to the meaning of human existence; it provides interpretive categories relevant to all life situations. Moreover, part of the theological

---

37. See A. Roy Eckardt, "A Note on Theological Procedure," *Journal of Bible and Religion*, Vol. 29 (1961), 313.

task is the systematic exploration of the implications of revelation; religious beliefs have the broadest possible scope in the sense that they provide a coherent account of all phases of reality. Here the relation of the particular to the general is somewhat like that in science, though the theologian is not seeking laws of a scientific sort, and he assuredly does not claim that revelatory events could have been predicted. Nor does he, like the seientist, leave the particular behind when the general is reached, for science loses the unique in abstracting its recurrent features. None of the parallels should be pressed too far, because both the uniqueness and the universal significance of revelatory events consist in the fact that it is God who is revealed in them.

3. The Problem of Particularity

Christianity has always faced "the scandal of particularity" in attaching special significance to certain historical events. One of the problems raised thereby is the relation of Christianity to *other religions*. There are those who assert that there is no knowledge of God except through Christ or that there is no salvation outside the church. Such assertions of superiority have in the past led to dogmatism and intolerance, and they always run the danger of spiritual pride; exclusive claims for one's own theology or church are ruled out if one believes that every human perspective and institution stands under God's judgment.

At the opposite extreme are statements that *all religions are essentially the same*. This position overlooks significant differences on which members of other religions would rightly insist. We have, for example, noted the belief of Western religions that history is the primary arena of God's activity, as against the nonhistorical character of Eastern religions. Again, the world religions do not diagnose man's dilemma in the same way. For Buddhism and Hinduism it is the self as such which is the problem, and man should escape the self by detachment from all desires and emotions, or by loss of individuality in absorption in the divine; for Christianity, however, self-centeredness rather than selfhood itself is the problem, and love toward God and man is the true fulfillment of individuality. Because of these significant differences in their basic concepts, one simply cannot state that all religions are identical.

The only way to give recognition to the distinctiveness of Christianity without indulging in defensive claims of superiority is to adopt *a confessional attitude*, saying: this is what has happened in our lives, and this is how things look from where we stand. Such an approach recognizes the relativism and finitude of every human viewpoint and maintains the existential stance of faith itself. H. Richard Niebuhr has written at length on the dangers of self-justification and defensiveness, and he commends and exemplifies such confessionalism:

> Such theology in the Christian church cannot, it is evident, be an offensive or defensive enterprise which undertakes to prove the superiority of Christian faith to all other faiths; but it can be a confessional theology which carries on the work of self-criticism and self-knowledge in the church. . . . We can proceed only by stating in simple confessional form what has happened to us in our community, how we came to believe, how we reason about things and what we see from our point of view. Whenever the revelation idea is used to justify the church's claim to superior knowledge or some other excellence, revelation is necessarily identified with something that the church can possess. Such possessed revelation must be a static thing and under the human control of the Christian community—a book, a creed, or a set of doctrines. It cannot be revelation in act whereby the church itself is convicted of its poverty, its sin and misery before God. Furthermore, it cannot be the revelation of a living God. . . . We are enabled to see why we can speak of revelation only in connection with our own history, without affirming or denying its reality in the history of other communities into whose inner life we cannot penetrate without abandoning ourselves and our community.[38]

We can only say that we have made a mess of things, but are moved to start again because of events symbolized by a cross; one who saw his role as "suffering servant" disclosed a new possibility for our lives, a new pattern of human existence before God and man.

Let us recall, finally, that revelatory events are *in history as interpreted*. The meaning of a historical event is not contained in the bare happening, but in the way it is related to other events, which can be represented only in interpretive categories. Any attempt to identify revelation with "objective facts" faces great difficulties; for our only records about Christ (except brief references by Jewish and Roman historians) were written a generation later by his devoted disciples and obviously reflect their viewpoint.

---

38. Niebuhr, *The Meaning of Revelation*, pp. 18, 41, 82. Used by permission of The Macmillan Company.

Besides, since many of Christ's contemporaries—from Pontius Pilate and Caiaphas on down—met him and rejected him, it is clear that revelation does not consist simply in historical details alone. Christians may welcome all the factual evidence that historical research can disclose about the life of Christ, but they cannot expect its claims to be "objectively" proven by such research. Revelation lies in interpreted history which involves subject as well as object. Only if we find God in the present do we find him in the past.

Yet even after adopting a confessional attitude and acknowledging the relativism of historical judgments and the impossibility of proving revelation, the Christian must insist that his affirmations are *not purely subjective* or arbitrary. Revelation starts from interpreted *events* and the experience of a community, not from private preferences. Universal intent is implied in the assertion that this set of beliefs makes more sense of all the evidence than any other. There are, of course, grave dangers in any missionary or evangelistic undertaking; but if a person has made a genuine effort to understand another man's religious tradition, and recognizes that it embodies much that is valid, and that he himself does not possess any final truth, it is surely then legitimate for him to want to share what has happened in his life. He can express his convictions in word and deed without forcing them on the other person or violating his integrity, for he believes that he worships the God of all men, not his own private deity. Both particularity and universality are present in biblical religion, and neither can be ignored.

IV. INTERIM CONCLUSIONS

Our final conclusions concerning the comparison of methods in science and religion must await the next chapter. But we can make an interim assessment of where things stand at this point, using the three broad classifications of Chapter 5: "Contrasts," "Parallels," and "Derivations." The *"Derivations"* of religion from science, in the tradition of *natural theology*, bear little resemblance to what actually goes on in the religious community. In the biblical understanding, God acts primarily though not exclusively in the sphere of the personal; he can reveal himself more adequately through the lives of individuals and communities, and through the life of

Christ, than through the order of nature. Natural theology does not lead to the personal involvement and dependence on revelatory events which characterize the Western religious tradition. (The specific arguments of recent natural theology will of course have to be examined in detail from the scientific side in Part Three).

Between "*Contrasts*" and "*Parallels*," however, the evidence at this stage seems fairly evenly matched. In Section I we followed the pattern of liberal theology in looking for parallels, which we found in the roles of experience and interpretation, individual and community, analogy and model, and so forth. In Section II, personal involvement in religion appeared at first to constitute a major contrast, as existentialists claim; but we ended by portraying it as a difference in emphasis rather than an absolute dichotomy. We suggested that faith and reason (or commitment and inquiry) are not mutually exclusive, though we have yet to explore the role of reason. Next, revelation as God's initiative in history was seen to be without parallel in science, as neo-orthodoxy insists. Yet we found that revelation is always humanly interpreted in the context of man's total life, and it in turn illuminates present experience; hence particularity must not be stressed at the expense of universality. At this point in the argument we have noted both similarities and differences in comparing science and religion. But the final problem yet remains, and on it depends the outcome. Is there anything in religion comparable to "empirical verification" or even "intersubjective testability" in science? Are the functions of science and religion totally different, as many linguistic analysts hold, or do they share a common dedication to truth?

9

The Languages
of Science and Religion

In the previous chapter it was suggested that religion, like
science, can be thought of as having an experiential and an interpretive component. The distinctive character of personal involvement and revelatory events was described; but it was maintained
that neither religious faith nor revelation is divorced from interpretive concepts and cognitive beliefs. We must now ask whether
there are any criteria in religion, as there are in science, for testing these interpretations. Section I, "Verification and Religious
Language," outlines recent treatments of this question by philosophers: first the positivist's "verification principle," according to
which scientific language is normative and all religious statements
are dismissed as meaningless; then the linguistic analyst's understanding of the diverse uses of language, according to which
religious language serves legitimate but predominantly noncognitive functions. We will contend that these functions presuppose
religious beliefs which are intended as assertions about reality.
In Section II, "The Evaluation of Religious Beliefs," the applicability of criteria of coherence, comprehensiveness, and relevance
to evidence is discussed. Naturalistic interpretations of religion
are criticized in terms of these criteria. The limitations on any

process of evaluation in religion are also indicated; and the dangers in identifying religious beliefs with any metaphysical system are pointed out. A final section summarizes our conclusions about the parallels between the methods of science and religion.

I. VERIFICATION AND RELIGIOUS LANGUAGE

The relation of science and religion has been extensively debated by recent philosophers, but the dispute can only be understood in the light of the discussion of "verifiability" in earlier decades. For this reason we will present in greater detail the logical positivist position to which Chapters 5 and 6 have alluded, especially the requirement of "verification by sense-data" and the claim that religious propositions are meaningless. We then trace the rise of linguistic analysis, wherein the diversity of functions of language in human life is recognized. We will see that religious language is now said to recommend a way of life, or to evoke and express worship and self-commitment—functions very different from those of science, but nonetheless significant. We will suggest, however, that in addition religious language often includes, and always pre-supposes, cognitive assertions and religious beliefs. Hence the question of verification cannot be completely dismissed, even though the earlier formulations of it are unacceptable. Several recent attempts to retain this cognitive component of religion are noted.

1. Verification by Sense-Data (Logical Positivism)

In the writings of the "Vienna Circle" in the 1930's, and in such presentations as A. J. Ayer's *Language, Truth and Logic*, a particular view of scientific discourse was taken as the norm for all language, and religious language was considered neither true nor false but cognitively "meaningless." Logical positivism represented a revival of extreme empiricism combined with interest in formal logic. It was asserted that the only meaningful statements are (a) empirical propositions verifiable by sense-experience ("it is now raining outside") or (b) formal definitions, tautologies, and linguistic conventions ("a triangle has three sides").[1]

---

1. See, e.g., Herbert Feigl, "Logical Empiricism," in Feigl and Sellars, eds., *Readings*; Gustav Bergmann, *The Metaphysics of Logical Positivism* (New York: Longmans, Green & Co., Inc., 1954), Chap. 1; Rudolph Carnap, *Philosophy and Logical Syntax* (London: Routledge & Kegan Paul, Ltd., 1935).

This *"verification principle"* turned out to be difficult to formulate precisely. A "strong" form stated that apart from definitions all meaningful statements must be at least potentially capable of *conclusive* verification. But this excluded universal statements and scientific laws, so it was modified to a weaker version: statements are acceptable which can be adjudged more or less *probable* because of some possible sense-data; that is, there must be observations relevant to the determination of their truth or falsity. The important question to ask concerning any statement is: what sensory evidence would count for or against it? What difference would be observable if the statement were true? A meaningful sentence was said to be logically equivalent to—and hence must be translatable into—sentences about procedures for making observations.

Propositions that are not sensibly verifiable were said to be *meaningless.* Most traditional assertions of philosophy, and all those in metaphysics, ethics, and theology were held to be neither true nor false, but vacuous "pseudostatements" devoid of any cognitive significance. Propositions that are not empirically verifiable assert nothing and have no factual content; they are expressions of personal preference and subjective feeling. Like laughter, they serve an expressive but not a referential function. "Moral" statements ("murder is wrong") are really only indications of individual taste ("I dislike spinach and I dislike murder") or rhetorical devices aimed at persuading or enjoining ("keep smiling and don't murder"). Ayer wrote: "In every case in which one would commonly be said to be making an ethical judgment, the function of the relevant ethical word is purely 'emotive.' It is used to express feelings about certain objects, but not to make any assertion about them."[2] Moreover, "all utterances about the nature of God are nonsensical"; hence atheism is just as meaningless as theism.

It should be noted that here *philosophy* supposedly does not judge the truth or falsity of particular statements, the investigation of which is the task of the various sciences; its job is rather to delineate the acceptable forms of statements in general, to clarify the logic and language of the sciences, and to analyze the structure of legitimate propositions. The influence of logical positivism has in some ways been beneficial, particularly in fostering greater rigor in the use of language. It has also led to caution

---

2. Ayer, *Language, Truth and Logic,* p. 108.

about claiming too much for the metaphysical implications of scientific discoveries. Moreover, the dogmatism of the early positivists gave way to self-criticism, and significant modifications arose from within the movement itself. We can indicate three kinds of criticisms which logical positivism faced.

First, *the status of the verification principle itself* is problematic. How should one classify the central proposition: "Only verifiable statements and definitions have meaning"? This proposition is not itself scientifically verifiable by sense-data. It is not an empirical generalization formulated after exhaustive study of individual metaphysical statements; and "meaninglessness" is hardly an observable property. Is it then a definition? But definitions make no factual assertion about the way things are; they are either tautologous or arbitrary. Why not adopt some other definition of "meaning"? Moreover, branding a proposition "meaningless" derives much of its force from the usual derogatory connotations of the word ("unintelligible," "nonsense"); "meaningful" is simply not synonymous with "empirically verifiable." Critics called this "persuasive definition,"[3] because it used loaded terms to make the distinction between empirical and nonempirical sentences.

If *the verification principle* is itself neither verifiable nor simply a definition, the only possibility left, by its own criteria, is that it is an emotive statement, an expression of taste or feeling. The central principle of logical positivism thus appears to undermine its own status. The dilemma can be escaped only at the price of consistency. Ayer himself later spoke of the principle as "a definition, but not an arbitrary one,"[4] and other authors called it a "recommendation" or "a program for action." But these terms introduce new categories of meaningful statement, which are forbidden by the principle itself—whose intent is precisely to rule out any third classification. A "recommendation" is surely a normative proposal with criteria of importance presupposed—unless it is merely an expression of personal preference. To its critics, the procedure seems rather like making up the rules in order to disqualify an opponent before the game starts. The principle appears to be an arbitrary restriction, a decree that only scientific language is respectable. Perennial problems are dismissed "wholesale," without detailed discussion of them individually.

---

3. Charles Stevenson, "Persuasive Definitions," *Mind*, Vol. 47 (1938), 339.
4. Ayer, *Language, Truth and Logic*, p. 16 (preface to 2nd ed.).

Second, the positivist's *overemphasis on sense-data* has been criticized. In Chapter 6 we listed some difficulties in the view that scientific theories are summaries of sense-data, and stated that sense-experience is by no means a simple "given" which can be the indubitable starting point of certainty; it is already conceptually organized and "theory-laden." We pointed to the complex interaction of experience and interpretation, and the use of abstract mental constructions far removed from observation. We maintained that no scientific theory is "empirically verified"; rather, whole constellations of concepts and data are contextually tested in networks, with empirical and rational criteria employed concurrently. None of the attempts to translate scientific statements into a "neutral observation language" were successful. Later empiricists themselves recognized that strict operationalism could not account for the role of concepts and theories in science.[5] We have suggested that this exclusive emphasis on sense-data results in even more serious problems in other fields. The positivist is primarily interested in the extension of reliable empirical knowledge, but this commendable motive is expressed in an oversimplified understanding of objectivity and an undue fear of the role of the subject. All phases of subjectivity are held to be devoid of cognitive content, and significant human experience is narrowed to sense-experience.

This leads to a third difficulty: though logical positivism rejects all metaphysical questions as meaningless, it has *an implied metaphysics* of its own. It claims to deal only with questions of language, yet it makes covert and uncritical ontological assumptions. H. J. Paton comments: "It is no new thing to find men who are prepared to believe only in what they can see and touch or in what can be proved by scientific method. It is not easy to see why it becomes a more serious argument simply because it appears in a linguistic dress."[6] Some positivists have a phenomenalistic metaphysics wherein all statements are to be reduced to statements about sense-data. The vehemence of the positivist's attack on theology and the unproven assumption that all inquiry must conform to a particular image of science perhaps indicate that these implicit commitments function as an alternative world-view rather than as neutral instruments for the clarification of language.

5 E.g., Carl Hempel, *Fundamentals of Concept Formation in the Empirical Sciences* (Chicago: University of Chicago Press, 1952).

6. H. J. Paton, *The Modern Predicament* (New York: The Macmillan Co., 1955), p. 42.

The verification principle, if strictly applied, *eliminates from serious discussion* whole areas of human experience, thought, and language. Ethical decisions are left to arbitrary and irrational preference or cultural mores, and the existence of God is ruled out from the start; problems relevant to man's daily life are neglected. The critics of logical positivism point out that its excessive caution and fear of error restricted inquiry to those questions in which certainty (or high probability) is possible. In order to ensure that one does not say something erroneous, one ends by excluding the most significant questions. Awareness of such difficulties on the part of the philosophical community itself contributed to the adoption of a new approach in which empirical verification is no longer taken as the criterion of meaning.

2. The Diverse Uses of Language (Linguistic Analysis)

In linguistic analysis, which is dominant in British and American philosophy today, the new motto runs: "Don't ask about the meaning of a statement, ask about its use." What are people doing when they make a particular type of statement? Already in Wittgenstein's later writings the wide *diversity of functions of language* (or "language games," as he called them) was described. The positivist had assumed that only sentences reporting empirical facts were cognitively important; therefore scientific statements were taken as the model of all significant discourse. But in linguistic analysis in the 1940's it was recognized, as J. O. Urmson puts it, that "language has many tasks and many levels: we may not be trying to describe the world, and when we do we may do it in radically different ways not reducible to each other."[7] The value of an explanation depends on what one wants to do with it. Since different languages reflect different interests—artistic, moral, religious, scientific—each field must use the approach it finds most appropriate for its purposes. It was asserted that "every type of language has its own logic."

Moreover, concern about *the uses of language* brought renewed interest in the social context, which we have often noted in this volume. The essentially social character of language, the ways in which specific communities employ statements, and the varying roles of language in the affairs of men have received extensive

---

7. Urmson, *Philosophical Analysis*, p. 180; see also G. J. Warnock, *English Philosophy Since 1900* (London: Oxford University Press, 1958; PB).

examination. If "the meaning of language is its use," then the context must be taken into account, and analysis must deal with the functioning of language in accomplishing specific human purposes. In devoting attention to the users of statements, prominence was given to the relation of language to the activity of the subject. Philosophers wrote many articles analyzing the logic embodied in sample sentences illustrating the accepted usage of a term in ordinary discourse. Thus where positivism took a narrow view of science and sought the elimination of religion, linguistic analysis considers both science and religion as legitimate enterprises—but it usually ends by representing them as totally unrelated to each other. Statements in both science and religion are to be judged not for their truth but for their usefulness in accomplishing their respective functions.

In the case of science, most (though not all) linguistic analysts advocate *the "instrumentalist" view of scientific theories* described in Chapter 6. The question of whether electrons exist is bypassed in favor of asking how the word "electron" functions in the activity of the scientific community. The most common interpretations depict *prediction* and *control* as the main goals of science; theories are conceived to be primarily calculating devices for accurate prediction and practical tools for technical control. It will be recalled that we criticized this instrumentalist view for ignoring the question of the relation of theories to reality. We maintained that the goal of science is to understand as well as to control. Most scientists, we said, view theories not as useful fictions but as attempts to represent the world.

The functions of religious language, according to linguistic analysts, are very different from those of scientific language. We look first at the contention that religious propositions are neither true nor false, but are *recommendations of a way of life.* For Braithwaite "the primary use of religious assertions is to announce allegiance to a set of moral principles."[8] The function of religion is *moral*; but it is not "merely emotive," for it expresses the intention to act in specific ways. Religious statements, he holds, are "declara-

---

8. R. B. Braithwaite, *An Empiricist's View of the Nature of Religious Belief* (Cambridge: Cambridge University Press, 1955), p. 19. In Paul van Buren, *The Secular Meaning of the Gospel* (New York: The Macmillan Company, 1963), the empirical content of Christianity is said to include historical perspectives and attitudes toward human existence as well as ethical recommendations.

tions of commitment to a way of life," or ways of "subscribing to a policy of action"—in the Christian case, an intention to act with love. Particular "stories," such as the life of Christ, have the function of evoking the proper ethical attitudes; they are psychologically effective in encouraging self-commitment and in inspiring people to adopt policies associated with the stories, whether or not the latter are believed to be true. "Indeed," Braithwaite writes, "a story may provide better support for a long-range policy of action if it contains inconsistencies."[9] The stories are useful fictions which are not asserted or believed, but are used as a source of inspiration to action. Religion serves a valuable function without making any assertions about reality. In a similar vein, many sociologists have spoken of religious ideas as useful fictions accomplishing important social purposes, such as the undergirding of value systems that provide social cohesion and stability.

Or again, religious statements are said to have *an exclusively existential use*, related only to man's life-and-death problems and the formation of his attitudes and orientations.[10] "Faith provides no new knowledge, but a new existence," we are told. Religious statements must never be considered apart from the questions of "ultimate concern" around which personal life is organized. Their influence on attitudes is varied; some statements are reassuring, helping the individual face an unknown future; others are challenging, stirring him to courage; still others are judging, engendering humility and penitence. But on this reading they all serve functions which can be described in terms of man's inner life and orientation.

Other authors have portrayed a more distinctively religious function of language in *the expression and evocation of worship*. Language arises from the activity of a community and cannot be divorced from the purposes for which it is employed; religious language not only grows out of, but serves to bring about, the response of worship. Its job is "praising God, not describing him." Religious language also furthers personal *religious experience*. "It points hearer and speaker alike back to the experiential source in which it is rooted." Its distinctiveness is its ability to engender religious attitudes and to lead others to fresh experience.

---

9. *Ibid.*, p. 29.
10. E.g., D. M. MacKinnon, "Death," in Antony Flew and Alasdair Mac-Intyre, eds., *New Essays in Philosophical Theology* (London: SCM Press, 1955; Macmillan PB).

The theologian Ian Ramsey finds that the distinctive function of
religious language is *the evocation of commitment*. Its logical
structure is similar to that of statements about dominant personal
loyalties: a man's devotion to his nation, a captain's loyalty to his
ship, a man's love for his wife. Religious commitment is more
total, and is evoked by the powerful symbols and images to which
we respond:

> So we see religious commitment as a *total* commitment to the *whole*
> universe, something in relation to which argument has only a very
> odd function, its purpose being to tell such a tale as evokes the "in-
> sight," the "discernment" from which commitment follows as a re-
> sponse.... So our conclusion is that for the religious man "God" is
> a key word, an irreducible posit, an ultimate of explanation expres-
> sive of the kind of *commitment* he professes.[11]

Paul Holmer draws an absolute contrast between the language *of*
religion (in which he includes theology) and disinterested language *about* religion, which can be a branch of objective scientific
knowledge. He translates familiar existentialist themes into the
terminology of language analysis. The language of religion an-
nounces a commitment and "proposes a new and radical passion
by which to live our lives." It "has a different satisfaction in view
than that provided by cognition." Holmer defines the function of
religion in these phrases:

> The test of a sound moral and religious passion is whether it gives
> confidence and overcomes despair in the presence of the multitude
> of distractions the world provides.... The point of the religious dis-
> course is in part served when it both suggests and testifies to a human
> life dominated and unified by a master ethico-religious passion....
> Just as the language of the lover needs no scientific explanation and
> no certification outside of the immediate passion, so the language of
> faith earns its own way and has its own meaning and use.[12]

In a similar vein, Zuurdeeg[13] says that religion uses *the language
of conviction*. A man's convictions, around which his life is organized, are intimately bound up with his own self-appraisal, and

    11. Ian Ramsey, *Religious Language* (London: SCM Press, 1957; Macmillan
PB), pp. 37, 47.
    12. Paul Holmer, "Scientific Language and the Language of Religion," re-
printed from *Journal for the Scientific Study of Religion*, Vol. 1, No. 1 (1961),
47, 53.
    13. Willem Zuurdeeg, *An Analytical Philosophy of Religion* (Nashville:
Abingdon Press, 1958).

are constitutive of selfhood. Zuurdeeg writes that the object of conviction is "real to the speaker," but that beyond this we cannot say anything about its validity.

3. Cognitive and Noncognitive Functions in Religion

The theologian has reason to be grateful to the linguistic analyst. Religion is once again a respectable topic for philosophers to deliberate. Moreover, *the "functional" view of language* encourages a close examination of what language-using communities are actually doing. We noted in Chapter 6 that "instrumentalists" have been more sensitive than positivists to the diversity of procedures and thought-processes which scientists employ. In religion the linguistic analysts have taken cognizance of the context of the worshiping community; such functions as ethical dedication, existential orientation, worship, and self-commitment are indeed central in religion, as we saw in the preceding chapter. The positivist's attempt to make science the norm for all discourse has been repudiated.

In addition, this approach provides a ready solution to any issue between *science and religion*: the two fields cannot possibly compete or conflict, since they serve *totally different functions*. A hammer will not be replaced by even the best of saws, since they are used to perform dissimilar tasks. When religion is doing its proper job it has nothing to fear from science, which does a different job. A clear-cut separation is achieved, without any overlap; the function of scientific language is prediction and control, whereas that of religious language is worship and life-orientation. Each can achieve its own purposes in its own way. We will in future chapters give a number of examples of the fruitful employment of the "two-language" approach—for instance, in the analysis of "creation" and "evolution."

There is, however, a serious difficulty in these instrumentalist interpretations of religion, as a number of linguistic analysts have recognized: all *cognitive functions* of religious language are dismissed. All the functions outlined above are essentially noncognitive, and questions of truth and falsity are not raised; we are left with a plurality of unrelated languages. Religious beliefs are viewed as instrumental to other goals. But surely in some religious discourse, claims about reality are proffered. If one held, with Braithwaite, that religious "stories" are fictional, they would lose the very power to produce moral action for which he commends them. On his view one could belong to several religions at once, since one does not have to believe any of them. We would suggest, in reply, that ethical principles are always closely linked to *beliefs* about the nature of reality; the recommendation of a way of life implies that the universe is of such a character that this way of life is appropriate.

Again, the "language of worship" includes *assertions about what one worships*. Commitment presupposes some understanding of that to which one commits himself. We must ask, in other words, about the relation of religious language to the object of worship and commitment, and not simply to the subjects who use it. Inquiry must be directed to the validity of the object of ultimate concern, as well as to the function of ultimate concern in human life. If people did not accept the truth-claims of religion, its varied "uses" would disappear, for religious language is referential in intent. And in the absence of all cognitive elements, commitment would be arbitrary caprice. Religion is never merely intellectual assent, but it always presupposes the latter. Crombie writes:

> Christianity, as a human activity, involves much more than simply believing certain propositions about matters of fact, such as that there is a God, that He created this world, that He is our judge. But it does involve believing these things, and this believing is, in a sense, fundamental; not that it matters more than the other things that a Christian does, but that it is presupposed in the other things that he does.[14]

Despite the differences in their languages, science and religion share a common *dedication to truth* and *desire to understand*. The questions asked in the two fields are radically different, but both make cognitive claims, and both are realistic in intent. In the terminology of Chapter 6, we seek in religion, as in science, a *critical realism* which preserves what is valid in both positivism and linguistic analysis, without being restricted to "summaries of sense-data," on the one hand, or "useful fictions," on the other. The task of evaluating the cognitive claims of religion cannot be escaped, even though no simple process of "empirical verification" is applicable. In theology, in particular, the status of religious beliefs as well as their function must be investigated.

---

14. Ian Crombie, "The Possibility of Theological Statements," in Basil Mitchell, ed., *Faith and Logic* (Boston: The Beacon Press, 1957), p. 31.

4. Theism and Verifiability

Can *the cognitive functions* of religious language be defended? If we reject the positivist's identification of cognitive significance with strict empirical verifiability, can we specify other types of cognitive functions that religion performs? We will indicate the efforts of several philosophers to reinterpret and broaden rather than completely abandon the idea of verification in religion.

A first step toward granting *a limited cognitive* function to religious statements is evident in John Wisdom's famous essay, *Gods*; he grants that religious statements are experimentally unverifiable, and yet holds that they have an objective reference and not a purely subjective one: their function is *to direct attention to patterns in the facts*. Religious language is not just emotive, for religious attitudes influence interpretations and suggest "models with which to 'get the hang of' the patterns in the flux of experience":

> It is possible to have before one's eyes all the items of a pattern and still miss the pattern. . . . And if we say as we did at the beginning that when a difference as to the existence of a God is not one as to future happenings then it is not experimental and therefore not as to facts, we must not forthwith assume that there is no right and wrong about it, nor rationality or irrationality, no appropriateness or inappropriateness, no procedure which tends to settle it, nor even that this procedure is in no sense a discovery of new facts. After all even in science this is not so.[15]

Religious beliefs are not mere matters of feeling, since "reasons for or against them may be offered." Wisdom compares them with legal decisions in which the judge makes no simple logical deduction, yet his decisions are not arbitrary. Religious discourse involves drawing attention to connections, making analogies, comparing alternative interpretations, pointing out patterns, and portraying the features that fit the theistic model. Other authors have spoken of the realization of a sense of contingency as "a new way of seeing familiar facts," comparable to the sudden realization of beauty in a landscape, or recognition that a pattern of lines on paper represents a three-dimensional cube. Such an "attention-directing"

15. John Wisdom, "Gods," *Proceedings of the Aristotelian Society*, Vol. 45 (1944); reprinted in his *Philosophy and Psychoanalysis* (Oxford: Basil Blackwell, Ltd., 1953), pp. 153, 159.

function is related to empirical evidence, but no direct verification is expected.

Might one at least specify events whose occurrence would show religious assertions to be *false?* In Chapter 6 we noted Popper's reformulation of the verification principle. For a statement to have meaning, he insisted, it must be compatible with some states of affairs and not with others; and if a hypothesis is to be tested, there must be some conceivable evidence whose occurrence would *falsify* it, or at least count against it. Antony Flew[16] recently initiated an interesting debate by stating that religious assertions are *unfalsifiable*; they are so formulated that no possible evidence could count against them. The Christian may say that "God loves his children," but there is no conceivable situation with which the statement is incompatible; neither the death of children from cancer, nor the destruction of cities in earthquakes, nor any other imaginable event would be accepted by the Christian as disproof of the statement. But if there is no observable difference between "God loves his children" and "God does not love his children," the assertions are vacuous, Flew maintains.

Crombie replies that religious beliefs are *"falsifiable in principle,"* which indicates that they are not vacuous, even though in practice the relevant evidence is not available:

> Does anything count against the assertion that God is merciful? Yes, suffering. Does anything count decisively against it? No, we reply, because it is true. Could anything count decisively against it? Yes, suffering which was utterly, eternally, and irredeemably pointless. Can we then design a crucial experiment? No, because we can never see all of the picture. Two things at least are hidden from us: what goes on in the recesses of the personality of the sufferer, and what shall happen hereafter.[17]

Crombie here takes the position, developed more fully by John Hick,[18] that "verification in principle," even in "the world to come," is all we require; "to fully understand a statement I must know what a test of it would be like," even if the test cannot actually be carried out. But we would suggest that although dis-

---

16. Antony Flew, "Theology and Falsification," in Flew and MacIntyre, *New Essays,* p. 96.

17. Ian Crombie, "Theology and Falsification," in Flew and MacIntyre, *New Essays,* p. 124. Used by permission of SCM Press, Ltd.

18. John Hick, *Faith and Knowledge* (Ithaca, N.Y.: Cornell University Press, 1957).

cussion of verification "in principle" may clarify the *meaning* of a statement, it does not help us in evaluating its *truth*, which requires verification "in practice." Crombie seems to have a stronger case, therefore, when he goes on to say that the Christian "claims that in the religious life, of others if not as yet in his own, the divine love may be encountered, that the promise 'I will not fail thee nor forsake thee' is, if rightly understood, confirmed there."[19] In another essay Crombie says that religious images aid our understanding of the world: "The more we try to understand the world in the light of this image, the better our understanding of the world becomes."[20] Crombie seems to hold that religious beliefs have a cognitive function and are subject to at least some kind of testing "in practice" as well as "in principle."

Basil Mitchell[21] takes a further step in maintaining that *evidence does count* for and against religious beliefs. He holds that "pain and suffering do count against the assertion that God loves man," but they *do not count decisively* for the person who has committed himself to belief in God. Mitchell tells a parable about a man who has met a Stranger in the resistance movement during an enemy occupation; later the Stranger appears to be working for the enemy, but the man is convinced that the Stranger is really loyal. Now we may suggest that there are three considerations in the belief held by the man in Mitchell's parable: (a) positive evidence of the Stranger's loyalty (from personal encounter with him); (b) a partial "explanation" of the contrary evidence, which renders it more compatible with his belief (the Stranger may want to secure information from the enemy); and (c) the judgment that any "unexplained" contrary evidence is outweighed by the positive evidence. The third point, though not stressed by Mitchell, seems essential; for it implies that sufficient negative evidence could lead to a reversal of judgment. The total pattern of evidence of all kinds *does "count decisively."*

Perhaps *evidence bears on religious beliefs* also in this three-fold way. Purposeless suffering does "count against" God's love (as it did for Job). On the other hand, love is not totally incom-

---

19. Crombie, in Flew and MacIntyre, *New Essays*, p. 129.

20. Ian Crombie, "The Possibility of Theological Statements," in Mitchell, ed., *Faith and Logic*, p. 81.

21. Basil Mitchell, "Theology and Falsification," in Flew and MacIntyre, *New Essays*, p. 103; see Howard Burkle, "Counting Against and Counting Decisively Against," *Journal of Religion*, Vol. 44 (1964), 223.

patible with the presence of suffering (no truly loving father would
want a child brought up in a nursery with all his wishes granted
—nor would he put him in a torture chamber). But the balance of
evidence must bring in many other factors and it may eventually
change "decisively"; people do change in their religious beliefs.
There are elements of belief and unbelief in all of us. We would
submit that there is a more total process of evaluation than any
of these authors indicate; even in science, we suggested, no simple
"falsification" of theories occurs. The later phases of the "verification" debate are very different from the earlier ones, but they have
not entirely escaped the positivist's preoccupation with sense-data.
We need a broader picture of the cognitive contribution of religious beliefs and a more comprehensive process of testing than any
considered above.

II. The Evaluation of Religious Beliefs

We propose first that religious beliefs are interpretations of religious experience and revelatory events, and that they may be
evaluated by the same criteria as scientific theories: relation to
data, coherence, and comprehensiveness. Religious beliefs, however, appear to be relevant primarily to personal and social life-
situations. These criteria are then used as a basis for criticism of
Freud's naturalistic interpretation of religion. Next, the limitations
of any such evaluative process are discussed: the influence of interpretation on experience, the possibility of intersubjective testability
only within a particular religious community, and the tension between the attitudes required in worship and those in critical evaluation. Finally, the differences between religious beliefs, "world-
views," and metaphysical systems are discussed; some dangers that
arise when religion is too closely identified with metaphysics are
pointed out.

1. Criteria for Evaluating Religious Beliefs

In the first section of the previous chapter it was proposed that
religious beliefs may be analyzed along these lines: (1) The initial
data are *religious experience* and *revelatory events* in the life of a
community. (2) *Models* provide a unified and readily comprehended interpretation of experience; vivid images are also powerful
in evoking human responses. For theism in general, the dominant

model of God is taken from characteristics of personality, such as intelligence and will; for Christianity, Christ's self-giving love is the central model. (3) Interpretation by concepts allows statement in propositional form, namely *religious beliefs*, which are more formally developed and interrelated in systematic theology.

Let us consider ways in which *criteria for religious beliefs* might parallel *criteria for scientific theories*[22]—though we will have to note later some of the points at which the comparison breaks down. In Chapter 6, three criteria were presented: (1) *Relation to data.* Scientific theories must be testable through some correspondence, however remote, with public sense-data. Religious beliefs are derived from historical events as interpreted in a particular community and from religious experience as interpreted in a particular theological tradition. We indicated, for example, three aspects of the transformation from alienation to reconciliation. Obviously the crucial question is whether anything so subjective can be called "data." (2) *Coherence.* Internal consistency was defined as the absence of contradiction, coherence as the presence of connections and relations of implication between statements, together with simplicity of conceptual structure. The same criteria, we would suggest, are applicable to religious beliefs. (3) *Comprehensiveness.* Scientific theories are judged by their generality, their fruitfulness in ordering new data, their extensibility to new domains. Religious beliefs serve to interpret not only religious experience but other areas of personal life; we will argue that they also contribute to a wider interpretive framework or "world-view," though they do not constitute a complete "metaphysical system."

It was stated that science is not primarily a search for facts, but a *search for pattern*: scientific theories order experience intelligibly. Religious concepts also result in an intelligible ordering of experience, though the relevant experience is more closely related to the personal lives of subjects. It will be recalled that scientific concepts and theories can be *tested only in networks*. Webs of interdependent constructs are evaluated as total systems. The fabric of interlocking religious beliefs must also be contextually tested; ideas of God, self, society and nature are not independent. An interpretive scheme is evaluated indirectly by the convergence of many lines of

22. Cf. Ferré, *Language, Logic and God*, pp. 160–65; also Kent Bendall and Frederick Ferré, *Exploring the Logic of Faith* (New York: Association Press PB, 1962), pp. 163–81.

inquiry. In the natural sciences there are no "crucial experiments" that allow one hypothesis alone to be decisively proven or disproven; likewise there are no conclusive tests of rival social or psychological theories. There is clearly no "crucial experiment" in the evaluation of religious beliefs.

The criterion of *coherence* is also applicable. The ideas of systematic theology are interconnected; in the explication of any one concept it soon becomes necessary to refer to most of the other concepts. As a minimum, coherence requires consistency, which is a demand of human thought and a corollary of the idea of a rational Creator. The so-called "paradoxes" of theology are not contradictions, but only the statement of ideas in apparently contradictory form to serve as a challenge for further thought and clarification. If someone says "I was both pleased and displeased with the outcome," his remark calls for further discrimination concerning his reactions. The scriptural sentence "Whoever would save his life will lose it," calls for further analysis of the terms "would" and "will," "save" and "lose." Even the "paradox" of the person of Christ is not a contradiction but a challenge for further reflection.

Concerning the criterion of *extensibility*, it appears that religious beliefs have their greatest relevance in *personal and social life-situations*. Theological concepts serve to interpret not just religious experience but all events in our lives as existing persons. The Bible is a compendium of diverse life-situations *interpreted in relation to the model of a personal God*. Religious beliefs are at least partially vindicated by the organizing pattern they produce in human life. The particular data to which they direct attention are the experiences of active selves in decision. A distinctive perspective is brought to new areas of life, contributing to an understanding of oneself, man and society, love and hate, joy and tragedy, life and death. H. R. Niebuhr refers to "progressive validation in contemporary life," but makes it clear that he is always speaking of the experience of participating selves:

> The pattern, to be sure, is discovered in our personal and communal history; it is applicable to events as these are known by participating selves and never primarily or directly applicable to events as seen by nonparticipants. The obscurities which it explains are not those which bother us as observers of life but those which distress moral agents and sufferers. . . . It is progressively validated in the individual Chris-

tian life as ever new occasions are brought under its light, as sufferings and sins, as mercies and joys are understood by its aid.[23]

Although religious beliefs are thus applicable primarily to the interpretation of personal life, they also provide *a coherent view of all reality*. Theology is not, as some existentialists hold, restricted to the discussion of events in our inner lives; even the meaning of personal existence involves our understanding of the character of the universe. The model of a personal God is used not just to interpret religious experience and life-situations, but as a clue for interpreting the nature of reality. This comprehensiveness is a demand not only of the human desire for coherence, but of biblical theology itself. For in biblical thought God is the Creator of all things and the Lord of every area of life. If one is to subscribe to a Christian world-view, it must make more sense of all the available evidence than any other world-view. We will return shortly to these wider implications.

2. Naturalistic Interpretations of Religion

We have described religious beliefs as the interpretation of experience. Wherever there is human interpretation there is the possibility of misinterpretation. We must be prepared therefore not only to consider the theistic view of religious experience, but to assess *alternative interpretations*. It is not the purpose of this volume to carry out such a task in detail, but we will comment briefly on a view which is often believed to have scientific support: the Freudian theory that dismisses religion as entirely subjective and interprets it within a philosophy of naturalism.

In the nineteenth century Ludwig Feuerbach had claimed that the idea of God is *a product of man's imagination*, a personification of his needs, and a rationalization of his desires: "Gods are the wishes of men represented as real beings. God is nothing but man's drive for happiness, satisfied in imagination." Sigmund Freud held the same view, namely, that God is a subjective illusion, but supported his claim by the theory that theism is the product of a subconscious father-complex. Every child, he suggested, is helpless and dependent on his human father. As the child grows up, he finds he cannot depend on his father for protection from a hostile and

23. Niebuhr, *The Meaning of Revelation*, pp. 94, 133. Used by permission of The Macmillan Company.

intolerable world. In his continuing insecurity, he imagines a divine being, the "father image" projected on a cosmic scale, to which he can turn for security and comfort. "It would indeed be very nice if there were a God who was both creator of the world and a benevolent providence, if there were a moral order and a future life; but at the same time it is very odd that this is all just as we should wish it ourselves."[24] Freud saw religion as "wishful thinking" growing out of man's search for security. Belief in God as a cosmic ally is the prolongation of an infantile dependence, whereby the harsh realities of life are evaded.

In evaluating this interpretation, we must acknowledge that there is indeed much *rationalization in religion,* as in all human enterprises. There is ample clinical evidence of the use of religion in ego-defense mechanisms. We often do delude ourselves, making God the cosmic chum who will answer our selfish prayers. Prophetic religion has been the first to condemn this tendency to use God for man's purposes. Here is *immature* religion which is escapist and self-centered. But there is also *mature* religion, which, instead of leading to escapism, increases a person's honesty with himself and which, in place of self-centeredness, increases the capacity to love. Religion can be regression to childhood, but it can also be an organizing framework conferring integration upon personality, a source of courage in working for ideals, and an expression of concern for intellectual integrity. Freud's sweeping attack fails to distinguish different levels of religious maturity. What of the prophet's reluctance to accept his call, or the saint's sacrifice of his life for his faith, or the presence of demands and ideals in religion that run precisely counter to man's desires? Biblical religion usually sees God's will as the opposite of man's wishes, challenging our conventional morality and destroying our complacency and our pretenses. The wish-projection theory can account for such occurrences only by introducing additional assumptions—which again seem to be plausible in some cases but not in others.

Moreover, the *truth or falsity* of a belief can never be determined simply by examining *its relation to human wishes.* Some desires do correspond to reality and others do not. Some, such as craving for food, or desire for truth and justice, are valuable, whereas

---

24. Sigmund Freud, *The Future of an Illusion* (New York: Doubleday PB, 1957), p. 57.

others, such as the wish for status or for vengeance, are more ambiguous. We inevitably have to select from among conflicting desires. The validity of a belief can be neither proved nor disproved from its psychological origins or motives alone. Furthermore, the theory of rationalization is *inconsistent*, for it undermines the critic's own position. If he claims that basic beliefs are the rationalization of wishes, would this not imply that his own atheistic beliefs may be equally the rationalization of *his* wishes, the product of unconscious forces and childhood experiences? Perhaps his atheism derives from the desire to be self-sufficient, or from the wish that there be no God who makes moral demands, or from rebellion against his parents and their convictions. He can exempt his own position from criticism only at the price of consistency.

Although it purports to be neutral, objective, and purely scientific, Freud's writing reveals *a naturalistic world-view*, an alternative faith that is his starting point as much as his conclusion. Occasionally his philosophical position is explicitly stated; more often it is implicit. It seems to be reflected in the selectivity of his data: most of his illustrations are from pathological cases or primitive religions, with almost no mention of the great saints of the Western tradition; much of what he attacks is a caricature of biblical religion. Here, as always, disagreement between adherents of naturalism and theism is basically not an argument between science and religion, but between two ultimate commitments, two interpretations of the nature of the universe and the significance of human life. As a reminder of the universal tendency to rationalization present in every human enterprise including religion, Freud's theory needs to be heard. But as an over-all explanation of religion, his theory has serious shortcomings when judged by the criteria of consistency, comprehensiveness, and adequacy to the evidence. Freud's view as well as other naturalistic interpretations of religious experience should of course be examined in much greater detail than space here permits; our purpose has been simply to illustrate the applicability of the criteria we have outlined.

3. *The Limits of Evaluation*

Returning to our main theme, we should indicate that although there are points of similarity between the processes of evaluating religious beliefs and scientific theories, there are also some far-reaching differences that warn us against pressing the comparison too far. First, *the influence of interpretation on experience* is far greater in religion than in science. To be sure, there are no un-interpreted facts in science; the "barest" data are already "theory-laden." In the social sciences, the selection of variables and assessment of results reflect theoretical considerations. Only total systems of experience-plus-interpretation can be tested. In religion, however, the "feedback" from interpretive to experiential components is far greater, for interests and commitments profoundly influence the religious life of individuals and communities. With some interpretations of religious experience, worship would suffer or cease; with others, corporate sensitivity might be heightened. There is a tendency for any set of basic beliefs to produce evidence that can be used in its own support, and hence to be self-confirming. There are also wide variations in individual temperament and life history that influence a person's religious as well as his artistic and intellectual responses. A person experiences the world differently when he sees it in terms of new basic categories.

Second, *criteria of evaluation are themselves influenced by religious beliefs.* To a limited extent the same situation prevails in science, where varying weights are assigned to such features as intellectual beauty and simplicity. In the social sciences, criteria are even more dependent on presuppositions. Now the outcome of the evaluation of basic beliefs depends on the relative weight given to diverse aspects of experience, and this can never be a purely empirical question. If *pragmatic* criteria are introduced, and beliefs are judged by their effects on behavior, the variations are even greater. Does a particular philosophy of life encourage creative love, social harmony, ethical conduct, maturity and integration of personality? William James finds that religion is a source of moral power, inward peace, and "saintliness." Tillich holds that "idolatrous faiths do not fulfill the promises they make" and are destructive and divisive, whereas commitment to the true ultimate is creative and integrating. But all of these claims already presuppose value-judgments; the consequences are assessed in terms of the goals of the life-affirming Western tradition. Criteria of evaluation thus embody standards that are themselves influenced by religious beliefs.

Third, *intersubjective testability occurs only within particular religious communities.* We suggested that objectivity in science consists of intersubjective testing within a community that shares the same goals, standards, and procedures. The scientific community is potentially universal in the sense that members of various cultures can come to hold these assumptions; but in the process they may have to abandon a number of the assumptions held by their culture (science is not universal in the sense of being compatible with all cultural presuppositions). Similarly, religion is the response of a community, not a private affair; beliefs are tested against the corporate experience of the worshiping community attempting to understand itself. The Christian community as the context of social corroboration is international and may be said to be potentially universal; but it exists alongside other religious communities, whereas the scientific community has no rivals serving functions similar to its own. Niebuhr points to the possibilities and limits of intersubjectivity:

> Furthermore, historic faith, directed toward a reality which appears in our history and which is apprehended by historic beings, is not private and subjective and without possibility of verification. Every view of the universal from the finite standpoint of the individual in such a society is subject to the test of experience on the part of companions who look from the same standpoint in the same direction, as well as to the test of consistency with the principles and concepts that have grown out of past experience in the same community. . . . We remind ourselves of the relative standpoint we occupy in history and faith. We are not trying to describe a common human certainty gained in a common human experience; yet on the other hand we are not seeking to set forth a private and mystic assurance which is not subject to the criticism of our community, that is all those who occupy the same standpoint and look in the same direction toward the same reality to which we look as individuals.[25]

The limitations on the intersubjective testability of religious beliefs are not altogether unlike *the limitations on the testability of paradigms* in science. We saw that paradigms embody basic presuppositions as to what types of concept and what kinds of procedures are acceptable to a scientific community. They affect the scientist's thought-patterns and his mode of experiencing the world. Paradigms are not rationally proven, and their alteration constitutes a "scientific revolution"; often this involves seeing the old data in a new way. However, we suggested that science is in

---

25. Niebuhr, *The Meaning of Revelation*, pp. 21, 141. Used by permission of The Macmillan Company.

general a cumulative process, and that many of the assumptions
of an old paradigm, and much of the work done under its guidance, are carried over after the "revolution." Between different
systems of religious belief there are perhaps fewer common assumptions. In this respect they are more like the axioms of a geometrical system; one does not try to prove axioms, but one asks
what happens if one assumes them.

It is thus apparent that *no unambiguous evaluation of religious
beliefs can be made.* There is of course no certainty in science;
theories are not unambiguously determined by facts, and personal
judgment enters at various points. But there is obviously a far
greater degree of consensus and intersubjective testability in
science than in religion. Yet here it must be stressed that the possibilities for the evaluation of a religious world-view should be
compared not with those for scientific theories, but *with those for
alternative world-views.* No world-view, theistic or naturalistic,
is capable of demonstrable proof. There is an element of risk in
commitment to any world-view; but risk is inevitable—on such
questions there may be greater risks in a policy of caution. Moreover, there are implicit affirmations in any activity; the choice is
not whether to hold such basic beliefs, but which ones to hold.

Finally, there are *specific attitudes in biblical religion* which
might seem to prevent a person from even attempting any kind of
evaluation. Theistic beliefs not only arise from *worship* but lead
back to worship; to believe in God is not merely to accept an
interpretive hypothesis, but to acknowledge one who is worthy of
worship and devotion. Our faith is in God, not in our own religious
experience. There is a corrective for intellectual pride in the sense
of *mystery* which reminds us that we do not have God encom-
passed in our conceptual systems. We earlier advocated a *"confessional"* attitude and pointed to the dangers of defensiveness in
trying to prove the superiority of one's own beliefs. We spoke of
the necessity of *personal involvement,* and the deficiencies of the
speculative approach of natural theology. *Revelation* is something
given to us to which we respond in gratitude, not an intellectual
conclusion we have established on our own.

Yet we submit that none of these features of biblical religion
is incompatible with the evaluative process described. In the last
chapter it was maintained that *religious commitment* and *reflective
inquiry* are in tension but are not irreconcilable; and that faith

and doubt, properly understood, are not mutually exclusive. There can be in religious inquiry an attitude of self-critical questioning, and a dedication to a truth transcending individual preferences, which is not unlike that of the scientist. And if God is a mystery not captured in our statements, we should be all the more critical of our theological formulations, tentative in our claims, and aware of the limited and symbolic character of our language. The motive of reflective inquiry must always be our own search for truth, not the desire to prove ourselves superior to others. We can acknowledge that revelation is not our own doing, and yet admit that it is recognized partly by its ability to illuminate events in our lives. None of the distinctive features of biblical religion need rule out this process of reflective inquiry which, despite its limitations, is the only way in which the cognitive component of religion can be evaluated.

4. World-Views and Metaphysical Systems

What is *the intended scope* of religious beliefs? To what kinds of experience are they relevant? We have indicated that the primary context in which religious beliefs function is that of religious experience, worship, and the interpretation of revelatory events in the life of a community. Further, religious beliefs serve to interpret personal and social life-situations. In these areas, religious concepts are closely tied to personal experience. But religious beliefs also serve a wider function as interpretations of the general character of reality; assertions are made about nature, man, and God. This universal scope is implicit in the ultimacy of any object of worship, and more specifically in the biblical understanding of God. Religious beliefs refer to all events—but only insofar as they are related to ultimate concern.

We may use the term "*world-view*" to designate such a set of basic beliefs about the fundamental character of reality. World-views are realistic (they purport to refer to reality) and inclusive (they include all of reality), but they represent only the features deemed significant as a framework for life-orientation. A *metaphysical system*, on the other hand, tries to represent exhaustively the most general characteristics of all events, and it arises from a more theoretical interest. But the distinction is never a sharp one, since world-views use metaphysical categories, and metaphysical systems reflect ultimate commitments which provide life-orientations. We would suggest, then, that a set of religious beliefs is more than an interpretation of personal experience, but less than a metaphysical system; we will call it a "world-view." Historically, various metaphysical systems have been used to express the Christian world-view. There are some systems that are incompatible with Christianity and others that seem to be more compatible, but there is no unique "Christian metaphysics." There are dangers in the establishment of any tight and inflexible synthesis (such as the fusion of biblical theology and Aristotelian metaphysics in the Middle Ages). Yet if we seek a coherent view of reality and not a multiplicity of unrelated languages, explicit analysis of metaphysical categories is inescapable. In Part Three we will argue that the categories of process philosophy are consonant with the personalistic concepts of biblical religion. But any such theological use of a metaphysical system must be very tentative and cautious, and must avoid the temptations of grandiose system-building.

Metaphysics is the search for a coherent set of categories for the interpretation of all experience.[26] Systematic connectedness is sought among areas of inquiry usually considered in isolation. Insofar as it succeeds, the power of such a conceptual synthesis lies in its ability to integrate and illuminate a wide range of experience—in science, history, art, ethics, religion, and so forth. But metaphysical categories are inevitably highly abstract, for they are applicable to very diverse types of experience. Moreover, the metaphysician, in attempting to achieve an all-inclusive system of great generality, is always tempted to misrepresent or distort some types of experience in order to fit them into a conceptual framework derived primarily from other types of experience.

Metaphysical systems are based on *models* and *analogies* of wide scope. The separate facts of existence do not organize themselves into unambiguous patterns of meaning; every system takes its clues from particular kinds of experience. Dorothy Emmet[27] suggests that *"coordinating analogies"* drawn from one area of experience are used as an interpretive scheme in other areas. She writes that perhaps today no one analogy is comprehensive enough to encompass the great diversity of modern life, and hence we may

---

26. Cf. Whitehead, *Process and Reality*, Chap. 1.
27. Emmet, *The Nature of Metaphysical Thinking*, Chap. 9.

have to use several analogies only loosely related to each other. Pepper[28] contends that every philosophical system has at its heart a *"root-metaphor"*—for example, the world as a "machine" or an "organism"—which cannot be empirically proven, but which can be compared in its adequacy to alternative "root-metaphors." Any such system embodies judgments of importance and expresses in its conceptual categories a "vision of reality."

Because of its unlimited scope, a metaphysical system is never *falsifiable* in any simple sense. It is impossible to specify an event which would falsify it because all the major types of experience have already been taken into account in formulating it—and presumably no radically new types are likely to be found. No isolated fact will yield a decision between two systems—not even in science, and certainly not in metaphysics. In the history of philosophy, metaphysical systems appear to have been not disproved but abandoned; a system is like a castle which is not taken by frontal attack but which one day is found to be unoccupied. Again, metaphysics does not lead to predictions of events beyond those which entered the construction of the system, for the general characteristics of reality are not time-dependent. A metaphysics is not a pseudoscientific super-theory, for it deals with the most general characteristics of various types of experience. Metaphysics does not try to do the job of either science or religion.

It is not surprising that today *many persons take a dim view of metaphysics.* Scientists are apprehensive lest interpretive categories which are alien to their work be imposed on scientific thought; conversely, they are in general cautious about extending scientific concepts to do jobs for which they were not originally intended. Similarly contemporary theologians resist the use of conceptual structures imported from other fields; having seen the speculative character of metaphysical systems and the pretentious claims often made for them, they prefer to go no further than to affirm a religious world-view of restricted scope. Philosophers, aware that past philosophical debates have been inconclusive, are content to trace the functions of a variety of unrelated languages; if concepts are "useful fictions" serving diverse purposes, there is no possibility of attaining a coherent view of reality. Yet there are signs that the

28. Stephen Pepper, *World Hypotheses* (Berkeley: University of California Press, 1942; PB).

"ban on metaphysics" among linguistic analysts is weakening; a number of recent works represent tentative explorations in metaphysics.[29]

We have, in earlier sections, defended the realistic intent of both scientific and religious language, the inescapability of metaphysical categories, and the legitimacy of the search for wider coherence. But our goal should be modest; we must not expect to achieve a total integrated system of thought of the kind developed during the Middle Ages. Any conceptual synthesis will be partial and tentative. Human experience is diverse and varied, and each field of inquiry must have its own autonomy; any limited synthesis will have to allow for considerable pluralism. The connection of both science or religion with any metaphysical system must be a loose one, and the integrity of both fields must be respected.

III. CONCLUSIONS:
ON METHODS IN SCIENCE AND RELIGION

Before attempting to draw together our conclusions we should underscore a fact which is implicit in previous chapters: *the selective character of both science and religion.* Even between the various sciences, theories can be virtually independent of each other (in physical geology and molecular biology, let us say) because each field has a selective interest—though the sciences represent similar types of interest. Between science and religion, however, radically different types of interest are represented; they arise from dissimilar areas of experience which reflect dissimilar aspects of reality, despite the presence of certain parallels in their methodologies. Men ask diverse kinds of questions, and the kind of answer sought always depends on the context of inquiry.

The *selectivity of science* is evident from Chapter 6. The scientist is interested in regular patterns that are at least statistically lawful; the individuality and concreteness of particular events are of course omitted from his analysis. A process that has occurred

---

29. See D. F. Pears, ed., *The Nature of Metaphysics* (London: Macmillan and Co., Ltd., 1957); Ian Ramsey, ed., *Prospect for Metaphysics* (London: George Allen & Unwin, Ltd., 1961); P. F. Strawson, *Individuals: An Essay in Descriptive Metaphysics* (London: Methuen & Co., Ltd., 1959; Doubleday PB); cf. Huston Smith, "The Death and Rebirth of Metaphysics," in W. L. Reese and E. Freeman, eds., *Process and Divinity* (LaSalle, Ill.: Open Court Publishing Co., 1964).

only once (for example, the evolution of man) can be studied only insofar as it exhibits repetitive and orderly features. Moreover, the scientist starts from publicly observable sense-data. Though the "data" of his research are never free from interpretation, they are reproducible within a scientific community because of the reliability of observation-processes and the lawfulness of the events being studied. Whenever possible he uses concepts that can be treated quantitatively. Another kind of selectivity arises from the fact that science studies what is, not what ought to be. (Science is "ethically neutral" in the sense that its findings can be used in the service of a variety of human goals. Although the scientific enterprise embodies within its own activities many human values—such as cooperation, honesty and freedom of inquiry—it does not provide a basis for decisions in personal and social ethics. We will touch on this question later, though ethical problems as such are beyond our purview.)

The scientific community is *abstractive*, for like every community of inquiry it has its own symbolic language by which it represents those aspects of experience in which it is interested. Whitehead warns of the temptation to assume that only those qualities which science can analyze are real:

> The disadvantage of exclusive attention to a group of abstractions, however well-founded, is that by the nature of the case you have abstracted from the remainder of things. Insofar as the excluded things are important to your experience, your modes of thought are not fitted to deal with them.[30]

A symbol-system in which a small group of variables is abstracted can often be very exact, but its representation is likely to be far removed from the complexity and variety of levels of meaning in human experience. The laboratory situation is highly artificial in the sense that it deliberately excludes the "extraneous influences" that are always present outside the lab. Often the problems most significant to man cannot be analyzed quantitatively or with precision. (For example, it is suggested by Polanyi that historical studies are justified despite their inherent inaccuracy by the intrinsic interest of their subject matter and its breadth of implication; the atom is simple in comparison to the human personality.) If the scientific community *deliberately selects* only certain kinds

---

30. Whitehead, *Science and the Modern World*, p. 59. Used by permission of The Macmillan Company and Cambridge University Press.

of variables for inclusion in its symbol-system, then one cannot decide on the basis of that system alone whether the scientific description of existence is potentially exhaustive and complete. The point is delightfully illustrated in Eddington's parable[31] about a zoologist, studying deep-sea life by means of a net of ropes on a two-inch mesh, who after repeated expeditions concluded that there are no fish smaller than two inches in the sea! (Or, if you prefer, take the story of the man who, late at night, endlessly searched the ground in the circle of light under a street lamp looking for his lost keys; a passerby asked, "Are you sure you lost them here?" and the man replied, "No, but here I can see better.") Von Weizsäcker says that the scientific picture of the world "is wrong not in what it asserts but in what it omits."[32] A person may believe that "only that with which science deals is real," but he must defend this belief as part of a naturalistic world-view and not as a conclusion of science itself. Campbell writes: "It must always be remembered that science does not attempt to order all our experience; some parts of it, and the part perhaps that is of most importance to us as active and moral human beings, is omitted altogether from that order."[33]

Religion is also selective. It asks about the objects of a man's trust, loyalty, and worship, his "ultimate concern." What are the powers operating in the world for good and evil, and the forces of fulfillment and destruction in human life? What are the personal and social goals men should serve? Religious beliefs are relevant primarily to existential questions about man's orientation in a framework of meaning, the fundamental character of man and the world, personal identity and destiny, time and history. The life of the religious community centers in the great "transitions" (birth, marriage, death), the service of man and society (love, justice), the celebration of formative historical events (sacraments, festivals), and above all the worship and service of God. Such differences between science and religion concerning the type of interest represented would lead us to expect that although there may be some parallels between their methods, the differences will in the last analysis be more significant.

  31. Eddington, *Philosophy of Physical Science*, p. 16.
  32. Carl F. von Weizsäcker, *History of Nature* (Chicago: University of Chicago Press, 1949; PB), p. 2.
  33. Campbell, *What is Science?*, p. 71.

Let us then *summarize the comparison of methods* in science and religion in Part Two, listing first some *similarities*. (1) In both cases there is a two-way interaction between experience and interpretation, though the two components are never clearly separable. We have noted the contribution of the subject (knower) to all inquiry. Models and analogies aid the formation of conceptual propositions. (2) The community is essential in both science and religion, and its paradigms govern the presuppositions of its members. The interpretive language of both communities is used realistically and referentially; it is neither a "summary of data" (positivism) nor a "useful fiction" (instrumentalism). Yet it provides no literal representation, since it is always partial and symbolic (critical realism). (3) Interconnected networks of concepts are evaluated together, using simultaneous criteria of coherence, comprehensiveness, and adequacy to experience. Religious beliefs should be evaluated primarily as interpretations of historical events, religious experience, and life-situations; any contribution they make to a broader synthesis or metaphysical system should be viewed more cautiously.

Some *differences* between the methods of the two fields have also been presented. (1) The degree of personal involvement and the range of selfhood affected are greater in religion than in science —though the distinction is not as absolute as existentialists claim. (2) Revelation in historical events has no parallel in science— though the role of revelation in human understanding is not as isolated from experience and interpretation as neo-orthodoxy asserts, and particularity must not be stressed at the expense of universality. (3) The function of religious language is primarily the evocation and expression of worship and self-commitment— though religious beliefs also serve a cognitive function, which linguistic analysts tend to neglect. (4) The intersubjective testability of religious beliefs is severely limited as compared to that of scientific theories or even scientific paradigms—though this need not lead to the abandonment of critical evaluation, since testability in religion should be compared not with that in science but with that of competing interpretations of religious experience and alternative world-views (the choice is not between theism and science but between theism and naturalism). The first three differences above are likely to seem crucial to the theologian as he defends the distinctiveness of religion; the fourth point (intersubjective testability) is likely to seem crucial to the scientist as he defends the distinctiveness of science.

This comparison leads us to the conclusion that in considering any specific problem *the contrasts of science and religion must always be kept in mind.* Any account that neglects personal involvement, revelation, or the special functions of religious language will fail to portray accurately the life of the religious community. We can thank existentialism, neo-orthodoxy and linguistic analysis for insisting on these differences. Religion does predominantly employ "actor-language," whereas science is (despite the contribution of the scientist as person) predominantly expressed in "spectator-language." We have recorded in Part One some of the conflicts that arose in the past when these distinctions were ignored. When the "God of the gaps" was introduced to complete a scientific explanation, a religious concept was used to answer a scientific question—and both scientists and theologians had every right to object. The reverse error occurred when a scientific theory such as evolution was uncritically transformed into the central concept of a world-view—whether in naturalism or in natural theology. In future chapters we shall criticize some recent instances of similar "category mistakes."

But we must immediately go on to say that *the contrasts are not as absolute as most recent theologians and philosophers have maintained.* We have argued that science, on the one hand, is a more human enterprise than is usually assumed, and that there is a "spectrum" of degrees and types of personal involvement in various fields of inquiry. Religion, for its part, presupposes cognitive assertions which are subject to critical evaluation. Such evaluation does not yield conclusions with the reliability of scientific results, to be sure, but we have argued that some of the same criteria are applicable; one's beliefs must be as coherent, comprehensive, and adequate to experience as alternative world-views. Reason is fulfilled, not abrogated, by revelation; reflective inquiry can coexist with religious commitment. Furthermore, we have defended the legitimacy of the wider search for coherence and synthesis which leads to a concern for metaphysics; the compartmentalization of thought thwarts the quest for unity. The critical realist cannot remain content with a plurality of unrelated languages; but at the same time he will recognize the limitations of all human concepts and the dangers of grandiose claims on behalf of any neat metaphysical system. The theologian, in turn, should be unwilling to settle for a solution that makes the gospel immune from attack at the cost of isolating it from contemporary intellectual life, or of destroying bridges of communication between theology and "secular culture."

These conclusions will guide the treatment of particular problems in the chapters ahead. We will, for example, confront a number of polarities: freedom-determinism, purpose-mechanism, mind-brain, creation-evolution, and providence-natural law. In each case the *"alternative languages"* approach is taken as the starting point of a satisfactory solution; it allows both terms of each polarity to be retained and used in their appropriate language-systems, since the alternative languages are not regarded as mutually exclusive. (Thus "mind" and "brain" would be terms for the same events viewed from within and from without; an act would be "free" when described in actor-language, and "determined" when described in spectator-language.) This approach avoids reductionism (in which the behavior of any entity is explained exclusively in terms of the laws governing its components) and dualism (in which two distinct and contrasting entities are postulated). But in each case we will not stop with such a solution; we will go on to ask about *the structures of man and the world* which make such diverse languages appropriate. We will attempt to formulate a coherent interpretation of experience.

In Part Three, then, we will not expect to derive a natural theology directly from science; nor will we assume, at the opposite extreme, that science can have no implications which theology should take into account. Let it be granted that the scientist is interested in nature as a lawful structure, whereas the theologian is interested in nature as related to God and to man's life-orientation. Despite the divergence of their interests, it is (according to critical realism) the same natural world to which they look, so their inquiries cannot be totally independent. If the theologian speaks of God's activity in nature, his statements cannot ignore the scientist's discoveries about the character of the natural order. Again, the theologian raises distinctive questions about the character of human existence; but he is referring to the same creature whose relation to nature is under scrutiny by the scientist. We have proposed, moreover, that both scientific and religious concepts can contribute to the search for a consistent set of metaphysical categories—though both disciplines must resist any pressure to conform to the requirements of a superimposed metaphysical system. The project must be a more modest and open-ended one: *dialogue between two communities that respect one another's integrity.*

We will not be advocating a natural theology of the sort that flourished in earlier centuries. Nor will we be content with a theology that ignores nature, as recent religious thought has tended to do. We seek rather *a theology of nature* that can preserve the distinctive contributions of both science and religion.

PART THREE

Religion and
the Theories
of Science

10

Physics and Indeterminacy

Science as a general method and its relation to religion occupied us in Part Two. We now turn to science as a particular group of theories which are the content of current "scientific knowledge." In the next few chapters the implications of specific theories in physics and biology are considered. The following are examples of some of the conclusions we will reach:

1. *Naive realism* is no longer tenable. Examination of particular theories, especially in physics, adds support to the argument of previous chapters that scientific concepts are partial, abstractive, and symbolic. But the need to use "alternative languages" to deal with the world should not lead us to abandon the search for a unified account.

2. *Reductionism* is challenged by the evidence that "the whole is more than the sum of the parts." Study of the components—for example, the basis of living processes in molecular biology—is an essential task, but does not replace the need for distinctive concepts and theories dealing with integrated systems at higher organizational levels. The concept of "emergence" in evolution allows for both continuity of development and the occurrence of genuinely new phenomena.

3. *The significance of time* is a recurrent theme. The atom is a sequence of vibratory patterns, and its future is indeterminate; only the passage of time will disclose which of its alternative

potentialities will be actualized. Organisms display purposeful activity guided by anticipation of future goals. The evolution of living forms shows nature as a dynamic process of continual change and novelty.

In these chapters we intend to trace the relevance of such assertions for theology as it deals with *man's relation to nature* and *God's relation to nature.* The biblical understanding of man is threatened if he is taken to be just a biochemical machine, his brain essentially a complex computer, his existence the product of blind evolutionary forces, his actions determined by his past. We must of course acknowledge the power of the biochemical and evolutionary approaches; but at the same time we will insist that there are in man's life higher levels of activity which cannot be analyzed in such terms. Similarly we will suggest that the new picture of nature as a dynamic process requires a concept of continuing creativity rather than a doctrine of once-for-all creation. In a later chapter we will ask how nature as understood by contemporary science can be the scene of God's activity; how may we interpret the idea of providence in the light of what we know about the world? Part Three is thus an attempt to move toward a doctrine of man and a theology of nature which can take both scientific and theological ideas into account.

The present chapter starts from current theories about the constituents of the universe at the atomic level—far removed, perhaps, from the concerns of theology, but a first step in considering the contribution of science to a total view of man and nature. Section I, "The Strange World of the Atom," describes the radically new conceptual schemes by which the structure of matter is represented in quantum physics; Bohr's Complementarity Principle and Heisenberg's Indeterminacy Principle are also briefly set forth. In Section II, "Implications of the New Physics," it is argued that quantum theory has considerable significance for epistemology (the limitations of commonsense concepts and the involvement of the observer, for example), but provides no justification for positivism or metaphysical idealism. The extension of the idea of "complementarity" beyond the realm of science is also viewed with caution. It is suggested, however, that even within physics there are system-laws (such as the Pauli Exclusion Principle), which cannot be derived from the laws of component parts; thus reductionism seems questionable already in the atomic world.

The last half of the chapter is devoted to the problem of indeterminacy and freedom. Section III, "Interpretations of Indeterminacy," presents three schools of thought among physicists, who attribute atomic uncertainty respectively to human ignorance of detailed causes, conceptual limitations of human thought, or objective indeterminacy in nature itself. The latter view is defended, according to which there is present in the world a range of future possibilities, a plurality of genuine alternatives. But in Section IV, "Indeterminacy and Human Freedom," it is maintained that the concept of freedom cannot be identified either with determinism or with chance, but must derive from analysis of the activity of the person as agent.

I. The Strange World of the Atom

Usually science grows by small increments within the framework of accepted assumptions. Occasionally new discoveries produce ideas so revolutionary that the paradigms of a portion of the scientific community are replaced. Atomic physics effected a break with classical physics which—although it was not as complete as the break between Newtonian and Aristotelian science—did bring about a similar reexamination of basic asumptions about the status of scientific theories and the character of the world. In this section these changes within twentieth-century physics are described in nontechnical language as a basis for the discussion of their significance in subsequent sections.

1. The Background of Nineteenth-Century Physics

Galileo's view of matter-in-motion and its development into the mechanical and deterministic conception of nature held by Laplace were outlined in earlier chapters. Physics in the nineteenth century (up to 1890) consisted in the further elaboration of Newtonian mechanics, together with the introduction of new types of conceptual scheme (such as those of electromagnetic theory and the kinetic theory of gases) whose basic assumptions were still those of classical physics. Nineteenth-century physics was *deterministic*, for the future states of all its systems could in principle be calculated from their present states. It was *reductionistic*, for all laws seemed to be derivable, if not from the mechanics of particles, at least from the laws governing a few kinds of particles and fields.

The ideal was "to reduce everything in the whole universe completely and perfectly to purely quantitative changes in a few basic
entities which themselves never change qualitatively."[1]

Nineteenth-century physics was *naively realistic* in its epistemology; scientific theories were taken to be literal and objective replicas of the world as it exists independently of the process of knowing it. It was assumed that one can separate the object from the
subject—the knower imagined as external spectator and passive
observer. "A first postulate," writes de Broglie, "was that it must be
possible to arrive at a description of the material world which
does not in the least take into account either the scientist who
experiments and reasons, or the means of investigation which he
uses to observe the phenomena."[2] Experimental errors, it was believed, can be reduced indefinitely, enabling a one-to-one correspondence between the external world and our picture of it to be
progressively approached. Commonsense notions of space and time
and the continuity of the paths of objects were presumed applicable throughout the universe.

It might appear that *kinetic theory* violated the assumption of
determinism, for it described the behavior of gases in terms of
probability. This procedure was, however, considered to be only
a convenience in calculation. It was believed that the motions of
all the gas molecules, pictured as tiny billiard balls, are precisely
determined by mechanical laws. But because these individual
motions would have been much too complex to calculate, kinetic
theory derived statistical laws for the average behavior of large
groups of molecules. The presuppositions of kinetic theory were
thus no exception to the deterministic, reductionistic, and naively
realistic approach of classical physics. An attitude typical of his
times is reflected in Lord Kelvin's statement that we do not really
understand something until we can make a mechanical model of it.

By 1890 it appeared that physics was nearly through its task.
Greater experimental accuracy might still be achieved here, a further refinement of existing theory there, but no radically new types
of phenomena or theories were to be anticipated. A physicist at
the Bureau of Patents deserted science because he "wanted to get
into a field with a future." But developments in the subsequent

1. David Bohm, *Causality and Chance in Modern Physics* (Princeton, N.J.:
D. Van Nostrand Co. 1957; Harper PB°), p. 47.
2. Louis de Broglie, *Physics and Microphysics*, trans. M. Davidson (New
York: Pantheon Books, 1955; Harper PB°), p. 114.

generation produced a revolution that altered such expectations and cast doubt on all three assumptions listed above.

2. The Quantum Theory

Between 1890 and 1900 several discoveries were made quite unlike anything previously known: *electrons, X rays,* and *radioactivity.* These were novel phenomena, but they seemed to fit into the general framework of classical categories of analysis. They opened up whole new fields of investigation, although at first they did not suggest the need for any revisions of previous assumptions.

Then between 1900 and 1910 several puzzling experiments were carried out which could be explained only on the very unclassical assumption that energy is *quantized,* that is, capable of having only certain discrete values. (To use an analogy, United States currency is "quantized," for it has only discontinuous values that change by steps; I can pay 5 cents or 6 cents but not 5.3 cents, because one cent is the smallest unit in any transaction.) Planck showed that the spectrum of radiation from a hot object could be accounted for if one assumed that its atoms can vibrate not with just any amount of energy, but only with quantized energy values. In 1913 Bohr developed his well-known *model of the atom;* he pictured a heavy nucleus, around which revolve electrons following only orbits having quantized energies. Note that the Bohr model had one feature that was totally inexplicable classically—the assumption that only discrete energies are possible, and that orbits with these energies are stable; but in all other respects his model represented atomic structure in classical and mechanical terms. It resembled a miniature "planetary" system and obeyed similar laws.

The development of *quantum theory* during the 1920's brought a much more radical break with the past.[3] Einstein had shown that the photoelectric effect could be explained if light, which is usually thought of as a wave, is assumed to travel as a quantum or packet of energy. Compton had shown that such a light quantum has momentum and behaves very much as a particle would. Now de Broglie suggested that if light waves could behave like

---

3. There are many popular accounts in inexpensive editions, including George Gamow, *The Atom and its Nucleus* (Englewood Cliffs, N.J.: Prentice-Hall PB, 1961); Selig Hecht, *Explaining the Atom,* rev. by E. Rabinowitch (New York: Viking PB, 1960); Banesh Hoffman, *The Strange Story of the Quantum,* 2nd. ed. (New York: Dover PB, 1959).

particles, perhaps particles such as electrons might behave like waves. Schrödinger derived the equation that such waves would have to satisfy, and calculated the wave-pattern for the simplest case, the hydrogen atom. The energy of the waves turned out to be quantized, not by the introduction of an arbitrary assumption as in Bohr's scheme, but as a direct consequence of the mathematics of wave representation. (The quantization is not unlike the restrictions that govern waves in a violin string of a given length, which can vibrate only with an integral number of loops and hence can produce only certain possible harmonic overtones arising from specific modes of vibration.)

Instead of the "planetary model" of electrons traveling in definite orbits around the nucleus, a complex *wave-pattern* throughout the region surrounding the nucleus was used to represent the atom. But it was not immediately clear what physical interpretation was to be given to these hypothetical waves, which, though never directly observable, could account for the quantized energy levels of the atom. Many additional experiments could be correlated when the amplitude of the Schrödinger wave at a given point was interpreted as a measure of the *probability* that the system behaves as if there were a localized electron at that point when a measurement of some kind is made. In general, the wave-pattern permits the calculation of a probability-distribution (but not an exact value) for a series of observations of any variable.

To illustrate this concept of *probability*, let us take an example from nuclear physics. Neither in theory nor in practice is it possible to predict the moment when an *individual* radioactive atom will disintegrate after removal from activation in an atomic pile. All one can calculate is the probability that it will disintegrate during the first minute, the somewhat smaller probability that it will disintegrate during the second minute, or the third, and so forth. If there is a *group* of radioactive atoms, these unpredictable individual disintegrations will occur at random during any brief time interval; if the emitted radiations trigger a Geiger counter activating a loudspeaker, the resulting "clicks" will have the familiar erratic distribution in time. But if *a very large number* of atoms is involved, these statistical irregularities will tend to average out, and the over-all behavior of the total aggregate over a period of time will be found to conform accurately to that calculated from the probability-distribution.

Such a *probability-distribution* might be compared to an *actuarial table* of human mortality rates, from which for a given year (1) one *cannot* predict whether an individual will die, (2) one *can* predict accurately the probability that an individual will die, and (3) one *can* predict accurately for a large group how many will die. The only exact laws are statistical. Quantum mechanics also describes individual phenomena by probabilities, such as the probability for a radioactive atom to disintegrate at a particular time, or for an electron to be observed at a particular point in a wave-pattern. The wave-patterns change with time in a rigorously predictable manner; but their connection with individual events is statistical, and the particular instance is a matter of chance. In the human case we assume that there are various unspecified causes of the death of individuals, and that probabilities are a derivative mathematical device for summarizing data about individuals; but in the atomic case the probability-waves seem to have a more fundamental status.

3. The Heisenberg Principle and the Wave-Particle Dualism

Instead of exact values for predictions, quantum theory can give only probabilities, but the magnitude of the resulting uncertainty varies greatly. It can be shown from the postulates of quantum theory, and has been confirmed experimentally, that certain pairs of variables are related to each other in a peculiar way: the more accurately one of the quantities is known, the less accurately the other quantity is predictable. For example, the more accurately the position of an electron is measured in an experimental arrangement, the greater is the uncertainty in any prediction of its velocity. This is the famous *Heisenberg Uncertainty Principle* or *Principle of Indeterminacy*.

It will be instructive to describe a typical experiment which illustrates both the Heisenberg Principle and the wave-particle dualism. Although it may sound rather complicated, it is actually a very simple experiment. A beam of electrons is shot at a metal screen containing *two narrow parallel slits*. A photographic plate a few inches beyond the screen registers a very small black mark wherever it is struck by an electron that has passed through the slits. After bombardment with electrons, the photographic plate shows a series of bands; dark bands composed of many tiny electron-marks alternate with light bands having few marks. Though the marks within any small area are distributed at random, their average density is alternately high (in dark bands) and low (in light bands) and conforms exactly to the probability-distribution calculated if the electrons in transit are represented not as particles but as probability-waves spread out in space. (The over-all pattern is in fact similar to that of water waves passing through two small openings in a barrier such as a breakwater—behind the barrier there are some points at which no waves are present because a

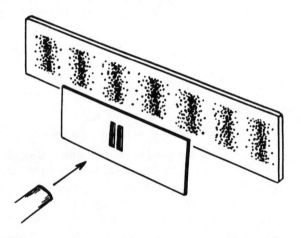

wave "peak" from one opening always arrives simultaneously with a "trough" from the other opening, canceling out its effect, whereas at other points the peaks from the two openings always arrive together and reinforce each other. Analogous "interference patterns" of alternate bright and dark bands occur after a light beam passes through two very small adjacent openings in an opaque screen.)

But now consider what happens to *an individual electron* in our experiment if a short exposure and a very weak source of electrons is used. The point at which this lonely electron will strike the photographic plate is unpredictable, though we know the probability for it to strike at any given point. The electron makes only one tiny mark, so it seems to reach the screen as an individual *"particle,"* discontinuous and localized. Moreover, since its electric charge cannot be divided, it must have gone through either one slit or the other but not both. Yet the presence of the second slit, through which, if it were actually a "particle," it could *not* have passed, somehow influenced its behavior drastically. (A very different pattern, without interference bands, would be found if we alternately opened the left slit alone and then the right slit alone.) A *"wave"* would of course pass through both slits and form precisely the interference pattern that the probability-distribution displays. In everyday life we have waves (such as those in water) without particle-like features, and we have particles (e.g., if we shoot machine-gun bullets at two slits in an iron plate) without wavelike features. But very small entities at the atomic level paradoxically display the properties of both waves and particles.

Finally, by varying the experimental arrangement we can see Heisenberg's Principle in action. Suppose we are interested in making predictions about the lateral position (left and right) and lateral velocity of an electron *just after it has passed through the slits.* Since we cannot tell through which slit the electron will pass, the uncertainty in predicting its position is just the distance between the slits. Now if this distance is great, the bands on the photographic plate are found to be very close together, which means that the direction of the electron's motion, and hence its lateral *velocity* on leaving the slits, can be predicted rather accurately. On the other hand, if we use a screen with slits close together, so that there is less uncertainty about the *position* of the electron, the probability-pattern will be spread through a wide angle—meaning that there is great uncertainty in predicting the electron's lateral velocity. In other words, a small slit-distance (position uncertainty) gives a large probability-pattern (velocity uncertainty), and vice versa. We can predict position or velocity, but not both in the same experimental arrangement.

If the two slits are so close that they merge into a single slit, the *position* is defined accurately and we have "particle-like" behavior; but the probability-function has now spread out at all angles covering the whole photographic plate uniformly so we cannot predict the lateral *velocity* at all, and the "wave-like" pattern of bands has disappeared. We can imagine the trajectories of "particles" or the interference of "waves," but not both at the same time. One physicist suggested that on Mondays, Wednesdays, and Fridays the electron is a wave, and on Tuesdays, Thursdays, and Saturdays it is a particle! Many other experiments lead to comparable difficulties in any attempt to visualize in familiar terms the character of the atomic world.[4]

4. The Principle of Complementarity

The wave-particle dualism of electrons in the above experiment is a feature of other entities also. Light in some situations (for example, interference effects) behaves as a wave, in others (for example, photoelectric effects) as a particle. Bohr used the word "complementarity" to refer to such sharply contrasting concepts, of which he writes:

> However far the phenomena transcend the scope of classical physical explanation, the account of all evidence must be expressed in classical terms. The argument is simply that by the word "experiment" we refer to a situation where we can tell others what we have done. . . . This implies the impossibility of any sharp separation between the behavior of atomic objects and the interaction with the measuring instruments which serve to define the conditions under which the phenomena appear. Any attempt of subdividing the phenomena will demand a change in the experimental arrangement, introducing new possibilities of interaction between objects and measuring instruments which in principle cannot be controlled. Consequently, evidence obtained within a single picture must be regarded as *complementary* in the sense that only the totality of the phenomena exhausts the possible information about the objects.[5]

Bohr's rather complex argument can be separated into the following points: (1) We cannot avoid the use of conventional concepts in describing the *experiment*, which employs apparatus and observations in space and time. (2) No sharp line can be drawn between *the process of observation* and what is observed; thus conventional concepts inevitably enter our attempts to picture what is going on in the atomic world. Moreover, the process of observation influences what is observed, so we cannot form a picture of the atom-in-itself apart from the total experimental situation. No clear line can be drawn between subject and object; various lines can be drawn for purposes of analysis, yielding alternative representations. We are actors rather than spectators, and we freely choose the experimental arrangement we will employ. (3) Familiar concepts, such as wave and particle, are inescapable and useful in referring to the atomic world, but we have to *use different models*

---

4. See, e.g., Frank, *Philosophy of Science*, Chap. 9.
5. Niels Bohr, *Atomic Physics and Human Knowledge* (New York: John Wiley & Sons, 1958; PB), p. 39.

in different experimental situations. Their alternate use is "*complementary*," rather than contradictory, since they do not occur in the same experimental situation. (4) We cannot make from conventional concepts a unified image of the atomic world, because of *the limitations of such concepts* when applied in a new range of dimensions.

Documenting the third point, Bohr goes to great lengths to show that the *experimental arrangements* in which behavior can be visualized as predominantly wavelike exclude arrangements under which particle-like behavior is dominant, and vice versa. He stresses the interaction between measuring instrument and the atomic system under investigation; thus the experimental context of any statement must always be specified. "The position of a particle" is a property not just of the particle but of the total experimental situation; and any situation in which this property is meaningful excludes situations in which the expression "velocity of a particle" might be meaningful.

Developing the fourth point, many authors have asserted *the limitations of concepts* drawn from the everyday world. Bohr is willing to apply such concepts, but holds that we must use successive and incomplete complementary pictures that cannot be neatly unified. He believes that we must abandon the search for a single picture of the microphysical object and accept a set of mutually exclusive representations appropriate under different circumstances. Other physicists go further than Bohr and urge the total abandonment of such commonsense language. We are not able to imagine what happens in the atomic world between observations, but we can at least write a unified set of equations for the observations themselves. The attempt to visualize atoms in conventional terms must be abandoned, according to these interpreters. Here were new scientific findings, then, which seemed to require a reformulation, not only of our view of matter, but also of our understanding of how theories are related to the world.

II. Implications of the New Physics

Classical physics, we said, was naively realistic, reductionistic, and deterministic. In discussing the new physics, we will first survey its *epistemological* implications—the abandonment of naive realism, the loss of picturability, and the recognition of the involvement of the observer. We will criticize the claim that these developments provide support for a metaphysics of idealism. Next, we will examine the idea of complementarity, and question the positivist interpretations it has received, as well as the applications of the concept beyond the borders of science. Finally, it will be suggested that in its approach to the relation of parts and wholes, quantum theory provides the beginning of an answer to reductionism, as well as a new view of time. The challenge to determinism is the topic of Section III.

1. The Downfall of Naive Realism

The nineteenth-century assumption that scientific theories are *literal descriptions* of nature as it is in itself can no longer be accepted in physics. The "planetary model" of the atom could still be visualized, for its components were held to be particles with such "primary qualities" as size and position. Enlarged a trillion times, the atom as Bohr first pictured it would consist of basketball-size electrons whirling in orbits a hundred yards in diameter around a dense nucleus the size of a pinhead. But in quantum theory moving particles are replaced by wave structures described by differential equations, abstract mathematical representations that cannot be visualized at all. If one tried to imagine such an atom, it would be a pattern of probability-waves filling the whole region in harmonic relationships in space and time, which might be compared with a three-dimensional symphony of musical tones of incredible complexity. However, the analogy would be inadequate—there is simply nothing in everyday experience comparable to this strange atomic realm.

This *loss of picturability* is a striking feature of the new physics. Our tendency to conceive of the atom's components as similar to things perceivable by the senses has to be given up. Not only is atomic structure inaccessible to direct observation and inexpressible in terms of sensory qualities, but we are unable even to imagine it in terms of space, time, and causality. The domain of the very small seems to be a radically different kind of reality from the domain of everyday experience, and our commonsense concepts are not applicable to it. We can describe by mathematical equations what happens in experiments, but we cannot ascribe familiar attributes to the inhabitants of the atomic world. The wave-particle dualism is only one among many instances of the difficulties which arise when we try to form a unified model of events in the submicroscopic realm.

Recognition of *the involvement of the observer* in the knowledge-situation is a characteristic of atomic physics on which we have previously commented (Chapter 7). Classically, it was assumed that a sharp separation could be made between the object and the subject; man was a spectator describing an independent external world. Today, as Margenau puts it:

> The new fact is that the search for truth modifies truth, that there is an effect of the knower on the known, that knowledge, too, is action. Four decades ago the typical observation of science was the measurement of the position of a star, an act wholly detached from the celestial object far away, and insignificant to its further motion. Today, with our principal concern about the atom, we regard such observations as atypical, as limiting cases.... When the genius of Heisenberg first confronted the physicist with this interpretation of the measuring process, he evinced a shocked reaction, for his whole concept of objectivity was shaken and his neat distinction between spectator and spectacle broke down.[6]

The role of the observer is also prominent in relativity. From Galileo's day through the nineteenth century, the "primary qualities" of mass, length, and velocity were held to be objective properties of the world independent of the knower (and were thus the basic attributes ascribed to the particles of which the real world of matter-in-motion was believed to be constituted). But in relativity these very properties, which had been assumed to characterize the object in itself, were found to depend on the relationship of the object to the observer; the data vary according to the frame of reference from which they are viewed.[7] Science arises from the interplay between nature and ourselves; we have no access to things as they would be apart from our investigation. No clear separation of subject and object is possible. Hanson maintains not only that all data are theory-laden but also that "all properties are observer-dependent."[8]

We might mention in passing the sense of *the unboundedness of nature* that recent physics has encouraged. In the nineteenth cen-

---

6. Henry Margenau, "The New View of Man in his Physical Environment," *The Centennial Review*, Vol. 1 (1957), 24. See also Henry Margenau, *Open Vistas* (New Haven, Conn.: Yale University Press, 1961; PB), pp. 201f.

7. Among popular accounts of relativity are Lincoln Barnett, *The Universe and Dr. Einstein* (New York: New American Library, Mentor PB, 1952); C. V. Durell, *Readable Relativity* (London: G. Bell & Sons, 1926; Harper PB).

8. N. R. Hanson, "The Dematerialization of Matter," in Ernan McMullin, ed., *The Concept of Matter* (Notre Dame, Ind.: University of Notre Dame Press, 1963), p. 549.

tury it appeared that the task of physics was almost done, except for the filling in of details; science seemed to form a convergent series. Like the expanding frontier of the nation, the advances of science seemed to leave less and less territory still to be discovered. But today each scientific discovery raises a dozen new questions, and each problem solved becomes the starting point of a dozen others. It looks more like a divergent than a convergent series; far from tapering off, science seems to be following an accelerating curve. There is a sense of inexhaustible challenge, of surprises yet to come, and of permanent mystery remaining. There is no end in sight among the particles and antiparticles which once were called "elementary." In 1955 some thirty types of "fundamental nuclear particle" were known; by 1965 more than a hundred had been discovered. There seemed to be no order in this chaotic assortment of what were officially called "strange particles" until a totally new theory was developed (known variously as "the eightfold way" because it uses eight quantum numbers, or as "SU3" because it uses the mathematics of special unitary groups of three elements.)[9] In other fields recent discoveries have been equally unexpected; in 1955, who would have dreamed of the four-letter genetic code of DNA, or of a single radio-star that emits a hundred times the energy of our entire galaxy of a hundred billion suns?

But to return to our topic: *the inadequacy of naive realism* in quantum physics. In many cases the relation between theoretical concepts and experimental observations is so indirect that scientists have been forced to reexamine the status of scientific theories. Positivists and instrumentalists, focusing attention on the *experimental* side, and emphasizing the unobservability of theoretical terms, argue that theories tell us nothing about reality—they are only summaries of the data or calculating devices for making predictions about observable phenomena. We will consider shortly such positivistic interpretations of complementarity. Idealists, on the other hand, direct attention to the *theoretical* side as a self-consistent, formal, mathematical system, and find support therein for the claim that reality is essentially mental.

2. "Idealist" Interpretations of Physics

A number of writers have maintained that the new physics provides support for metaphysical idealism, or even for "a spiritual

---

9. See Geoffrey Chew, Murray Gell-Mann, and Arthur Rosenfeld, "Strongly Interacting Particles," *Scientific American* (February 1964), p. 74.

view of the universe." There seem to be three types of argument which have been advanced. First, *the new role of the observer* is taken to imply the primacy of the mental over the material. Barnett interprets relativity to mean that "space has no objective reality except as an order or arrangement of the objects we perceive in it, and time has no independent existence apart from the order of events by which we measure it."[10] Similarly, atomic phenomena are said to depend on the subject and his mind. (It is interesting to recall that after hearing such idealist interpretations Lenin and other Marxists for many years denounced relativity itself, and also quantum theory, as unacceptable "reactionary theories" incompatible with dialectical materialism.)

In reply to these claims, we have already argued that the "involvement of the observer" refers to *observation-processes* and not to mental states as such. The "frame of reference" means the measuring apparatus—clocks, meter sticks, photographic plates—not minds or persons. It is indeed true that we deal with interactions and relationships rather than isolated objects, but we investigate by means of physical instruments. It is the detection apparatus, not the observer as a human being, which influences the measurement obtained. Moreover, recognition of the contribution of the subject to the data need not lead one to neglect the contribution of the object.

A second claim is that *matter is now insubstantial.* The apparent solidity and endurance of matter once seemed the assurance of its reality. But now we know that atoms consist of empty space and probability-waves. Mass, far from being indestructible, is, in the theory of relativity, a temporary manifestation of nonmaterial energy. All forms of matter can be "dematerialized" into energy (as occurs partially in the atomic bomb reaction, and totally in the mutual annihilation of a positive and negative particle to form electromagnetic radiation). Thus one author, after listing such findings, concludes:

> If the Christian view is true, surely we should expect to find the evidence of the Holy Spirit in the physical sphere in just such signs of dynamic energy and activity as are indicated by modern physics. If energy is the essential basis of the whole material world, this is to the Christian a clear manifestation of the active, creative Spirit of God in the physical realm.[11]

---

10. Lincoln Barnett, quoted in Frank, *Philosophy of Science,* p. 176.
11. Arthur Smethurst, *Modern Science and Christian Belief* (Nashville: Abingdon Press, 1955), p. 81.

Sullivan, following Eddington, finds spiritual significance in the downfall of materialism; he holds that physics now studies the form but not the nature of reality:

> The fact that science is confined to a knowledge of structure is obviously of great "humanistic" importance. For it means that the problem of the nature of reality is not prejudged. We are no longer required to believe that our response to beauty, or the mystic's sense of communion with God, have no objective counterpart.[12]

In reply to this proposition, we must criticize *the ambiguity of the term "immaterial."* To be sure, the modern atom lacks many of the properties formerly attributed to matter, and time plays a more fundamental role than in the classical view. But the term "immaterial" has misleading connotations of "mental" and "spiritual." Frank's rejoinder to Sullivan seems justified: "It is hardly more plausible to regard beauty and mystical communion with God as de Broglie waves than to regard them as material masses."[13] Energy, electric fields, radiation, and probability-waves are as physical as billiard-ball atoms, and they are always related to experimental observations. We should remember that there were those in Newton's day who argued that gravitation is a spiritual power because it is invisible and acts at a distance. Moreover, as Stebbing observes,[14] the statement "matter is not really solid" mixes the languages of physics and of familiar experience; the floor is just as solid as it ever was, since by "solid" we mean that it can support heavy objects and resist blows. Conversely, "mass" in physics is not a commonsense term, but a technical concept correlating experimental situations. We may correctly say that the constituents of the atomic world are not picturable and that they do not have the properties of everyday objects; but we should be cautious about applying the adjective "immaterial." Objections may also be raised from the theological side, for biblical religion accepts material existence as part of the created order (see Chapter 12) and does not assert that the whole world is somehow mental or insubstantial.

A third variation is the statement that *the mathematical character* of modern physics shows that reality is essentially mental. Jeans

---

12. J. W. N. Sullivan, *The Limitations of Science* (New York: The Viking Press, 1933; Mentor PB°), p. 142.

13. Frank, *Philosophy of Science*, p. 239.

14. L. Susan Stebbing, *Philosophy and the Physicists* (London: Methuen & Co., 1937; Dover PB), Chap. 3.

holds that these theories are "structures of pure thought incapable of realization in any sense which would properly be described as material." "The universe begins to look more like a great thought than like a great machine. Mind no longer appears as an accidental intruder in the realm of matter."[15] From this he infers that the world must be a thought in a Universal Mind. Now, it is indeed true that formal properties play an impressive part in modern physics (for example, symmetry, topological forms, invariance to transformations, generalized multidimensional spaces) and that the symbolism is highly abstract. But it is misleading to speak of physics as "pure mathematics," for its axioms are not arbitrary, and there is always the test of experiment, even if observations are only very indirectly and remotely tied to the mathematical equations of the theory.[16]

Behind all these arguments lies a more fundamental question. For what reason do we reject the mechanistic world-view that once claimed support from classical physics: (a) was the mistake a *scientific* one, which we now reject because of new scientific discoveries, or (b) was it a *philosophical* and *epistemological* mistake involving an uncritical transition from physics to metaphysics? In the second case we would conclude that a mechanistic world-view never did have legitimate justification, even when it claimed to be based on the best science of its day; and the lesson from the past would lead us to be wary today about extending modern physics into a new metaphysics. If, as we suggested earlier, mechanism was wrong on both scores—that is, it made an invalid extrapolation from a now outmoded science—then we can see in atomic theory a genuine challenge to a mechanistic world-view, but we will not claim that it provides the basis for idealism, or any alternative metaphysical system.

Thus the primary significance of modern physics lies not in any disclosure of the fundamental nature of reality, but in the recognition of *the limitations of science*. The selective and abstractive character of scientific concepts is today widely discussed. The contemporary scientist is aware that any theory is partial, tentative, and incomplete. Humility and caution in extending a particular theory into a total philosophy of life are more prevalent. The new physics is no more adequate for the exhaustive description of all

---

15. Jeans, *The Mysterious Universe*, p. 186.
16. See also our discussion of Eddington's idealism in Chapter 6, Section III.

existence than was the old. To elevate wave-functions to a central metaphysical status is just as dubious as to make matter-in-motion the ultimate category. It is "misplaced concreteness" to take the abstractions of any theory, old or new, as an all-inclusive clue to reality. Neither classical nor modern physics—nor any other specialized science—can do justice to all aspects of human experience or provide a comprehensive world-view. The most we should expect from physics is a modest contribution to a view of nature at one limited level.

3. The Significance of Complementarity

We have indicated the downfall of naive realism in modern physics and the attempt to replace it by an idealist interpretation. The peculiar epistemological difficulties of quantum theory have also been taken by some authors as a vindication of *positivism*, as we saw in Chapter 6. The positivist stresses the empirical side of science, and is impressed by the unobservability of the theoretical terms such as wave-functions. He notes the use of complementary models, such as wave and particle, and the absence of any unified, consistent model, and finds support for his conviction that we should *dispense with all models*—except perhaps as temporary aids in setting up equations with which to organize observations. A theory, he maintains, is not a description of reality, but only a useful calculation device from which one can make predictions— at least on a statistical basis. One cannot say anything about what happens between observations (we do not know "what the electron is doing" after passing through the slits before it reaches the photographic plate, or "how the atom behaves" in the interval between the times it is observed). According to the positivist, it is meaningless to ask questions about intervening events in nature that occur between experimental observations. We should discard models and be content with equations that correlate observables.

Most physicists, however, would probably subscribe to Bohr's advice: *retain both wave and particle models but recognize their limitations.* "A complete elucidation of one and the same object," Bohr writes, "may require diverse points of view which defy a unique description."[17] A duality of representation is required, since differing aspects of the structure of events are interpretable by

---

17. Niels Bohr, *Atomic Theory and the Description of Nature* (Cambridge: Cambridge University Press, 1934; PB), p. 96.

differing models, each of which is incomplete and applicable only to certain experimental situations. We noted earlier Mary Hesse's defense of models as a fruitful source of new ideas for the extension of theories; she has also defended their use in atomic physics, insisting that every model has some features that are inapplicable.[18] It is legitimate to use alternative models under mutually exclusive experimental conditions, even though they cannot be combined into one all-purpose model.

Bohr himself believes that the epistemological lesson of atomic physics can be extended to other phenomena susceptible of analysis by *alternative conceptual schemes*. Thus in biology there is validity in both a *mechanistic* approach (study of physico-chemical components) and an *organic* approach (study of the integrated functioning of the total organism). Often the isolation of one part of the organism for investigation entails the death of the living unit—which Bohr sees as another example of the influence of the observer:

> In biological research, references to features of wholeness and purposeful reactions of organisms are used together with the increasingly detailed information on structure and regulatory processes. . . . It must be realized that the attitudes termed mechanistic and finalistic are not contradictory points of view, but rather exhibit a complementary relationship which is connected with our position as observers of nature.[19]

He finds a similar complementarity between *behavioristic* and *introspective* viewpoints in psychology, where the difficulty in drawing a line between subject and object is obviously acute. *Free will* and *determinism* constitute alternative interpretations of man as seen from mutually exclusive observational positions. "The place for the feeling of volition is afforded," Bohr suggests, "by the very circumstance that situations where we experience freedom of will are incompatible with psychological explanations where causal analysis is reasonably attempted."[20]

A number of physicists have followed Bohr in this *wider use of the idea of complementarity*. Oppenheimer employs it in relation to mechanistic versus organic analyses of life-processes, and also

---

18. Mary Hesse in David Bohm *et al.*, *Quanta and Reality* (Cleveland, Ohio: World Publishing Co., Meridian PB, 1964), p. 56.

19. Bohr, *Atomic Physics and Human Knowledge*, p. 92. Used by permission of John Wiley & Sons, Inc.

20. Niels Bohr, "On the Notions of Causality and Complementarity," *Science*, Vol. 111 (1950), 54.

behavioristic versus introspective descriptions of personality.[21] Coulson applies it to the problems of mind versus brain, free will versus determinism, and teleology versus mechanism. "Mind and matter are different ways of looking at the same set of phenomena."[22] In each case the apparently conflicting accounts are seen as alternative but not contradictory descriptions, and are valuable in differing contexts.

The German physicist, Gunter Höwe, applies the concept of complementarity to various descriptions *within theological discourse*. He is impressed particularly by Barth's dialectical treatment of the attributes of God. An American physicist compares complementarity in physics with the presence of seemingly contradictory ideas in theology, such as the traditional statement that Christ was both fully human and fully divine.[23] Pollard sees complementarity in the paradox of human freedom and divine providence.[24] Some authors employ the concept in an even broader way, referring to various disciplines as complementary perspectives on a single reality; Coulson gives the analogy of a sheaf of diagrams of a single building:

> For the building stands for the reality God, who is being described in the separate disciplines (or diagrams). The modes of description vary greatly, and may sometimes even appear to be wholly different from one another; but at other times there will be common elements. . . . If we can agree on this, then we can see how it comes about that science, art, history, and so on, are to be called authentic revelations of God. . . . In all this we have spoken of art, poetry, history, science, and philosophy as modes of description of the one reality.[25]

In a similar vein, science and religion are sometimes spoken of as "complementary views of reality."

How are we to evaluate such *extensions of the idea of complementarity*? There are several reasons for caution. First, it should be made clear that use of the Complementarity Principle outside physics is *analogical not inferential*. There must be independent grounds for justifying in the new context the value of two alterna-

---

21. J. Robert Oppenheimer, *Science and the Common Understanding* (New York: Simon and Schuster, 1954), Chaps. 4, 5, 6.

22. Coulson, *Science and Christian Belief*, p. 74.

23. Van der Ziel, *The Natural Sciences and the Christian Message*, Chap. 9.

24. William G. Pollard, *Chance and Providence* (New York: Charles Scribner's Sons, 1958), Chap. 4.

25. Coulson, *Science and Christian Belief*, pp. 67–68. Used by permission of University of North Carolina Press.

tive sets of constructs. (No direct link has been established, for example, between the wave-particle dualism at the atomic level and the mechanistic-organic dualism at the biological level.) Insofar as the extended use of complementarity represents an epistemological generalization, the principle must be supported by evidence from other fields, rather than simply transferred to them from physics—which would repeat in a new form the early mechanists' mistake of imposing on other disciplines the methodological assumptions of physics.

Second, the principle within physics refers to *different ways* of *analyzing a single entity* (such as an electron) under varying conditions. The principle might perhaps be extended to refer to the mind and the brain as two manifestations of one system, but it appears more dubious to refer to various disciplines as complementary, unless they are all assumed to analyze the same set of events. (Thus science and religion are not simply two views of one world—unless one subscribes to pantheism and denies transcendence—for God and the world are different modes of being, not different modes of knowing a single being.) Moreover "wave" and "particle" are similar types of term; they yield alternative conceptual schemes that serve the same function within a single (scientific) language, not two languages with differing functions.

Third, the idea of complementarity must not be taken as a veto to *the search for unity*. It provides no justification for premature and uncritical acceptance of dichotomies, or for allowing alternative analyses to be kept in watertight mental compartments without further elucidation of the relationship between them. In addition, the paradoxical element in complementarity should not be overemphasized. After all, we do not say that an electron *is* both a wave and a particle, but only that under varying circumstances it exhibits wave-like and particle-like behavior. The mathematical formalism of quantum mechanics does provide a unified correlation of all the observable phenomena and a method of calculating predictive probabilities, even if it gives no consistent picturable representation of the atomic world.

Fourth, although complementarity has often been given positivist interpretations, it is by no means incompatible with the *critical realism* we advocated earlier. Bohr himself dwells on epistemological problems and avoids ontological ones; he renounces the characterization of objects and stops with complementary accounts from alternative viewpoints. For him, the atomic world, like the Kantian thing-in-itself, is inherently inaccessible to the scientist, who can deal only with the appearances as interpreted in classical concepts (which Bohr calls "forms of perception"). We have argued, on the contrary, that although naive realism is untenable, and a comprehensive picture of reality is indeed impossible, nevertheless the use of scientific concepts is always realistic in intent. Moreover, the scientist does continually try to unify his concepts as much as possible—whereas with Bohr's interpretation there would be no reason (except economy of thought) even to attempt the construction of a unified account.

Our conclusion, then, is that *the idea of complementarity* in physics underscores the abstractive and symbolic character of concepts, the indirectness of their relation to observable phenomena, the limitations of models, and the inadequacy of attempts to visualize reality in terms of the categories of everyday experience. When other fields do provide independent evidence of the value of using alternative conceptual schemes for analyzing the behavior of a single entity under differing conditions, one may legitimately see some analogy with the Complementarity Principle in physics. The principle provides no justification, however, for the easy acceptance of dualisms, for abandonment of the search for synthesis, or for a positivist interpretation of scientific theories.

4. The Whole and the Parts

We have discussed at some length the downfall of the naive realism of classical physics. We now examine more briefly the challenge to the classical postulate of *reductionism*, that is, the assumption that the functioning of any system can be exhaustively explained in terms of the laws governing its component parts. Laplace's statement—that "all future events" could be predicted from knowledge of the present position and velocity of every particle—was reductionistic as well as deterministic, for it assumed that all events can be completely described and understood in terms of such information about the separate components. The inadequacies of reductionism will be considered more fully in later chapters, but they begin to appear, in a limited way, even in modern physics. These aspects of atomic theory do not, when taken alone, seem to have any great significance, and should not be extrapolated beyond the bounds of physics. But as part of a pattern that appears at various levels of existence they warrant comment here.

In quantum theory *the atom must be represented as a whole* rather than as a collection of parts. Consider the helium atom, which has a double-charged nucleus and two electrons. In the "planetary model" it was pictured as a nucleus around which circled two separate identifiable electrons; the atom's parts were clearly distinguishable, and the laws of its total behavior were derivable from analysis of the behavior of these components. But in quantum theory the helium atom is a total pattern with no distinguishable parts. Its wave-function is not at all the sum of two separate single-electron wave-functions. The electrons have lost their individuality; we do not have electron A and electron B, but simply a two-electron pattern in which all separate identity is lost. (In the statistics of classical physics, an atom with electron A in an excited energy state and electron B in a normal state counts as a different configuration from the atom with electrons A and B interchanged, but in quantum theory it does not.) De Broglie writes:

> The particles which form these systems seem to lose the individuality and the autonomy with which our very conception of the idea of particles seemed bound to endow them; these particles are in some way built into the systems which incorporate them and from diverse points of view the system appears to be more than the totality of particles of which it is formed. . . . The system thus appears as a sort of unit of higher order in the heart of which the constituents are so much the more difficult to isolate in that they are more strongly united between themselves by the interactions.[26]

If we consider more complex atoms with additional electrons, we find that their configurations are governed by the *Pauli Exclusion Principle*—a law concerning the total atom which cannot conceivably be derived from laws concerning individual electrons. The principle states that in a given atom no two electrons can be in identical states (or have identical quantum numbers specifying energy, angular momentum, orientation, and spin). To this remarkable and far-reaching principle can be attributed the periodic chemical properties of the elements. When another electron is added to a given atom, it must assume a state different from all electrons already present, even if this necessitates a very different energy (as occurs in starting a new "row" of the familiar periodic table). If one used classical reasoning, one would have to assume

---

26. De Broglie, *Physics and Microphysics*, pp. 111, 135. Used by permission of Random House, Inc., and Hutchinson & Co., Ltd.

that the new electron is somehow influenced by the states of all the other electrons; but this "exclusion" does not resemble any imaginable set of forces or fields. By quantum reasoning any attempt to describe the behavior of the constituent electrons is simply abandoned, and the properties of the atom as a whole are analyzed by new laws unrelated to those governing its separate "parts," which have now lost their identity. Margenau gives this summary:

> The essence of mechanistic reasoning is seen to cluster around two beliefs: first that entities are divisible into parts, and second that these parts are localizable in space and time. . . . Prior to [the exclusion principle], all theories had affected the *individual* nature of the so-called "parts"; the new principle regulated their *social* behavior. With respect to a single particle it has nothing to say. And what it says for aggregates, though most important, cannot be expressed in terms of *dynamic* regulation. It is as though here, for the first time, physics had discovered within its own precincts a purely social law, a law that is simple in its basic formulation and yet immense in its collective effects. Mechanistic reasoning, already far behind, has gone out of sight as a result of this latest advance. . . . In the Pauli principle is a way of understanding why entities show in their togetherness laws of behavior different from the laws which govern them in isolation. . . . The emergence of new properties on composition is a rather general phenomenon in modern physics and owes its occurrence to the exclusion principle.[27]

There are other cases in which *analysis of a system as a whole* is required in physics. The energy levels of an array of atoms in the solid state (such as a crystal lattice) are a property of the whole system rather than of its components. Again, some of the disorder-order transitions, and the so-called "cooperative phenomena," have proven impossible to analyze atomistically—for example, the process whereby, when a metal is cooled, elementary magnetic units suddenly line up with each other. Such situations, writes one physicist, "involve a new organizing principle as we proceed from the individual to the system," and result in "qualitatively new phenomena."[28] There seem to be system-laws that are not derivable from the laws of the components; there are distinctive explanatory concepts characteristic of higher organizational levels—as we shall see

---

27. Margenau, *The Nature of Physical Reality*, pp. 442, 444. Used by permission of McGraw-Hill Book Company.

28. E. Purcell, "Parts and Wholes in Physics," in D. Lerner, ed., *Parts and Wholes* (New York: The Free Press of Glencoe, Inc., 1963).

again in the next chapter. Interpenetrating fields and integrated totalities replace self-contained, externally related particles as fundamental images of nature. The being of any entity is constituted by its relationships and its participation in more inclusive patterns. Such examples allow us to begin to give a more precise meaning to the statement that "the whole is more than the sum of its parts."

It is thus frequently necessary in modern physics to consider *an organized system as a whole*, whereas in classical physics its elements could be considered separately. We have seen that observer and observed can no longer be assumed to be separable. Again, time and space are indissolubly united in a space-time continuum. Matter and energy must be taken together as matter-energy, and according to relativity matter-energy is simply a distortion in the structure of space. In quantum theory, separate particles seem to be temporary and partial manifestations of a shifting pattern of waves that combine at one point, dissolve again, and recombine elsewhere; a particle begins to look like a local outcropping of a continuous substratum of vibratory energy. As more complex systems are built up, new properties appear that were not foreshadowed in the parts alone. Each of two separate hydrogen atoms will attract a third hydrogen atom; but when the two combine to form a molecule, the third atom will be repelled. New wholes do not of course contain any mysterious entities in addition to their parts, but they do have distinctive principles of organization as systems, and therefore exhibit properties and activities not found in their components.

Finally, the central role of *time* at several points in modern physics deserves mention.

a. Classically, matter was thought to consist of inert particles that could be rearranged in space without themselves undergoing any change; a particle does not require any temporal duration in order to be. In the new physics, time is constitutive of the being of atoms as *vibratory patterns*; a wave or a musical note requires time in order to exist—a note is nothing at an instant. Matter seems more like a sequence of events than a collection of substances.

b. Classically, time was an independent variable, separate from and essentially extraneous to spatial relationships. In relativity, the four-dimensional *space-time manifold* is a fusion of space and time. Just as "vertical" and "horizontal" dimensions of a box vary according to its orientation relative to the observer, so the "spatial" and the "temporal" components of the separation of two events will vary for observers moving with respect to each other. Since "simultaneity" is not absolute and there is no cosmic "now," there are no purely spatial or geometrical relationships in nature, but only spatiotemporal ones.[29]

c. If indeterminacy is a characteristic of nature, as will be suggested below, then only the passage of time discloses which of the various atomic probabilities or *potentialities* is actualized. The future is not inexorably contained in the present; time is not the unwinding of the predetermined scroll of events, but the spontaneous and novel coming-into-being of the unpredictable in an unrepeatable history. Thus in the new view of matter—as in the evolutionary picture of the universe which we will examine later—time plays a more constitutive role than in the science of earlier centuries.

III. Interpretations of Indeterminacy

We have indicated that modern physics has challenged naive realism and reductionism. The challenge to determinism is more problematical, for the significance of the Heisenberg Principle is still debated. Clearly, Laplace's claim that all future events could be predicted from knowledge of the present is abandoned in quantum theory; for we cannot predict both exact position and exact velocity, and we can calculate only probabilities for the future. But is this uncertainty the result of indeterminacy in nature—or is it only a confession of human ignorance? Does it mean that there are no exact laws in the atomic world—or only that we have not yet discovered such laws? Is the uncertainty, in other words, objective or subjective in character?

Three answers have been given: (1) Uncertainty is attributed to *temporary human ignorance*, in the conviction that there are exact laws which will eventually be discovered. (2) Uncertainty is attributed to *inherent experimental or conceptual limitations*, for the observer inevitably disturbs the system he is observing, and theories of the atom inescapably utilize the concepts of everyday experience; the atom in itself is forever inaccessible to man.

---

29. See Milič Čapek, *The Philosophical Impact of Modern Physics* (Princeton, N.J.: D. Van Nostrand Co., 1961), Chaps. 10–13.

(3) Uncertainty is attributed to *indeterminacy in nature*; there are alternative potentialities in the atomic world. The first position is realistic (in epistemology) and *deterministic* (in metaphysics); the second is positivistic and *agnostic* (since we can never know how the atom itself behaves between observations); the third, which we will defend, is realistic and *indeterministic*. The implications of indeterminacy for human freedom are treated in the subsequent section.

1. *Uncertainty as Human Ignorance (Einstein, Bohm)*

Some of our uncertainties may reflect our lack of knowledge about systems that conform to precise laws. Uncertainty about the weather may be no more than a confession of human ignorance of meteorology. One cannot predict the toss of a coin; but perhaps the prediction could be made if one knew enough (how hard the coin was flipped, how much air resistance there was, and so forth). The uncertainty would be entirely *subjective*, representing incompleteness of information; objectively, the system is determined. Probability would then be epistemological rather than ontological in origin, a measure of our lack of knowledge rather than of anything in nature itself. (Kinetic theory took just this view of probability; statistical laws for large groups of molecules were developed on the assumption that the motions of all the individual particles, though precisely determined by mechanical laws, were too complex to calculate. Randomness, which appears to be chance, was ascribed to variable combinations of many independent determinate forces.)

A minority of physicists, including Einstein, Planck, and more recently, de Broglie,[30] have maintained that the uncertainties of quantum mechanics are similarly attributable to *our present ignorance*. They believe that there are detailed subatomic mechanisms which are rigidly causal and deterministic; some day the laws of these mechanisms will be found and exact prediction will be possible. Einstein wrote: "The great initial success of quantum theory cannot convert me to believe in that fundamental game of dice. . . . I am absolutely convinced that one will eventually arrive at a theory

---

30. On de Broglie, see n. 2 above. See also Ernst Cassirer, *Determinism and Indeterminism in Modern Physics*, trans. T. Benfy (New Haven, Conn.: Yale University Press, 1956); M. Planck, *The Universe in the Light of Modern Physics* (New York: W. W. Norton & Co., 1931).

in which the objects connected by laws are not probabilities but conceived facts."[31] Einstein was an epistemological realist, holding that the concepts of physics must "refer to things which claim real existence independent of perceiving subjects." He was confident that nature follows precise laws which our future theories will express.

David Bohm[32] has recently attempted to construct a new formalism, using what he calls "*hidden variables*" which escape present observation but determine observed results. He wants to develop a theory which would provide a detailed deterministic mechanism at the subatomic level. So far, his calculations yield no empirical conclusions that differ from those of quantum mechanics, though Bohm hopes that in the future the "hidden variables" may play a detectable role. He acknowledges von Neumann's proof that indeterminacy is an inescapable feature of existing quantum theory and cannot be removed by simply adding terms to it; but he anticipates the restoration of determinism in a totally new theoretical structure. The apparent randomness at the atomic level would arise from variations in the concurrence of exact forces at the subatomic level (comparable to the situation assumed in kinetic theory). Bohm speculates that the postulated subatomic laws might in turn be the statistical averages of sub-subatomic randomness, arising from fluctuations in even more basic lawful mechanisms, and so on. But the net effect of Bohm's proposal would be deterministic, since the uncertainty at any level could be removed by analysis of the exact laws of the next lower level. The uncertainty at any stage would represent a temporary state of human ignorance.

Most scientists are *dubious about such proposals*. In the absence of any clear experimental evidence, the defense of determinism rests largely on philosophical grounds. (Einstein expressed his own faith in the order and predictability of the universe—which in his rationalistic perspective would be marred by any element of chance.) We must grant that in the history of science many uncertainties turned out to be the result of inaccuracy in man's knowledge. But the exact laws discovered in the past were often statistical averages for large numbers of atoms, and we cannot necessarily apply the lesson of history to the study of individual atoms; the atomic world seems to be very different from that of ordinary experience. To be sure, there are other reasons for dissatisfaction with the present state of quantum theory, apart from the question of uncertainty (for example, for very high energies certain equations give expressions with infinite values or an infinite number of solutions, which only an arbitrary "renormalization" procedure removes). However, most physicists expect these deficiencies to be corrected not by discarding but by developing further the existing probabilistic quantum theory, which has proved its power in case after case over the last forty years. Unless someone can actually develop an alternative theory that can be tested, we had better accept the theories we have and give up our nostalgia for the certainties of the past. As Hanson puts it:

> Speculation is never an alternative to a working theory, however imperfect that theory may be. . . . There is as yet no working alternative [to quantum mechanics]. Ask your nearest synchrotron operator. . . . Expressions of discomfort at this juncture are often ways of announcing that one likes his physics deterministic, orthodox, Newtonian.[33]

2. Uncertainty as Experimental or Conceptual Limitations (Bohr)

Many physicists are convinced that uncertainty is not a product of temporary ignorance, but a fundamental limitation on human knowledge which permanently prevents us from knowing whether events in the atomic domain are determinate or not. The first version of this position claims that the difficulty is an experimental one: *the uncertainty is introduced by the process of observation.* Suppose that we want to observe an isolated electron. To do so we must bombard it with a quantum of light, which disturbs the situation we were attempting to study. (The use of light quanta of shorter wavelength permits more accurate location of the electron's position; but such quanta have higher energy, causing a greater disturbance of the electron's velocity—the Heisenberg Principle again.) The disturbance of the system is unavoidable, since there must be at least a minimal interaction of the observed and the observer. (The "observer," as we have indicated, here refers to an experimental process, not to a mind; the act of measuring, not the act of apprehending, is the locus of the problem.)

---

33. N. R. Hanson in D. Bohm *et al.*, *Quanta and Reality*, p. 92 (used by permission of the American Research Council and Hutchinson & Co.); and in *Philosophy of Science: Readings Selected, Edited, and Introduced* by Arthur Danto and Sidney Morgenbesser. Copyright © 1960 by the World Publishing Company. Reprinted by arrangement with the World Publishing Company, Cleveland and New York—a Meridian Book, pp. 455, 463.

Although this interpretation fits many experiments, it appears unable to account for *uncertainties when nothing is done to disturb the system*—for example, the unpredictability of the time at which a radioactive atom spontaneously disintegrates, or the time at which an isolated atom makes a transition from an excited state. Quite apart from any measuring process, a system may lose one form of precision and gain another—for example, in the spontaneous "diffusion of wave packets." Moreover, the idea of "disturbing the system," even when it applies, does not in itself explain the element of unpredictability. Even in classical physics there were disturbances that could not be eliminated—yet they could be allowed for in calculating what the situation would have been without them (for instance, in measuring the heat capacity of a very small object one could allow for the disturbing influence of the thermometer). The unpredictability of the atomic realm, then, is a distinctive feature of quantum mechanics—from whose postulates the Heisenberg Principle can be derived without reference to disturbances introduced by the observer.

The second version of the argument *attributes uncertainty to our inescapable conceptual limitations.* Man as thinker and knower, not as experimenter, is the source of the difficulty. It is held that interpretive concepts are derived from everyday commonsense experience—and are then used to formulate theoretical models of the atomic world. We have encountered this view already in Niels Bohr's rendition of the Complementarity Principle. Von Weizsäcker says that "we ourselves have created the perceptible forms of the real through our experiment."[34] By our choice of experimental situations we decide in which of our conceptual schemes (wave or particle, exact position or exact velocity) an electron will manifest itself to us. In particular, the structure of the atomic world is such that we must choose either causal descriptions (by probability-functions which evolve deterministically) or spatio-temporal descriptions (by individual localized observations which are only statistically connected)—but we cannot have both at once.

The authors writing in this vein usually subscribe to a *positivist view* of science. Probability-functions are useful calculating tools for coordinating observations, not representations of the real world:

> The salient point is that according to Bohr every state or arrangement can be "interpreted" by particles, but he does not claim that particles

---

34. Von Weizsäcker, *The World View of Physics*, p. 57.

"exist." . . . The interpretations lead us into deep water, however, if we take them too seriously, which means if we regard them as statements about reality. We invite trouble if we ask the question, what are the "real" physical objects. . . . Bohr would refuse to give the "phenomenon" or the psi-function [probability distribution] the attribute "real." . . . According to him, these are two descriptions of the same atomic object which serve different purposes.[35]

This interpretation is therefore *agnostic* as to whether the atom itself, which we can never know, is determinate or indeterminate (though a particular author expounding it may favor one assumption or the other on other grounds). The ontological question of the character of the world is ignored or dismissed as meaningless. We have indicated in Chapter 6 our reasons for rejecting this positivist view.

3. Uncertainty as Indeterminacy in Nature (Heisenberg)

The first position above expresses the fundamental conviction that nature follows deterministic laws, and ascribes uncertainties to temporary human ignorance. The second ascribes uncertainty to inescapable experimental or conceptual limitations, which will always prevent us from knowing what the atom itself is like. A third position endorsed by many physicists holds that *indeterminacy is an objective feature of nature*, and not a limitation of man's knowledge. These men maintain that since quantum theory has been tested in thousands of experiments it must, like other accepted theories, be taken as a reliable portrayal of the world. Such a viewpoint would accord with the critical realism we have advocated in which scientific theories are held to be representations of nature, albeit limited and imperfect ones. These limitations help to remind us that the denizens of the atomic realm are of a very different sort from the objects of everyday experience— but this does not mean that they are less real. Instead of postulating that an electron has a precise position and velocity which is unknown to us, we should conclude that it is not the sort of entity which has such properties at all.

Margenau[36] holds that "the uncertainty does not reside in the imperfection in our measurements, nor in man's ability to know;

35. Frank, *Philosophy of Science*, p. 244. Used by permission of Prentice-Hall, Inc.

36. H. Margenau, "Advantages and Disadvantages of Various Interpretations of the Quantum Theory," *Physics Today*, Vol. 7 (1954), 6f. See also his *Open Vistas*, Chaps. 6, 7.

it has its cause in nature herself." There is no exact causal connection between observable events, since measurement consists in
extracting from the existing distribution one of the many *possibilities* it contains. "The act of measurement is a human ingres-
sion into the state of a physical system which has the consequence
of calling position into being, into actuality." The "influence of
the observer," on this view, does not consist in disturbing a previously precise though unknown value, but in forcing one of the
many existing potentialities to be actualized. The observer's activity becomes part of the history of the atomic event, but it is an
objective history, and even the spontaneously disintegrating atom,
left to itself, has its history. Heisenberg writes similarly that "the
transition from the 'possible' to the 'actual' takes place during the
act of observation."[37]

Some authors speak of individual atomic events as *uncaused*,
since they are not strictly determined. But "uncaused" seems to
imply that the future springs up *de novo*, unrelated to its antecedents; this is not the case, for the probabilities at one instant are
precisely and unambiguously determined by the wave-functions at
earlier instants. On the other hand we cannot speak here of *absolute causation* or necessary connection, for the past passes on to
the future a set of probabilities. One alone out of these many
potentialities can be realized. Perhaps such a relation between
events, in which the range of probabilities but not the particular
occurrence is determined, can be called *a weak form of causality*,
distinguishing it from a determinate relation which would be a
strong form of causality.[38]

If this interpretation is correct, indeterminacy is an ontological
reality. Heisenberg calls this "the restoration of the concept of
potentiality." In the Middle Ages the idea of potentiality referred
to the tendency of an entity to develop in a particular direction.
Heisenberg does not accept the Aristotelian manner of describing
a potentiality as a striving to attain a future purpose, but he does
suggest that the probabilities of modern physics refer to tendencies
in nature that include *a range of possibilities*. This is a merging
of aspects of Aristotelian potentiality and Newtonian causality in
a distinctive way that differs from both previous views. The future

---

37. Werner Heisenberg, *Physics and Philosophy* (New York: Harper and
Brothers, 1958; PB), p. 54.
38. See F. S. C. Northrop's Introduction to Heisenberg, *ibid*.

is not simply unknown, it is "not decided"; but it is not completely "open," since the present determines the range of future possibilities. Reichenbach[39] suggests that this requires modification of the traditional two-valued logic (in which a statement is actually always either true or false, though our knowledge of it may be uncertain), in favor of a three-valued logic, in which uncertain means "not decided" and hence neither true nor false. If indeterminacy is thus an attribute of nature, more than one alternative is open and there is some opportunity for unpredictable novelty. Time involves a unique historicity and unrepeatability; the world would not repeat its course if it were restored to a former state, for at each point a different event from among the potentialities might be actualized. Potentiality is objective and not merely subjective.

IV. INDETERMINACY AND HUMAN FREEDOM

It is a long jump from the atom to man. The status of life and mind should be discussed before considering man's freedom. But because determinism at the atomic level has been interpreted as excluding freedom, and indeterminacy as allowing it, we will take issue with both claims here. The implications of indeterminacy for the representation of God's activity in nature will be taken up in Chapter 13. We consider first several versions of determinism, and then some difficulties in the identification of freedom with indeterminacy. Finally, a view of the self as agent is proposed. Freedom is a topic on which many volumes have been written, and we can do little more than indicate why it cannot be analyzed in the categories of physics.

1. Assertions of Determinism

The most common version of determinism, sometimes referred to as "hard determinism," assumes that (a) all events are determined, (b) freedom is the absence of determinism, and thus (c) freedom is illusory. The first point was once defended by assuming that classical physics provides an exhaustive description of reality, as in Laplace's contention that all future events could be predicted from knowledge of the present state of all particles. Although such prediction is impossible in quantum physics, we have seen that one can still reason that events themselves are

39. Reichenbach, *The Rise of Scientific Philosophy*, Chap. 11.

RELIGION AND THE THEORIES OF SCIENCE

determined and our knowledge is incomplete. If atomic events
follow exact laws, and if the laws of all entities can be expressed
without remainder in terms of the laws of their component atoms,
then every event is determined.

In *behaviorism* it is specifically assumed that all human actions
are determined. Man is taken to be a complex stimulus-response
mechanism, whose behavioral output is the product of the forces
acting on him. His acts are lawful functions of external factors
impinging on him. Only when we do not know the causes of an
act do we in our ignorance attribute it to a supposed free and
active self. B. F. Skinner asserts:

> If we are to use the methods of science in the field of human affairs,
> we must assume that behavior is lawful and determined. We must
> expect to discover that what a man does is the result of specifiable
> conditions and that once these conditions have been discovered, we
> can anticipate and to some extent determine his actions. . . . The self
> is most commonly used as a hypothetical cause of action. So long as
> external variables go unnoticed or are ignored, their function is as-
> signed to an originating agent within the organism. If we cannot show
> what is responsible for a man's behavior, we say that he himself is
> responsible for it.[40]

Freedom, like indeterminacy, is said to be another name for our
ignorance of operative causes. Other determinists in the psycho-
analytic tradition point to the influence of subconscious forces on
actions and suggest that no person can be held responsible for
his acts, since character is the product of childhood experiences
over which he had no control; a murderer may be expressing ag-
gression because as a child he never knew love and security. In
this view, punishment and blame have no justification except as
pragmatic expedients used by society to deter future antisocial
behavior.[41]

Another version, sometimes called "*soft determinism*," assumes
that (a) all events are determined, (b) freedom is not the absence
of determinism, but a particular kind, namely *self-determination*,
and thus (c) freedom so defined is compatible with determinism.

40. B. F. Skinner, *Science and Human Behavior* (New York: The Macmillan Co., 1956), pp. 6, 283.
41. See essays by Paul Edwards and John Hospers in S. Hook, ed., *Determinism and Freedom* (New York: New York University Press, 1958; Collier
PB).

Responsibility for one's actions, far from implying that they are undetermined, requires that actions be determined by one's own motives.[42] To say of an act, "I did it freely," means that there was no external compulsion or constraint—not that there were no motives for doing it. Freedom is not the absence of causation, but the absence of any interference in carrying out one's intentions:

> I am free when my conduct is under my own control, and I act under constraint when my conduct is controlled by someone else. My conduct is under my own control when it is determined by my own desires, motives, and intentions, and not under my control when it is determined by the desires, motives, and intentions of someone else.[43]

Acts are determined by motives, and *motives are determined by earlier events*, on this reading. Could I have acted otherwise than I did in a particular situation? Yes, if I had wanted to, that is, if I had had different motives. But from the motives I had, the action followed unalterably. The "soft determinists" construe *motives* in various ways. For some, they are comparable to physical forces whose resultant is a single specifiable force—"the strongest motive wins out." For others, motives are not causes but simply tendencies to act in a certain way. Or again they may be understood to be dispositions and attitudes existing antecedent to and independent of acts; the enduring set of such attitudes is called "character." Without continuity and stability of character a person's actions would be chaotic and random. Some authors[44] holding this position have given careful attention to the dynamics of personality, and in some cases their concept of selfhood has approached the view we will defend shortly. Nevertheless this school of thought seems to have preserved an image of causality of which deterministic forces in classical physics are the model.

2. Freedom as Indeterminacy

Early in the century, before the advent of quantum theory, Charles Peirce postulated small *chance variations* in physical causality in order to account for the spontaneity of the world and the activity

42. See J. Laird, *On Human Freedom* (London: G. Allen & Unwin, 1947).
43. University of California Associates, "The Freedom of the Will," in G. P. Adams *et al.*, *Knowledge and Society* (New York: D. Appleton-Century, 1938); reprinted in Feigl and Sellars, eds., *Readings*, p. 599.
44. E.g., A. Ewing, "Indeterminism," *Review of Metaphysics*, Vol. 5 (1951), 221.

of the mind. William James felt that the idea of a real future requires some "looseness" or "disconnectedness" in the universe; man's experience of moral responsibility, he held, implies genuine alternatives of choice. Bergson urged that if there is change and "becoming" in the world there must be essential novelty and unpredictability.[45]

More recently the defenders of freedom have often invoked *the Heisenberg Principle*, taken as an expression of objective indeterminacy in nature rather than subjective uncertainty in man's knowledge. Physics, which had always been the prime witness for determinism, could now testify to indeterminacy at the most basic level. Eddington, for example, links quantum uncertainties to man's consciousness of volition; "at some brain center the course of behavior of certain atoms or elements of the physical world is directly determined for them by mental decision."[46] Volition decides which of the probabilities is actualized, without violating the laws of physics. Arthur Compton writes that volition is not itself causally determined by physical states; and in turn atoms that are physically identical (having the same wave-functions) will produce differing results (such as electron velocities):

> A knowledge of the initial conditions does not enable us to predict what will happen, for with the same initial conditions we cannot consistently produce the same effect. . . . The matter in our brains may occur in conditions which though physically indistinguishable nevertheless correspond to distinguishable states of consciousness.[47]

Thus what appears random to the scientist may be caused by a mental state within which there is freedom.

Several questions must be raised about this association of *indeterminacy* with *freedom*. First, do *individual atoms* play a significant part in the activity of the brain? Most biological phenomena involve large numbers of atoms, for which predictable (statistical) laws would hold. There are also various mechanisms that provide stability against random fluctuations (for example, thresholds for nerve excitation prevent the transmission of small spurious

---

45. Charles Peirce, *Chance, Love, and Logic* (New York: Harcourt, Brace, 1923); William James, "The Dilemma of Determinism," in *The Will to Believe* (New York: Longmans, Green and Co., 1921; Dover PB); Henri Bergson, *Time and Free Will* (London: George Allen & Unwin, 1950; Harper PB).

46. Eddington, *The Nature of the Physical World*, p. 332.

47. Compton, *The Freedom of Man*, pp. 37, 44. Used by permission of Yale University Press.

signals).[48] But there are some cases in which a small variation is "amplified," or a minute change "triggers" a large one. According to some biologists[49] it is not implausible that a few atoms (for which Heisenberg indeterminacy would be pronounced) at critical neural junctions could start a switchover from one pulse-conduction pattern to another. A single cosmic-ray particle can produce an unpredictable gene mutation, resulting in large-scale changes in an organism, because its effects are "amplified" in the process of growth. It is possible that atomic indeterminacy plays a role in biological phenomena, but little is known about it at present.

Second, the identification of indeterminacy with freedom may be questioned *on philosophical grounds*. To the physicist, the outcome among quantum probabilities is strictly a matter of *chance*. The electron's behavior shows randomness, not freedom. To be sure, both freedom and chance result in unpredictability, but they have little else in common. We would hardly attribute freedom to a roulette wheel simply because its stopping point is not predictable. A breach in causality does not in itself yield a significant concept of freedom; uncaused action would be chaotic and random, not at all what we mean by responsible choice. Within physics the only alternatives are determinate cause and indeterminate chance, and freedom cannot be equated with either. It is reductionistic to seek the clue to human freedom in a property of isolated atoms—a property, moreover, shared by all atoms, including those of "inanimate objects." But if one introduces mind as a distinctive nonmaterial cause which somehow influences electrons, one is led to a mind-body dualism (see below), for which the indeterminacy of the physical world is really irrelevant. In such a scheme the brain (whether determinate or indeterminate) is controlled by the mind, and it is the freedom and independence of the mental realm, not the physical, on which one's case would depend.

3. *Freedom as an Alternative Language*

Neither determinism nor indeterminacy in physics seems to provide a suitable model for human freedom. The defense of freedom must start, not from the properties of the atom, but from the human

---

48. See A. Bachem, "Heisenberg's Indeterminacy Principle and Life," *Philosophy of Science*, Vol. 19 (1952), 261.

49. E.g., J. C. Eccles, *The Neurophysiological Basis of Mind* (London: Oxford University Press, 1953), pp. 271f.

experience of deliberation, decision, and the initiation of action. Man's creativity is unpredictable in principle as well as in practice. To have predicted a Beethoven symphony would have required writing it before Beethoven did; to have foreseen Newton's laws would have meant discovering them before Newton. For a person to predict his own decision before it is made would require that he had made it already. Furthermore, freedom is a precondition of moral and intellectual responsibility. The laws of civilized societies distinguish between actions performed with deliberate intent and those which are involuntary or unintentional.[50] Man's radical freedom to take responsibility for his own actions has of course received vigorous defense from the existentialists, for whom authentic human existence consists precisely in commitment and decision, creativity and individuality, courage and resolve.

If we start from such distinctive human experiences of freedom, how can we also allow for the predominantly deterministic findings of science? The classic solution, systematically developed by Descartes, was the *mind-body dualism*. Mind is a distinctive substance, a free rational intelligence, a separate self-contained entity that controls the body. Matter, including man's body, follows exact mechanical laws (indeterminacy in matter, if it occurs, would in this scheme only be a hindrance to the mind's ability to use the body in carrying out its free choices). We shall suggest in the next chapter some difficulties in such a dualism; in particular, if mind and body have no properties in common, what kind of interactive link between them can there be? Here we note that dualism, like both the determinism and indeterminacy described earlier, does attempt to provide a set of metaphysical categories applicable to all entities in the world; all three schools of thought assume a realist epistemology.

But many contemporary thinkers abandon any such attempt to describe in a unified set of categories the structure of reality. They assert that our concepts serve more limited functions in the fulfillment of specialized purposes. On this view, freedom and determinism are concepts in *two different languages*. A choice is free when described from within, in first-person "actor-language"; it

50. See William Barrett, "Determinism and Novelty," in Hook, ed., *Determinism and Freedom*; Austin Farrer, *The Freedom of the Will* (New York: Charles Scribner's Sons, 1960). A massive classification of issues and extensive bibliography is given in Mortimer Adler, *The Idea of Freedom*, 2 vols. (Garden City, N.Y.: Doubleday & Co., 1958, 1961).

is determined when described in the "spectator-language" of the scientist observing the same events externally. Despite the tension between them, both languages are needed to describe human experience. Bohr and other physicists speak of freedom and determinism as "complementary descriptions" of man—extending, as we have seen, the idea of complementarity from the wave-particle dualism. The psychologist Carl Rogers writes:

> Behavior, when it is examined scientifically, is surely best understood as determined by prior causation. This is one great fact of science. But responsible personal choice, which is the core experience of psychotherapy, and which exists prior to any scientific endeavor, is an equally prominent fact in our lives. To deny the experience of responsible choice is, to me, as restricted a view as to deny the possibility of behavioral science. That these two important elements in our experience appear to be in contradiction has perhaps the same significance as the contradiction between the wave theory and the corpuscular theory of light, both of which can be shown to be true even though incompatible.[51]

It has been proposed by a number of *linguistic analysts* that determinism is a useful postulate within science; it is not a universal truth about the world, but a "fruitful maxim" or "rule of procedure" for scientific inquiry. For if the scientist assumes that every event has a cause, and searches for regularities, he is more likely to achieve his goals of prediction and control. But other languages, such as those of daily affairs, are fruitful for other purposes, which may be achieved more fully by assuming that some human acts can be described as free by those who perform them. In understanding human actions other types of explanation—for example, attention to "reasons" or "goals"—may be more useful than causal explanations.[52] The idea of "complementary languages" here derives, not from the Complementarity Principle in physics, but from analysis of the varying functions of language in human life.

This idea of *complementary languages* does not postulate two distinct entities or substances in man, and thus avoids a metaphysical dualism. Moreover, it acknowledges the limitations of all our conceptual categories; to describe diverse aspects of human

---

51. Carl Rogers and B. F. Skinner, "Some Issues Concerning the Control of Human Behavior," *Science*, Vol. 124 (1956), 1057.

52. See the symposium on "Motives and Causes" in *Proceedings of the Aristotelian Society*, Sup. Vol. 26 (1952); also articles by Philippa Foot and Richard Taylor in S. Morgenbesser and A. Danto, eds., *Free Will* (Englewood Cliffs, N.J.: Prentice-Hall PB), which has an excellent bibliography.

experience one may have to use concepts that cannot be fitted into a single neat system of ideas. Nevertheless the demand for coherence of thought, as well as the image of man as a unitary being, seems to require us to analyze further the relationships between the aspects of man which give rise to such diverse languages. We have suggested that "complementarity" does not have to be interpreted positivistically, nor need it cut short the search for unity.

4. Freedom as Act of the Total Person

None of the preceding positions—determinist, indeterminist, dualist, or even the "two language" view—provides a satisfactory model of selfhood, a concept of the total person as an active, integrated system.[53] The act of decision is not an automatic summation of motives, like the resultant of physical forces. Nor does it resemble a random process such as the physicist's "chance." Nor is choice made by a separable part of man—his mind, or some faculty of "free will" or "volition"—but by the whole person. The "two languages" solution does indeed permit the dynamics of selfhood to be more faithfully transcribed, but it fails to give any unified view of man. We have said that the critical realist must seek *a coherent picture* while recognizing that all language-systems are selective and abstractive. Scientific language abstracts the regular and lawful aspects of reality (including statistical laws within which it postulates chance), and personal language abstracts the aspects of human activity most intimately reflected in conscious life; but the two accounts are not unrelated.

It must first be granted that past events *condition the activity of the person.* The reasons one gives for an act may be largely rationalizations of unconscious motives. There is a continuity between formative experiences and the resulting personality structure, as there is between personality and its acts. Without this stability of ongoing character, choice would be arbitrary and chaotic. Yet, as Whitehead insists, the influences of the past can be received, synthesized, and responded to in more than one way. The person is not a passive stimulus-response mechanism, but *an active self-*

---

53. See C. A. Campbell, *On Selfhood and Godhood* (New York: The Macmillan Co., 1957), Chap. 9, and his "In Defense of Free-Will," in M. Munitz, ed., *A Modern Introduction to Ethics* (Glencoe, Ill.: The Free Press, 1958).

organizing system with at least limited autonomy and spontaneity. An artist's work reflects forces in his past, yet he has the capacity to create an original painting. Such novelty is not discontinuous from antecedent events, but neither is it completely specified by them. Moreover, as we saw in discussing uniqueness in history, each individual represents an unrepeatable configuration of memories, attitudes, and purposes.

Moreover, human choices are influenced by *moral and intellectual ideals.* Man's reflection concerning ideal ends and his commitment to them do shape his behavior. Decisions are based, at least in part, on values adopted. Man as rational thinker responds to abstract ideas and envisages ideal possibilities. He has a distinctive capacity for imagination and anticipation; he can reflect on alternative ends and conceive of new ways of achieving them. In deliberation, attention can be directed among a variety of types of consideration. Man acts in terms of future goals—which does not mean that the future somehow influences the present, but that the present envisagement of alternative potentialities, and intentions to achieve particular purposes, does modify human actions. Freedom involves not only the absence of external compulsion (freedom *from* constraint) but the positive power to act (freedom *to* achieve goals), which has internal conditions. Freedom to love, for example, requires some measure of personal integration, harmony, and maturity. Psychotherapy indicates great diversity in the extent of self-knowledge and awareness of personal attitudes, but it presupposes at least some capacity to examine oneself, and to take responsibility for one's own life once one has recognized the power of influences from the past.

How is such *activity of the self* related to *the laws of atoms?* Reductionists, holding that the laws of higher levels can in principle be derived from the laws of lower levels, believe that behavior can be explained in physico-chemical terms. If atoms are determined, so are people; if atoms are indeterminate, so are people. Dualists, on the other hand, postulate a realm of selfhood the behavior of which is quite independent of the laws of atoms. The view of *levels*, which we will develop in the next chapter, is neither reductionistic nor dualistic. The theories and laws of a higher level of organization are not derivable from those of lower levels, but there are no separate entities or substances at higher levels. Other examples will be given of the emergence of organized "wholes" whose behavior cannot be deduced from the behavior of their "parts." Mental events, in particular, are aspects of higher integrated systems that have distinctive properties not found in atoms.

Atomic indeterminacy and *human freedom* are not, on this view, directly related to each other, and occur on very different levels. But they exhibit a number of common features. They are both examples of "weak causality" in which a set of potentialities is determined. Since the set is determined absolutely, continuity is assured; but since there is more than one alternative open within the set, novelty can occur. Again, *individual* events display some unpredictability, whereas exact laws are the result of large numbers. Insofar as man is a collection of particles, atomic indeterminacy is lost in statistical regularities. But insofar as human experience is an integrated event, it displays a new type of unpredictability—not derivative from atomic indeterminacy, but from its unitary organization at a higher level. Perhaps coordinated individual events, at various levels, have multiple potentialities, though only at higher levels is there freedom.[54] In the next chapter this hypothesis will be explored further.

V. Conclusions: On Implications of Physics

We have suggested that modern physics has important implications for epistemology, but that its implications for metaphysics are more modest. Let us summarize first its *epistemological significance*. A recurrent theme has been the involvement of the observer in the results of observation. Another striking feature is the symbolic nature of the concepts used and the absence of visualizable models. A theory is no longer taken to be a literal representation, as in naive realism. Because the connection between theory and experiment is very indirect, it is understandable that some physicists, stressing the theoretical and mathematical side, have found encouragement for philosophical idealism; whereas others, stressing the empirical side, have concluded that theories are only useful fictions for coordinating observations. The limitations of

---

54. See Ian Barbour, "Indeterminacy and Freedom: A Reappraisal," *Philosophy of Science*, Vol. 22 (1955), 8; Charles Hartshorne, *Reality as Social Process*, Chap. 5, and *The Logic of Perfection* (LaSalle, Ill.: Open Court Publishing Co., 1962; PB), Chap 6.

theoretical concepts are dramatized in the Complementarity Principle. We maintained, however, that the principle does not lead to positivism, and that its application to problems outside physics sometimes hinders the search for coherent interpretations. The principle is nevertheless a valuable reminder of the partial character of human knowledge and the inadequacy of our models. In the critical realism which we have defended, theories are acknowledged to be highly abstract and symbolic, but are taken to be attempts to represent the structure of nature.

Concerning *metaphysical implications*, we have taken issue with some of the more far-reaching claims made for quantum physics. We rejected arguments for idealism based on the role of the observer, the prominence of mathematics, and the new view of matter. Probability-waves may be less "substantial" than billiard-ball atoms, but the new atom is no more "mental" or "spiritual" than the old. If science is indeed selective and its concepts limited, it would be as dubious to attempt to build a metaphysics of idealism on modern physics as it was to build a metaphysics of materialism on classical physics. We also maintained that the attempt to found a concept of human freedom on atomic indeterminacy is as guilty of reductionism as was the earlier denial of freedom on the basis of classical physics. Such metaphysical claims for quantum theory seem unwarranted.

Yet we submit that contemporary physics does contribute to *a new view of nature*. One should not expect that the metaphysical categories in which such a view is expressed will be direct conclusions from the scientific data of any one field, but rather that such categories will be relevant to the coherent interpretation of theories from various fields of inquiry. Among the ideas put forward tentatively in this chapter and explored more fully in the following ones is the thesis that *"the whole is more than the sum of its parts."* As against reductionism, which seeks to explain the activity of complex entities in terms of the laws of their components, we have maintained that higher organizational levels involve distinctive patterns of behavior. The Pauli Exclusion Principle which links physics to chemistry—but which cannot be derived from the laws of single particles—was offered as an illustration of this thesis.

It was also proposed that *alternative potentialities* exist for individual events. We urged, in accordance with critical realism,

that the Heisenberg Principle is an indication of objective indeterminacy in nature rather than the subjective uncertainty of human
ignorance. In both quantum physics and relativity, *time* is a more
constitutive aspect of reality than in the classical representation.
It was suggested, however, that human freedom must be approached through the distinctive experience of the self in decision,
for which no model taken from physics is satisfactory. Freedom
and indeterminacy thus occur at very different levels, but both
exhibit the novelty and openness of the world. On this reading,
physics makes only a modest contribution to an inclusive view of
reality; but this is perhaps all that should be expected from a field
that studies inanimate objects at the lower levels of existence. It
is at least clear that physics can no longer be the chief witness
called on behalf of reductionism or determinism.

11

Life and Mind

As the physical sciences have influenced conceptions concerning the nature of matter, so the biological sciences have raised fundamental questions about the nature of life and mind and our view of man. One of the greatest challenges to the Christian faith today is the reductionistic image of man as a complex machine whose operation can in principle be exhaustively explained by the laws of physics and chemistry. We will first survey recent evidence concerning the physical basis of life and mind: the discovery of the DNA molecule, which is said to hold "the secret of life," and the progress of research on the physiology of the brain. Next, in Section II, we will examine the problem of the reduction of biological concepts to physico-chemical ones. The emergence of new relationships at higher organizational levels is discussed, and the logic of parts and wholes presented. We will conclude that concepts and theories at various levels of analysis are not mutually exclusive. In Section III we will argue that teleological explanations and causal explanations are not incompatible. We will look to biologists on the directiveness of organisms, cyberneticists on the operation of self-guiding mechanisms, logicians on the functions of teleological explanations, and process philosophers on the self-creative character of all entities. In the final section it will be suggested that mind and brain are two aspects of the same set of events.

I. The Physical Basis of Life

This section presents some scientific findings relevant to the status of life and mind. We will note first the impossibility of drawing any clear line between living and nonliving forms. The breakthrough in molecular biology is then described, especially work on the role of DNA. Some theories on the functioning of the brain are also summarized. This brief sampling can do no more than indicate the kind of evidence that must be taken into account in interpreting the nature of life and of mind.

1. The Living and the Nonliving

Biology texts often propose lists of *"distinctive characteristics of life"*: reproduction (self-duplication), growth (by reorganization of environmental materials), irritability (response to stimuli), and self-regulation (active self-maintenance and adaptation). Analogies of each of these properties—but not all of them together —can be found in systems usually regarded as inanimate. There is no sharp line between living and nonliving, however, and the distinction seems to be meaningless in the border zone. *Viruses* can be stored indefinitely with no evidence of life, being unable to reproduce in most environments. But within specific host cells they can replicate; half an hour after a virus enters it, a cell may burst and release 200 newly formed viruses. Moreover, viruses can undergo mutation and hence are capable of evolutionary development. In most properties they thus bridge the gap between animate and inanimate.

Nor can *the second law of thermodynamics* be used to distinguish the nonliving from the living. The law states that any closed system tends to increase in *disorder* (or more technically, entropy). Thus when a hammer strikes a block of metal, the energy of its orderly downward motion is converted into heat—that is, into the random motion of molecules in the metal. It might seem that living things violate this law, for they show an increase in *order*; but careful analysis shows that this is always at the cost of a decrease somewhere else.[1] Even in the clearly "inanimate" realm, one part of a system can increase in order (for instance, a liquid with

---

1. See Harold F. Blum, *Time's Arrow and Evolution*, 2nd ed. (Princeton, N.J.: Princeton University Press, 1955; Harper PB), Chaps. 11, 12.

randomly moving molecules solidifies into an orderly crystal lattice), but at the price of increased disorderliness in the surrounding parts (in this example, heat is given off during crystallization). So too a growing plant represents an increase in order, but the sun, soil, and air must be included in the "system" if the second law is to be applied. Animals feed on various organic nutrients with a high content of both energy and order. As Schrödinger puts it: "The device by which an organism maintains itself at a fairly high level of orderliness really consists in continually sucking orderliness from its environment."[2] He holds that such activity does not violate the second law.

Another feature of living things for which distinctiveness has been claimed is *self-regulation*. Higher organisms have many complex control processes for maintaining specific equilibrium conditions—temperature, blood alkalinity, oxygen content, and so forth.[3] The similarity of these biochemical *homeostatic* systems to man-made control mechanisms such as thermostats will be discussed later. But the coordination of developmental processes in the·*growing embryo* is without parallel in the inorganic world. The differentiation of cells follows exact spatial patterns and temporal schedules as the various organs come into being. At certain stages cells retain their ability to differentiate (a second limb will form after the normal one has been amputated, or a piece of epidermis grafted over the optic cup will become an eye lens). At a later stage, specialization has been fixed (a limb bud transplanted to a new site continues to grow as a limb). In most of these distinctive activities of living things, it now appears that DNA molecules play a central role.

2. DNA and the Genetic Code

The crucial properties of genes have long been known: (a) replication and (b) control of developmental processes. A number of converging lines of evidence showed genes to be Deoxyribonucleic Acid (DNA), containing groups of atoms called *nucleotide* units formed from one of the four bases: adenine (A), thymine (T), guanine (G), or cytosine (C). In 1953, Watson and Crick[4] inferred

2. Erwin Schrödinger, *What is Life?* (Garden City, N.Y.: Doubleday PB, 1956), p. 72.

3. Walter B. Cannon, *The Wisdom of The Body* (New York: W. W. Norton & Company, 1939; PB).

4. J. D. Watson and F. H. C. Crick, "A Structure for Deoxyribose Nucleic Acid," *Nature*, Vol. 171 (1953), 737.

from X-ray diffraction data a model of the DNA molecule as a twisted (helical) double strand; at regular intervals along each strand there is a projecting nucleotide that is linked by hydrogen bonds to a nucleotide in the opposite strand (forming cross-links like rungs on a twisted ladder). An A unit on one strand is always linked to a T unit on the other, and a G always to a C unit. Here was a possible mechanism for replication: if the two strands separate (by breaking the hydrogen bonds), every nucleotide in each strand could attract a partner nucleotide (floating around in the surrounding fluid) and build up a new partner-strand identical to the old—with A, T, C, and G units in exactly the same order. The self-duplication of genes could be accounted for along such lines.

But how do genes regulate developmental processes? All protein molecules throughout living organisms are built out of simpler building blocks, the 20 *amino acids*. The mechanism by which the DNA of the genes controls the assembly of amino acids into proteins was clarified during the 1950's. The DNA itself remains in the cell nucleus, but its pattern is duplicated by a strand called *messenger-RNA* (Ribonucleic Acid) which travels throughout the cell. Next, there are short *transfer-RNA* segments with nucleotide projections on one side that match those of the messenger-RNA, and bonds that attract specific amino acids on the other, holding them in place until they link together. Thus the amino acids are assembled into protein chains in the precise order determined originally by the nucleotide sequence of the DNA.[5]

The problem of *"cracking the genetic code"* was to understand how sequences of the 4 nucleotides (the "letters" of the DNA "code") could in varying combinations represent the 20 amino acids. With 4 different letters it is possible to form 4 one-letter "words" or 16 two-letter "words" or 64 three-letter "words" (triplets). Groups of three units (AAA, AAC, ATC, and so forth) would provide more than enough different combinations to represent the amino acids. Recent experiments have identified the triplets corresponding to particular amino acids—for example, TTT corresponds to phenylalanine.[6] A long DNA segment is thus a chain

5. For summary accounts, see T. H. Jukes, "The Genetic Code," *American Scientist*, Vol. 51 (1963), 227, and Vol. 53 (1965), 477; Isaac Asimov, *The Genetic Code* (New York: New American Library, Signet PB, 1963).

6. M. W. Nirenberg, "The Genetic Code: II," *Scientific American*, Vol. 208, No. 3 (1963), 80f.

of nucleotides grouped in triplets (AAA: TTT: AGC: ATA. . . .) whose order determines the order in which the amino acids are to be assembled into protein chains by the transfer-RNA. An "alphabet" of just four "letters" (A, C, G, and T units) grouped in three-letter "words" (each specifying one of the 20 amino acids) is arranged in "sentences" (specifying particular proteins). One can make thousands of different "sentences" (and thus proteins) of varying length and "word order" from the 20 basic "words." It appears that chains made up of the four nucleotides—identical but for their order—constitute the genes of all organisms from microbe to man. DNA, then, is a chemical structure which by the spatial arrangement of its parts carries the genetic information or "instructions" for all forms of life.

Though the basic structure of the genes is thus relatively simple, the ways in which their codes are *"translated" into life processes* are exceedingly complex. A single human chromosome (a string of thousands of genes) contains on the order of 100 million nucleotide triplets—which is several times the number of words in a set of the *Encyclopaedia Britannica.* Each cell in the body is continuously making hundreds of different kinds of protein, and each protein may contain hundreds of amino acid units—there are 574 in the hemoglobin molecule in blood, for example. Even a simple cell is a very complicated community with a vast and diverse population of interacting molecules. There must be many interlocking regulatory systems whereby the rates of production of specific proteins are inhibited or stimulated. If the differentiation of cells and the coordinated development of the embryo are considered, it is apparent how fantastically complex must be the "translation" or "read-out" processes whereby the genetic "instructions" result in the growth of the right kind of cell at the right place at the right time with respect to the total growing organism. The interaction of the various components of such systems and the role of spatial patterns and fields are at present but little understood. Only in popular accounts is it claimed that "the secret of life has been discovered."

Nevertheless most biologists believe that life processes are in principle *explicable in physico-chemical terms* without invoking any distinctive vital substance or life-force. It appears probable that scientists will eventually produce self-replicating molecules from simpler substances. This would still be a long way from even

the lowest single cell, but there appears to be no obstacle in principle to the laboratory synthesis of life.

3. The Physiology of the Brain

Like the physical basis of life, the physiological basis of mind
has been the object of intensive research in recent years.[7] The
human brain contains some ten billion *neurons* on each of which
converge many nerve fibers connecting with other neurons. Some
neurons produce an output pulse only when they receive several
input pulses simultaneously, or when excitatory signals predominate over inhibitory ones. In general it appears that information
is transmitted through temporal and spatial distributions of pulses,
which are themselves fairly uniform. (Increasing the intensity of
sensory stimuli increases the frequency, but not the amplitude, of
the resulting train of nerve impulses. Moreover, if nerves from
organs of taste and hearing are interchanged, the subject is conscious of a taste rather than a noise when a bell rings.) Let us
consider what happens to sensory input signals coming into the
brain.

Millions of impulses from all over the body would provide an
overwhelming mass of data if they were not *selected* and *organized*. In some cases there is already considerable selectivity within
the sensory organs. Single fibers in the optic nerve of frogs were
found to be activated only when an object moved in the field of
vision. In similar experiments on cats, nerves from the retina were
found to be connected through successive neural networks; in the
output from the third such stage of "data processing" there are
fibers that respond only to particular configurations in the visual
field—e. g., a band of light slanting at 30°.[8] Higher cortical centers
must somehow integrate information from both eyes, and then
from various senses, and finally relate it to memory images.

Little is known about *the physical basis of memory*. Some evidence favors precise localization of memory traces (for example,
vivid details of long-forgotten scenes can be evoked by electrical
stimulation of particular points on the exposed cortex during brain
surgery). But there is other evidence against localization (for in-

---

7. See, e.g., M. A. B. Brazier, ed., *Brain and Behavior* (Washington, D.C.:
American Institute of Biological Sciences, 1961), Vol. 1.

8. David Hubel, "The Visual Cortex of the Brain," *Scientific American*,
Vol. 209, No. 5 (1963), 54.

stance, large portions of the cortex can be removed without impairing memory, which implies that either memory-patterns are not localized or there is duplication of traces in several locations). According to one theory, memory storage is achieved by conductivity patterns in neural circuits or networks. Another theory postulates storage in coded micropatterns in molecules, possibly in nucleotide sequences; perhaps the organism's memory is stored as a molecular code similar in structure to the genetic code which carries "the memory of the species."[9] With molecular storage, a very rapid "read-out" mechanism would be required, since the myriad details of a complex visual image can be recalled almost instantaneously.

The *electrical stimulation of the brain* by the insertion of tiny electrodes through the skull has produced many interesting effects.[10] In sensory areas, sensations of sound or taste are engendered; in the temporal lobe, vivid memories are evoked. Stimulation in the motor area can cause the subject to raise his arm automatically. In another area, word-recall is inhibited without any paralysis of speech, and the subject is puzzled at his inability to name a common object. In stimulation of deeper brain areas, patients have reported feelings of happiness, anxiety, or anger. A cat can be made to fly into a rage and attack a dog, or to react with fear and panic at the sight of a mouse. There are centers of pleasure whose stimulation an animal finds almost irresistible; if a brief current, activated by pressing a lever in his cage, goes to an electrode in such a center, a rat will press the lever at the fantastic rate of 8,000 times an hour until he is exhausted.

There are of course many other lines of research—such as the influence of drugs on animal and human behavior—which provide further evidence concerning the *physiological basis of mind.* The increased power to control human personality, which such knowledge is beginning to provide, raises important ethical and social problems[11] that lie beyond the scope of this volume. We will be concerned only with the impact of these scientific findings on our view of the nature of man. If both life and mind are increasingly

9. See H. F. Harlow and C. N. Woolsey, eds., *Biological and Biochemical Bases of Behavior* (Madison: University of Wisconsin Press, 1958).

10. Daniel E. Sheer, ed., *Electrical Stimulation of The Brain* (Austin: University of Texas Press, 1961).

11. See S. M. Farber and R. H. Wilson, eds., *Control of The Mind* (New York: McGraw-Hill PB, 1961).

explained by the laws of biochemistry, must we not conclude that man is a complex machine?

II. Emergence versus Reduction

New discoveries, of which we have given only a sample, show the power of the biochemical approach in the study of living things. Does such evidence support the claim that all phenomena of life are explicable in physico-chemical terms? The "organismic" biologists, avoiding the extremes of both mechanism and vitalism, have asserted the distinctiveness of organisms as total interacting systems. Philosophers of science have analyzed the "logic of reduction"; they have often defended the value of characteristically biological concepts and the emergence of new phenomena at higher levels of organization. Scientists have advocated multi-level analysis and the search for inter-level laws. Similar conclusions have arisen from considering the relation of parts and wholes. We will be looking here at the nature of organisms in general, but many of these comments will be applicable in our subsequent discussion of the status of mind and of man; thus a careful exposition of issues, even in their more technical philosophical aspects, seems justified.

1. Vitalism, Mechanism, and Organicism

We start with the historical background of the debate. In *vitalism* life was held to be a distinctive entity or substance, a non-material agency. In the last century the Romantic idea of intuition into the organic wholeness of nature (e.g., in Goethe) influenced the *Naturphilosophie* which dominated early biology on the Continent; it was assumed that life and matter are separate realms governed by opposing principles. In this century, Driesch[12] interpreted his experiments in embryology as evidence of a vital agent within the developing embryo directing events in anticipation of future goals. He postulated a purposeful *"entelechy"* which adjusts processes, in spite of obstacles, to achieve its intended plan. A newt's ability to grow a new limb after an amputation seemed inexplicable without some directing agency. But the idea was vague and offered no testable hypotheses for particular cases; since anything unexplained can be ascribed to entelechies, they are not amenable

---

12. Hans Driesch, *Science and Philosophy of the Organism*, 2nd ed. (London: G. Allen and Unwin, 1930).

to investigation. Vitalism has been scientifically unproductive and is a dead issue in biology today. The supposed "gaps" in the scientific account are being gradually filled in.

Mechanism in biology was clearly enunciated by Descartes: living beings including the higher animals are complex machines, nonconscious automata, assemblies of moving particles. (In man alone, he held, there is an additional substance, a nonspatial mind, interacting with a body that is mechanical.) In the nineteenth century, the chemical approach to biology was increasingly fruitful. In 1828 Wohler synthesized the first organic compound from inorganic substances; after Schwann and Schleiden formulated the cell theory, the importance of cell metabolism was recognized. Bernard maintained that "all the phenomena which make their appearance in a living being obey the same laws as those outside it." Early in the present century, Loeb articulated the belief that all living processes "can be unequivocally explained in physicochemical terms."[13] Recent work in molecular biology and brain physiology have given further support to the conviction that all aspects of life and mind will be explained by the laws of physics and chemistry. W. S. Beck writes:

> With this sort of beginning in the biological approach to the problems of ethics, it seems not a very large jump to a future in which neurophysiology will have finally achieved a deeper understanding of the physical basis of mental activity. It is this development to which we may reasonably look for explanations of altruism, goodness, and love in terms of bioelectric circuits.[14]

The term *"mechanism"* has been used with several distinguishable meanings including the following assertions: (a) *Biological explanations are reducible to mechanics.* This Laplacian program seems implausible, since it has been rejected within physics itself. (b) *The machine is the best analogy for the organism.* This is vague, but has the merit of emphasizing structure and organization, so characteristic of man-made machines. (c) *Biological laws are reducible to physico-chemical laws.* We define reduction as the

13. Jacques Loeb, *The Mechanistic Conception of Life* (Chicago: University of Chicago Press, 1912); see also L. Hogben, *The Nature of Living Matter* (London: Routledge, 1930); J. Needham, *Order and Life* (New Haven, Conn.: Yale University Press, 1936).
14. W. S. Beck, *Modern Science and the Nature of Life* (New York: Harcourt, Brace & World, Inc., 1957; Doubleday PB), p. 286; reprinted by permission of Harcourt, Brace & World, Inc., and Macmillan & Co., Ltd.

deduction of theories or laws in one area of inquiry *from* theories or laws formulated in another area (usually at a lower level and involving parts or components). This is the most plausible meaning of mechanism, and we will examine it in detail below. Since it refers to laws and theories, it is overtly a methodological proposal about scientific inquiry; but it often becomes a metaphysical assertion about the nature of reality, that is, a form of materialism and atomism. (As in eighteenth-century materialism, this is "making a metaphysics out of a method.") Among factors contributing to its acceptance have been the excesses of vitalism, the desire for the unification of the sciences within a single set of principles, and of course the amazing success of biochemistry.

Organicism, (or "organismic biology") seems to be a compromise between mechanism and vitalism, but at crucial points differs from both. Its proponents agree with mechanists in rejecting all non-material vital agents; life is a type of organization, not an entity or substance. "Living things are ordinary chemicals organized in extraordinary ways." There is no impassable gulf between the living and the nonliving, but rather a continuity of levels. Reference to entities that are by definition outside the scope of science can only hinder biological inquiry; all concepts must be judged by their ability to suggest testable hypotheses. The case must rest, not on failures in explanation (as in vitalism) nor on hoped-for future explanations (as in mechanism), but on the actual character of biological theories. Here organicists diverge from mechanists, insisting that biologists do in fact use distinctive biological concepts not defined in physico-chemical terms—concepts that are neither vitalistic nor mechanistic but *organismic*. An organism is an integral whole with a hierarchy of levels of organization—a fact overlooked by the mechanist (who sees only one level) and neglected by the vitalist (who turns out to be a mechanist at heart, since he merely adds an invisible agent to run the machine!).

A major theme of organicism is that *the parts are influenced by the whole.* Typical slogans are "the whole is more than the sum of its parts" and "organic unities are not additive aggregates." J. S. Haldane[15] holds that the biologist "must always keep the whole

---

15. J. S. Haldane, *The Philosophical Basis of Biology* (New York: Doubleday and Co., 1931); see also W. E. Agar, *A Contribution to the Theory of the Living Organism*, 2nd ed. (Melbourne, Aus.: Melbourne University Press, 1951); R. S. Lillie, *General Biology and the Philosophy of Organism* (Chicago: University of Chicago Press, 1945).

organism in view." J. Smuts[16] urges a "holistic" approach to organisms as integrated systems of dynamically interrelated parts. The parts of a machine are unchanged when they are separated from other parts; but the parts of an organism have properties *in situ* which they do not have in isolation. There is mutual causal interdependence and interaction, and changes in one part influence many other parts. These authors give particular attention to phenomena without parallel in the physical world—reproduction, embryological development, self-maintenance, evolution and animal instinct. Note that organicism, like vitalism and mechanism, has usually been understood as a claim about reality, rather than a methodological statement about scientific knowledge.

Living organisms are also said to have *emergent properties* not predictable from the properties of their constituents. Such emergence is a general feature of higher levels, and not unique to life as such. C. D. Broad states that the wetness of water or the smell of ammonia could not be deduced from the properties of atoms of hydrogen, oxygen, and nitrogen; such properties "could not even in theory be deduced from the most complete knowledge of the behavior of its components taken separately or in other combinations, and of their properties and arrangements in this whole."[17] A related claim has been made by Alexander, Morgan, and other proponents of "emergent evolution" (see next chapter), who say that historically there have come into being new levels of reality with novel qualities unpredictable from knowledge of the previous state of the world.

2. The Logic of Reduction

The organicists' advocacy of *distinctive biological concepts and laws* has appeared in a modified form in the writings of recent philosophers of science. Their reasoning is clearly based on methodological rather than metaphysical considerations. They do not minimize the value of reductionistic analysis, but they do defend the usefulness of a variety of types of explanatory model. No claim is made for the uniqueness of life as such; instead, the logical prob-

16. Jan Smuts, *Holism and Evolution* (New York: The Macmillan Co., 1926; Viking PB).

17. C. D. Broad, *Mind and Its Place in Nature* (London: Routledge and Kegan Paul, Ltd., 1925; Littlefield, Adams & Co. PB°), p. 59; see also A. Lovejoy, "The Meaning of 'Emergence' and Its Modes," in P. Wiener, ed., *Readings in Philosophy of Science* (New York: Charles Scribner's Sons, 1953).

lems of the reduction of laws in any field are discussed. (Such problems are more common in biology but they occur even within physics; the case is strengthened, rather than weakened, if there are analogies and parallels in the inorganic world.) These arguments can be summarized under three headings:

1. *Reduction is a function of the theories available.* "Reducibility" and "irreducibility" are not, as the earlier debate assumed, absolute features of reality, but are characteristics of theories and are relative to the state of knowledge. Thus the valences of chemical elements and the specific heats of solids are not derivable from classical physics, but they are derivable from quantum theory. Contrary to Broad's contention, many properties of compounds have been predicted before they were observed—predicted not from "the properties of their constituents" but from new theories. On the other hand, the impossibility of deducing a particular biological theory from existing physical theories cannot be simply ascribed to "temporary ignorance," nor can one assert that it is "deducible in principle given sufficient knowledge"; one can only talk about deduction from given theories, and leave the extent of deducibility to further inquiry.

However, the *irreducibility* of theories involving biological concepts not defined in terms of physico-chemical concepts can be asserted on purely logical grounds. Deduction requires common terms, since a conclusion cannot contain terms not present in the premises. Often coordinating definitions can be introduced, independent postulates that connect levels can be proposed, or "composition laws" can be discovered empirically—but none of these is derivable from the lower-level theory itself, as strict reductionism would demand. For example, the laws of thermodynamics can be derived from those of kinetic theory only if molecular kinetic energy is identified with temperature (a term that is meaningless at the molecular level). Nagel points out that many higher-level laws refer to properties about which physics and chemistry make no statements, and he concludes: "We have thus admitted the essential correctness of the doctrine of emergence when construed as a thesis concerning the logical relations between certain statements."[18] The existence of "composition laws" and connective theories between levels undermines both strict "reductionism" (which wants to derive everything from the lower level) and strict "emergence"

---

18. Nagel, *Structure of Science*, p. 372.

(which denies laws connecting the concepts of different levels

2. *Reduction does not mean that higher-level activities are unreal.* Nagel states that "the reduction of one science to a second does not wipe out, or transform into something 'merely apparent,' the distinctions and types of behavior which the [first] discipline recognizes."[19] Concepts on various levels are useful, and alternative modes of analysis, explanatory models, and methods of simplification should be retained. Any set of concepts is abstractive and selective, and none is exhaustive. Nagel suggests that even where reduction is possible it may have little scientific importance, and higher-level theories may be more fruitful. Physicists still use thermodynamic equations because calculations on individual molecules would be prohibitively complex; chemists still find atoms and molecules more useful for many purposes than wave-functions. Nagel writes:

> The main conclusion of this discussion is that organismic biologists have not established the absolute autonomy of biology or the inherent impossibility of physico-chemical explanations of vital phenomena. Nevertheless, the stress they place on the hierarchical organization of living things and on the mutual dependence of organic parts is not a misplaced one. For, although organismic biology has not convincingly secured all its claims, it has demonstrated the important point that the pursuit of mechanistic explanations for vital processes is not a *sine qua non* for valuable and fruitful study of such processes.... The protest of organismic biology against the dogmatism often associated with the mechanistic standpoint in biology is salutary.[20]

Mechanism was often associated with an *atomistic and materialistic metaphysics* in which the true nature of any entity was said to be manifest in its lowest level or its smallest parts. But the chemical composition of an entity does not show what it "really is"; it provides a particular type of information in terms of a restricted set of abstracted concepts. Woodger believes that many biologists still have "a nineteenth-century view of matter" as a collection of little particles. He endorses the thesis of process philosophy that activity and not matter, relationships and not objects, processes and not components, are fundamental. Functions as well as structures—i.e., temporal as well as spatial factors—are constitutive. Even an inanimate object that can readily be analyzed chemically may

19. *Ibid.*, p. 366.

20. *Ibid.*, pp. 444, 445. Used by permission of Harcourt, Brace & World, Inc., and Routledge and Kegan Paul, Ltd.

organization and a function which cannot be de-
̷̷ical terms:

̷̷se the iron has the form of a poker or a padlock, then although
̷̷e iron is still chemically analyzable in the same way as before, it
cannot be fully described in terms of chemical concepts. It now has
an organization above the chemical level. In the same way an organism is a physical entity in the sense that it is one of the things we
become aware of by means of the senses, and it is a chemical entity
in the sense that it is capable of chemical analysis just as is the case
with any other physical entity, but it does not at all follow from this
that it can be fully and satisfactorily described in chemical terms.[21]

3. *Hierarchies of organizing relations involve distinctive problems.*
"Mutual interaction" and "causal interdependence" are not (as
organicists often imply) unique to organisms—they are exhibited
by the solar system or by an electrical network, for example. Even
a machine or a watch must be analyzed by system-laws; we cannot
explain its action from knowledge of the parts separately, unless we
know their configuration, their organization, and the principles of
their interaction. However, organisms display a greater range in
levels of organization than do machines. Woodger indicates that
when a single cell divides to form two cells, new relations not
previously possible for it (namely, intercellular relations) come
into being; "the very first cleavage raises the level of organization
of the developing organism." Embryological differentiation introduces additional patterns of parts in wholes; the genetic endow-
ment of a cell may allow it to develop in various ways depending
on its relation to other cells. An organism exhibits complex hierarchies of levels of organization (atom, molecule, cell, organ, organism) so that its over-all behavior is several levels removed from
the chemical level; and it is integrated by many systems (for example, hormonic, metabolic, and nervous systems). Such complexity need not prevent the discovery of interconnections between
levels, but it does show why higher-level theories may be useful.
Woodger states:

The properties of a part are different when it is in place in the organic
hierarchy from what they are removed from it. . . . An entity having
the hierarchical type of organization such as we find in the organism
requires investigation of all levels, and investigation of one level can-

21. J. H. Woodger, *Biological Principles* (London: Kegan Paul, Trench,
Trubner and Co., 1929), p. 263.

not replace the necessity for investigation of levels higher up in the hierarchy.[22]

A careful discussion of the value of *higher-level concepts,* defined in terms of larger patterns rather than physico-chemical constituents, has been given by Beckner. Some properties, such as weight, are possessed by parts; others, such as integrative functions, are not specifiable in the parts alone. These concepts permit a simplified analysis of activities which at the atomic level are unmanageably complex, and they provide a vantage point for formulating hypotheses that can be tested. Beckner suggests that organicism can be reformulated as a proposal to "describe the parts of organic wholes in their activities qua parts by employing concepts that are defined by reference to the higher-level phenomena exhibited by the whole, or at least by larger segments of the whole."[23]

3. Levels of Scientific Analysis

These three theses about *the relation of biology to chemistry* were derived from the logic of reduction. Similar conclusions have been presented by a number of biologists, who believe that the exciting prospects in molecular biology are producing a bandwagon trend which could lead to the neglect—both in research and in university curricula—of the study of the whole organism (for example, population genetics, physiology, embryology). The "new biologists" trained in mathematics, physics, and chemistry may have little familiarity with living things. Simpson[24] acknowledges the value of *reduction;* but he holds that the resulting information is often applied only in the context of the lower level, so that one ends by describing not organisms but reactions in test tubes. There must be a simultaneous concern for *composition,* in which attention is directed up the scale to higher levels. Simpson wants reduction and composition to be used conjointly, but "all approaches must take into account the organization of organisms, and so must both depart from and lead to the level of whole organisms."

Grobstein makes a similar plea for the importance of *multi-level analysis.* "Sophisticated biological investigation thus involves a con-

---

22. *Ibid.,* pp. 310, 316.

23. Morton Beckner, *The Biological Way of Thought* (New York: Columbia University Press, 1959), p. 187.

24. G. G. Simpson, "The Status of the Study of Organisms," *American Scientist,* Vol. 50 (1962), 36.

tinuous cross-feed of information between analyses proceeding at several levels." He gives examples from embryology of the dangers in using results from only one level (for example, in drawing conclusions about cell differentiation from tissue transplanted to a culture). The coordination whereby the right enzyme is released at the right place at the right time—so that genetic differences are translated into physiological ones—is an inter-level problem which involves emergence:

> What we must do is to recognize that we have a multi-leveled phenomenon, and that part of our problem is to unravel the relationship between the levels. This we can do only by approaching the phenomenon with tools and concepts appropriate to each of the several relevant levels. . . . I submit that a theory of development cannot be complete, or even adequate, without the concept of *emergence* in some form, and that it is the business of developmentalists not to avoid the concept but to give it specific and concrete meaning. It is, indeed, at the very root of the translational devices which gradually convert the bare abstraction of genetic programming into the fully realized living organism. . . . Cohesiveness among cells clearly is a new property, for it cannot be displayed by a single cell. It is only when the cell divides that the question of coherence arises; it emerges as a factor *in the new context* produced by cleavage.[25]

Another reason for the importance of multi-level analysis is the fact that *randomness at one level* often has no connection with randomness at other levels; thus both the probabilities for individual events and the statistical laws for large populations must be formulated independently for each level. For example, the randomness of molecular motion has no connection with the randomness of quantum-mechanical observations. Again, the randomness of the combination of genes in the mating of two given organisms (from which the Mendelian probabilities are calculated) is quite independent of the randomness in the pairing of mates in a genetic population (from which the Hardy-Weinberg Law is derived). "We may conclude," writes Bentley Glass, "that the statistical laws of one level of organization are not reducible to the statistical laws of another."[26]

As a final example, we may cite Von Bertalanffy's contention that the central task of biology is *the search for system-laws*. He is very

25. C. Grobstein, "Levels and Ontogeny," *American Scientist*, Vol. 50 (1962), 52, 53.
26. Bentley Glass, "The Relation of the Physical Sciences to Biology: Indeterminacy and Causality," in Baumrin, ed., *Philosophy of Science*, Vol. 1, 243.

critical of vitalism, which puts life outside the sphere of science. But he holds that mechanists look too exclusively to the atomistic analysis of component parts and tend to neglect the action of larger units and the role of organization, coordination, and hierarchies of levels:

> This biological order is specific and surpasses the laws applying in the inanimate world, but we can progressively approach it with continued research. It calls for investigation at all levels: at the level of physico-chemical units, processes, and systems; at the biological level of the cell and the multicellular organism; at the level of supraindividual units of life. At each of these levels we see new properties and new laws. . . . In every system forces of a higher order are *potentia* present which, however, become manifest only if that system becomes part of a configuration of a higher level.[27]

Furthermore, Von Bertalanffy suggests, the mechanist tends to assume that biology will be reduced to physics and chemistry in essentially their present form. But in the history of science, understanding of lower levels was itself often modified when higher levels were taken into account:

> The incorporation of new fields into physics is usually accomplished not by a mere extrapolation of given principles, but in the way that first there is an autonomous development in the new field and that, in the final synthesis, the original field is also broadened. . . . We cannot foretell what extensions of the conceptual system of physics will be necessary before a final synthesis of both realms can take place.[28]

4. Parts and Wholes

Because emergent events are often associated with *unified systems* which have *component parts*, the problem of emergence and reduction may also be approached by considering the relation of wholes to parts. The selection of a "whole" is of course relative to the investigator's problem, since any given system is always part of a yet more inclusive whole (ultimately, the universe); often a key step in research is judging when wider interactions may legitimately be ignored. In the previous chapter, a whole (the atom) was said to be more than the sum of its parts (nucleus and electrons) in a specific sense: the Pauli Exclusion Principle could not conceivably be stated in terms of forces acting on separate elec-

27. Ludwig Von Bertalanffy, *Problems of Life* (London: C. A. Watts and Co., 1952; Harper PB°), pp. 20, 150.
28. *Ibid.*, p. 161.

trons. The atom must be analyzed as a total vibratory system, and the electrons do not even have any continuing self-identity. We have seen that in general a whole exhibits properties and activities not found in its parts, because it has a distinctive form of organization.

The wide diversity of types of whole is conveniently represented by the flexible term *"society."* The social analogy is discussed by the Whiteheadian philosopher Hartshorne, who calls an organism a "society of cells."[29] In some societies (for example, a pile of sand grains) all members are of the same grade and there is almost no over-all structure; the whole has less unity than each of its parts. Other societies consist of loose aggregates (for example, a sponge, or even a tree) whose parts are still relatively independent; plants have a less complex integration than their constituent cells. (They might be compared with an ant colony in which there is some coordination and division of labor but no central agent, or with a confederation of states without a strong central government.) Other societies are well-unified wholes with radically dominant members and complex internal organization. Even in a man, however, each cell has considerable independence; various organs and sub-systems (heart, endocrine system, and so forth) function apart from any conscious control and are tied into the whole organism in other ways. In embryonic development there is some autonomy among the sub-units (as when the eye structure develops from its own local coordinating center); only with the growth of the nervous system is the unification of the experience of the whole organism achieved.[30]

The degree of subordination of part to whole thus varies widely. In the hierarchy of "societies" (electron, atom, molecule, cell, organ, organism, group, community), the "organism" is the unit of reproduction and usually has a more complex integrative organization than levels above or below it. But there is great diversity in the kinds of integration which can occur at any of these levels. Consequently, there are variations in the extent to which a part preserves or loses its autonomy and its identity when it contributes to a larger whole. In general, an activity at any level is influenced by patterns

---

29. Hartshorne, *Reality as Social Process*, Chap. 1; *The Logic of Perfection*, Chap. 7.
30. See Agar, *Theory of the Living Organism*, Chap. 5; J. T. Bonner, *Morphogenesis* (Princeton, N.J.: Princeton University Press, 1952; Atheneum PB).

of activity at both higher and lower levels. In this sense one can say that there is mutual influence of the activity of part and whole without implying that the whole is somehow an entity existing independently of the parts. We can stress the idea of wholes without minimizing the value of conceptual analysis into parts, and without denying the possibility of the laboratory synthesis of wholes from parts. System analysis and component analysis are mutually illuminating.

We mention parenthetically that *the importance of "wholes"* can be illustrated in almost any field of inquiry. The anthropologist considers a culture to be an integrally functioning system with its own inner consistency; any one aspect can be abstracted conceptually, but its actual role depends on the social context. Kluckhohn maintains that a culture is a total configuration governed by distinctive clusters of social values. "Anthropologists," he writes, "are sure that valid propositions can be constructed about a whole culture that will not emerge from any seriatim listing of its parts."[31] Economic behavior occurs within a matrix of noneconomic beliefs and institutions which may or may not be significant in studying a particular problem.[32] Or again, the clinical psychologist deals with the whole personality structure of an individual; in Chapter 7 we noted Allport's view of a person as an integrated dynamic system in which the operation of any aspect, such as intelligence, is dependent on its place in the total personality configuration.

In sum, the scientist must consider wholes as well as parts, systems as well as components, higher levels as well as lower. Contrary to reductionism, we have defended the use of theories that are not deducible from theories at lower levels; contrary to most versions of emergence, we have defended the importance of inter-level laws. Let us draw together our conclusions in this section by looking at *the idea of levels* in the light of our remarks in previous chapters:

1. *Levels of Analysis.* Since scientific symbols are *selective* and *abstractive*, theories at two different levels may be used concurrently; both of them may satisfy the criteria of evaluation (rational and empirical), and they need not be viewed as mutually exclusive. Here "level" is a methodological rather than a metaphysical concept; "levels of analysis" are relative both to the state of knowledge and to the problem under investigation. The presence of inter-level

31. Clyde Kluckhohn, "Parts and Wholes in Cultural Analysis," in Lerner, ed., *Parts and Wholes*, p. 114.

32. Simon Kuznets, "Parts and Wholes in Economics," in *ibid.*

laws, connecting the concepts of two levels of analysis, does not imply that the properties associated with the higher level are unreal. Now we could readily leave the issue here, as instrumentalists (including most linguistic analysts) would urge. We could, on this basis, recognize the power and fruitfulness of the chemical approach to biology and yet maintain the integrity of distinctively biological concepts and theories. When we come to higher levels of mind and man, the same principle would allow the acknowledgment of physical and chemical laws, without the threat to man's status which reductionism is usually taken to imply. Alternative symbol-systems may be employed even within science; and alternative languages among diverse areas of thought may serve diverse functions in human life.

2. *Levels of Organization. Critical realism* makes the additional assumption that "levels of analysis" reflect "levels of organization" in the world. "Level" is here intended to refer objectively to nature, that is, to a *"level of being"*; it is a metaphysical and not simply a methodological concept. Mechanism was nominally a methodological program, but it frequently turned into a one-level metaphysics (materialism or atomism); vitalism, in its day, expressed a dualistic or two-level metaphysics, with an ontological gap between the living and the nonliving. Organicism, which we are defending, postulates significant differences among levels, but no sharp breaks or gaps. A level, like an arbitrary portion of a continuous spectrum, has no sharp boundaries; there are no separate strata marked off in nature. To the critical realist, the concept of level is indeed an abstraction, and is relative to the context of inquiry, but it reflects in a limited and partial fashion the real structure of the world.

3. *Levels of Activity. Process philosophy* leads us to consider "levels of activity" rather than entities or spatial "wholes" as such. We can grant that a man is indeed composed of nothing but atoms, and that the behavior of these atoms does not violate the laws of physics and chemistry. But then we can go on to say that in man there are patterns of organization with which physics and chemistry do not deal; and more important, there occur in man *types of events* which differ from any event that occurs in an isolated atom. The analogy of the spectrum is particularly appropriate in process philosophy, which portrays genuine differences among processes without any absolute dichotomies. It insists, as we shall see shortly, that low-level events must be interpreted in terms of the categories

usually associated with high-level events, as well as vice versa; "inanimate" and "animate" characteristics are present at all levels, though in varying degrees. "Levels of activity," like "levels of organization" and "levels of analysis," are not mutually exclusive. Thus the concept of level, whether taken methodologically with the linguistic analysts or metaphysically with the process philosophers, allows full recognition of both the laws of molecular biology and the presence of distinctive higher-level phenomena in man.

III. Teleology versus Mechanism

In addition to these ideas of levels and whole-part relations, various interpretations of *purposiveness* have been proposed as distinctive features of biological organisms. Some biologists have argued that living things display anticipation and activity directed toward the attainment of future goals. Many biologists and philosophers, on the other hand, have tried to avoid the concept of purpose because it has often been interpreted anthropomorphically or introduced in place of efficient causes. But it has been suggested in a number of recent volumes that properly defined teleological concepts do have a valid scientific role, and process philosophers have given them a prominent place among their metaphysical categories.

1. Four Meanings of Purpose

We are *not* considering here the problem of "design," or of direction in the evolutionary process—that is, the question of divine purpose, which is the subject of the next chapter. Restricting ourselves to *the purpose of an organism or organ*, it is important to distinguish behaviorally the diverse meanings which are often confused:

1. *Functional behavior.* When it is said that "the purpose of the kidney is to purify the blood," there is no explicit reference to a purposeful agent, and the word "function" could be substituted. Functional concepts call attention to the contribution that a part or process makes to the activity or maintenance of the whole. Beckner points out that in anatomy the definition of an organ, such as the kidney, must be general enough to include a wide range of species; hence, as a defining characteristic, function is more useful than size and shape. Again, animal behavior (for example, building a nest or escaping from a predator) is almost infinitely complex and variable if described in terms of detailed muscle movements;

but if described in terms of functions performed, regularities are evident and testable hypotheses can be formulated.

Simpson[33] and Mayr[34] defend *functional concepts* from the standpoint of evolutionary theory. One may legitimately ask "what an organ is for," since it would probably not have survived natural selection unless it contributed to the welfare of the organism. These authors maintain that in reacting against final causes, biologists have gone too far in rejecting this type of "purpose." However, we will not be interested here in "purpose" in this sense of function, since it entails no explicit reference to goals.

2. *Self-regulating behavior*. Consider a control system in which deviations from a "standard condition" are compensated for through a "feedback" mechanism. In a household thermostat, when the temperature falls a switch is activated to ignite the furnace, which raises the temperature again. The furnace controls the temperature, but is in turn controlled *by* the temperature—*via* the thermostat, that is, a "sensing" device which provides "information" about the system's performance. Homeostatic systems in the human body (such as regulation of temperature or blood alkalinity) seem to be similar in principle. A self-guiding missile "seeks its target" by modifying its direction of flight according to the predictive extrapolation of information (from radar or infra-red signals) concerning the target's motion. Some cyberneticists claim that such servomechanisms display all the characteristics of purpose. "Teleological behavior thus becomes synonymous with behavior controlled by negative feedback."[35] This can be called "teleological" in at least a rudimentary sense, since (a) behavior can be analyzed in terms of an end state not yet attained, and (b) there is some flexibility of response to changing external conditions.

It is widely accepted that both *teleological* and *mechanical* explanations can be given for such processes. Sometimes this is interpreted as proof that purpose is nothing but mechanism. But more often the value of teleological representation is defended: Thus Arthur Pap states: "The feud between mechanists and teleologists is unnecessary; both types of explanation satisfy cognitively, in

---

33. G. G. Simpson, "Biology and the Nature of Science," *Science*, Vol. 139 (1963), 81.

34. E. Mayr, "Cause and Effect in Biology," *Science*, Vol. 134 (1961), 1501.

35. A. Rosenblueth, N. Wiener, and J. Bigelow, "Behavior, Purpose, and Teleology," *Philosophy of Science*, Vol. 10 (1943), 24; see also G. Sommerhoff, *Analytical Biology* (London: Oxford University Press, 1950).

that they subsume diverse phenomena under constant laws."[36] Nagel concludes: "The difference is one of emphasis and perspective in formulation. If this account is sound, the use of teleological explanations in the study of directively organized systems is as congruent with the spirit of modern science as is the use of non-teleological ones."[37]

3. *Goal-directed behavior.* This can be defined as "persistence toward a goal under varying conditions." Although not separated by any sharp line from "self-regulation," there is greater plasticity and flexibility as to types of action in achieving the goal, and greater sensitivity to the conditions that support or impede its attainment. A rough identification of the "goal" allows the observer to note "persistence" under varying conditions, and vice versa, by successive approximations, at the behavioral level, that is, without direct reference to desires or intentions. From observed regularities in such behavior (for example, food-seeking in animals or mouse-chasing in cats) and its relation to other activities, hypotheses can be formed and tested. Braithwaite believes that such teleological laws are scientifically acceptable: "It seems ridiculous to deny the title of explanation to a statement which performs both of the functions characteristic of scientific explanations—of enabling us to appreciate connections and to predict the future."[38] The question why an event or activity occurs "can be answered by specifying a goal or end toward the attainment of which the event or activity is a means."

We would submit, moreover, that such behavior *cannot* be adequately represented by *the cybernetic model of a goal* as a source of guiding "signals." The goal-object sought may even be nonexistent. An animal may seek food when there is none; the cat may wait at an empty mousehole. Braithwaite[39] proposes an alternative model of goal-directedness as a plurality of causal chains all ending in the same terminal state; here the plasticity of the system is stressed. But the sets of initial conditions and causal chains converging to the end state may be infinite and unspecifiable (the cat may be ingenious at finding new ways to catch the mouse). Moreover, this model, like most of those proposed, does not allow

36. Arthur Pap, *An Introduction to the Philosophy of Science* (New York: Free Press of Glencoe, Inc., 1962), p. 362.
37. Nagel, *Structure of Science*, p. 422.
38. Braithwaite, *Scientific Explanation*, p. 334.
39. *Ibid.*, pp. 319f.

for cases where the goal object exists but is not attained. Surely the cat's action is no less teleological if the mouse gets away. Scheffler[40] suggests that activity oriented to future goals is often based on learning. Memory of past sequences and their outcomes leads to *anticipation* of future occurrences—which serve as goals for present action even if the expected goal-object is absent or not attained.

4. *Purposive behavior.* We have reserved the word "purposive" for cases in which there are desires, intentions, and beliefs concerning goal-ideas. We maintain that in man there is evidence, both from the actions and statements of other persons and from introspection, that behavior is influenced by conscious goals. Men desire particular future events to occur and behave in ways they believe appropriate to their achievement.[41] Here there clearly can be goal-ideas for which there are no goal-objects (for example, the "short route to India," which Columbus sought, or the elusive "fountain of youth," or other operative expectations based on erroneous beliefs). In an earlier discussion of the field of history we defended the ascription of *motives and reasons* to agents. Many questions about human actions call for explanations in terms of intention. "Why is Jones climbing the mountain?" is in most contexts answered by: "In order to see the view from the top." Reference to purposes does not mean that the future influences the present or that goals are agents in their own realization. It is the present intention, the existing desire to attain an objective, and the mental anticipation of expected outcomes that influence behavior. This is not the denial of causality, but specification of a particular type of causality.

What do these three kinds of teleological behavior ("self-regulating," "goal-directed," and "purposive") have in common, and wherein do they differ? In each case there is *flexibility of response* to changing external conditions, and this response can be analyzed in terms of *an end state not yet achieved.* Reference is made not to the future as such (for the goal may never be achieved), but rather to a representation of present activity in terms of possible future states; this yields a significant and scientifically justifiable type of intelligibility, which we have called "teleological explana-

40. Scheffler, *The Anatomy of Inquiry*, pp. 115f.
41. See C. J. Ducasse, "Explanation, Mechanism, and Teleology," in Feigl and Sellars, eds., *Readings.*

tion." Previous remarks about the relation of part to whole are applicable here in the temporal dimension; present changes can be analyzed as phases of a total pattern covering a span of time. Even self-regulation can usefully be described as a system's progress toward an end state by modifying its activity as external conditions vary (for example, the missile adjusts its course to a moving target). Moreover, in each case there are other kinds of regularity that can be formulated with respect to past states of the system (for example "feedback of information," "learning from experience," "the formation of motives"). Now if the selective character of scientific concepts is recognized, we can say that *teleological explanations* are compatible with *causal explanations*; each mode of analysis directs attention to a particular kind of pattern in events ("goals" or "causes") but neither excludes the other. They are two ways of regarding the same occurrences. If we adopt the "alternative language" approach we would leave the matter here.

But there are also *differences among the three types of teleological behavior* that encourage us to move beyond "levels of analysis" to consider "levels of activity." There are differences in (a) the way the end state is represented in the present, and (b) the degree of flexibility of response to changing conditions. Purposiveness as we have described it is characteristic only of high levels of organization in life and mind. In man it has attained the form of conscious envisagement of alternative future possibilities. In animals and birds, the ability to devise highly novel and circuitous means of achieving an end (when normal paths to it are blocked) seems to indicate a rudimentary form of orientation toward the future, as well as imagination in devising new ways of circumventing obstacles. We must ask, not just about the observer's analysis of a system in terms of states not yet achieved, but about the agent's reference to such states, that is, the organism's mode of orientation toward the future.

2. *The Directiveness of Organisms*

Animals display what we have called goal-directed and purposive behavior which suggests the presence of anticipation and intention. Most biologists attribute sentience and elementary mental life to creatures as low as insects. Sinnott goes considerably further in applying *the concept of purpose* to amoeba, individual cells, plants, and the early stages of embryos; but he is open to criticism for failing to distinguish different meanings of teleology. He says that "development in an orderly fashion" or "conformity to a pattern" is "a primitive sort of goal-seeking and purposiveness, and thus a manifestation of mind." "Something presides over development, something to which these activities tend to conform, a norm, a standard, a goal or end."[42] But surely "conformity to a pattern" is a very general characteristic of even inorganic events, such as crystal growth, and is no indication of any of the types of teleology we have outlined. Many of Sinnott's concrete examples would correspond only to what we termed "self-regulating behavior"—for example, a plant's tendency to seek the light or to regenerate a root. Moreover, the idea of purpose is often introduced as if it explains phenomena which he claims would otherwise be "inexplicable," such as regeneration of an amputated limb in a frog embryo; "purpose" becomes another name for scientific ignorance, like the vitalists' "entelechy."

Some biologists[43] have given more cautious analyses of *goal-directed activity*. W. E. Agar[44] recognizes the operation of detailed mechanisms in developmental processes. He holds that the embryo has no "central agent," and the subject of unified experience emerges only gradually from the integration of diverse organs. Plant movements are ascribed to differential growth under chemical stimulation, not to purposive responses to external conditions. Nevertheless Agar urges that all organisms should also be considered as feeling, experiencing subjects. He suggests that perception involves *anticipation*; things are perceived in relation to intended responses. A rat deciding between two paths, in one of which he will receive an electric shock, hesitates as if imaginatively anticipating future consequences. There is some foresight even amidst largely instinctive actions; a wasp building a nest undertakes long sequences of actions toward the completed whole, and shows considerable ingenuity in devising new methods when difficulties arise. Agar holds that *rudimentary mental life* should be attributed even to cells, not because it is evident in their behavior, but for the sake of the consistency of our conceptual categories. If in evolu-

---

42. Edmund Sinnott, *Matter, Mind and Man* (New York: Harper and Brothers, 1957; Athenaeum PB°), p. 35; see also Edmund Sinnott, *Biology of the Spirit* (New York: The Viking Press, 1955; PB).

43. E.g., E. S. Russell, *The Directiveness of Organic Activities* (Cambridge: Cambridge University Press, 1945).

44. Agar, *Theory of the Living Organism*, pp. 19f.

tionary history cells eventually led to minds, and if in embryological development a single cell produces a mind, then we must
assign mentality to cells, even though their margin of freedom
and responsiveness is small. "We accept the proposition that mental
processes cannot emerge from nonmental."[45]

Sewall Wright argues that in the spectrum of behavior from
higher to lower organisms there is *no discontinuity*; since we cannot draw a line at any point, we must assume the universal presence of something akin to *mind*. There is no discontinuity in the
development of minds from simpler structures in either the history
of the world (evolution) or of the individual (embryology). "The
emergence of even the simplest mind from no mind seems to me
utterly incomprehensible."[46] Wright concludes that at all levels
an entity is *mind* to itself and *matter* as viewed by others. Living
things are tightly knit organic hierarchies in which observable
spontaneity can occur—both because there are trigger mechanisms
whereby an action in a minute portion can lead to actions of the
whole, and because the whole can influence the parts. But the
unique creativity of each individual event and its essential nature
as will or mind inevitably escapes the scientist, who deals only
with regularities and sees only the external side of things.

Proposals of this kind avoid most of the pitfalls that have led
biologists to be wary of *teleological concepts*. In the past, teleology
has often hindered scientific advance, especially in studying inanimate objects (recall Aristotle's assertion that the increasing
velocity of a falling stone is caused by its jubilation in approaching
its natural resting-place). But such scientists as Agar and Wright
do not neglect the role of lawful regularities and efficient causes.
Again, the idea of goals as final causes has sometimes been thought
to imply that the future can influence the present; but it is clear
that these authors hold that events are influenced by the present
anticipation of future possibilities, not by the indeterminate and
nonexistent future as such. They have avoided gross anthropomor-
phism by postulating only exceedingly rudimentary forms of mental
life at lower levels. In the past an anthropomorphic image of the
inanimate world led to the neglect of mechanical relationships;
today there is an opposite danger, that a "mechanomorphic" image

---

45. *Ibid.*, p. 101.
46. S. Wright, "Gene and Organism," *American Naturalist*, Vol. 87 (1953),
14. See also his essay in Reese and Freeman, eds., *Process and Divinity*.

of the animate world will exclude teleological concepts which, if suitably qualified, can contribute to our understanding of organisms. We may agree, then, that concepts of anticipation, purpose, and mind can, in attentuated form, be extended far down the scale of life. "Time" and "alternative potentialities" are central categories in organismic biology as in modern physics, but they are represented at a new level that can be associated with incipient mentality.

There are three basic reasons for assuming a rudimentary mental life in lower organisms. (a) Mental events are *known to us from within*, with an immediacy that cannot be dismissed despite the epistemological problems involved (see Section IV). It is reasonable to consider an organism as a center of experience (though not necessarily of consciousness) even if such experience can never be directly accessible to us. (b) Mental events are *a product of the evolutionary process*, and hence an important clue to the nature of reality (see the next chapter). By definition metaphysical categories cannot evolve, since they are formulated to be applicable to all events; however their relative importance may vary drastically, so that types of behavior, which had never been evident previously, may appear in evolutionary history. (Correspondingly there may be laws for higher-level phenomena that cannot be derived from laws at lower levels.) (c) *The continuity of the levels of reality* is a basic metaphysical assumption, but one in whose support considerable evidence can be adduced (for example, the continuity of the organic and the inorganic; or, in the present context, analogies in the behavior of organisms of one level with those of a somewhat higher level, on up to man). From this one might conclude that organisms are matter-like (which indeed they are, in some respects), or that molecules are life-like or even mind-like. One may interpret the lower in terms of the higher, as well as vice versa.

3. Spontaneity and Self-Creation (Whitehead)

Among modern systems of thought, process philosophy assigns the most prominent role to teleological concepts. Let us consider *the general categories* by which Whitehead portrays[47] how any new event arises, and then examine the application of his scheme

---

47. Whitehead, *Process and Reality*; for additional references, see Chapter 5, Section II, above.

to the activity of organisms. We recall his understanding of reality as a dynamic web of interconnected events. Not separate self-contained particles touching externally, but interpenetrating fields of influence provide the basic image of nature. Any entity is a sequence of events each of which is initially constituted by its relationships. But Whitehead also wants us to look at the world from the point of view of each event itself, considered as a moment of experience that takes account of other events and responds to them. He proposes a very general scheme that he believes is applicable, with suitable modifications, at any level of activity.

Summarizing Whitehead's detailed analysis, we may say that *causality* is a complex process in which many strands are interwoven: (a) Every new event is in part the product of *efficient causation*, which refers to the influence of previous events on it. There are objective "data" from the past which are given to each present event and to which it must conform; but there are alternative ways in which it can do so. (b) There is thus an element of *self-causation* or self-creation, for an event unifies its "data" in its own manner from its unique perspective on the universe. Every event contributes something of its own in the way it appropriates its past, relates itself to various possibilities, and produces a novel synthesis that is not strictly deducible from the antecedents. (c) There thus occurs a creative selection from among alternative potentialities in terms of goals and aims, which is *final causation*. In brief, every new occurrence can be looked on as a present response (self-cause) to past events (efficient cause) in terms of potentialities grasped (final cause).

Whitehead describes the *self-creation* of each new event as an individual instant of experience under the guidance of its "subjective aim." Even the influence of the past on the present, which can be viewed externally as efficient causality, can also be considered the action of the present entity as a momentary subject conforming to the objectified past and reproducing or reenacting its pattern. Each such subject has at least a modicum of creative freedom in shaping the particular unity of experience into which its past inheritance is woven and integrated. During its brief existence it is autonomous, closed to any additional data and on its own in making something of itself—even if its activity essentially repeats that of its predecessors in a routine and "mechanical" fashion. Efficient causality thus characterizes the transition between

events while final causality dominates the momentary internal
growth of the event itself as it progressively actualizes its own
synthesis, embodying a particular pattern of forms (which Whitehead calls a "conceptual prehension"):

> In the formation of each occasion of actuality the swing-over from
> reaction to anticipation is due to the intervening touch of mentality.
> Whether the ideas thus introduced by the novel conceptual prehen-
> sion be old or new, they have this decisive result, that the occasion
> arises as an effect facing its past, and ends as a cause facing its future.
> In between there lies the teleology of the Universe.[48]

Is such ascription of self-creation *to all entities* tenable? In defense of Whitehead, it should be noted that: (a) Many of his seemingly "subjective" or "mental" terms have *technical definitions*
that bear only remote resemblance to their common usage ("feelings," for example, include all the modes by which one entity is
affected by another—even electromagnetic energy transmitted from
one electron to another). (b) In inert objects such as atoms any
"mental" aspects are vanishingly small and may for all practical
purposes be considered absent. Whitehead specifically denies the
presence of consciousness in any but the most complex types of
experience. In any case, "mind" and "matter" are not two separate
substances, but two different patterns of events which we abstract
from a single complex process. (c) The internal life of an entity is
not accessible to scientific investigation. Whitehead stresses the
selectivity of science and the abstractive character of its concepts,
which only the perpetrator of "misplaced concreteness" identifies
with the real world: "Science can find no individual enjoyment in
nature; science can find no aim in nature; science can find no
creativity in nature; it finds mere rules of succession. These nega-
tions are true of natural science; they are inherent in its methodology."[49]

Whitehead's systematic use of concepts that are at least remotely
analogous to aspects of *human experience* seems to stem from his
conceptions of: (a) metaphysics as the elaboration of a set of general categories *applicable to all events*, (b) the universe as *continuous and interrelated* (particularly, man as a part of nature), and
(c) human experience as the one portion of reality that we know

---

48. A. N. Whitehead, *Adventures of Ideas* (New York: The Macmillan
Company, 1933; Cambridge: Cambridge University Press, 1933; Mentor PB),
p. 196.
49. A. N. Whitehead, *Modes of Thought* (Cambridge: Cambridge University Press, 1938; Putnam PB), p. 211.

directly *from the inside.* In order to give a unified account of the
world, Whitehead employs categories ("self-creation," "subjective
aim") which in very attenuated forms can be said to characterize
physical events, but which at the same time have at least some
analogy to our awareness as experiencing subjects. Such a procedure might be defended on the ground that if we want to use a
single set of categories, we should treat lower levels as simpler
cases of complex experience—rather than always try to interpret
higher levels by concepts derived from the inanimate world. In
addition, we have seen that there is a continuous spectrum of
complexity in organisms, from man down to amoeba and beyond,
and it is difficult to set any absolute limits to the range of applicability of any particular concept. Human experience is an
extreme instance of an event in nature, and hence is taken to
exhibit the generic features of all experience.

It appears at first sight that Whitehead's use of such a very
general conceptual scheme does not allow adequately for *the
diversity among levels of activity* in the world. He has taken
categories most appropriate for a "middle range" in the scale of
being (biological organisms) and extended their use both "up"
and "down" the scale; consequently his concepts seem to be in-
sufficiently "personal" to express the enduring unity of human
selfhood, but too "personal" to be applicable in the inorganic
realm. However, we must remember that he assigns radically varying weights to the roles of the basic metaphysical categories in
the diverse realms of being. A stone will never be anything but a
stone, for efficient and mechanical causation are overwhelmingly
predominant in its history, and any novelty in self-creation is so
vanishingly small as to be effectively absent. Whitehead holds that
consciousness, even in rudimentary form, is present only in the
higher forms of organic life. We will return to these problems
inherent in process philosophy in Chapter 13.

IV. The Status of Mind

Much of the general discussion of reduction, emergence, wholes,
and levels in Section II would apply to the analysis of mental
events. In analyzing teleological concepts (Section III) we found
ourselves dealing with simple forms of mentality in organisms.
But we must now give more explicit consideration to the status
of the human mind. In addition to evidence from brain physiology

already mentioned, the striking advances in the "artificial intelligence" of computers should also be indicated. We will then compare briefly some alternative ways of representing the relation of mind to brain (the classical "mind-body problem"), and conclude that "mental" and "physical" should be considered as two aspects of a single process.

1. Computers and Minds

Can an "electronic brain" think? Do the capabilities of computers suggest that the human brain is "just a complex machine"? Consider first the authors who defend *the potentialities of artificial intelligence* and its similarities to human thought. They insist that any comparison of brain and machine must be based on *observations of behavior*. By "thought" we should refer only to performance (that is, the results of thinking), since consciousness, subjective feelings, or internal experience are inaccessible to others. This behavioristic criterion is embodied in the famous "Turing test,"[50] in which a scientist communicates (by sets of telegraph wires) with a computer and with a person, in adjacent closed rooms. Turing predicted that by the end of the century computers will be so far advanced that from the answers received in five minutes' interrogation the scientist will in the majority of cases be unable to tell which wires go to the computer and which to the person. Expressed here is another theme: the brain should be compared not to present computers, but to extrapolated hopes for the future, for computer technology is a very young science.

Machines already display *impressive achievements* which, if manifest in men or animals, would be said to evidence intelligence. A checker-playing computer consistently beats the world's checker champion. Samuel's chess-playing computer offers a creditable game. Moreover, there are new computers that *learn from experience*; such a "self-improving" machine can modify its own program in the light of its past performance.[51] For example, the chess

---

50. A. M. Turing, "Computing Machinery and Intelligence," *Mind*, Vol. 59 (1960), reprinted in A. R. Anderson, ed., *Minds and Machines* (Englewood Cliffs, N.J.: Prentice-Hall PB, 1964). A popular account is W. Slukin, *Minds and Machines*, rev. ed. (London: Penguin PB, 1960).

51. Among recent volumes on the intellectual capabilities of computers are E. A. Feigenbaum and J. Feldman, eds., *Computers and Thought* (New York: McGraw-Hill Book Co., 1963) (see especially Minsky's review article); K. M. Sayre and F. J. Crosson, eds., *The Modeling of Mind: Computers and Intelli-*

machine can readjust the weight given to various criteria of decision (value of pieces, defensive position, flexibility in offense) and can "catch on" to tricks of its opponents. Such a "higher-order" machine in effect alters its own wiring; interconnections have adjustable probabilities of functioning, so that successful patterns persist but new patterns are occasionally tried. The future activity of a computer of this type is not predictable by its designer. Scriven concludes his appraisal: "Despite the difficulties, there can be no grounds for radical pessimism about the possibility of combining the devices of originality with those of learning, to produce a machine that is cognitively a match for the human being."[52]

At the opposite extreme are those who stress *the limitations of artificial intelligence.*[53] They point out that even if a machine modifies its own program, it does so by specified rules and it does only what it has been told to do. Insofar as it duplicates human performance it testifies not to its own intelligence but to that of the mind which designed it. Again, the behaviorist postulate has been challenged; there is evidence in man, but not in machines, for the presence of consciousness and feeling. The behaviorist finds that mind resembles machine largely because he starts by dismissing consciousness. But man is a creature who perceives, wills, loves, and makes free choices.[54] A machine, these critics hold, is *incapable of originality.* How could a machine form a new scientific hypothesis or theory? How would it select promising candidates from the infinite class of possible hypotheses? (Perhaps the use of analogy is partly susceptible to logical exploration, but judgments of similarity as well as criteria of simplicity and elegance resist systematization.) Music and poetry composed by computers have not been impressive, perhaps in part because of the subtlety of tonal relationship and poetic metaphor, the effects of which on the listener seem to defy formal specification.

One can point to other human capabilities that have proven unexpectedly recalcitrant to mechanization. Despite some three

gence (Notre Dame, Ind.: University of Notre Dame Press, 1963); H. Borko, ed., *Computer Applications in Behavioral Science* (Englewood Cliffs, N.J.: Prentice-Hall, Inc., 1962); S. Tomkins and S. Messick, eds., *Computer Simulation of Personality* (New York: John Wiley & Sons, 1963).

52. M. Scriven, "The Compleat Robot," in S. Hook, ed., *Dimensions of Mind* (New York: New York University Press, 1960; Collier PB°), p. 123.

53. E.g., Mortimer Taube, *Computers and Common Sense* (New York: Columbia University Press, 1961; McGraw-Hill PB).

54. See A. Samuel, letter in *Science,* Vol. 132 (1960), 740.

million dollars a year spent for a decade trying to develop a *mechanical translator* for foreign scientific articles, no acceptable translations have been achieved. Bar-Hillel,[55] the first full-time researcher on this problem, finally gave up, because the choice among meanings of a word derives from a context that often involves many sentences and many areas of the reader's experience (for example, computers have trouble distinguishing the meanings of "pen" in the two sentences "the pen is in the box" and "the box is in the pen"). Not all investigators share this pessimism; perhaps further understanding of linguistic structure will eventually permit mechanical translation,[56] but it has been a far more difficult problem than was anticipated. *Pattern recognition* programs have also been disappointing. Mechanical readers can identify special numbers on bank checks, or letters printed in a particular type, but cannot read all type fonts, much less handwritten letters. How do we recognize the configuration of a face, though the details of lighting, angle, and expression vary? Little progress has been made on such questions.

Between these two extremes—the scientists who stress similarities of brain and computer, and those who stress differences—is *a middle group* that recognizes the huge gap separating man and machine, but is unwilling to set any limits on computer potentialities for specific types of operation. It has been suggested[57] that *human thought is a many-dimensional continuum*; it includes a large repertoire of processes and diverse types of thought requiring a multiplicity of criteria of evaluation; in some dimensions (such as speed of mathematical calculation) machines surpass man, whereas in others (such as artistic creativity) man surpasses machine. There are distinctive characteristics of human mentality, such as cumulative cognitive development in the maturational sequences of a child's growth or the association of emotion and feeling with thought. Man's cognitive processes occur in relation to the complex needs and experiences of the individual; the machine's intellectual processes do not develop in this manner and hence cannot be expected to resemble man's very closely. "The

55. Yehoshua Bar-Hillel, *Current Research and Development in Scientific Documentation*, No. 5 (Washington, D.C.: National Science Foundation, 1959).

56. Victor Yngve, "Computer Programs for Translation," *Scientific American*, Vol. 206, No. 6 (1962), 68.

57. P. Armer, "Attitudes toward Intelligent Machines," in Feigenbaum and Feldman, eds., *Computers and Thought*.

very concept of 'artificial intelligence' suggests the rationalist's assumption that man's intelligence is a faculty independent of the rest of human life; happily it is not."[58] Thinking cannot be identified with the narrow range of capacities that can be subjected to the Turing test; judgments about the feelings or experiences of other persons depend on total theoretical interpretations based on observations in many contexts.[59] This middle group, we suggest, gives a balanced appraisal of computers by recognizing both their possibilities and their limitations in comparison to man.

There are various indications that *the operation of the brain is unlike that of any computer* existing or contemplated. Von Neumann holds that the logical approach and structure of brain and machine "may be expected to differ widely";[60] the language of the brain is not the language of mathematics, and its operation is fundamentally different from either digital or analog computers. Little is known about the basic processes in the brain itself, but physiological research will probably reveal some features that can be duplicated in computer design and other features that involve distinctive properties of neural nets or protein molecules. But even a more complete physical explanation of the brain will not, D. M. MacKay[61] suggests, obviate the use of mental categories; physical and mental languages are "complementary descriptions" of the same activity from the viewpoint of observer and actor respectively. We must turn then to the question of the status of mind in man.

2. The Mind-Body Problem

The relation of mind to brain (or to matter) has been a question of perennial interest to philosophers. We indicate first the traditional alternative answers (a complete list should include *idealism*, which in varying forms takes matter to be a manifestation of human or divine mind):

1. *Dualism.* Descartes' view of mind and body as two distinct

---

58. U. Neisser, "The Imitation of Man by Machine," *Science*, Vol. 139 (1963), 197.

59. K. Gunderson, "The Imitation Game," in Anderson, ed., *Minds and Machines.* See also Norbert Wiener, *God and Golem, Inc.* (Cambridge, Mass.: The M.I.T. Press, 1964), Chaps. 5–6.

60. John von Neumann, *The Computer and the Brain* (New Haven, Conn.: Yale University Press, 1958; PB°), p. 52.

61. D. M. MacKay, "On Comparing the Brain with Machines," *American Scientist*, Vol. 42 (1954), 261; also D. M. MacKay, "Mentality in Machines," *Aristotelian Society Supplementary Volume 26* (1952), p. 61.

entities that interact causally has had many adherents. The characteristics of mental and physical events are radically different; awareness of the color red does not have the properties of a red object, an electromagnetic vibration, or an electrical impulse in the brain. Mental events are inherently private rather than publicly observable, and are nonspatial rather than spatially extended. Mental life as experienced includes pains and sensations, thoughts and emotions, memories and anticipations. The interrelations among mental events (such as logical deduction of ideas or coordination of means to ends) do not resemble forces between physical objects. But how, it may be objected, could two such dissimilar substances interact? How could a nonspatial mind exert an influence in space? The reply is given that causality does not require similarity of cause and effect; and in any case there are always physical as well as mental conditions necessary for a volitional act to occur.[62]

Such a *mind-brain dualism* has been adopted by many prominent neurophysiologists. In a British symposium, all the scientists[63] agree that the neural activity of the brain somehow interacts with the private world of the mind. Penfield, for example, postulates "a spiritual element of different essence capable of controlling this mechanism. ... Something else finds its dwelling place between the sensory complex and the motor mechanism; there is a switchboard operator as well as a switchboard." Eccles[64] believes that "the mind-brain liaison occurs in the cortex"; man's will can close neural circuits without violating physical laws because the energy involved is within the limits of the Heisenberg Uncertainty Principle. He suggests that there might be either an influence of mind on individual quantum events (whose effects are "amplified" by a kind of "trigger action"), or, more probably, a coordinated shifting of probabilities in many such events. In either case, patterns of neural activity are changed by a separate "nonphysical factor." Such mental influence, others have said, does not violate the conservation of energy because only the patterns of distribution of chemical or electrical energy already present are altered.

62. See Broad, *Mind and Its Place in Nature*, Chap. 3.
63. Sherrington, Adrian, Clark, Brain, and Penfield in P. Laslett, ed., *The Physical Basis of Mind* (Oxford: Basil Blackwell, 1950); see also C. S. Sherrington, *Man on His Nature* (Cambridge: Cambridge University Press, 1951; Mentor PB); W. Penfield, "The Physiological Basis of Mind," in Farber and Wilson, eds., *Control of the Mind*.
64. Eccles, *The Neurophysiological Basis of Mind*.

2. *Epiphenomenalism.* Here it is asserted that a mental realm exists but has no causal efficacy. Consciousness accompanies but never influences material events in the brain (just as a shadow accompanies a moving object but never influences it—and of course a shadow does not influence other shadows). Mental events are "epiphenomena" that do not affect any other events, physical or mental; the only real causes are physical events (electrical impulses, chemical changes in neurons). This position is reductionistic, since all events are to be exhaustively explained in physicochemical terms. It is very close to a metaphysics of materialism, since nonmaterial phenomena, though held to be in some sense "real," play no role in the course of events. In criticizing this view, Feigl[65] asks how the laws of concomitance of such superfluous "danglers" or impotent by-products could be accounted for. Why was consciousness selected in evolutionary history if it makes no difference in the organism's activity? And are not mental concepts (ideas, attitudes, and motives) more useful than concepts of neural activity in describing introspective experience and even in understanding the activity of other persons?

3. *Behaviorism.* Basic to this view is the conviction that the postulation of "private" events inaccessible to public observation violates the canons of science. J. B. Watson and B. F. Skinner urge us to avoid reference to thinking and feeling, and to translate "mentalistic" concepts into statements about bodily behavior and observable responses. This view is reductionistic, but in a manner different from epiphenomenalism, in that "mental" phenomena are to be analyzed not in terms of neural activity in the brain but in terms of the overt behavior of the organism. It is nominally a methodological program rather than a materialistic metaphysics; but it leads to materialism if all mental concepts are assumed to be replaceable by stimulus-response correlations. In Ryle's modification, mental concepts are really statements of dispositions to behave in particular ways. "To find that most people have minds (though idiots and infants in arms do not) is simply to find that they are able and prone to do certain sorts of things."[66] Ryle does not follow the strict behaviorists who want to eliminate mental concepts, for he thinks such concepts are useful and economical,

65. Herbert Feigl, "Mind-Body, Not a Pseudoproblem," in Hook, ed., *Dimensions of Mind.*
66. Gilbert Ryle, *The Concept of Mind* (London: Hutchinson's University Library, 1949; Barnes & Noble PB), p. 61.

though they can always be translated into concepts referring to observable behavior. A person's verbal testimony as to what he would do in various situations is valuable evidence, but his use of mental terms is a linguistic convention. As children we learned to use "private" concepts when, on the basis of "public" clues, others applied to us words that we then applied to ourselves (for example, we were told that we were angry).

There are many *difficulties in behaviorism*, some of which were pointed out in Chapter 7. Surely I do not find out that I have a pain by observing my own behavior or other people's reactions to me. There is no logical contradiction in saying that I behave exactly as if I had a pain, but have none (I am a good actor), or that I have a pain but have vowed to give no indications of it (I am a Stoic). Hence behavior, although it is a common sign of pain, cannot be equated with it. Similarly, thinking and remembering as such are not externally observable; as Feigl insists, when I report emotions or ideas I am referring to direct experience. And how can a mental event that occurs only once and is not related to actions (a dream, say) be equivalent to a "disposition to behave"? Even attitudes related to actions (such as anger) can be correlated only with an indefinite range of possible actions. The attempt to solve the mind-body problem by eliminating the concept of mind has not been successful.

4. *Parallelism.* Here the distinctiveness of mental experience is recognized, but it is held (contrary to dualism) that there are no mental events without corresponding physical changes. Mental and physical phenomena are concomitant aspects of a single process of activity. We distinguish two forms. In *universal parallelism* (*panpsychism*), *all* events are said to have both mental and physical aspects, though in varying degree. Since there are no sharp lines in the scale of life, mentality is extrapolated below the level at which its effects are evident. Rudimentary mental qualities in the inorganic world are not detectable; as we have suggested, their presence is postulated on the assumption that mental phenomena could not have developed unless matter already had at least the barest beginnings of mentality.

In *limited parallelism* it is held that mental phenomena occur only at higher levels of organization; they involve new relationships not describable by the concepts and theories of lower levels. Some phenomena are purely physical (for example, in stones), some are both mental and physical (in brains)—but there are no purely mental events without physical concomitants. There is no special problem of "interaction" between "mind" and "brain," but only the general problem of the relation between levels (which have both mental and physical aspects). We will consider these two forms of parallelism below.

Let us summarize the four alternatives outlined, designating *physical* events by capital letters, *mental* events by lowercase letters, and causal relations by arrows. In dualism, physical events are said to cause mental ones ($A \rightarrow b$, for example, sensations) or vice versa ($c \rightarrow D$, for example, volitional actions), whereas some mental events without physical concomitants are causally connected ($b \rightarrow c$, for example, reflective decisions). In epiphenomenalism there is no direct connection between mental events b and c, which are inoperative by-products of the physical chain of events. In this fashion, we might represent typical sequences as follows:

Dualism: $A \rightarrow b \rightarrow c \rightarrow D$

Epiphenomenalism: $A \rightarrow B \ (\rightarrow b) \ \rightarrow C \ (\rightarrow c) \rightarrow D$

Behaviorism: $A \rightarrow D$

Parallelism (universal): $Aa \rightarrow Bb \rightarrow Cc \rightarrow Dd$

(limited): $A \rightarrow Bb \rightarrow Cc \rightarrow D$

3. A "Two-Aspect" Theory

Following the procedure that should by now be familiar, we will look for a constructive solution first along the lines of *a two-language approach* in which mental and physical concepts are taken as differing symbolic schemes referring to the same events. Feigl says that one and the same event can be described as an immediate experience or as a neural excitation: "Instead of conceiving of two realms or two concomitant types of events, we have only one reality which is represented in two different conceptual schemes."[67] He recognizes that precise correlations of introspective data with patterns of activity in cerebral neurons have not yet been discovered experimentally, but he postulates that they exist. A sensation simply is a brain process of a certain sort, though we cannot yet give it an exact physiological specification.[68] The same events are known as mind from within and brain from without.

---

67. Feigl, in Hook, ed., *Dimensions of Mind*, p. 41.
68. Cf. J. J. C. Smart, "Sensations and Brain Processes," in V. Chappell, ed., *The Philosophy of Mind* (Englewood Cliffs, N.J.: Prentice-Hall PB, 1962).

The *two-language theory* has the merit of recognizing that the logic of mental concepts is different from the logic of physical concepts, and yet it avoids a dualistic metaphysics. It also takes cognizance (as behaviorism fails to do) of processes in the brain that cannot be equated with overt behavior or even "dispositions to behave." In itself, the theory leaves open the question of whether events follow laws of the kind associated with mental concepts, or with physical concepts, or with both. If one assigns the primary ontological significance to the physical description, then of course one is back to epiphenomenalism, but this need not occur. Thus MacKay[69] sees "observer-language" and "actor-language" as two complementary descriptions; the constructs of physiology and of introspection must then be taken with equal seriousness. Once again, we could stop at this point, but critical realism prompts the search for relationships between the two languages, in terms of the processes both languages describe.

An interesting proposal, which might be called *a "two-attribute" theory*, has been worked out by Strawson. Ordinarily, he writes, we do not ascribe mental attributes to one discrete entity (a mind) and physical attributes to another (a body); rather we ascribe both kinds of attributes to a single entity: a *person*. "What I mean by the concept of a person is the concept of a type of entity such that predicates ascribing states of consciousness *and* predicates ascribing corporeal characteristics, a physical situation, etc., are equally applicable."[70] The idea of person (in reference to either oneself or another individual) thus has a distinctive logical status, namely that the very same grammatical subject has both mental and bodily predicates. So too all "personal" concepts cover both what is felt and what is observed in others; the concept of depression includes both depressed behavior and feelings of depression. Moreover, we apply these compound ideas equally to ourselves and to other persons, who apply them to themselves and to us (though of course we do not find out about others in the same way we find out about ourselves).

The *"two-attribute" theory* focuses on the idea of person. It keeps a balance between mental and physical predicates, and preserves the unity of man as a thinking, willing, and acting individual. It is based on the "ordinary language" of everyday life,

69. MacKay, n. 61 above.
70. P. F. Strawson, "Persons," in H. Feigl, M. Scriven, and G. Maxwell, eds., *Minnesota Studies in the Philosophy of Science* (Minneapolis: University of Minnesota Press, 1958), Vol. 3. See also his *Individuals*.

which has grown out of the experience of selfhood and interpersonal relatedness. The multiple logic of "person-language" is testimony to the presence of multiple aspects in the activity of man. Thus we are led a step further to speak of *two aspects of events.* If we postulate no mental events without physical concomitants, we avoid dualism. This would be essentially a form of *parallelism,* in which the mental and the physical are dual aspects of a single set of events. Here the primary reality consists of events; the abstractive character of the mental and physical concepts in which they are interpreted is recognized (as in the two-language theory), but the realistic intent of both languages is also stressed.

This viewpoint would lead to several conclusions concerning the comparison of *man* and *computer.* The existence of similarities between brain and machine does not show that man's mental life is epiphenomenal, but rather that in computers there are relatively high levels of organization in which there can occur complex types of activity that in some respects resemble human thought. We should not overestimate these similarities, for human mentality is many-dimensioned, and computers differ from brains in both their mode of operation and their complexity (the most advanced computer has fewer circuit elements than the brain of an ant). On the other hand, we cannot draw any limits to the capacities of machines for any particular type of operation, and there is no reason to deny the use of mental concepts in the interpretation of their activity. Their parts are "inanimate"—but so are the "parts" of man. We can expect that communication theory and systems research, which deal with "higher-level" integrated activities and computer operations considered as "wholes," will make important contributions to the understanding of the brain in both its physical and mental aspects. Can we not then assume that events in computers also have both physical and mental aspects (though both may have only limited resemblances to human phenomena)?

V. Conclusions: On Man and Nature

In the previous chapter we outlined four types of solution of the problem of human freedom: *reductionistic* views (stressing either determinism or indeterminacy at the atomic level); *dualistic* views; *"two-language"* views; and finally *a metaphysics of levels*—which we only began to develop—that interprets the self as the total person in its unified pattern of higher-level activities. We may now apply these same classifications to the problems of this chapter and draw some conclusions about the implications of the biological and cybernetic data for the Christian understanding of man. We group together similar types of answer to the main topics discussed: (a) emergence versus reduction, (b) teleology versus mechanism, and (c) mind versus body.

1. DUALISTIC VIEWS. In common, these interpretations assert that there are in the world radically contrasting kinds of entity which follow principles unrelated to each other. (a) In *vitalism* the ontological gap lies between life and matter. In most versions of *emergence* there are said to be no laws connecting phenomena of higher and lower levels. (b) *Teleology* and *mechanism* are taken to be mutually exclusive; the operation of purposes is understood to require a gap in the chain of physical causes, in which factors of another kind can enter. (c) *Mind-body dualism* represents mind as a distinctive entity interacting with matter in the brain. On this assumption, a computer, since it is a physical system, can have no truly mental characteristics; the dualist emphasizes the limitations of "artificial intelligence." We have suggested, however, that these various "gaps" and dichotomies (living-nonliving, mind-brain, and so forth) are difficult to maintain in the face of recent scientific evidence (such as DNA, brain physiology, and computer technology).

2. REDUCTIONISTIC VIEWS. Here it is believed that the behavior of any system can be exhaustively explained in physico-chemical terms. (a) *Mechanists* and extreme *reductionists* hold that all biological theories are in principle deducible from the laws of physics and chemistry. This position is often coupled with a metaphysics of materialism. (b) "Purpose" is equated with a particular type of mechanism, of which *the cybernetic model* (the target-seeking missile) is taken as typical. Higher-order "purposive behavior" is understood to be distinguished therefrom only in its complexity. (c) In *epiphenomenalism* causal efficacy is assigned only to physical events; in *behaviorism* all "mental" concepts must be translated into statements about observable behavior. If one anticipates that computers will be able to duplicate all types of human behavior, and if one admits only behaviorist criteria, one concludes that there is no significant difference between man and machine. Man, in short, is a complex mechanism whose operation

is predictable from physical laws. We have suggested that this view is unsatisfactory even within science.

3. "Two-language" views. Every language is selective and serves distinctive functions; conceptual schemes that seem to be mutually exclusive should be taken as alternative modes of analysis. The concern here is methodological rather than metaphysical. (a) *Multi-level analysis* is often fruitful in science, and a variety of types of models and symbol-systems can be employed concurrently. The biologist uses distinctive higher-level theories involving concepts that cannot be defined in lower-level terms, but he also seeks inter-level laws. Even where reduction is possible there is no reason to assume that the phenomena to which the higher-level concepts refer are less real than phenomena at lower levels. (b) *Teleological* and *mechanical explanations* are not mutually exclusive. Purpose and mechanism are two ways of regarding the same system; patterns in events can be analyzed in terms of either "goals" or "causes." (c) *"Mental"* and *"physical" languages* are two ways of regarding man—from within and from without, in "actor-language" and "spectator-language" respectively. In each of these cases we found much to commend this approach, which acknowledges that science is abstractive and that concepts must be employed in interpretive contexts. It provides a ready solution to other issues which will arise in the remaining chapters. Moreover, there is no problem here (as there is in any metaphysical dualism) as to how two dissimilar substances or principles could interact; it is man's language, not reality itself, which is dual. But we were driven beyond this position by our commitment to "critical realism" and by our understanding of the unity of man. In other words, one must ask about the activities within man's total being which give rise to these diverse languages.

4. A metaphysics of levels. We suggested that "levels of analysis" reflect "levels of organization" and "levels of activity" in nature. (These terms seem preferable to "levels of being," which has a more static connotation and might seem to refer to separate entities or objects.) The important point is that "levels," like "languages," are not mutually exclusive. Since any representation of a level is admittedly an abstraction, this approach differs from that of "alternative languages" only in its insistence on ontological reference. (a) *Organicism* in biology stresses the presence of system-laws and the distinctive activities of *wholes,* as well as hierar-

chies of organizing relations in unified systems. Although the laws of these higher levels cannot be derived from studying lower-level phenomena among the separate parts, the activity of the whole is always dependent on that of the parts. (b) *Purpose* is found at various levels, which differ both in the way the future is represented in the present and in the kinds of flexibility of response displayed in goal-seeking. But we need not deny that there are some features common to these various levels of purpose, nor that there are causal factors at work in all of them. (c) *Parallelism* takes the mental and the physical to be two aspects of one set of events. Whereas the advocates of metaphysical dualism and "alternative languages" find the extension of mental concepts beyond the human sphere problematical (even for the animal kingdom), advocates of psychophysical parallelism ascribe low levels of mentality at low levels of organization—in organisms or in computers. Recognition of both the diversity of activities at various levels and the continuity between levels enables us to avoid the ontological discontinuity of dualism as well as the one-level metaphysics to which reductionism usually leads. The analogy of a "spectrum" suggests not only the value of interpreting the lower in terms of the higher, and the higher in terms of the lower, but also the need for distinctive categories at various levels.

Such an interpretation of levels can contribute to *a view of man* which takes both the scientific and the biblical understanding into account. It can allow for DNA and neurons, but also for personality and selfhood, the highest levels in man, to which both the religious tradition and human experience testify. Yet this many-leveled complexity must be seen within the total unity of man, to which biological science and biblical theology alike bear witness. Any general conclusions about the nature of man are of course beyond the compass of this book; they would require a discussion of the findings of the social sciences, an exploration of the many facets of the biblical understanding of human nature, and a comparison of religious and psychological concepts (such as sin and guilt, love and self-fulfillment). We will, however, consider briefly the relation of *the biblical view of man* to the biological evidence.

The Old Testament sees man as *rooted in nature*, sharing the finitude, creatureliness and death of all living things. "You are dust and to dust you shall return."[71] Man and beasts are equally

71. Genesis 3:19; *cf.* Isaiah 31:3, 40:6; Job 14:1–17.

perishable. Yet man is distinguished from the animal world by his special relationship to God. Man alone is *a responsible self* who can be addressed by God. Man, as a free purposeful agent who can respond to the demands of righteousness and justice, is made "in the image of God." Man's "breath" or "spirit" is not a separate entity but the animating principle of the total person, the vitality of the whole individual in his biological, mental, and emotional life. Biblical scholars are agreed that "there is no dichotomy or division into body and soul, for these various functions are not considered as distinct notions."[72] "Opposition between body and soul is not to be found in the Old Testament; man is a psycho-physical being."[73] "Biblical man, from the standpoint of a psychological approach to his nature, is a *unitary* being. He is body, spirit, self, feeling, mind and heart."[74] "Characteristic of the Old Testament, the idea of human nature implies a unity not a dualism. There is no contrast between the body and the soul such as the terms instinctively suggest to us."[75]

The biblical view of *the unity of man* is also evident in the fact that when belief in a future life finally developed, it was expressed in terms of *the resurrection of the total person,* not the immortality of the soul. (A future life is affirmed in a few late Old Testament passages, a number of intertestamental writings, and of course repeatedly in the message of the early church.) Cullmann has shown that in the New Testament the future life is seen as a gift from God "in the last days," and not an innate attribute of man. "The Jewish and Christian interpretation of creation excludes the whole Greek dualism of body and soul."[76] Even Paul, who was strongly influenced by Greek thought, speaks of the dead as "sleeping" until the day of judgment when they will be restored—not as physical bodies nor as disembodied souls, but in what he calls

72. T. C. Vriezen, *An Outline of Old Testament Theology* (Oxford: Basil Blackwell, 1958), p. 203.

73. Edmund Jacob, *Theology of The Old Testament,* trans. A. W. Heathcote and P. J. Allcock (New York: Harper and Brothers, 1958), p. 157.

74. Otto J. Baab, *The Theology of The Old Testament* (Nashville: Abingdon Press, 1949; PB), p. 68.

75. H. Wheeler Robinson, *Religious Ideas of the Old Testament* (London: Gerald Duckworth & Co., Ltd., 1913), p. 83; cf. Walther Eichrodt, *Man in the Old Testament,* trans. K. and R. Gregor Smith (London: SCM Press, 1951).

76. Oscar Cullmann, *Immortality of the Soul or Resurrection of the Dead?* (New York: The Macmillan Co., 1958), p. 30.

"the spiritual body."[77] Such views of the future life may be problematical for modern man, but they do testify that our faith must
be in God and not in our own souls, and that man's whole being
is the object of God's saving purpose.

Paul's contrast of *"flesh"* and *"spirit"*[78] at first seems to support
a dualistic view of man, but more careful analysis shows that this
is not the case. He never portrays a body which is inherently
evil and a soul which is inherently good. Sin is in the will, which
governs man's whole being; "spiritual" sins such as arrogance and
ingratitude are prominent in Paul's account. Similarly, the power
of the Holy Spirit transforms man's *total* life, the inner and the
outer man.[79] (To be sure, Paul does speak of an inherited impulse
to evil, and of the occasions of temptation presented by the body;
but "the flesh" is a symbol of the weakness of human nature in all
its dimensions, rather than of any intrinsic evil associated with
matter or the body as such.) Only in later Gnostic and Manichaean
movements was a strong dualism developed in which matter was
understood to be evil. This trend was influenced by the Greek
idea (evident already in Plato's *Phaedo,* and prominent in the
Hellenistic world) that the body is a prison from which death
liberates the soul. There were other forces in the declining Graeco-
Roman culture which aided the growth of asceticism, monasticism
and rejection of the world, and the search for individual salvation and escape from worldly existence. But these tendencies ran
counter to the *affirmative attitude toward the natural,* which is
predominant in the biblical record, wherein there is no counsel to
disown the body or escape into otherworldly withdrawal;[80] there
are no monasteries in the Bible. As Reinhold Niebuhr suggests,[81]
sin may indeed take the form of sensuality which exploits others
or evades one's own responsibilities (man is "absorbed into nature"
and his higher potentialities are denied); but it may equally take
the form of spiritual pride, self-righteousness, or the idealization

77. I Corinthians 15.
78. E.g., Romans 8.
79. Frederick C. Grant, *An Introduction to New Testament Thought* (Nashville: Abingdon Press, 1950; PB), pp. 160–70; cf. Sydney Cave, *The Christian
Estimate of Man,* (London: Gerald Duckworth & Co., Ltd., 1944), Chap. 1.
80. Cf. Amos Wilder, *Otherworldliness and the New Testament* (New York:
Harper and Brothers, 1954); J. A. T. Robinson, *The Body* (London: SCM
Press, 1952).
81. Niebuhr, *The Nature and Destiny of Man,* Vol. 1, Chap. 7.

of human reason (man denies his natural and bodily existence and refuses to acknowledge his finitude). No aspect of man is evil in itself, but only in its misuse. The inherent goodness of the material order, in which man's being fully participates, is, as we shall see, a corollary of the doctrine of creation.

Among the contemporary options, a *dualism* that assigns *the body* to science and *the soul* to religion might seem to allow man to participate in both realms. The soul would be an immaterial entity inaccessible to science, which in turn would be confined to the study of man's body. But such a dichotomy may be challenged on other grounds besides biblical exegesis. If mind is integral to the soul as the rational principle in man, we are faced with all the problems of a mind-body dualism. Again, we know that genes, environmental influences, and chemical changes can drastically influence human personality in its psychosomatic unity. Thus one must either say that chemicals can alter the soul, or else postulate that the soul is an unchanging entity untouched by personality changes, and thus apparently unrelated to personal existence as we know it.

The idea of man as *a many-leveled unity* seems to us more consonant with both the biblical and the scientific viewpoints. The highest level of man's total being may be represented by the concept of *the self*, conceived not as a separate entity but as the individual in his unified activity of thinking, willing, feeling, and acting. The self is described not in terms of static substances but of dynamic activities at various levels of organization and functioning. It is this integral being whose whole life is of concern to God. Whereas the soul is usually imagined as a self-contained individual unit, which is only incidentally and externally related to anything else, a selfhood that is social in character is portrayed in the biblical view. A person is constituted by his relationships—he is who he is precisely as father, husband, citizen, and servant of God. The dominant image of person-in-community emphasizes this corporate dimension of selfhood without absorbing the individual into the collective. It was noted earlier that selfhood as we know it, including language and symbolic thought, would be impossible without society. We will find that many biologists today recognize man's nature as a social being, and assert that human evolution is now cultural rather than biological.

The presence in man of *levels of activity not found among other creatures* has been widely acknowledged by biologists, as will be seen in the next chapter. In the capacity for abstract thought and symbolic language there is a radical distinction between man and animal. Self-conscious awareness, critical self-reflection, and creative imagination are found nowhere else in nature. In memory of the past, anticipation of the future, and envisagement of ideal potentialities he transcends his immediate environment. He is unique in his search for truth, concern for moral values, and acknowledgment of universal obligations—and above all, in his relationship to God. As we take up the problem of evolution, we will consider further the issue of man's relation to nature, as understood by both biology and biblical theology.

We will find also that *the uniqueness of each individual* can be defended on purely biological grounds. Each human being represents a novel genetic combination not duplicated elsewhere in the universe, and his life history is an unrepeatable set of events; in Chapter 7 it was suggested that such uniqueness is compatible with the existence of lawful regularities. Moreover our account has surely not exhausted the mystery of self-consciousness, whereby each of us is aware of himself as a unique center of experience. Even if I matched someone else identically in every empirical description, I would never confuse myself with him; this distinctiveness is reflected in the logical peculiarities of first-person language. The biblical conviction of the uniqueness of each person derives, of course, from other considerations, especially the idea of God's love for each man as an irreplaceable individual. The sacredness of personality and the fundamental equality of man are rooted in the value of every person in God's sight. The belief that each man is a special creation of God must be seen today as an assertion of individuality, novelty, and dependence on God, rather than as a denial of genetic and evolutionary continuity.

12

Evolution and Creation

Four issues raised in the nineteenth century by Darwin's work were discussed in an earlier chapter: (1) the challenge to design, (2) the challenge to human dignity, (3) the challenge of evolutionary ethics, and (4) the challenge to scripture. Four types of response were also described, those (from "right" to "left") of traditionalism, liberalism, modernism and naturalism. In the present chapter, after a brief summary of new scientific evidence, each section examines contemporary forms of one of these theological perspectives, and at the same time takes up one of the issues raised earlier. In Section II, "Traditional Theism and the Doctrine of Creation," Roman Catholic and neo-orthodox views of evolution and its relation to scripture are presented. In Section III, "Liberal Theology and the Argument from Design," reformulations of the teleological argument by DuNouy, Henderson, and Tennant are set forth. Section IV deals with "Evolutionary Theism and the Immanence of God" in the writings of Bergson, Teilhard, and others. In Section V, "Evolutionary Naturalism and the Status of Man," we find evolutionary ethics defended by Huxley and criticized by Simpson and Toulmin.

I. THE EVOLVING UNIVERSE

Since Darwin's day there has been a vast accumulation of scientific data supporting the fact of evolution, and there have been many significant advances in understanding the factors which

have contributed to evolutionary change. Moreover, biological
history is now seen within a wider picture of the history of the
universe, to which many fields of science have contributed. From
astronomy have come theories about the origin of the universe;
from biochemistry, clues as to the origin of life; from genetics and
molecular biology, information about the role of genes and mutations in organic evolution; from paleontology, a partial reconstruction of human ancestry. From this wealth of data we have selected
a few findings important for their bearing on the character of the
evolutionary process and the origins of the universe and of man.

1. *Theories of Creation in Astronomy*

Astronomers today are divided between two rival scientific
theories concerning the origins of the universe. Gamow's *instantaneous creation* (or "big bang") theory[1] assumes that the universe
started as a single exceedingly dense concentration of neutrons, a
gigantic "primeval nucleus," which within half an hour decayed
radioactively to produce atoms. On the basis of known nuclear
properties and plausible assumptions, the relative abundance of
the atomic elements in our galaxy can be accounted for. Expanding from this initial explosion, matter slowly collected into stars,
which continued to move outward. Gamow proposes no theory for
the origin of the "primeval nucleus"; it is simply treated as a
"given." He suggests that it might represent an "absolute beginning," in which case time would be finite. Or it might represent
a "relative beginning," the start of an expansive phase of a cosmic
cycle having an earlier contracting phase; with such an oscillating
universe, time might be either finite or infinite.

The rival *continuous creation* (or "steady state") theory has been
expounded by Hoyle[2], Bondi, and Gold. They postulate that matter has always been coming into being uniformly, throughout infinite time and unbounded space. These newly formed isolated
atoms continually condense into stars. But stars die or escape
from possible observation (by approaching the velocity of light)
at the same rate that they are being born. In this "steady state"
situation, the structure of the universe would appear identical when

1. George Gamow, *The Creation of the Universe* (New York: The Viking
Press, 1952; Mentor PB); see also Milton Munitz, *Space, Time and Creation*
(Glencoe, Ill.: The Free Press, 1957; Collier PB).
2. Frederick Hoyle, *The Nature of the Universe* (New York: Harper and
Brothers, 1950; Mentor PB). He has subsequently modified his view.

observed from any point in space or time. No explanation is proposed by Hoyle for the continuous creation of hydrogen atoms; matter "simply appears," at a very slow rate, throughout the universe.

Between these two theories *astronomers are divided* at present, and the data are insufficient for any clear decision. Some argue for instantaneous creation from the second law of thermodynamics: if entropy is always increasing, time must be finite. But there are many disputed questions (whether the law is applicable to the whole universe, to "open" systems, to relativistic velocities, and so forth). Further, the "continuous creation" of matter violates the conservation of energy-matter, and no satisfactory "mechanism" of origination has been proposed; but the divergence from an absolute conservation law would be far too small to detect directly—one atom per century in a 50-yard cube. Again, the speed of recession of stars increases uniformly with distance as the steady-state theory requires; however, data from near the present limit of observation seem to show a deviation from linearity. Extremely powerful radio-stars (quasars), found only at very great distances, may represent vast explosions long ago when the universe was young—which would imply "instantaneous creation."

Some naturalistic defenders of the steady-state theory have claimed in its favor that it "avoids *metaphysical* and *theological* biases" associated with a beginning in time. And some Christian authors have defended the "big bang" theory as more consistent with the biblical doctrine of creation.[3] We would submit, however, that both theories are capable of either a naturalistic or a theistic interpretation. Both theories push explanation back to an unexplained situation which is treated as a "given"—the "primeval nucleus" in Gamow's case, the "continual creation" of matter in Hoyle's. The question of the creation of time (finite or infinite) is not raised by either theory. Bondi claims that the steady-state hypothesis fulfills what he calls "the perfect cosmological principle" of complete uniformity, since it postulates no distinctive point in space or time; but it is doubtful whether an empirical question can be settled by such an *a priori* principle. Moreover, defense of the infinity of time often displays a naturalistic "metaphysical bias,"

3. Pollard, *The Cosmic Drama*; Edmund Whittaker, *Space and Spirit* (London: Nelson, 1946); Pius XII, allocution to the Pontifical Academy of Sciences (see Chap. 5, n. 21 above).

as if nature, having taken the place of God, must itself be infinite. We will suggest that the Christian need not favor either theory, for the doctrine of creation is not really about temporal beginnings but about the basic relationship between the world and God. The religious content of the idea of creation is compatible with either theory, and the debate between them can be settled only on scientific grounds, when further data are available.[4]

2. From Matter to Man

We have indicated that many fields of inquiry have contributed to our knowledge of the history of the universe. The astronomer can offer at least some hypotheses concerning the development of galaxies, stars, and planetary systems. The geologist reconstructs for us the early history of our planet earth. Next, the chemist introduces ideas of "chemical evolution," the building up in warm primeval seas of the complex compounds and molecular chains, utilized by subsequent organic forms. The biochemist has at least a few limited clues about *the origin of life*.[5] We have seen that the gap between the living and the nonliving has been greatly narrowed by the study of viruses and recent work in molecular biology. The possibility of a transition from matter to life in the early history of our planet no longer appears inconceivable. Urey and Miller, in their laboratory in Chicago, passed sparks through a capsule containing only a mixture of simple gases, similar to those that might have been present on the early earth, and found that they had produced many of the amino acids, which are the building blocks of life (though still a long way from the simplest cell). Problems of the biochemistry of living cells are incredibly complex, but they do not seem to be insoluble in principle.

It may be noted in passing that there seems to be no biblical warrant for asserting a sharp line between *living* and *nonliving* entities. One occasionally hears it said that we can know on theological grounds that the laboratory synthesis of life is impossible ("Only God can cross the line between nonliving and living," or "The creation of life is a miracle God alone can perform"). But

---

4. A similar view is taken by Mascall, *Christian Theology and Natural Science,* Chap. 4. See also C. F. von Weizsäcker, *The Relevance of Science: Creation and Cosmogeny* (London: Collins, 1964), Chap. 9.

5. A. I. Oparin, *The Origin of Life* (New York: The Macmillan Co., 1938; Dover PB); H. E. Blum, *Time's Arrow and Evolution*; J. H. Rush, *The Dawn of Life* (Garden City, N.Y.: Doubleday and Co., 1957; Signet PB).

actually throughout most of Christian history no such line between life and matter was assumed (for example, in the Middle Ages it was believed that frogs generate spontaneously from mud). The vitalist's portrayal of a distinctive "life-principle" contrasting with "inert matter" is theologically as well as scientifically indefensible.

The long slow *development of living forms* has been amply documented from the study of fossils.[6] Successive epochs were dominated by protozoa, simple invertebrates, fishes, amphibians, reptiles and dinosaurs, mammals and birds, and finally primates and primitive man. Of particular interest are discoveries that may represent some of the "missing links" of man's immediate ancestry.[7] Of these, the earliest are specimens of *Australopithecus* who lived in South Africa, possibly as much as a million years ago, and was intermediate between modern man and ape in brain size, skull shape, type of teeth, and partly erect posture; there are some signs that he may have used very primitive implements. *Sinanthropus* in China, like *Pithecanthropus* in Java, perhaps half a million years ago, had a brain somewhat smaller than modern man, a sloping forehead, protruding jaw, and erect posture; he used fire and roughly shaped tools. The *Swanscombe* skull, though fragmentary, is quite advanced in form, and dates back 250,000 years. But *Neanderthal* man, after the start of the last glacial period, still shows heavy eyebrow ridges, jutting jaw, and thickset bones. Finally, a number of discoveries dating from the last 50,000 years, such as *Cro-Magnon* man who drew paintings and held burial rituals, are fully *Homo sapiens* in form and culture.

The exact *reconstruction of man's ancestry* is by no means clear, and there have been differences of opinion about many of these specimens and their relationship to each other. A generation ago it was customary to picture a single line of descent from ancient ape to modern man. Today it appears more likely that the resemblance of man and ape signifies not the descent of one from the other, but a common ancestry in some earlier, lower form of life. Moreover, there was probably not just one line of development, but diversification along collateral lines. For example, Neanderthal man is later but appears to have been less human than the owner

6. E.g., Gaylord G. Simpson, *The Meaning of Evolution* (New Haven, Conn.: Yale University Press, 1949; PB), Pt. I.

7. Theodosius Dobzhansky, *Mankind Evolving* (New Haven, Conn.: Yale University Press, 1962; PB); W. E. LeGros Clark, *The Fossil Evidence for Human Evolution* (Chicago: University of Chicago Press, 1955).

of the Swanscombe skull, and may represent a branch line that remained more primitive and died out. Although many of the details remain obscure, the continuity of man with lower forms has indeed been impressively documented.

3. Genes, Mutations, and Natural Selection

We saw that variations and natural selection were the two key factors in Darwin's theory of evolution. *Modern genetics* has greatly advanced our understanding of the causes of variations, about which Darwin could only speculate. The laws of heredity had been discovered in 1866 by Mendel, but were virtually ignored until the twentieth century. In 1901, Hugo de Vries studied the random appearance of new varieties of plants and animals differing markedly from their parents. T. H. Morgan found among many generations of pink-eyed fruit flies an occasional white-eyed individual; it was later discovered that the frequency of such mutations increased with exposure to X rays, heat, and certain chemicals. By the 1930's, many people had contributed to the merging of genetics and evolutionary theory, including Fisher and Haldane in England, Wright in America, and Chetverikov in Russia. Population genetics became a highly developed theoretical system supported by extensive data obtained both in the laboratory and in studies of natural populations.[8]

We have seen that genes are *DNA molecules* that carry coded information governing the growth of the organism. In the long process of evolution each set of genes has been "programmed" with a genetic code whose "instructions" control the embryonic development, physiological structure, and instinctive behavior of the individual organism. In this view, mutations are caused by damage to a portion of the DNA molecule, or defective duplication of its code. In addition to mutations, the *recombination of genes* is an important source of variations. Since in bisexual reproduction each individual arises from the combination of sets of genes from two parents, the number of possible new genetic complexes is enormous. If a set contains 1,000 genes, each with 10 possible forms, there could be 10^{1000} different combinations—far more than the number of atoms in the universe. Each man has his own

---

8. See J. A. Moore, *Heredity and Development* (London: Oxford University Press, 1963); T. Dobzhansky, *Evolution, Genetics and Man* (New York: John Wiley and Sons, 1955).

gene pattern (genotype), and every face and fingerprint is unique. Because the integral development of the organism is governed by the total constellation of its genes, every new individual is a genuinely novel occurrence.

A subject of continuing debate is the relative importance of *large* and *small variations.* The neo-Darwinian school (Huxley, Simpson, Mayr,[9] and others) holds that evolution is the result of the accumulation of many small changes. Dobzhansky and Fisher[10] agree but suggest that while results due to small mutations can be repeated over and over in the laboratory, there may be somewhat larger jumps that are rare and hence not predictable from statistical laws. The more extreme school (Goldschmidt, Schindewolf,[11] and others) insists that laboratory studies have documented only changes within species, not the formation of new species, and that there have been found few fossils of transitions between species, much less between major types (classes or phyla). These critics believe that new species and phyla arise suddenly from exceedingly rare cases where a viable creature is produced by gross "systemic" mutations—which perhaps modify an early stage of the embryo's development, drastically altering its structure. But there is no direct evidence for such major transitions, and the integration of a radically mutant individual into a population is problematical.

Variations from both mutation and genetic recombination are today generally held to be *random* with respect to the needs of the organism. There have been three versions of the opposing claim, namely that variations are (a) controlled toward a preconceived goal, by divine intervention, or (b) urged in a constant direction, by an immanent vital force, or (c) modified favorably to the needs of the organism, by the Lamarckian inheritance of changes in the individual during its lifetime. The first two claims will be examined later; any assertion that mutations are produced by God must reckon with the fact that individual mutations are very erratic and predominantly injurious or lethal. The third, or Lamarckian, thesis has been the subject of long and bitter controversy.

9. E.g., J. Huxley, A. C. Hardy, and E. B. Ford, eds., *Evolution as a Process* (New York: The Macmillan Company, 1954; Collier PB).

10. R. Fisher, *Creative Aspects of Natural Law* (Cambridge: Cambridge University Press, 1950).

11. R. Goldschmidt, *Theoretical Genetics* (Berkeley: University of California Press, 1955).

Suffice it to say that repeated claims for the inheritance of acquired characters have rested either on data that subsequent investigators were unable to reproduce, or on interpretations of the data that most biologists have not accepted. The preponderance of evidence favors the conclusion that the genes which an organism will pass on are not influenced by its life experience.

In addition to such data on variations, there has also been new evidence about the second factor in Darwin's theory, the operation of *natural selection*. The appearance of novel strains as a result of changes in the environment has actually been observed. For example, among a species of light-colored moths, there occurs a rare dark mutation, which is normally more conspicuous against light-colored tree trunks and is picked off more rapidly by birds. But on the soot-darkened trees of industrial areas, the dark moth is less conspicuous than the light moth, so that in the past century it has completely supplanted the original light-colored species in certain parts of England. Another example of a rapid process of selection is the production of bacteria that are resistant to antibiotics. Among "normal" bacteria there are rare mutant cells resistant to streptomycin—a capacity which is not ordinarily useful, but which suddenly becomes useful when streptomycin is present; these mutations flourish while other forms die out, so a new strain comes into being. There are many other illustrations of a potential for change latently present in the gene pool of a population, but only evoked by a modification in the environment.

Another development since Darwin's day is awareness of the role of *cooperation* as well as competition in natural selection. "The survival of the fittest" no longer implies a gladiatorial view of nature, for survival now means reproductive success; not the conqueror, but the parent with the largest number of progeny reaching parenthood, is the fittest. Kropotkin, Allee, and others[12] have demonstrated the importance of parental care of the young, social habits in animal and insect communities, and other cooperative relationships between organisms. Some of the complex patterns of interdependence among individuals, among species, and between individuals and their total environment have been traced. Several of these problems will be discussed further when we treat of the major theistic and naturalistic interpretations of evolution.

12. Petr Kropotkin, *Mutual Aid, a Factor of Evolution* (New York: McClure, Phillips and Co., 1907); W. Clyde Allee, *Cooperation Among Animals* (New York: Schumann, 1951).

II. Traditional Theism
and the Doctrine of Creation

We have scanned evidence from astronomy, paleontology, and genetics concerning our evolving universe. We turn now to the first theological issue, "the challenge to scripture," especially regarding the doctrine of creation. We will be dealing with scholars who derive their religious beliefs from revelation, who take scripture seriously but not literally, and who accept the evidence for evolution. Although the fundamentalist rejection of evolution has continued to have its supporters, it has generated few new ideas; little would need to be added to the description of fundamentalism given in Chapter 4. But there have been significant new approaches in neo-orthodoxy and Roman Catholic theology (philosophical writings of Catholic authors and the views of Teilhard will be considered later).

1. The Origins of Man (Roman Catholicism)

The Catholic view of scripture and the increasing acceptance of "higher criticism" have already been described. In interpretations of the creation story a distinction is often made between the inspired religious message the ancient authors intended to convey, and the prescientific cosmology and Near East symbolism in which that message was expressed. According to one theologian: "It is possible that the scientific notions of the author of Genesis are erroneous, drawn as they are from his contemporary science, but it is not these notions that he is affirming or implying. It is not the intention of sacred scripture to teach us cosmogony."[13]
In 1909 the Pontifical Biblical Commission listed among *the "fundamental truths" of the Genesis story*: the creation of all things by God at the beginning of time; the special creation of man; the formation of the first woman from the first man; and the transgression of a precept given by God to the first man. An address of Pius XII in 1951 cited with approval the views of several astronomers that the universe had a beginning in time. In general, it is maintained that the creation of both the universe and the first man and

---

13. R. W. Gleason in W. Ong, ed., *Darwin's Vision and Christian Perspectives*, p. 106. See also C. Hauret, *Beginnings: Genesis and Modern Science*, trans. E. P. Emmans (Dubuque, Iowa: Priory Press, 1955).

woman were historical events, but that the biblical portrayal of these events is figurative. *Humani generis* (1950), the first papal encyclical to deal with evolution, states:

> Thus, the teaching of the church leaves the doctrine of evolution an open question, as long as it confines its speculations to the development, from other living matter already in existence, of the human body. (That souls are immediately created by God is a view which the Catholic faith imposes on us.) In the present state of scientific and theological opinion, this question may be legitimately canvassed by research, and by discussion between experts on both sides. . . . Christians cannot lend their support to a theory which involves the existence, after Adam's time, of some earthly race of men, truly so called, who were not descended ultimately from him, or else supposes that Adam was the name given to some group of our primordial ancestors. It does not appear how such views can be reconciled with the doctrine of original sin, as this is guaranteed to us by scripture and tradition, and proposed to us by the church. Original sin is the result of a sin committed, in actual historical fact, by an individual man named Adam, and it is a quality native to all of us, only because it has been handed down by descent from him.[14]

This encyclical permits belief in the evolutionary origins of man's body, but insists on *the special creation of Adam's soul*. The Catholic tradition holds that the soul, as a spiritual substance, comes directly from God, who creates it immediately in each individual case. As the Jesuit anthropologist F. J. Ewing puts it: "This is one occasion on which God has to step in with his primary power, because matter cannot produce a spiritual soul."[15] Father Gleason points out that if God took matter for the formation of Adam, not from dust, but from a suitable near-human animal body slowly evolved under his direction, and then infused a soul into it, both the long preparation and the final act of intervention were God's doing. He suggests that the story of Eve's creation from Adam's rib is "figurative," and that Adam was only the "exemplary cause" or model for Eve; in any case the religious message concerns woman's basic equality with man and their common human nature. The Catholic understanding of original sin, as a

---

14. Pius XII, *Humani Generis* (1950), trans. R. A. Knox, paragraphs 36, 37.
15. F. J. Ewing, "Current Roman Catholic Thought on Evolution," in S. Tax, ed., *Evolution After Darwin* (Chicago: University of Chicago Press, 1960), Vol. 3, 26. See also his article in *Anthropological Quarterly* (October 1956), p. 91.

taint from Adam's fall inherited by all mankind, requires his existence as an actual historical individual.[16]

In *Evolution and Christians*, P. G. Fothergill, an outstanding Catholic botanist, presents extensive scientific data on evolution, and in a final chapter discusses their theological significance. He believes that under God's guidance evolution produced a creature fit to receive a soul; Adam's body came from prehuman parents very near to man in physical structure. Nevertheless a great intellectual and spiritual gulf separated Adam from his parents. Fothergill asserts that the human brain evolved, but man's mind and soul, being immaterial, could not be the product of evolution:

> There is a vast impassable gulf between the mind of man and the "mind" of any animal no matter what its state of development.... The ancient forms of fossil men, such as *Pithecanthropus*, sometimes called prehominids, are therefore fully human from the first moment of their appearance. There can be no true link between a lower animal and a creature who has crossed the threshold of thought, except perhaps structurally.... Hence we may say that the creation of a new spirit, when infused into a certain one of the end products of evolution that is physical man, formed an intellectual soul and produced the first rational human being. The human soul thus has no necessary connection with the life-principle, or organization, of the organisms that preceded its creation (except insofar as this organization was perfect enough to receive the soul). Hence there was no break in the chain of nature as such, for the advent of the human soul is a fact above natural happenings; it is a gratuitous addition to nature.[17]

In the Catholic view, then, the scientific facts about evolution can be accepted, and the special creation of man is an additional truth *known only by revelation*. The existence of a unique human ancestor is in principle incapable of scientific proof or disproof, because only the human body and not the soul could be an object of investigation by paleontologists. (Many scientists think that man arose in only one geographical region rather than independently on different continents, but they can make no assertions about a single ancestral couple.) The existence of a historical Adam is

---

16. R. W. Gleason in W. Ong, ed., *Darwin's Vision and Christian Perspectives*. See also R. Nogar, *The Wisdom of Evolution* (Garden City, N.Y.: Doubleday and Company, 1963). Two useful earlier volumes are E. C. Messenger, *Evolution and Theology* (New York: The Macmillan Co., 1932), and *Theology and Evolution* (Westminster, Md.: The Newman Press, 1952).

17. P. G. Fothergill, *Evolution and Christians* (London: Longman's, Green & Co., Ltd., 1961), pp. 286, 290, 334.

a revealed truth; but it is not defended simply by an appeal to scripture as such. In many biblical passages (Jonah and the whale, for instance) a purely allegorical interpretation is permitted. The Genesis story, however, is not interpreted completely allegorically or symbolically, as by many Protestants, nor completely literally, as by fundamentalists, but rather as what is termed "allegorical history," that is, a story about events that really took place, narrated in a form different from that in which they actually occurred.

Thus we may say that in recent Catholic thought the existence of an ancestral pair is really a conclusion, not from science, nor from scripture alone, but from *theology* as developed from scripture and tradition interpreted by the church. One crucial doctrine is the inheritance of *original sin,* understood as a condition caused by the transgression of a single ancestor and transmitted in a quasi-biological way to the whole human race. A second doctrine is the discontinuity of *the human soul* from the order of nature. Only man is rational, moral, spiritual, and immortal; these attributes are held to be totally absent from the animal kingdom, and could only have been introduced supernaturally by divine intervention. Many Protestants, by contrast, give greater emphasis to the unity of the human person, and hold that God created man's total being by the long gradual operation of secondary causes, without any point of absolute discontinuity. They view Adam's fall not as a historical event but as a mythical representation of the human condition, along the following lines.

2. *The Religious Meaning of Creation (Neo-Orthodoxy)*

In Catholic thought, evolution in science and the doctrine of creation in theology are linked by two actual events in history: the beginning of the universe and the advent of man. In neo-orthodoxy no such links exist, for the opening chapters of Genesis are taken not as history—not even "allegorical history"—but as an entirely symbolic expression of religious truths which are on *a totally different level* from evolutionary history. The doctrine of creation here has nothing to do with temporal origins; it is an affirmation concerning the fundamental relation between God and the world. Its theological content can therefore be set forth without reference to evolution, though we will want to raise some questions afterward about this total separation of the two areas of thought.

In accordance with the *neo-orthodox view of revelation*, the doctrine of creation is based on the understanding of God and human existence made known in Christ. One should start where the Gospel of John does: "In the beginning was the Word . . . and the Word was made flesh." This was the event in which the purpose of creation and the creaturely nature of man were disclosed. Barth asserts that "the creation is the establishment of a place for the history of the covenant of grace," a preparation for the redemption initiated in Israel and fulfilled in Christ.[18] Historically, God was acknowledged first as Lord of Israel, and then of all mankind, and finally, as a sort of corollary, as Lord of nature; the first chapter of Genesis comes from a late document and stands as a preface to the history of the covenant. Similarly, Brunner insists that the doctrine of creation is not a hypothesis about origins, but one form of the basic affirmation that God is sovereign Lord.[19]

In Gilkey's *Maker of Heaven and Earth*, which is perhaps the best recent exposition of the doctrine by a Protestant theologian, the basis of religious knowledge is revelation in history, but creation is not such a historical event. "The idea of creation is an inference from the nature of God as he is revealed in those events; it is not itself a part of revelation."[20] Faith in God as redeemer and sovereign implies belief in God as creator. Gilkey distinguishes religious questions from scientific ones along existentialist lines; in questions of ultimate concern our own personal existence and the meaning and destiny of our lives are at stake, and we ask as participants not as spectators. In this light, the idea of creation is an extension of the acknowledgment of our own dependence on God. It is not really about temporal origins in the past, but about the basic relationship between God and the world in the present. In Genesis these religious insights were expressed as a myth about beginnings, in the images of a prescientific cosmology. Their meaning, however, consists in *affirmations about the character of God and the world*, which we might organize (drawing from Gilkey and other authors) under four headings:

1. *God is sovereign and transcendent.* God's status is defined in relation to all else by the primary ontological distinction of crea-

---

18. Karl Barth, *Church Dogmatics* (Edinburgh: T. & T. Clark, 1958), Vol. 3, Pt. 1.

19. Emil Brunner, *The Christian Doctrine of Creation and Redemption* (Philadelphia: Westminster Press, 1952), Chap. 1.

20. Langdon Gilkey, *Maker of Heaven and Earth* (Garden City, N.Y.: Doubleday and Co., 1959; PB), p. 271.

ture and creator. The concept of creation "out of nothing" signifies that God is not finite or limited by materials that happened to be available. (In most creation myths—Plato's *Timaeus*, for example— God imposes form on the matter which is given to him, and reworks the primeval stuff on which he is dependent. But in the biblical myth God is unconditioned, self-sufficient and independent; no additional principle limits him, for everything else owes its existence to him alone.) Transcendence means that God is distinct from the world, and not a part of it or a force within it; monism and pantheism are excluded. Gilkey suggests that without such transcendence the divine would lack the holiness which alone can evoke worship; man's sense of finitude and dependence points to the difference between creature and creator. The same point is emphasized by neo-Thomism: creation is fundamentally a doctrine about absolute ontological dependence, a relation between the world and God rather than an event (though in the context of Catholic thought a historical beginning is assumed).

2. *God is free and purposeful.* He is not an automatic process or an impersonal structure, nor a victim of forces within the world. This freedom and independence is symbolized by speaking of God's initiative in judging, redeeming—and creating. In analyzing human actions or historical events, intentions and motives are crucial categories of explanation; God's actions are also described in terms of purposes—love, self-communication, the goal of "the Kingdom of God." God's relation to the world is not describable in purely metaphysical terms (such as "power" or "ground of being"), so we employ personal terms of will and purpose, as in the creation story. One product of the biblical belief that God has purposes in history is the conviction permeating Western thought that time and history are significant and directional, rather than static or cyclical as in most Greek and Oriental thought.

3. *The world is real and orderly.* A created world is dependent but real; natural causes are effective, and creatures are centers of genuine activity and freedom. Individuality and selfhood are real and in themselves good—not illusions or evils to be overcome by absorption in the infinite. (By contrast, the Hindu doctrine of *Maya* asserts that finite existence is essentially illusory; Buddhism has tended to deny the reality and value of individuality, seeking liberation from selfhood in undifferentiated union with God.) It will be recalled that the attitudes toward nature engendered by the doctrine of creation are generally held to have contributed to the rise

of science in the West. The world is orderly and dependable because God is trustworthy and not capricious; but the details of the world must be found by observation rather than rational deduction because God is free and did not have to create any particular kind of universe.

4. *The world is essentially good.* If everything is God's creation, no entity can in itself be evil. Of every created thing in the Genesis story it is said, "And behold, it was very good." Judaism and early Christianity had an affirmative attitude toward the world, though this was modified by later trends toward otherworldliness and life-denial. The Bible itself gives a positive valuation of matter; the body, for example, is not something to be shunned or escaped, though like any aspect of man's being it can be used in ways destructive of human fulfillment. This does not deny the reality of evil; but it does—in contrast to the sense of meaninglessness and futility so widespread today—undergird the conviction that there are opportunities for significant activity because man's existence participates in a wider fabric of coherence and purpose. The first two chapters of Genesis are considered to be a mythical representation of such religious affirmations.

Concerning *the story of Adam's fall*, we can only list without discussion the ideas to which Genesis 3, taken with other expressions of the biblical view of man, is understood to point. Adam is interpreted by most Protestant writers not as a historic individual but as a symbol of Everyman's journey from innocence to responsibility, sin, and guilt. Man's given structure is basically good, made "in the image of God." The locus of evil lies in man's will and his freedom—not in his body or intellect, nor in society or external necessity. Everyman's sin is compounded of prideful egocentricity and disobedience to God; self-centeredness and turning from God are two sides of the same act. The Genesis story goes on to indicate man's experience of anxiety, evasiveness, and sense of guilt. (To these facets of individual sin, other biblical passages, especially in the Prophets, add the corporate dimension of social injustice and alienation from fellowman; failure to love God and neighbor are seen as inseparable from inordinate self-love.) This chapter of Genesis, then, is understood as a mythical representation of fundamental characteristics of human nature, just as the opening chapters are taken as a mythical representation of the basic relationship of God and the world.

It was indicated in Chapter 5 that neo-orthodoxy leads to a radi-

cal separation of scientific and religious questions. The view of
creation outlined above leaves *complete freedom for the scientific
investigation of evolution.* The doctrine excludes no scientific theories; it excludes only alternative interpretive assertions—for instance,
"God is part of nature," "the world is illusory," or "matter is ultimate." Gilkey emphasizes that creation is a relationship, not an
event; the doctrine deals with ontological dependence, not temporal history. Though traditionally these ideas were expressed in a
story about origins which assumed that time is finite, their real
theological meaning, he holds, would not be invalidated should it
be discovered that time is infinite:

> The myth of creation does not tell us about a first moment of time,
> any more than the myth of the Fall tells us about a first human being.
> What it does tell us is that every moment of time, like every contin-
> gent thing, comes to be from the creative power of God. The question
> of the first moment of chronological time is a question for the astro-
> physicist, not for the theologian, just as the question of the first *Homo
> sapiens* is a question for the anthropologist, not for the biblical scholar.
> The event of creation of which we speak in theology is not just an
> initial event within a first moment of time; rather it points to the rela-
> tion of all events to their eternal source.[21]

Gilkey would like to see the creation story retained but *read as
a myth.* God is represented as if he were a being acting in space
and time; but all trace of literalism is avoided if no actual historical
occurrences are claimed. The biblical myth makes use of analogies
from human acts of creation; but at the same time it bespeaks the
limitations of analogy, for creation "out of nothing" has no parallel
in human creativity. Gilkey urges us to keep the mythical language
of temporal action, with its dramatic and personal categories; for
the philosophical language of ontological structure neglects God's
dynamic character, his purposeful freedom, his transcendent mystery, and his existence outside of time.

3. Creation and Evolution as Unrelated Languages

For Roman Catholics (and for many traditionalist Protestants)
the doctrine of creation is associated with special acts of supernatural intervention in the origination of the universe and of man,
which would represent gaps or boundaries in the scientific account.

---

21. From p. 260 of *Maker of Heaven and Earth* by Langdon Gilkey. Copyright © 1959 by Langdon Gilkey. Reprinted by permission of Doubleday and
Company, Inc.

For them, the doctrine is incompatible with certain types of scientific theory (specifically, "steady-state" theories in astronomy, in which time is infinite, and "polygenist" theories in paleontology, which postulate that man arose independently on more than one continent). Neo-orthodoxy, in contrast, asserts that the theological meaning of creation does not exclude any conceivable scientific theory, since the doctrine is concerned only with the ontological status of man and the world in the present, not with beginnings in the past. Two other versions of this *total separation of theological from scientific assertions* are given by existentialism and linguistic analysis. We mention them only briefly here and discuss them more fully in the next chapter.

The *existentialist* confines the meaning of creation to present personal confession, and he excludes all reference to purported actions of God in space and time. Thus Bultmann wants to "demythologize" the idea of creation and recover its existential significance as an acknowledgment of present dependence on God, namely "the Lord is *my* creator":

> The affirmation that God is creator cannot be a theoretical statement about God as *creator mundi* in a general sense. The affirmation can only be a personal confession that I understand myself to be a creature which owes its existence to God. It cannot be made as a neutral statement, but only as thanksgiving and surrender.[22]

In the case of Adam's fall, mythical language can readily be translated into existential equivalents (as in the neo-orthodox rendition). We will suggest in the next chapter that although this method is valuable in representing the relation of man to God, it tends to bypass the problem of God's relation to nature—and in particular it says nothing about God's activity in nature.

The *linguistic analyst* tries to base his argument upon an examination of the functions served by language about creation. He concludes that such language is not an "account of origins" which might be in competition with scientific accounts but an expression and evocation of a distinctive orientation toward God and the world.[23] "To believe in creation is to see the world in a certain way." The creation story is an "imaginative vision" or "picture" that

---

22. Bultmann, *Jesus Christ and Mythology*, p. 69. Used by permission of Charles Scribner's Sons and SCM Press.

23. See Antony Flew and D. M. MacKinnon, "Creation," in Flew and MacIntyre, eds., *New Essays*.

encourages distinctive attitudes toward the world—for example, if the earth is seen as a gift not of our own making, a sense of stewardship is evoked. The creation myth is a "useful fiction"—or, if you prefer, a "parable"[24]—which expresses man's sense of creatureliness, finitude, and dependence on God, and encourages worship and reverence. Moreover, it involves looking at the world in a special way, namely "seeing it as a creation," that is, as the intentional and purposive self-expression of a person. Men will both regard and treat the world differently when they view it "as if created by God."

A thorough exploration of the doctrine from the standpoint of linguistic analysis has been made by Evans. He shows that *biblical language about creation* is always "*self-involving*"—that is, the speaker does not give assent to a proposition but declares an attitude:

> In the biblical context, if I say "God is my Creator" I acknowledge my status as God's obedient servant and possession, I acknowledge God's gift of existence, and I acknowledge God's self-commitment to me.[25]

To say "God is holy" is to express reverence and awe and to perform an act of praise and reverence. To say "God is creator" is to acknowledge his sovereignty and his evaluation of the world as good. To picture God as maker is to regard the world as purposeful and one's own existence as significant rather than meaningless. The creation story is a parable whose point is the suggestion of attitudes; to accept a *parable* is to adopt the attitude it proposes. For Evans, "the factual story which suggests a religious attitude becomes a nonfactual parable which expresses much the same attitude."

For most linguistic analysts, this focus on the human attitudes which religious language expresses leads to *the abandonment of propositional assertions* about God or the world. Evans manages to qualify this conclusion, however, by a suggestion which we may call "revelation through authoritative parables."[26] One does not simply say "Let's pretend God is maker," or "Act *as if* the world were a creation." For we have it on divine authority that even though the parable is in no sense factual, the attitudes it suggests are appropriate. God is *not* like a potter, builder, or maker in any

24. Miles, *Religion and the Scientific Outlook*, pp. 165ff.

25. Donald D. Evans, *The Logic of Self-Involvement* (London: SCM Press, 1963), p. 158.

26. *Ibid.*, Chap. 6.

specifiable way; but these biblical images lead to human responses toward God and the world which *are* authorized as fitting. (For example, we cannot assert any analogy between God and a potter, but we can say that our attitude toward God should be like the imagined attitude of a pot toward the potter.) Moreover, there are no events in time, "at the beginning" or subsequently, to which the parable applies; there is no "neutral core" of propositional truth which could be asserted without self-involvement, or which could have any relation to scientific accounts. The religious attitudes expressed in the idea of creation must be completely detached from all cosmological questions.

According to the scheme of the present volume, these views of "evolution" and "creation" as *alternative languages* provide the most suitable starting point for a constructive position. Thereby one avoids using theological ideas to answer scientific questions, and vice versa. Neo-orthodoxy, existentialism, and linguistic analysis all stress the religious significance of creation and divorce it from hypotheses about the beginning of the universe. The neo-orthodox interpretation also includes statements about the ontological status of nature, which we would hold are indeed part of the intent of the doctrine. But all these viewpoints leave out two features of the traditional concept: *creation as divine activity* and *creation as bringing-into-being.* Can we preserve the conviction that God acted in creating, and yet avoid assuming a temporal beginning? Can we develop an idea of *continuing creation* which is compatible with both biblical theology and evolutionary biology?

4. Continuing Creation

Let us state in preliminary form some of the reasons for considering a doctrine of continuing creation:

1. *Continuing creation is a biblical idea.* Almost every chapter of the Old Testament witnesses to the conviction of God's *continuing* sovereignty over history and nature (the events of the Exodus, c. 1300 B.C., are the paradigm), whereas there are relatively few references to primeval beginnings—and these are usually in late writings (Genesis 1 was written around 500 B.C.). The idea of creation "at the beginning" is an outgrowth of ideas of the covenant and providence, and remains subservient thereto. There are some texts that imply that creation is a completed process, Professor Jacob states, "but other texts, generally more ancient, draw much

less distinction between the creation and the conservation of the world and make it possible for us to speak of a *creatio continua.*"[27] In this conviction of a creative and creating God still at work in the world, Hebrew thought stood poles apart from Deism.[28] Many of the Psalms speak of God as creating in the present by natural means: "Thou dost cause the grass to grow for the cattle, and plants for man to cultivate ... When thou sendest forth thy Spirit, they are created."[29] Thus a thoroughly biblical notion informs the use of the present tense in the first affirmation of the "Statement of Faith" of the United Church of Christ: "We believe in God ... He calls the worlds into being, creates man in his own image, and sets before him the ways of life and death."

2. *Creation "out of nothing" is not a biblical concept.* Most scholars hold that it is not stated or implied in the biblical narrative.[30] At the opening of the Genesis story there is a primeval sea, a background of darkness and chaos. The church historian Pelikan shows that the idea of *ex nihilo* was developed post-biblically as a defense of the goodness of the world and the absolute sovereignty of God against Gnostic ideas regarding matter as evil or as the product of an inferior deity. "So began the identification of creation primarily or exclusively with *creatio ex nihilo* which crowded continuing creation out of the attention of theologians."[31] Priority in status was equated with absolute temporal priority. Pelikan traces the subordination of continuous to instantaneous creation through the Middle Ages, Reformation, and Enlightenment. "Deism carried to its conclusion the definition of creation as the original establishment of the universe *ex nihilo.*" He concludes that neglect of continuing creation has made it difficult for us to interpret evolution as the means of creation.

3. *Coming-into-being has been a continuing occurrence.* From the Middle Ages to the nineteenth century, creation was understood as the once-for-all origination of a completed, static world. The

---

27. Jacob, *Theology of the Old Testament*, p. 139; see also Vriezen, *An Outline of Old Testament Theology*, pp. 183–94.

28. H. Wheeler Robinson, *Inspiration and Revelation in the Old Testament* (London: Oxford University Press, 1946; PB), pp. 23f.

29. Psalms 104:14–30. Cf. 147:8–19, 139:13; Job 34:14–15.

30. Jacob, *Theology of the Old Testament*, p. 143; Robinson, *Inspiration and Revelation in the Old Testament*, p. 18; so also commentaries on Genesis by Gunkel, Driver, and Skinner.

31. Jarislov Pelikan, "Creation and Causality in the History of Christian Thought," in Tax, ed., *Evolution After Darwin*, Vol. 3 (also in *Journal of Religion*, Vol. 40 (1960), 250).

analogy of the maker of a finished object seemed appropriate. True, the analogy was qualified in various ways (God's creation was said to be *ex nihilo*, whereas human creation uses existing material; God's creation was not *in* time, for time began along with the world; God continues to sustain the world, whereas the results of a man's work exist in independence of the man). But the analogy of making a finished product remained basic; creativity was identified with the initial act, and divine preservation only sustained what already existed, without introducing essential novelty. Today the world as known to science is dynamic and incomplete. Ours is an unfinished universe which is still in the process of appearing. Surely the coming-to-be of life from matter can represent divine creativity as suitably as any postulated primeval production of matter "out of nothing." Creation occurs throughout time.

4. *"Continuing creation" merges with "providence."* Traditionally, the doctrines of creation and providence were distinct in three ways: (a) *temporally*, creation was God's initial act and providence referred to his subsequent acts; (b) *ontologically*, creation *ex nihilo* was God's act alone, establishing the creaturely status of the whole world, whereas in providence he acts along with or through other existing causes to guide particular events; (c) *theologically*, creation represented God's absolute sovereignty, transcendence, and freedom, whereas in discussions of providence these attributes were qualified (in varying degrees) by recognition of human freedom, the lawfulness of nature, and divine immanence. Now if creation is continuing, the first two distinctions vanish. If time is infinite, there was no initial act, no state of *"nihilo,"* and God has always been working along with other causes. Even if time is finite, creation occurs throughout its span and in the midst of other entities. Moreover, the existential meaning of the two doctrines is virtually identical.

Can the *theological affirmations* implicit in the traditional doctrine of creation be expressed by continuing creation and providence? In most theological systems the doctrine of creation has been the main point at which pantheism has been rejected and divine transcendence has been defended (in part, of course, by the sheer mystery of the primeval event that was postulated). But "continuing creation," like "providence," gives greater weight to immanence, and tends to qualify the absoluteness of God's sovereignty. In part this would mean a real shift in theological emphasis; in part it would simply mean that the defense of transcendence rests more heavily on other doctrines (especially the interpretation of Christ and religious experience). Beyond such doctrinal shifts, there are serious dangers in the idea of continuing creation. This concept lends itself to the abstract approach of metaphysical speculation, and the loss of the specifically religious context on which neo-orthodox, existentialist, and linguistic authors all rightly insist. (These theological questions are taken up in Chapter 13.) There is still another danger: will not any attempt to preserve the idea of continued divine activity in nature contradict science, or else invoke dubious gaps in the scientific account? Let us look at possible ways of relating continuing creation to evolution.

III. LIBERAL THEOLOGY
AND THE ARGUMENT FROM DESIGN

We have looked at the first issue raised by evolution—the challenge to scripture and the doctrine of creation. A second issue, the argument from design, has a long history of proponents (from Aristotle and Aquinas to Newton and Paley), as well as critics (notably Hume, Kant, and Darwin). Today, reformulated versions of the argument are most often found among Protestant liberals and in the philosophical writings of Catholic scholars. Conclusions about God are here inferred not from revelation but from nature; there are thus greater possibilities for interaction between science and theology—either in fruitful discussion, or in conflicting interpretation. First, we consider claims that there are various phenomena for which the theory of evolution cannot account. Next, we discuss the argument (developed by Henderson, Tennant, and others) that the existence of a system of laws and properties through which life and mind came into being is itself evidence of a cosmic purpose. Finally we examine the relation of teleology and mechanism in evolution in the light of recent writings by analytic philosophers.

1. Alleged Inadequacies of Evolutionary Theory

It has been maintained by some authors that evolutionary theory provides no explanation for certain features of evolution. These writers recognize that natural forces play important roles but hold that an additional teleological factor must be operative.

First claim: On the basis of chance alone evolution is highly improbable. For McCrady[32] evolutionary theory is like the adage that

---

32. E. McCrady, "Biology," in H. N. Fairchild, ed., *Religious Perspectives in College Teaching* (New York: Ronald Press, 1952).

if a billion monkeys pound typewriters for a billion years, one of them may happen to write Shakespeare's *Hamlet*. DuNouy calculates the probability for the chance occurrence of even the simplest protein molecule as one in 10^{321}—which would be fantastic odds against even one molecule forming. He writes:

> We will make use of the calculus of probabilities to demonstrate mathematically the impossibility of explaining today the birth of life by means of pure chance, that is to say, by our actual human science. ... It is *totally impossible* to account for all phenomena pertaining to Life, its development and progressive evolution; unless the foundations of modern science are overthrown, they are unexplainable.... Chance alone is radically incapable of explaining an irreversible, evolutive phenomenon.... The physical intervention of "anti-chance" was necessary, in spite of the prodigies of adaptation, to assure the ever-ascendant march of evolution.[33]

Reply: Evolutionary theory assumes chance and law—not "chance alone." DuNouy calculates the probability of atoms colliding as if each were added randomly and independently of previous configurations. But if there are laws governing the stability of chemical combinations and their ability to attract additional groups of atoms, then it is not legitimate to apply statistics that assume equal probabilities for all combinations. The probabilities with loaded dice simply are not the same as with unloaded ones; ten "sixes" in a row might be highly improbable in the one case, and fairly probable in the other. (Why the dice are loaded—or why there are laws of chemical affinity—is a separate question.) Similarly, in evolution there are chance variations *and* laws of natural selection. In the spurious example of monkeys pounding typewriters, chance alone operates; but if there were a mechanism which preserved a word every time one appeared, but destroyed other combinations—and then, shuffling the words, preserved only the combinations which made sentences, and the same with paragraphs—one might get a story. As Sir Ronald Fisher says, natural selection is a mechanism for making probable what would otherwise have been very improbable.[34]

Second claim: The simultaneous occurrence of interlocking organic changes is inexplicable. In some cases adaptive benefit would have accrued only from the simultaneous appearance of several

33. Lecomte DuNouy, *Human Destiny* (New York: Longman's, Green, 1947; Mentor PB), pp. 27, 36, 82, 224. Reprinted by permission of David McKay Company, Inc.
34. R. Fisher, "Retrospect of the Criticisms of the Theory of Natural Selection," in Huxley and Ford, eds., *Evolution as a Process.*

structural modifications, each of which would have been useless alone. An eye lens is of no use without a retina and all the other parts of the optical system; its value depends on the correlated presence of many intricate factors. Among examples cited by Canon Raven are "the five distinct properties of the cuckoo," all of which he says must be present concurrently if its habit of nest-piracy is to succeed. Again, a complex combination of physiological changes must occur before a land creature can be airborne. Raven concludes that natural selection "does not provide a convincing explanation of the appearance of wholly new forms of life in which the change of a number of elements in the structure of the organism must have taken place simultaneously."[35]

Reply: Changes need not be simultaneous to be advantageous. Most supposedly "interlocking" features could have arisen by a series of many small steps involving an improvement first in one feature and then in another. We do not have to assume that the eye appeared all at once in its present form; perhaps various aspects of a simpler structure were successively modified. Simpson[36] exhibits the variety of visual organs found today, from a single light-sensitive cell to a human eye, all of which are functional. The noted British biologist David Lack is a defender of Christian belief but is unwilling to base his case on any inadequacies in scientific explanation; after analyzing Raven's examples he concludes:

> In view of the evidence, it is reasonable to claim that flying birds could have evolved from flightless reptiles in a series of steps. Moreover, some of these steps were fully evolved before others began, so that there is no need to invoke the intricate synchronization of adaptations that Raven supposed was needed.[37]

Third claim: Natural selection is not a creative force. It is a negative limiting influence eliminating the unfit, but it cannot account for the positive direction of evolutionary advance. According to Raven, natural selection is a "sifting-process which eliminates the less viable mutants, rather than a means for improving and fixing stocks." DuNouy says that adaptation is a conservative force which

---

35. Raven, *Natural Religion and Christian Theology*, Vol. 2, 183. A similar argument is given in Errol E. Harris, *The Foundations of Metaphysics in Science* (London: George Allen and Unwin, Ltd., 1965), Chap. 12.

36. Simpson, *The Meaning of Evolution*, pp. 168ff.

37. David Lack, *Evolutionary Theory and Christian Belief* (London: Methuen & Co., Ltd., 1957), Chap. 5.

leads to static equilibrium; the individuals which evolve are not those best adapted but those with "a creative instability." Most flatworms did not change, but "one of those worms continued to evolve because it was less well adapted than the others." In McCrady's words:

Natural selection *permits* evolution in certain directions, *forbids* it in other directions, but cannot *initiate* it at all. When there is a change of external conditions affecting survival, natural selection destroys those species which do not adjust themselves successfully, and spares those which do, but it cannot cause any species to adjust itself successfully—i.e., to produce appropriate hereditary adaptations.[38]

Reply: The combination of natural selection and variation is creative. New species would not arise unless there were variations from among which selection is made. Sometimes there is latent in a population considerable hidden variability which is only evoked by a suitable change of environment (for example, antibiotic-resistance in bacteria). The contention that natural selection is only a "negative" force is perhaps a legacy of the emphasis on competitive struggle in evolution. It may be easier to accept the idea of creativity when it is recognized that genuinely new forms of life originate from novel combinations of genes, from unpredictable mutations, from reproductive success due to cooperative social arrangements, or from advantages conferred by instinct and intelligence.

Fourth claim: Nonadaptive changes cannot be accounted for. Two examples often cited are the Irish elk, whose huge antlers developed far beyond a functional size, and the saber-toothed tiger, whose canine teeth apparently grew too long to use. Another puzzling phenomenon is the disappearance of useless organs which are not actually harmful to the organism—for example, the atrophy of the eyes of cave-dwelling fishes. Apart from the negligible energy consumed in supporting such nonfunctional organs, there would have been no disadvantage in continuing them; to put it another way, the absence of such organs was not adaptive, yet the organs disappeared. Often the "explanation" offered for such problematic cases simply assumes (without any independent evidence) all the conditions and subsidiary hypotheses needed to make the theory fit. *Reply: Nonadaptive changes may accompany adaptive ones.* A detrimental organ may have been a by-product of beneficial changes, or vice versa. There is usually not just one gene for each anatomical feature; the total genetic constellation controls the total body development (once again, an example of the primacy of wholes over parts). Larger antlers were associated with larger body size, which might have been useful in a given ecological setting. The various subsidiary hypotheses introduced in such explanations are by no means confirmed, but they are capable of further investigation. We must admit the tentative status of many aspects of current theory.

But apart from particular cases, there is a principle at stake in all arguments from the inadequacy of evolutionary theory. We would submit that it is *scientifically stultifying* to say of any puzzling phenomenon that it is "incapable of scientific explanation," for such an attitude would undercut the motivation for inquiry. And such an approach is also *theologically dubious,* for it leads to another form of the "God of the gaps," the *deus ex machina* introduced to cover ignorance of what may later be shown to have natural causes. Coulson has aptly written: "When we come to the scientifically unknown, our correct policy is not to rejoice because we have found God; it is to become better scientists."[39]

2. Design in the Structure of the World

Instead of arguing from the inadequacies of evolutionary theory, other writers have seen evidence for design in *the whole system of laws* through which evolution has occurred. They hold that purpose is displayed by a universe whose processes could bring forth life and personality. Here design is envisioned as built into the structure of nature, not introduced by acts of intervention. The whole system of scientific laws provides an account which is potentially complete in its own terms, but which requires or suggests a more ultimate metaphysical justification.

We ask first whether evolution is *directional.* If we are looking for an unbroken straight-line progression we will be disappointed. There were short-term local trends at variance with long-term gen-

---

39. C. A. Coulson, *Science and Religion: A Changing Relationship* (Cambridge: Cambridge University Press, 1955), p. 2.

eral trends. Some species survived for long ages only to become extinct. There were divergent solutions when apparently identical organisms faced the same problem in different locations. In other cases similar ways of life were evolved by differing routes (as in the case of marsupial counterparts of placental mammals). Simpson is impressed with the "opportunism" of adaptations that exploit temporary advantages in existing circumstances—though they later turn out to be "blind alleys" when conditions change. But despite such diversity, an over-all direction of development can hardly be denied. Simpson finds an increase in awareness, versatility, and individualization as the most general trends. Teilhard describes the advance toward "greater complexity and consciousness." By almost any standard, man represents a higher level than primeval mud. Evolution, like a branching and meandering stream, seems to have a general orientation despite local deviations and deflecting obstacles.

The biochemist L. J. Henderson says that the fitness of the organism for its environment is a product of natural selection; but how, he asks, is *the fitness of the environment* for organisms to be explained? He elaborates the various chemical and physical properties on which life depends—properties that constituted a "preparation for life."[40] Carbon, for example, has a unique place in the organic world because of its variety of multiple bonds. Again, water has complex characteristics that make it the most universal solvent; even the anomalous expansion of water when cooled below 4°C has contributed to aquatic life, for lakes would freeze solid if water contracted on cooling as other liquids do. Henderson combines a *teleological view* of nature as a whole with a *mechanistic view* of the detailed operation of its processes. He is convinced that there is purpose reflected in the presence of so many conditions favorable to life. But he also holds that teleology is a sterile doctrine within science, where "only mechanical physical chemical forces are effective agents." He brings these two ideas together in the assertion that nature was so designed that the interrelations of its parts are mechanical. He suggests the analogy of a house of which we can

---

40. Henderson, *The Fitness of The Environment*. A recent version of the argument, elaborating the many environmental and molecular properties on which the possibilities of life and evolutionary development depend, is given by C. F. A. Pantin in I. T. Ramsey, ed., *Biology and Personality* (Oxford: Basil Blackwell, 1965).

give a complete description in terms of matter and energy without invoking the idea of the architect's design. The postulation of an over-all purpose is "a philosophical rather than a scientific act," and it derives from looking at "the whole story" rather than the working of its parts.

The "*wider teleological argument*" of F. R. Tennant[41] and P. Bertocci[42] dwells on the presence in the universe of conditions for distinctively human existence. The case is based on the interconnectedness of physical nature, life and human personality. The ways in which the structure of matter supports life are first described. Then self-regulatory systems are mentioned (temperature regulation, antibody production, healing of injuries); the "mechanisms" of many of these systems are known and show the harmonious coordination of different levels of existence. The argument moves on to the fitness of the world for moral behavior—which requires both dependable regularities, predictable consequences, and areas of freedom and choice. "The universe is of a sort which produces and sustains moral personality." The conditions are present for the realization of such values as love, justice, and friendship. The world is a system in which personal relationships can develop. Other instances of interconnectedness are man's response to beauty in the world, and the congruence between the human mind and the rational structure of nature. The presence of man's intelligence and moral awareness is the most significant clue to the ultimate character of existence. None of these arguments is held to be conclusive, but taken together they suggest an intelligent Designer. Several answers are given to the problem of suffering, cruelty, and waste in nature. The intensity of pain in lower organisms is actually very low, judging from the simplicity of their nervous systems. The suffering that is inescapably entailed as a condition of life is justified as part of the price of evolutionary advance culminating in free moral beings.

A similar point is made by advocates of the *alternative-language* approach, for whom *teleology* and *mechanism* in evolution are not mutually exclusive. Purpose may be displayed, not by gaps among natural forces or "scientifically unexplainable phenomena," but by the very operation of those forces. This is, of course, a very different question from reference to the purposes of natural agents, which

41. Tennant, *Philosophical Theology*, Vol. 2, Chap. 4.
42. Bertocci, *An Introduction to The Philosophy of Religion*, Chap. 13–15.

many analytic philosophers and biologists justify on methodological grounds—namely, concepts referring to the *teleological behavior of individual organisms*. In that context, the idea of purpose serves to direct the scientist's attention to particular aspects of patterns of events, and to suggest high-level concepts that can be used in testable hypotheses about them. Biologists formerly reacted violently against any mention of purpose because it was introduced in a way that hindered the search for lawful regularities. Today it is more widely recognized, as noted in the last chapter, that employment of teleological concepts of this kind does not preclude inquiry concerning physico-chemical mechanisms, but rather leads to alternative modes of analysis useful for dealing with the activity-patterns of total systems. A distinctive kind of intelligibility is provided by relating an occurrence to the goals of the organism or system itself.

It is quite another matter to talk about *a purpose external to the system observed*, as with an object produced by a purposeful agent. But purpose in this sense (which we did not mention at all in the previous chapter) is *also* compatible with mechanism. At the lowest level, mechanical explanation of a car's operation does not rule out recognition of (a) its coordinated functioning (where function refers to the contribution of the parts to the integrated activity of the whole), or (b) the purposes of the human designer who planned such functioning. So too the target-seeking missile was made according to the plans of an engineer, and can be regarded as an extension of his purposes; but the system, once designed, operates on its own. Now one might regard the evolving world as such a system, and God as its designer. The process is goal-seeking or directional, once on its own, not because of divine intervention but because of *laws built into its structure*. It would be precisely the operation of these laws—not their violation—which has brought about the intended result, and thereby displayed the divine purpose. As with the operation of the car or missile, there would be no gaps in the scientific account.

We may now comment on this revised teleological argument. First, in terms of *theological method*, we have previously indicated our conviction that *natural theology* cannot by itself do justice to the character of biblical religion. The new version of the argument can at best lead only to the conclusion Hume reached from the earlier version: the postulation of a divine intelligence "bearing some remote analogy to the human mind." We will, however, try to include within the context of a "theology of nature" the concern of these authors for the orderliness and interrelatedness of the web of life.

Second, the *concept of God* presupposed by the argument is essentially *deistic*. God is assumed to have provided the initial plan, the "built-in" design, the fixed laws according to which the world now operates on its own. More in keeping with the biblical conception is the Whiteheadian understanding of God as the source of novelty as well as order (as will be suggested in the next chapter). He pictures an active relationship between God and the world in every moment, which allows the representation of "continuing creation" as well as divine immanence and activity in nature. In Whitehead's scheme the teleological element is inseparable from the mechanical, and final causation passes into efficient causation (and vice versa) in the structure of every event.

Third, the *concept of nature* above is essentially *deterministic*. The reformulated argument does not, of course, assume a static universe in which everything was created in its present form; but it does stress the orderly and lawful character of evolutionary development. We will find below, however, that evolution is unpredictable and that the behavior of organisms does influence their own evolutionary history. These findings will require us to modify the idea of "design according to a preconceived plan," in favor of a more flexible and experimental sort of creativity.

IV. Evolutionary Theism
and the Immanence of God

The methodology of our first group (Catholic theology and neo-orthodoxy) relies on revelation. The second group draws theological conclusions from design in nature, but usually defends a traditional concept of God. A third group stresses divine immanence in the natural process; concepts of deity vary from Bergson's impersonal life-force to Teilhard's "Omega," which in many respects belongs with the previous group. Also characteristic of these men are the themes of novelty, creativity, and emergence in evolution. Their metaphysical categories resemble those of process philosophy; reality is conceived as a dynamic process of interrelated levels. Like the nineteenth-century modernists, these writers emphasize the continuity of God and nature, and of man and nature.

1. Emergent Evolution

Early in the century Bergson[43] maintained that evolution is a creative process developing spontaneously under the guidance of a *life-force* or *vital impulse* (*élan vital*) within nature. He ascribed genetic variations not to chance or to divine influence but to an immanent creative urge striving toward higher forms. Some of his arguments resemble those cited at the beginning of the previous section, namely reference to phenomena "which seem highly improbable if variations are accidental and uncoordinated." At other points he suggests that life in all forms is intuitively grasped by man because he understands freedom and vitality from his own experience. Like the vitalists, Bergson takes life and matter to be opposing principles. The life-force moves toward freedom and integration, and is hindered by matter, which is deterministic and tends toward randomness. He thus attacks what he calls mechanistic views of evolution, but he is equally emphatic in rejecting any idea of teleology which postulates a fixed plan. He sees evolution as guided but not completely controlled; it is novel and unpredictable, groping its way and modifying its course as it proceeds. Contrary to both natural and divine determination, the world is spontaneous and the future is open. Such purposefulness as it possesses is internal rather than external. The vital impulse is a creative immanent force that transcends individuals, but it is not conscious and does not transcend nature; it pushes blindly along divergent lines, with no definable end in view.

In the 1920's, three British authors gave more cautious presentations of *evolutionary emergence and novelty*, without Bergson's rather vague notion of *élan vital*, his dichotomy of life and matter, or his romantic intuitionism. For Alexander,[44] the new qualities of successive emergent levels—matter, life, and mind—are not predictable from the properties of lower levels; the ascent is not, as for Bergson, the result of an independent principle added to matter, but simply of the organization of matter itself into more complex patterns. The universe embodies "a tendency toward higher forms." Man can now only dimly conceive the next level, a future emergent which Alexander calls "deity." Since God is defined as the present

---

43. Bergson, *Creative Evolution*. See also additional references in Chapter 5, Section III, above.
44. Alexander, *Space, Time and Deity*.

world with its progressive striving (*nisus*) toward deity, God is temporal and not yet fully realized; but he is not merely immanent (as with Bergson) for he transcends the world by including an ideal beyond present actuality. To Lloyd Morgan emergence is not the introduction of some additional principle but "a new kind of relatedness" among already-existing entities. It is not peculiar to life as such, for "molecules are emergent with respect to atoms." At each level there is a new integration through the organization of previous components; yet the whole is not reducible to its parts, for it has a distinctive form of relatedness, both internally and externally. Similar ideas are elaborated by Jan Smuts, who postulates a "holistic principle" or "whole-making tendency" whereby the entities on a given level are organized in new ways into unpredictable syntheses. There is no fixed evolutionary plan, and the holistic tendency immanent in nature is itself evolving.[45]

A number of biologists have made a strong case for *indeterminacy* and *creativity* as characteristics of the evolutionary process. Sir Ronald Fisher[46] says that Bergson was right in rejecting determinism, but wrong in introducing the idea of the *élan vital* (which "serves no useful purpose in understanding evolution") and in overstressing the role of mutations. Fisher holds that it is the total process, variations plus natural selection, which must be viewed as creative since it brings forth unpredictable novelty. Dobzhansky[47] also views evolution as a creative process whose outcome is not predictable because gene recombination and mutations are unrepeatable events producing unique individuals. Every individual has a set of genes not duplicated elsewhere; of the billions of potential gene combinations that the offspring of two given parents might have, only one is realized. And in every genetic population (even in forms as simple and as plentiful as bacteria) there are many

45. Morgan, *Emergent Evolution*; Smuts, *Holism and Evolution*. Similar ideas, but in the context of philosophical idealism, have been developed in Errol Harris, *Nature, Mind and Modern Science* (New York: The Macmillan Company, 1954) and more recently in Harris, *The Foundations of Metaphysics in Science*. Harris sees in evolution an immanent teleology, a striving toward wholeness, and the unfolding of an integrative principle progressively realizing itself as mind.
46. Fisher, *Creative Aspects of Natural Law*.
47. T. Dobzhansky, "On Methods of Evolutionary Biology and Anthropology," *American Scientist*, Vol. 45 (1957), 390; also T. Dobzhansky, "Scientific Explanation: Chance and Antichance in Organic Evolution," in Baumrin, ed., *Philosophy of Science*, Vol. 1.

more gene combinations possible than there are individuals. In addition, environmental heterogeneity and the interdependence of genes in developmental processes make particular evolutionary histories distinctive. "Indeterminacy in biology is the outcome of the unpredictability of unique events."[48] Mayr similarly argues that evolutionary events "are neither predictable nor repeatable," and in addition defends "the emergence at higher levels of new qualities not logically predictable from the properties of their components."

The unrepeatability of evolution is also stressed by Simpson.[49] The history of evolution on earth has been influenced by long chains of contingent circumstances: mutations, gentic recombinations, competition between particular species, and environmental changes. The exact dates of successive ice ages, for instance, had a profound effect on the development of species. Again, nothing similar to dinosaurs has appeared before or since; the pattern does not repeat itself. Simpson holds that there is no scientific basis for expecting the presence of life as we know it, or anything remotely resembling man, on other planets in the universe. Evolution on each planet is a unique historical sequence and will no more duplicate that of another planet than the history of one human culture will duplicate that of another culture.

Finally, an idea which is essential to our argument has been reasserted by contemporary biologists: *the behavior of organisms does influence their own evolution.* Early in the century, M. Baldwin and C. Lloyd Morgan defended "organic selection"; they granted that the environment selects organisms, but pointed out that organisms also select their own environment. Waddington's idea of "genetic assimilation" underscores the importance of behavior, within a neo-Darwinian framework. Hardy clearly rejects the Lamarckian theory that an animal's activity directly produces physiological modifications that are inherited; he grants that no changes during an animal's life are transmitted genetically to its offspring. But he assigns great significance to an indirect effect whose long-term results are similar to Lamarckianism. Suppose that during a time of food scarcity a species of birds adopts a new habit of probing for insects under the bark of trees. Thereafter, those

---

48. Bentley Glass, "The Relation of the Physical Sciences to Biology: Indeterminacy and Causality," in Baumrin, ed., *Philosophy of Science*, Vol. 1, 244; E. Mayr, "Cause and Effect in Biology," *Science*, Vol. 134 (1961), 1501.

49. G. G. Simpson, *This View of Life* (New York: Harcourt, Brace & World, Inc., 1964).

mutations or variations associated with longer beaks will tend to survive more efficiently and will be selected. *Novel activities can thus bring about novel forms.* Functional changes may precede structural ones. Since there is always a vast latent variability in any genetic population, rapid development may result. A new behavior pattern can thus produce an evolutionary change, though not in the simple way which Lamarck assumed.[50]

Hardy contends that modern biologists have emphasized the mechanical role of external forces acting on random mutations, and have neglected the fact that *internal drives can decisively modify evolution* in the manner just described. This is no minor "side effect" and is probably the key factor in the development of new capacities (running, burrowing, swimming, flying, and the like). He discusses the curiosity and initiative of animals, their self-adaptation, instinct, and learning (for instance, the insight of birds learning to count objects), and other findings of ethology, "the science of the animal as a living whole." He concludes: "I think we can say, from the many different lines of argument, that internal behavioral selection due to the 'psychic life' of the animal, whatever we think about its nature, is now seen to be a most powerful creative element in evolution." If this is the case, the observations in our previous chapter concerning the distinctiveness of "wholes" and "higher levels," as well as teleological and mental activity, are not irrelevant to the discussion of evolution. We do not have to imagine that random mutations at the molecular level are the chief agent in the initiation of change; they may serve rather to perpetuate changes first introduced by the initiative of the organism itself.

The zoologist Birch maintains that such views of nature have important *implications for theology.*[51] Evolutionary history resembles a vast experiment more than a foreordained schedule. It is an unfinished universe, a world in birth, a dynamic process of trial and error. Struggle and suffering, accident and chance, uncertainty and risk are never absent. He holds that we must imagine a continuous and flexible creativity in the process, not an omnipotent purpose

---

50. C. H. Waddington, *The Strategy of the Genes* (New York: The Macmillan Company, 1957), pp. 171ff.; Allister Hardy, "Another View of Evolution," in Ramsey, ed., *Biology and Personality;* Allister Hardy, *The Living Stream* (London: Collins, 1965).

51. Charles Birch, *Nature and God* (London: SCM Press PB, 1965). Also "Creation and the Creator," *Journal of Religion*, Vol. 37 (1957), 85.

external to it executing a preconceived plan. For Birch this suggests the Whiteheadian God of persuasive love rather than coercive power, a God who influences and is influenced by the world and allows freedom in man and spontaneity in nature, a God deeply involved in the world and participating in its slow growth. Each stage builds on the previous ones, and creation is "the concrete actualization of potentialities" at each moment. Birch also adopts Whitehead's view that all entities have an inner aspect akin to mind; every entity is considered a center of at least rudimentary experience. He urges us to take man's self-awareness as an interpretive clue. We will examine these ideas of process philosophy at greater length in the next chapter.

2. The "Convergence" of Evolution (Teilhard)

The Jesuit paleontologist Teilhard de Chardin has powerfully expressed a vision of an evolutionary process which is basically spiritual in character. Because of the interest he has evoked, we shall consider his viewpoint in some detail. His thought was developed with an independence—even in coining words of his own— that precludes assigning him to any school of thought.[52] In *The Phenomenon of Man*, scientific data from many fields are presented within a total coherent synthesis of magnificent sweep and vivid imagery. Such a book cannot be summarized, but we can paraphrase three concepts relevant to our discussion:

1. *The continuity of the levels of reality.* Teilhard traces four stages of evolution (matter, life, thought, society) that are continuous with each other. His fundamental sense of the coherence of the universe leads him to picture "a single process without interruption," an integral development without gaps. Each level has its roots in earlier levels and represents the flowering of what was potentially present all along. The higher is already existent in the lower in rudimentary form: "In the world, nothing could ever burst forth as final across the different thresholds successively traversed by evolution (however critical they be) which had not already existed in an obscure and primordial way.... Everything, in some extremely attenuated version of itself, has existed from the very

52. Secondary sources on Teilhard's thought include Claude Tresmontant, *Pierre Teilhard de Chardin: His Thought* (Baltimore: Helicon Press, 1959); C. E. Raven, *Teilhard de Chardin: Scientist and Seer* (New York: Harper and Brothers, 1963); Olivier Rabut, *Teilhard de Chardin* (New York: Sheed and Ward, 1961).

first."[53] There is no sharp line between the nonliving and the living; there could be no life unless there was already incipient life in all matter. Similarly there is no line between life and thought; mindlike activity of an elementary kind reaches all the way down the scale of life, though it becomes imperceptible, "lost in darkness," as we trace it back. Teilhard does not, of course, impute self-consciousness or reflection to lower organisms; their "psychic life" is infinitesimal, but represents the beginnings of perception, sensitivity, and spontaneity. He assigns great importance to this inner aspect, the "*within of things*," which finally developed into mind. From our knowledge of ourselves we can reason that "since the stuff of the universe has an inner aspect at one point of itself, there is necessarily a double aspect to its structure, that is to say in every region of space and time." Here is a theme reminiscent of Whitehead.

But Teilhard also maintains that there have been a number of *thresholds* or *critical points*. These "crises" were not gaps or absolute discontinuities, but each marked a crucial breakthrough to a new level. Though the levels interpenetrate, there was real novelty in each new beginning (the word "emergence" is occasionally used). This idea of a critical point within a continuous process is vividly conveyed by the metaphors with which the book's second section closes, after the main branches (phyla) of primate evolution have been traced to the very threshold of reflective thought:

> We already knew that everywhere the active phyletic lines grow warm with consciousness toward the summit. But in one well-marked region at the heart of the mammals, where the most powerful brains ever made by nature are to be found, they become red hot. And right at the heart of that glow burns a point of incandescence.
> We must not lose sight of that line crimsoned by the dawn. After thousands of years rising below the horizon, a flame bursts forth at a strictly localized point.
> Thought is born.[54]

2. *The directionality of evolution.* There has been a trend toward greater *complexity* and greater *consciousness*. The increasing outward complexity of the nervous system and brain is correlated with the inward ascent to reflective thought. There is also a tendency toward personalization and individuation that is significant in

53. Teilhard de Chardin, *The Phenomenon of Man*, pp. 71, 78. Quotations here and below used by permission of Harper & Row, Publishers.
54. *Ibid.*, p. 160.

any extrapolation to the future. One of the most original aspects of Teilhard's thought is his idea of *convergence* at each evolutionary stage. He pictures phases of expansion, radiation, and diversification followed by phases of consolidation, unification, and "involution." Though human societies at first diversified, they are now converging toward interdependence and unification, which will lead to a single "inter-thinking" fabric of humanity. But Teilhard holds that despite directionality there has been much *groping* along the way. He speaks of the brutality of the process, its wastefulness, indifference to the individual, and excursions into blind alleys. "Groping" seems to imply a constant goal but a diversity of short-run directions. He defines it as "directed chance," "the blind fantasy of large numbers combined with the precise orientation of a specific target."

Teilhard apparently holds that *mutation* and *natural selection* play important roles in this directionality. "The universe ... proceeds step by step by dint of billionfold trial and error. It is this process of groping combined with the twofold mechanism of reproduction and heredity, allowing the hoarding and additive improvement of favorable combinations" which produces progress. The final outcome is uncertain because of "chance at the bottom and freedom at the top." The ability to use chance opportunities is in part a function of the internal life of the individual organism (instinct, intelligence, and the like); but *"the within of things"* also appears to be a channel for a transindividual upward striving that takes advantage of chance:

> The impetus of the world, glimpsed in the great drive of consciousness, can only have its ultimate source in some *inner* principle which alone would explain its irreversible advance toward higher psychisms. ... The long-term modifications of the phylum are as a rule so gradual, and the organs affected are sometimes so stable ... that we are definitely forced to abandon the idea of explaining every case simply as the survival of the fittest.[55]

3. *The convergence of evolution to the Omega Point.* An essential theme in Teilhard's message is the incompleteness of evolution. Creation is continuing; the universe is still in the process of being born. The social stage is moving toward a higher synthesis, the unification of mankind into a collectivity of consciousness, a global confluence into a single inter-thinking unit. This communal destiny

---

55. *Ibid.*, pp. 149–50.

of socialization into a kind of superorganism can be achieved without the loss of individuality which occurs in insect societies or totalitarian states. For the new humanity will maintain the integrity of personality, and its bond of union will be love.

Teilhard extrapolates these lines of convergence even further to the birth of a single hyperpersonal center, a focus of consciousness and personality which he calls *Omega*. If this were all one could say about it, Omega would be a future emergent, a distant summit, a contingent product of the evolutionary process:

> Accordingly its enormous layers, followed in the right direction, must somewhere ahead become involuted to a point which we might call Omega, which fuses and consumes them integrally into itself. . . . It remains understood or implied that it could not form itself save at an extremely distant future and in total dependence on the reversible laws of energy. . . . If Omega were only a remote and ideal focus destined to emerge at the end of time from the convergence of terrestrial consciousnesses, nothing could make it known to us in anticipation of this convergence.[56]

Such an emergent God might have some actuality already, since by the principle of continuity any new level must have always been present in some degree in lower levels, but like Alexander's "deity" he would exist now in only rudimentary form.

But *Omega is also a present reality*. This is in part an inference from evolutionary development:

> In Omega we have in the first place the principle we needed to explain the persistent march of things toward greater consciousness and the paradoxical solidity of what is most fragile. . . . By its radial nucleus it finds its shape and its natural consistency gravitating against the tide of probability toward a divine focus of mind which draws it onward. Thus something in the cosmos escapes from entropy, and does so more and more.[57]

Like Aristotle's Final Cause, Omega as future goal is a present influence, attracting from ahead, not pushing from behind. Moreover, only an already existent reality can initiate and maintain the love which universal convergence requires. Here the need for a unifying force seems to be taken as an argument for its existence. If it is to be immune to the threat of disappearance, it must be independent of death and of the collapse of forces within the process. "While being the last term of its series it is also outside

---

56. *Ibid.*, pp. 259, 268, 291.
57. *Ibid.*, p. 271.

all series." Its properties include autonomy, actuality, irreversibility, and transcendence. In an epilogue, Teilhard states that the same conclusions about God and about universal love are central convictions of Christianity.

3. Reactions to Teilhard

Among *biologists* there are many staunch defenders of Teilhard. In his introduction to *The Phenomenon of Man*, Huxley endorses most of its central ideas, with the exception of Omega. Waddington approves of the treatment of continuity, "the within of things," and man's role in evolution.[58] Dobzhansky closes a recent book with a long quotation from Teilhard, and writes: "To modern man, so forlorn and spiritually embattled in this vast and ostensibly meaningless universe, Teilhard de Chardin's evolutionary idea comes as a ray of hope."[59] This cosmic optimism is clearly one reason for Teilhard's wide appeal. His conviction that we live in an ascending universe contrasts with the pessimism toward the world and man's capacities often found in neo-orthodoxy, existentialism, and some versions of naturalism. Many scientists share his concern for coherence and synthesis, his conviction of the unity of truth, and his desire to avoid all rigid dualisms or watertight compartments of thought.

There have also been some *critical comments by biologists*. In one of the most intemperate reviews in the recent literature, Medawar writes that "the greater part of the book is nonsense, tricked out by a variety of metaphysical conceits," for Teilhard "cheats with words."[60] Other critics have stated that the book is "unscientific." It is true that Teilhard often uses scientific words metaphorically (for example, "psychic temperature," "radial energy"); it would have been helpful if confirmed scientific findings had been more clearly distinguished from speculative interpretations. Some reviewers may also have been misled by Teilhard's comment that he deals "only with the phenomena" and "avoids metaphysical questions." If one expects technical information alone, much of the book is indeed "unscientific." Teilhard's use of vague analogies in place of careful analysis is indeed disconcerting and gives some justification to those who classify his book as a poetic epic.

58. C. H. Waddington, *The Nature of Life* (London: Allen and Unwin, 1961).
59. Dobzhansky, *Mankind Evolving*, p. 348.
60. P. B. Medawar, *Mind*, Vol. 70 (1961), 99.

This criticism is moderated, however, if one views the volume *as an interpretation of the scientific evidence*. Teilhard's integral synthesis of evolutionary history and his concern for "the totality of the phenomenon of man" inevitably take him beyond the detailed facts of the specialized sciences. He attempts to view diverse data within a comprehensive interpretive framework. But it must be remembered that there are never absolute lines between fact and interpretation; every "fact" is "theory-laden," and the role of imaginative construction increases as more inclusive symbolic schemes are attempted. Teilhard himself was aware of this:

> During the last fifty years or so, the investigations of science have proved beyond all doubt that there is no fact which exists in pure isolation, but that every experience, however objective it may seem, inevitably becomes enveloped in a complex of assumptions as soon as the scientist attempts to explain it. But while this aura of subjective interpretation may remain imperceptible where the field of observation is limited, it is bound to become practically dominant as soon as the field of vision extends to the whole.[61]

His bold and imaginative vision of the total world process also transcends science in expressing a cosmic faith that gives meaning for existence, hope for the future, and motivation for action. It embodies what we have called an "ultimate concern" that goes beyond science—without making it "unscientific" in the sense of "conflicting with science."

The *responses of theologians* to Teilhard's book have also been mixed. Its publication was forbidden by Rome during his lifetime; but following his death it has been made the subject of dozens of books and articles, both sympathetic and critical, in the Catholic press. An official *monitum* in 1962 does not prohibit its circulation but warns that it should be read cautiously because of "ambiguities and doctrinal errors." Some of his critics[62] appear to have misjudged what he was trying to do. The objection that he does not discuss Adam was anticipated by Teilhard; he says in a footnote that belief in an ancestral couple is compatible with the data but must be justified on theological grounds outside the scope of his book. He has also answered the accusation of pantheism. He does, to be sure, suggest that God changes, and evolution constitutes "completion and fulfillment for the Absolute Being himself"; as

---

61. Teilhard, *Phenomenon of Man*, p. 30.
62. E.g., L. Cognet, *Le Père Teilhard de Chardin et la Pensée Contemporaire* (Paris: Flammarion, 1952).

in Whitehead's view, God fulfills himself in creating the world. Yet in most respects Teilhard's concept of God is traditional. The criticisms of his treatment of evil are perhaps more serious; he does tend to minimize the tragic and paradoxical character of human efforts, which might lead some readers (though never Teilhard himself) to conclude that divine forgiveness and redemption in Christ are not needed by man.

There have also been many *favorable responses by theologians*.[63] One of the best summaries of his thought is by the Catholic scholar Tresmontant, who especially commends his reverence for creation and concern for the sanctification of man's life in the world. He is sympathetic to Teilhard's thesis that Christ is not an unrelated intrusion into the universe but the continuation and fulfillment of a long cosmic preparation. Raven, a Protestant liberal, is also impressed by Teilhard's insistence that we live in one world rather than two, and contrasts this with "the unbridgeable chasm between science and religion in neo-orthodoxy." He agrees with what he calls Teilhard's "sacramental and incarnational" synthesis, in which divine love pervades nature and Christ's victory is the final stage of an integral, divinely guided process.

We may raise some questions, however, about three of our "issues." First, concerning *man's status in nature*, Teilhard does assert the importance of distinctively human reflection and capacity for love. Yet for him human culture, as the latest phase of an integral process, is fundamentally *continuous* with its earlier phases. Social and moral life are the extension of the patterns of biological life. But is Teilhard's use of biological categories in the human sphere (and vice versa) always helpful? He defines love as "the propensity to unite," so that attractive forces between atoms are "a form of love"; does this illuminate either love in human relationships or the laws of molecular bonds? Does Teilhard's system do justice to the characteristic features of man's personal existence, to which art, literature, and politics testify? He delineates human culture without mention of man as a worshiping creature, or religion as a social phenomenon. Could the distinctive aspects of human existence, which suffer by inclusion in an integral evolutionary scheme, be more adequately represented—without going to the opposite extreme, a dualism of man against nature?

Extrapolation from nonhuman to human spheres seems particular-

---

63. See n. 52 above.

ly dubious when *an ethic for the future* is derived from evolutionary trends of the past. Man is "evolution conscious of itself," directing its own future; we are enjoined to continue the previous trend
toward reflection and personalization. Yet Teilhard also recognizes
that evolution is now a psycho-social process, whose patterns are
transmitted by the culture rather than by genes, and whose course
is influenced by ideal goals chosen reflectively. Can future development, occurring by such a radically different process, be guided
by the laws of the biological past? Teilhard's optimism about the
future is in part based on extrapolation of the previous ascending
trend. He holds that if the world has progressed this far against
great odds, it would be absurd for it to abort now. Though he
grants that man has the power to destroy himself, he is confident
that this will not occur since "man's self-destruction would an-
nihilate an irreplaceable portion of the cosmic effort." Are man's
freedom and his unique potentialities for both good and evil sufficiently emphasized here?

A second "issue" is *God's relation to the evolutionary process.*
Teilhard describes a teleological ascent, but in general he does
not invoke divine intervention in gaps in the scientific account.
Omega is inferred from the trend of the whole process, not from
any specific "unexplainable" phenomenon. Since life was incipiently
present from the start, no special life-force has to supervene upon
matter (as in Bergson's philosophy). Divine creativity is immanent
in the natural order, not an interruption from outside it. Teilhard
wrote to Huxley in 1953:

> I fully agree that this game of chance involving its great numbers can
> propel a part of the universe toward the impossible, yet how do you
> explain this property of Natural Selection—that it persistently gives
> rise to unpredictable varieties more highly organized and consequently
> more consciously aware? Can it be by accident that the *weltstoff*
> shows itself to be endowed with a certain attraction which like gravity
> makes us fall or rather rise, taking advantage of every chance, to the
> level of a greater complexity and a more sensitive consciousness? If
> the *weltstoff* is not basically "loaded," how could it afford any oppor-
> tunity for Natural Selection?[64]

In some passages he implies that directionality is inexplicable unless we assume that some guiding force influences mutations. Other
passages describe Omega's function as luring the process toward

---

64. Quoted in Raven, *Teilhard de Chardin*, p. 135. Used by permission of
Harper & Row, Publishers, and Wm. Collins Sons & Co., Ltd.

its fulfillment (that is, as Final Cause) rather than entering as an efficient cause on the plane of natural forces. Teilhard does not, however, give any detailed discussion of the relation of primary and secondary causality, or of teleology and mechanism. He is more concerned to describe the cosmic process as he sees it than to explain its mode of operation. It would appear that he tried to combine a strictly Darwinian view on the level of mutation and selection with a Lamarckian interpretation of the role of "the within of things."[65] But he did not show how these factors are related to each other.

Finally, on the issue of *methodology*, the book has been viewed by some interpreters as a contribution to natural theology. There are indeed several passages in which the directionality of evolution is used as an argument for the existence of God; Teilhard's desire to communicate with his scientific colleagues and to avoid conflict with the church may have led him to claim support from science for conclusions at least partially derived from other sources. We would submit that his writing should rather be viewed as *a synthesis of scientific ideas with religious ideas derived primarily from historical revelation and religious experience*. Concerning Omega he says "doubtless I should never have ventured to envisage the latter or formulate the hypothesis rationally if, in my consciousness as a believer, I had not found not only its speculative model but also its living reality."[66] His other writings and his own life[67] make it clear that he was deeply informed by his Christian heritage and by his personal devotion which had something of the mystic's intensity and exaltation.[68] His convictions about the significance of man and personality and his cosmic optimism were surely also influenced by the Christian perspective which he brought to the interpretation of evolutionary history.[69]

But we should not neglect the reciprocal *influence of his evolu-*

---

65. Cf. P. F. Forsthoefel, "Beneath the Microscope," in R. T. Francoeur, ed., *The World of Teilhard* (Baltimore: Helicon Press, 1961); F. J. Ewing in *Theological Studies*, Vol. 22 (1961), 94.

66. Teilhard, *Phenomenon of Man*, p. 294.

67. The author's father was a close friend and colleague of Teilhard's over many years. See George B. Barbour, *In the Field with Teilhard de Chardin* (New York: Herder, 1965).

68. E.g., P. Teilhard de Chardin, *The Divine Milieu* (New York: Harper and Brothers, 1960; PB).

69. See Ernan McMullin, "Teilhard as a Philosopher," in *Chicago Theological Seminary Register*, Vol. 55, No. 4 (1964), 26f.

tionary perspective on his theological ideas. In its day, Aquinas' theology was influenced by Aristotelian philosophy and the assumption of an essentially static world created in its present form; he pictured God as the Unmoved Mover, the unchanging and omnipotent Absolute. Teilhard is convinced that ours is a dynamic world, an embryonic cosmos still in growth. In such a world, origins are less important than directions of development, and the past is less significant than the future. God is involved in continuous creation, in "cosmogenesis." We have suggested that such an attempted synthesis inevitably requires general categories for a coherent interpretation of all areas of experience—that is, metaphysics. Though Teilhard was not trained as a philosopher and did not elaborate a detailed metaphysical system, many of his basic emphases resemble those of Whitehead (whom he apparently never read)—the stress on temporality and change, the "within of things," man's continuity with nature, even the interaction of God and the world. In both cases God's immanence perhaps receives undue emphasis, but in neither case is the accusation of pantheism fair, for elements of transcendence are included. We will return to these theological questions in the next chapter.

V. EVOLUTIONARY NATURALISM
AND THE STATUS OF MAN

The authors in the first two groups preserve a traditional concept of God; those in the third group stress divine immanence and creativity. A final group rejects all concepts of God, and holds that nothing transcends nature. In looking at this position, we will also deal with the fourth of our issues: the status of man and the problem of evolutionary ethics. The leading exponent of evolutionary naturalism is Julian Huxley. Criticism of various aspects of Huxley's proposal have been given by Simpson, Dobzhansky, and Toulmin.

1. The "Evolutionary Vision" (Huxley)

In his convocation address[70] at the Darwin Centennial celebration, as in his writings over the past thirty years, Julian Huxley defends a vision of reality as *a natural evolutionary process* which

---

70. Julian Huxley, "The Evolutionary Vision," in Tax, ed., *Evolution After*

is continuous and unified, exhibiting the same basic principles throughout. In contrast to the reductionistic materialists of the late nineteenth century (such as Haeckel), Huxley recognizes the emergence of qualitatively new levels of existence, and he is deeply concerned about human life and social values. His view of the creativity of the universe has much in common with that of the "evolutionary theists" above—many of whom would concur with him in attacking supernaturalist concepts of God, though they propose alternative ideas of the divine which Huxley, in his rebellion against tradition, does not seem to have considered. He describes evolution as "blind and purposeless," yet there is a "trend toward sentience, mind and richness of being, operating so widely but so sparsely in the cosmos." Man is a product of this dynamic, interactive natural process.

In the last century, T. H. Huxley said that man differs but little from the higher apes; for Julian Huxley, his grandson, the idea of *man's continuity* with lower forms is modified by an appreciation of areas of *human uniqueness*. Man is indeed linked to all of life by genetic continuity and by common participation in a single natural matrix. The rudiments of higher capacities—social instincts, aesthetic response, learning and problem-solving—are all present in the animal kingdom. Yet a gulf in mental ability separates man from all other beings, and human language as symbolic communication goes far beyond the signals of animals. Moreover, Huxley acknowledges the theme that was prominent throughout the Centennial meetings: cultural evolution has now replaced genetic change as the main method of transmitting the past and modifying the present. Yet despite this recognition that man's advance will be psycho-social rather than biological, a large part of Huxley's address is devoted to analogies between past and present—analogies pushed somewhat further than in Teilhard's writing. As the amphibians long ago developed new organs when they crawled onto dry land, so man, having entered the cultural sphere, must "try to use his conscious thought and purposes as organs of psycho-social locomotion through the tangles of existence." Again, new ideas are compared to mutations that can be selected and passed on to new generations.

Having pictured this unified ascending process, Huxley com-

Darwin. See also Julian Huxley, *Evolution in Action* (New York: Harper and Brothers, 1953; Mentor PB).

mends his "evolutionary vision" as *the naturalistic religion of the future*. He not only attacks traditional religion but proposes an alternative understanding of human significance and destiny, a substitute source of hope and courage, an evolution-centered faith which he calls "a new religion."[71] Man's salvation lies in his own values and capacities; Huxley is confident in the ability of science to solve all man's problems. In making such pronouncements Huxley was speaking not as a biologist but as the advocate of a new world faith; he was criticized by both biologists and religious leaders for appearing to give to his personal philosophical viewpoint the authority of the scientific gathering at which he spoke.

Let us examine in particular Huxley's attempt to *derive ethical norms from evolution*. It will be recalled that Herbert Spencer saw in "the survival of the fittest" a justification for competitive economics, and defined the good as "that which increases the totality of life." The elder Huxley replied that the fittest in terms of competitive survival might be ethically bad; if nature is a scene of ruthless struggle, man should not follow it but oppose its tendencies. Today, however, mutual cooperation, community membership, and social behavior are taken to be as significant for survival as individual strength. The younger Huxley, holding many of the same ethical norms as his grandfather, can thus urge us to imitate the evolutionary process. His definition of the good is formulated to cover events in both human and subhuman spheres: "Anything which permits or promotes open development is right; anything which frustrates development is wrong."[72] Among the values that he derives at least in part from the trend and character of evolution are intelligence, self-awareness, cooperation, and the importance of 'the group rather than the individual. Another British biologist, C. H. Waddington,[73] takes the direction of evolution to be by definition the ethical norm: "Science can provide a secure basis for ethics by discovering and exhibiting reality to be an evolutionary process tending in a certain direction, action in conformity to which is taken as right conduct."

---

71. See also Julian Huxley, *Religion Without Revelation* (New York: Harper and Brothers, 1927; Mentor PB).

72. Huxley, *Evolution in Action*, p. 146; see also Julian Huxley, *Evolutionary Ethics* (London: Oxford University Press, 1943) and his chapters in T. H. Huxley and J. Huxley, *Touchstone for Ethics* (New York: Harper & Brothers, 1947).

73. C. H. Waddington, *The Scientific Attitude* (London: Penguin Books PB, 1941); also his introductory essay in C. H. Waddington, ed., *Science and Ethics* (London: Allen and Unwin, 1942).

2. Critiques of "Evolutionary Ethics"

Several biologists and philosophers have set forth their *reasons for rejecting evolutionary ethics*. Dobzhansky holds that "in giving rise to man, biological evolution transcended itself"; man's free choice occurs by principles totally unlike the laws of subhuman development. "The most important agents which propel human history are contained in that history itself." Culture shows traits *sui generis*, and the differences between cultures are not primarily biological:

> Attempts to discover a biological basis of ethics suffer from mechanistic oversimplification. Human acts and aspirations may be morally right or morally wrong, regardless of whether they assist the evolutionary process to proceed in the direction in which it has been going, or whether they assist it in any direction at all.... Moral rightness and wrongness have meaning only in connection with persons who are free agents, and who are consequently able to choose between different ideas and between possible courses of action.... This new evolution, which involves culture, occurs according to its own laws, which are not deducible from, although also not contrary to, biological laws. The ability of man to choose freely between ideas and acts is one of the fundamental characteristics of human evolution.[74]

G. G. Simpson shares Huxley's naturalistic world-view, but holds that *no ethical conclusions can be drawn from nature*. He maintains that the processes of cultural "evolution" are so different from those in biological evolution that it is misleading to apply the same word to both. Nature is neither immoral (T. H. Huxley) nor moral (J. Huxley) but amoral. "There is no ethics but human ethics, and a search that ignores this necessity that ethics be human, relative to man, is bound to fail."[75] Man is the only ethical animal because he alone makes a reflective choice of ends; moral principles cannot possibly be derived from nature in general. Further, any identification of ethical norms with survival begs the question of why survival is good, whereas any selection of specific biological trends as normative depends on prior criteria of selection.

Toulmin[76] attacks evolutionary ethics (and evolutionary naturalism as a whole) from the standpoint of analytic philosophy, with

---

74. T. Dobzhansky, *The Biological Basis of Human Freedom* (New York: Columbia University Press, 1956; PB), pp. 132, 134.

75. Simpson, *The Meaning of Evolution*, p. 154.

76. Stephen Toulmin, "Contemporary Scientific Mythology," in MacIntyre, ed., *Metaphysical Beliefs*. An earlier critique by C. D. Broad of J. Huxley's *Evolutionary Ethics* is included in Feigl and Sellars, eds., *Readings*. See also Anthony Quinton's essay in Ramsey, ed., *Biology and Personality*.

its sharp distinctions between *the various uses of language.* The biological evolution of particular species is a scientific theory, but Evolution (with a capital E) as a cosmic process is *"a scientific myth."* Toulmin says that a myth—whether constructed from pre-scientific or scientific materials—is a story told to answer ethical, philosophical or theological questions. "Scientific myths" can be recognized by the nonscientific motives which prompt them, and by their diversion of technical terms to "part-time jobs" which are outside their proper contexts and involve extended meanings that are not verifiable. "When we use terms of a scientific origin in an extended manner as the vehicles of some more-than-scientific attitudes to the world, science is neutral between all conclusions." Huxley's attempt to find guidance from biology for social and political change is subjected to lengthy criticism. "Which way," Toulmin asks, "is the cosmic bandwagon heading today? And should we jump on it or try to stop it?" Huxley, he suggests, is seeking support for ethical beliefs in a time of uncertainty; since God has failed, he will put his trust in Evolution as the supreme object of confidence—for such an ancient and venerable institution as the cosmic process is not likely to default.

Toulmin claims that Huxley *uses scientific terms for nonscientific purposes*—such as the restoration of confidence in a cosmic sanction for our moral ideas. But on such questions a scientist "off duty" is not an authority:

> We should soon notice if a tinker or a bus-conductor started laying down the law about things on which his calling did not make him an authority: it is as well to bear in mind that a scientist off duty is as much an "ordinary man" as a tinker or a bus-conductor off duty.... When we begin to look to the scientist for a tidy, a simple, and especially an all-purpose picture of the world; when we treat his tentative and carefully qualified conclusions as universal certainties; or when we inflate some discovery having a definite, bounded scope into the Mainspring of the Universe, and try to read in the scientist's palm the solutions of difficult problems in other fields—ethics, aesthetics, politics, or philosophy; then we are asking of him things he is in no position to give, and converting his conceptions into myths.[77]

A similar positivistic critique of evolutionary ethics is given by the historian of science, Charles Gillispie:

> It is the theologians who have learned to live with the theory of evolution. Whereas the ones who have not so learned, and cannot, are

77. Toulmin in MacIntyre, ed., *Metaphysical Beliefs,* pp. 77, 78. Used by permission of SCM Press, Ltd.

those atheists who would substitute nature for God as the source of morality and ethics, private or public. ... It is not the intellectual conflict between science and religion which has proved fundamental. It is the conflict between science and naturalistic social or moral philosophy. We must be clear about the nature of science as a description of the world, declarative but never normative.[78]

Even if Huxley's proposal is not ruled out on linguistic grounds, it fails, we submit, to answer unambiguously the two questions: *what is the direction of evolution*, and *why should man imitate it?* Since evolution displays many facets, it is not surprising that diverse inferences have been drawn. Spencer saw in it a justification for laissez-faire capitalism, Nietzsche for political absolutism, and Kropotkin for cooperative anarchism; Marx wanted to dedicate *Das Kapital* to Darwin for lending support to dialectical materialism. To Huxley, evolution and the UNESCO charter convey the same message. These conclusions seem to depend largely on the prior ethical commitments that lead an author to select particular aspects of evolution as definitive. Such a prior commitment is also evident in Sir Julian's comment that *if* the evolutionary process had the ruthlessly competitive character which it was thought to have in his grandfather's day, it would be legitimate for man to refuse to imitate it; this implies acknowledgment of a standard of judgment other than the process itself, and contradicts the principle of deriving ethics from evolution.

The values to which Huxley subscribes appear to have come less from the analysis of evolution than from *the heritage of the Western tradition.* It is doubtful whether concern for the sacredness of the individual person, which has been a dominant theme in Judaism and Christianity, can be justified from evolution (in which the species, not the individual, is important). Can this legacy of Western ethical values now be preserved within a naturalistic philosophy, in the absence of the theistic framework in which it was nurtured; or is it, like a cut flower, admirable while it lasts, but doomed to wither when severed from its original roots? Many of the forms taken by naturalistic ethics in this century seem to be more ruthless (e.g., Marxism) or more arbitrary (e.g., atheistic existentialism) than Huxley's genteel goodwill. The problem of motivation is also a serious one in naturalism. According to the biblical understanding, high ideals and rational intelligence are

78. Gillispie, *The Edge of Objectivity*, p. 350. Used by permission of Princeton University Press.

necessary but insufficient for creative action; moral change depends on a reorientation of the will from self-centeredness to genuine love. The view of human nature in evolutionary naturalism differs significantly from that in Christian thought.

VI. CONCLUSIONS: ON CONTINUING CREATION

In this chapter we have tried to do several things at once. We have brought up to date the discussion of the four sources of conflict in the nineteenth century: the challenge to scripture, to design, to ethics, and to the dignity of man. We have also surveyed representative responses across the theological spectrum from traditional theism through evolutionary theism to evolutionary naturalism. Let us now summarize our conclusions in the light of earlier remarks about *methodology*:

1. *Natural theology is scientifically and/or theologically inadequate.* We have rejected arguments for the existence of God from alleged shortcomings of evolutionary theory, or specific phenomena that are claimed to be "improbable" or "inexplicable" (DuNouy, Raven, Bergson). Most biologists object to these views as a hindrance to scientific inquiry; most theologians look on them as new versions of the "God of the gaps." Let us heed Coulson's counsel: when we come to a puzzling phenomenon within science, we should seek better scientific hypotheses rather than claiming that we have found God. No such objections can be raised against the "reformulated teleological argument" (Henderson, Tennant, Bertocci) or the more cautious exponents of "emergent evolution" (Alexander, Morgan), for whom design is assumed to be built into the process—the laws and properties through which life, mind, and personality emerged. But all such reasoning is subject to the general criticisms of natural theology raised in Part Two, as well as to the specific criticisms leveled against the teleological argument since Hume's day.

2. *Historical revelation and religious experience are the primary sources of theology.* We agree with neo-orthodoxy (Gilkey) that the doctrine of creation is not fundamentally a hypothesis about origins but an affirmation of our dependence on God, and of the essential goodness, orderliness, and meaningfulness of the world. The areas of experience which the theory of evolution makes in-

telligible are not the areas with which biblical thought is most centrally concerned; God is known in the sphere of the personal— in Christ, in religious experience, in reconciliation overcoming estrangement. Moreover, religious language is self-involving (Evans); for a person to speak biblically of God as Creator is to acknowledge his dependence and to receive his life as a gift. Linguistic analysis also rightly insists that scientific language serves specific purposes very different from those of religion; evolution is a theory in biology, answering delimited questions, and not an argument for either naturalism or theism. Toulmin's criticisms of Huxley's "evolutionary naturalism" would apply with equal force to attempts to derive theology from evolution. But we would argue that these distinctions are not absolute, and that there are certain points of overlap; having recognized the basic differences between ideas of creation and evolution, we must go on to deal with the problem of the relation of God and man to nature, and especially the idea of God's activity in the world.

3. *We seek a theology of nature.* Such a theology must take the findings of science into account when it considers the relation of God and man to nature, even though it derives its fundamental ideas elsewhere. At this point the evolutionary and indeterminate character of cosmic history (Fisher, Dobzhansky) is relevant, and is acknowledged in the theological reflections of Birch and Teilhard. These men realize that ideas of divine creativity and human nature must draw on both religious and scientific understanding. We would agree with them that a doctrine of continuing creation cannot ignore the evolutionary picture of the universe; in the next chapter the implications for our understanding of God will be discussed. Metaphysical categories should not be derived exclusively from evolution, but neither should evolutionary evidence be excluded.

We close by summarizing the views discussed in this chapter as to *the relation of God and man to nature,* using the classifications introduced in previous chapters:

1. DUALISTIC VIEWS. The metaphysical dualism of body and soul supported by Catholicism and much of conservative Protestantism involves an absolute discontinuity between man and all other forms of life, and requires a special act of divine intervention in evolutionary history. (We suggested that it is this view of the soul

together with the doctrine of the inheritance of original sin, rather than biblical literalism, which motivates the Catholic insistence on a historical Adam.) Another kind of absolute discontinuity is the assumed "beginning of the world," a boundary which scientific investigation might reach but not cross. Gaps *within* the scientific account of evolution are claimed by DuNouy and others, and allegedly "unexplainable" phenomena invoked as evidence of divine intervention.

2. REDUCTIONISTIC VIEWS. Julian Huxley sees man as essentially continuous with nature (though he gives more prominence than the elder Huxley did to distinctive human capacities). Extrapolation of past trends in evolution permits the derivation of an ethic for man, since we are part of a single natural process. Huxley says that his metaphysics is monistic and naturalistic, but he claims to have avoided materialism "by ascribing to the world stuff a potentiality for mind."

3. "TWO-LANGUAGE" VIEWS. Neo-orthodoxy, existentialism, and linguistic analysis all see creation and evolution as two unrelated languages that have nothing to do with each other. All are distrustful of metaphysics, though neo-orthodoxy is willing to make ontological statements about the world (dependence, goodness, orderliness). All avow a positivistic view of science, restricting its competence to technical descriptions of carefully delimited phenomena. In practice, however, these views tend to lead to dualistic portrayals of reality. In neo-orthodoxy, man and human history are taken to be very unlike nature and cosmic history; in existentialism, the personal realm of human existence contrasts sharply with the impersonal realm of natural events. Again, these men usually assume a mechanistic view of nature; consequently they often arrive at an essentially deistic interpretation of God's relation to nature, coupled with an existentialist understanding of God's activity confined to the sphere of man's personal life.

4. A METAPHYSICS OF LEVELS. We have welcomed the insights of the "two-language" schools concerning the distinctive functions of scientific and religious languages, but have suggested the need to go beyond them toward a unified metaphysics that is neither dualistic nor reductionistic. We must allow for both *continuity* and *discontinuity* between man and lower forms. Neo-orthodoxy, like Catholicism, has so stressed man's absolute uniqueness that his rootage in nature and the continuity of the web of life have been

overlooked—whereas for evolutionary theism and naturalism, man tends to be so absorbed into nature that the distinctive characteristics of human existence are neglected. Where the former have dwelt on man's sinfulness, the latter have achieved an overconfident optimism about man's future by extrapolating the upward trend in evolution. Protestant liberalism (Chapter 5) represents a more balanced position in its view of man. In addition it tries to combine the idea of God's *transcendence* (which neo-orthodoxy emphasizes, often to the virtual exclusion of any concept of God's activity in nature) with divine *immanence* (which evolutionary theism stresses—sometimes to the point of identifying God with the world process, to the jeopardy of transcendence).

We suggested that *higher levels of activity* in organisms do influence evolutionary history. The initiation of change is not attributable solely to random mutations at the molecular level. We noted the argument of Hardy and others that novelty may originate in patterns of behavior, which are subsequently aided and perpetuated by mutations or variations favorable to them. The internal life of the organism is significant in producing change, though not in the direct way Lamarck postulated. The arguments of previous chapters concerning "wholes," "purposive behavior," and mental activity are thus relevant to the discussion of evolution. Teilhard's stress on the importance of "the within of things" can be accepted, though he failed to indicate how it might be related to the factors which neo-Darwinian thought has emphasized. Hardy's analysis shows that random mutations, natural selection, and the higher levels of activity of the organism itself can all contribute to evolutionary development.

It was proposed that if we take seriously the new picture of nature, it would be desirable to merge the traditional doctrines of creation and providence into a doctrine of *continuing creation*. The universe is not complete but is still coming into being. The analogy of God as maker or craftsman is not a suitable image for portraying divine creativity in this kind of world. Creation refers not to one moment, but to every moment in time; if there is irreducible novelty and indeterminacy, perhaps God's activity is more flexible and experimental than traditionally assumed, and his sovereignty is not a coercive determination. God has participated in a long drama of growth and development; creation has been a slow and painful travail. Christianity has always maintained that God's involvement in the world's suffering is costly—surely this is part of the significance of the cross.

Such a doctrine of continuous creation entails two serious problems that will be discussed in the next chapter. (a) If we are not content with two unrelated languages, how should we represent *divine activity in the world*? Do we, in effect, postulate many little gaps in the natural order, while avoiding the few large gaps to which the scientist might object? Or do we say that God acts through and by means of natural forces, using "secondary causes" to bring about his purposes without violating the lawful regularities of nature? (b) Does the concept of continuing creation lead to the abandonment, or only to the modification, of the ideas of *divine freedom and transcendence* for which the traditional doctrine of creation *ex nihilo* stood (in both literal and mythical interpretations)? And are such modifications as are entailed consistent with biblical theology?

13

God and Nature

How can God act if the world is governed by *scientific laws?* What is God's relation to the causal processes of nature? Any answer to such questions presupposes a view of nature, and also a view of God's activity. The preceding chapters have dealt with modern science and its implications. In this chapter we start from the theological side, examining some of the ways in which God's action in the natural order is currently portrayed, and then evaluating these interpretations in the light of our previous conclusions.

There are many *theological problems* for which God's interaction with nature is crucial, in addition to the doctrine of creation already discussed at length. Can we still accept the idea of providence, God's governance of nature and history?[1] How is divine sovereignty operative in the midst of the natural forces by which we explain events today? Is a prayer for rain appropriate—does God influence meteorological processes? Again, is the concept of immanence, God as present and active in the world, compatible with the scientific understanding of nature? Many contemporary theologians reject the idea of God's intervention by the violation of laws of nature. Discussions of providence are usually confined to the

---

1. Three recent volumes on the idea of providence are Roger Hazelton, *God's Way With Man* (Nashville: Abingdon Press, 1956); Emil Caillet, *The Recovery of Purpose* (New York: Harper & Brothers, 1959); Georgia Harkness, *The Providence of God* (Nashville: Abingdon Press, 1960).

420 RELIGION AND THE THEORIES OF SCIENCE

realm of history, which is viewed as totally distinct from the realm of nature. We have suggested that the dominant viewpoint today combines a deistic representation of God and nature with an existentialist understanding of God's action in the sphere of personal selfhood.

As an example of the dilemma, consider *the deliverance of Israel at the Red Sea*. According to the commonest interpretation today, this was not a supernatural miracle, but a "strong East wind" (Exodus 14:21), which might easily have been explained as a natural phenomenon, but which Israel "interpreted as God's action." Does God then act in *all* winds, though only certain people are aware of it? Or does he act in *no* winds, but only in the religious response of a people? Or does he act in *some* winds *and* in the interpretation thereof? If "event as interpreted" is said to be the locus of revelation, how do we avoid emphasizing the interpretive activity more than the event in the world, so that the object of our study is Israel's faith rather than God's acts? Is divine sovereignty then reduced to "the inward incitement of a religious response to an ordinary event"?[2]

We will examine three broad types of answer. Each group of authors, despite its diversity, seems to have a common image of the world and of God's relation to it:

Section I presents *Classical Views: God as Sovereign Ruler of the Created Order*. In this group, God's sovereignty over nature is stressed. Barth defends divine omnipotence, scientific law, and human freedom, but makes few attempts to relate them to each other. Neo-Thomists, on the other hand, employ metaphysical categories for analyzing divine and natural causality. Pollard finds in atomic indeterminacy a point at which this sovereign control over all events can be effected.

Section II considers *Existentialist and Linguistic Views: God as Transformer of Personal Existence*. Here nature is in effect abandoned as a sphere of God's operation. The world as the scientist studies it is objective, lawful, and impersonal, standing in strongest contrast to the sphere of selfhood and history in which God acts. Some authors use linguistic analysis to show that religious state-

___

2. See Langdon Gilkey, "Cosmology, Ontology, and the Travail of Biblical Language," *Journal of Religion*, Vol. 41 (1961), 194, and "The Concept of Providence in Contemporary Theology," *Journal of Religion*, Vol. 43 (1963), 171.

ments do not make cognitive assertions about the world, but express and evoke personal commitment. Others, such as Bultmann, claim that any talk of God's action in objective events is a "myth" which must be replaced by accounts of the transformation of self-understanding by religious faith. Heim suggests that personal existence, as well as divine transcendence, are in a different "dimension" or "space" from the objective world.

Section III analyzes *Process Views: God as Influence on the World Process*. Thinkers influenced by process philosophy side with the first group in holding that God's activity in nature is significant, but they differ in two important respects. They view nature as a dynamic organic process characterized by indeterminacy, novelty, and emergence; and their analysis of God's interaction with nature leads to the disavowal of his omnipotent determination of all events. For Whitehead, God's influence is creative persuasion; for Hartshorne, it is sympathetic participation in the world process. These men develop a coherent metaphysical system that combines divine influence, human freedom, and both creativity and causality in nature. In a final section, we will argue that while neo-orthodoxy and existentialism have important insights concerning the basis of man's knowledge of God, they are deficient at the point where process philosophy has made a distinctive contribution: the development of metaphysical categories in terms of which divine activity can be related to the structure of nature as it is understood in recent scientific thought.

I. CLASSICAL VIEWS

For these authors, God is *the sovereign ruler of the created order*. He controls all events, and natural laws constitute no limitation of his omnipotence. In expressing this theme, Barth stays close to biblical images of God's freedom as "Lord" and "Redeemer" of the world; he cautions against any use of philosophical or scientific categories to explicate God's operation. Neo-Thomists give a metaphysical analysis of divine governance through natural causes, using terms more philosophical than biblical or scientific in origin. Pollard, on the other hand, avoids metaphysics but invokes science in defending God's power over nature: providence, understood in biblical terms, is the correlate of indeterminacy in science. Though their modes of reasoning differ widely, these authors all hold that the traditional claim for God's control of the world is compatible with modern science.

1. God as Sovereign Redeemer (Barth)

Karl Barth, who is still the dominant voice in European neo-orthodoxy, asserts *divine sovereignty over nature* in the strongest terms. God "rules unconditionally and irresistibly in all occurrence."[3] Nature is his "servant," the "instrument of his purposes." God controls, orders, and determines, for "nothing can be done except the will of God." God does not simply foreknow; he predetermines and foreordains. "The operation of this God," Barth writes, "is as sovereign as Calvinist teaching describes it. In the strictest sense it is predestinating." Events in the world are "decreed and brought to pass by him":

> As he himself enters the creaturely sphere—and he does not cease to do this, but does it in the slightest movement of a leaf in the wind—his will is accomplished directly and his decisions are made and fulfilled in all creaturely occurrence both great and small.[4]

Barth insists, however, that *divine omnipotence* must always be considered in the light of God's action in Christ. He feels that both Aquinas and Calvin represented sovereignty as absolute power in the abstract, which tended toward metaphysical necessity or arbitrary despotism. Our concern should be not omnipotence as such, but the power revealed in Christ, which is the power of love. God's power is simply the freedom to carry out his purposes, which center in the covenant of grace. Moreover, Barth defends both human freedom and the lawfulness of the created order. God respects the degree of independence he has given to his creatures. He preserves them in being, and does not absorb or blot out the creaturely activity, which "coexists" with divine activity. Again, Barth says that to speak of God as "cause" tends to make his operation too similar to mundane forces. The divine work is not just a higher potency supervening on a lower, but an activity "within a completely different order." God's governance is on another plane distinct from all natural causes.

Barth thus affirms both *divine sovereignty* and *creaturely autonomy*. All creaturely determination is "wholly and utterly at the disposal of his power." The creature "goes its own way, but in fact

3. Barth, *Church Dogmatics*, Vol. 3, Pt. 3, 148.
4. *Ibid.*, p. 133. Used by permission of T. & T. Clark.

it always finds itself on God's way." Concerning the structure of the world, Barth maintains that God

> uses it in the service of his kingdom, he coordinates and integrates it with his work in the kingdom, he causes it to cooperate in the history of this kingdom.... The activity of the creature along the way is simply a confirming of the divine activity.... Seeing that all things with their own particular activity must serve the activity of grace, their activity is a subordinate one even in its own autonomy.[5]

All causality in the world is thus completely subordinate to God. When a human hand writes with a pen, the whole action is performed by both—not part by the hand and part by the pen; Barth declares that creaturely causes, like the pen, are real but "have the part only of submission" to the divine hand which guides them.

Scientific laws, as Barth presents them, are very partial and limited compared to the power of total determination effected by divine foreordination. What a scientist calls a "law" is an ordering within man's knowledge, rather than within the world; it applies only to human experience and thought, though it does indeed point to some sort of underlying order in reality itself. In addition, a law has only a limited sphere of applicability, whereas God's ordination is all-encompassing. Moreover, "however valid a law may be, it cannot foreordain more than the order and form of an event which is already presupposed, and it cannot foreordain the event itself."[6] Barth seems to mean that a law describes regularities but does not in itself have any "power" or "efficacy" to make an event occur. Finally, he asserts that miracles are evidence of God's freedom to act in ways that do not even appear lawful to us. He adopts an essentially Kantian view of scientific laws as an order imposed on phenomena by the human mind; we are to imagine God as acting on the "thing-in-itself" which is inaccessible to science, though Barth insists that we cannot say anything about God's actual mode of operation.

After this summary of Barth's position, some questions about it may be raised. It would take us too far from the topic to ask whether *the existence of evil* is consistent with the idea that all events are foreordained. (Barth defines evil as directly contrary to God's will, and yet he says that all occurrences are God's will. Somehow evil is "unreal" and "nonexistent," and yet is a powerful

---

5. *Ibid.*, pp. 42, 94, 106.
6. *Ibid.*, p. 126.

force which "dominates the world.") But three issues that will concern us throughout this chapter can be indicated:

First, *is nature only the theatre of grace?* The world, Barth writes, "is the theatre of the great acts of God in grace and salvation. ... The theatre obviously cannot be the subject of the work enacted in it. It can only make it externally possible."[7] Barth would say, of course, that just in being the stage on which the drama of human redemption takes place, nature does have immense significance. But does not nature participate in a more direct way— is it not, in fact, part of the drama? Barth has drawn too sharp a contrast between creation and redemption, between nature and grace. For him, creation is finished and preparatory; nature is impersonal and inert. We have suggested that the idea of "continuing creation" may express the unity of God's creative and redemptive activity, and point to the continuity of man and nature which neo-orthodoxy underestimates.

Second, *how are human freedom and natural causation related to divine omnipotence?* Freedom in any significant sense surely requires the existence of genuine alternatives that would preclude predetermination of a unique outcome. In any interpersonal relationship the freedom of one person inescapably limits that of the other person. We will later suggest that God's creation of a world of freedom and law constituted a voluntary self-limitation. Perhaps the same conclusion might be reached by a more thoroughgoing application of Barth's own injunction to use the event of Christ as the model of God's power. For what is seen in the cross is the power of a love which accepts suffering, a love which, as Bonhoeffer puts it,[8] approaches apparent powerlessness in surrendering itself to man. Barth holds that God's operation on the world occurs "through his Word," of which a prime example is his Word to the prophets. But if the prophets acted by their own free response, might we not describe God's action in the Word as the power of communication, persuasion, inspiration, and evocation, rather than as "unconditioned and irresistible control"?

Third, *can metaphysical categories be avoided in portraying God's action in nature?* Barth himself does not escape metaphysical assumptions—such as the Kantian framework of his discussion of

---

7. *Ibid.*, p. 48.
8. Dietrich Bonhoeffer, *Prisoner for God* (New York: The Macmillan Co., 1953; PB edition entitled *Letters and Papers from Prison*).

the laws of science. He seems to be more successful in rejecting inadequate ways of describing God's activity—especially mechanical analogies—than in presenting a constructive alternative. If the same world is the subject of scientific regularities and of providential action, do we not have to show how natural and divine causality can be conceived to coexist? We can agree that the "language of grace," drawn from man's redemption in Christ, must remain central in Christian theology; but in the discussion of God's action in nature this need not prevent us from employing categories of thought that can be related to the terms in which the scientist describes the world.

2. God as Primary Cause (Neo-Thomism)

Neo-Thomism is similar to neo-orthodoxy in its claims for God's sovereignty, but differs in utilizing a distinctive metaphysical system for the discussion of divine and natural causality. The following summary draws from several recent writers in the Thomistic tradition, notably Gilson and Garrigou-Lagrange.[9] The first level of God's action in nature is *conservation*. If God ceased to sustain the world he created, it would lapse again into nothingness. Moreover, the powers of natural agents require a continual influx of divine power to be efficacious. Powers are only potentialities until they are actualized; every potency must be moved to act by God. Divine *concurrence* includes a more direct control over the actions of natural agents. Gerrity writes: "When water is placed over a flame and brought to a boil, God, says St. Thomas, (a) gives to the heat the powers by which it boils the water, (b) moves these powers to the actual operation of boiling the water, and (c) boils the water."[10] God operates in the operation of created agents. He foresees and predetermines every detail in the world, and he orders and governs every occurrence. His foreknowledge is itself the cause of all things.

No less emphatic, however, is the Thomistic defense of *the reality of secondary causes*. It is misguided to say that God is the only cause, or that what appear to be natural causes are only the occasions on which God produces the effects himself. As Gilson

9. Gilson, *The Christian Philosophy of Thomas Aquinas*; Reginald Garrigou-Lagrange, *God: His Existence and His Nature* (St. Louis, Mo.: Herder, 1934).
10. Brother Benignus Gerrity, *Nature, Knowledge and God*, p. 548.

points out,[11] God is not given greater glory if we belittle the activity of the world; it is a greater tribute to him to recognize his delegation of causal efficacy to his creatures. The world is active and organic, not passive and mechanical. In it there are genuine centers of activity, interrelated and dependent on each other as well as on God. Moreover, the conviction of the regularity of cause-effect relationships provides a basis for science. Aquinas wrote: "If effects are not produced by the action of created things but only by the action of God ... we are deprived of all knowledge of natural science, in which, preeminently, demonstrations are made through the effect."[12] Lawfulness obtains because each being has its essence, its natural way of behaving, and so always produces the same effect. In principle the world is amenable to scientific inquiry if secondary causes are real.

How then can the same effect be attributed to both *divine* and *natural causality?* The resolution must start by recognizing that these are not two actions doing essentially the same thing, not two causes on the same level working side by side like two men pulling a load, or each contributing to part of the effect:

> The mistake is due to the fact that we regard God as a cause like other causes, differing only in power, a Demiurge, whose action co-ordinates the action of creatures, works over the same ground, harmonizes with them, supports or runs counter to their very order. So considered, God's intervention would overrule all secondary causes, and thus deprive them of their natural action; hence there would no longer be any contingency, chance, or freedom.[13]

Rather, the whole effect is produced by both divine and natural causes, but under completely different aspects. Two causes can both be operative if one is instrumental to the other. As in Barth's example, both the pen and the man who uses it can be causes of the written letter because the pen's action is directed by the writer. God is *primary cause*, in a different order from all instrumental secondary causes. God can produce effects directly, as in the case of miracles; but usually he works through natural causes.

Does such divine control preclude *natural contingency* and *human freedom?* Aquinas asserted that "what the divine providence

11. Étienne Gilson, *The Spirit of Medieval Philosophy* (New York: Charles Scribner's Sons, 1940), Chap. 7.
12. Thomas Aquinas, *De Potentia*, III, Sec. 7c.
13. A. D. Sertillanges, *Foundations of Thomistic Philosophy* (Springfield, Ill.: Templegate Publishers, 1931), p. 154.

plans to happen contingently, happens contingently."[14] As Garrigou-Lagrange puts it, God "infallibly moves the will to determine itself freely to act." The apparent inconsistency of a foreordained free choice, which will "infallibly come to be contingently," is resolved as follows. A contingent event is defined as one which is not uniquely determined by its natural causes. If God were merely to calculate the future from the present, as we would have to, he could not know the future. Since God is eternal, however, the future is present to him as it will actually be, a single definite outcome. Because he is above time and his knowledge cannot change, he does not know the future as potentially and indeterminately contained in its worldly causes, but determinately as in his eternal decree. Within the world, an act is uncertain before it takes place. But for God there is no "before"; for him it has taken place.

Moreover, *divine causality* in Thomistic thought is rich and many-faceted, far from any simple mechanical coercion. We referred in Chapter 2 to the four basic types of cause: formal, material, efficient, and final. God is, of course, the origin of form and matter, but it is his role in final causation which we note here. He provides each being with a natural inclination which is genuinely its own, but which at the same time expresses his purposes. He endows every creature with an intrinsic nature and a way of acting, and leaves it free to follow the goal toward which it strives. He acts on each level of being in accordance with its character. Let us consider as an analogy the following natural influences, which form a sequence wherein the evocation of inherent activities progressively predominates over external constraint: a physical force; sunlight activating a seed; the intellectual influence of mind on mind; the power of human love. Similarly divine causality can occur at various levels. In the case of the human will, God moves it from within, inclining it toward the good, calling forth its own powers, so its free acts remain its own. Here his influence is the final causality of attraction to the good, and God's action becomes the power of love.

To the present author, this latter aspect of Thomistic thought is particularly significant. It escapes the tendency to picture God's action as coercive, which often accompanies discussions of "primary and secondary causality." The analogies associated with

---

14. Thomas Aquinas, *Summa Theologia*, I, q. 22, art. 4. See also q. 19, art. 4 and q. 105, art. 5.

"final causes" (such as human love) seem more apt than those used for "instrumental causes" (such as pen and writer) in which the total subordination of the instrument to its user minimizes the autonomy of secondary agents. Again, the idea of divine foreknowledge, despite the subtlety of its elaboration and the recognition of its mystery, seems to end by denying the reality of contingency and freedom. For if in God's eyes there is only one outcome, then ultimately there are no genuine alternatives. From the human perspective the future may be open, but from God's view, which defines reality, all things would be determined. Finally, we can agree with Thomists concerning the importance of metaphysical categories, but we will later suggest reasons for favoring a metaphysics of process, in which time brings unpredictable novelty rather than the unrolling of the already-written scroll of the future.

3. God as Controller of Indeterminacies (Pollard)

In *Chance and Providence*, the physicist and Episcopal priest, William Pollard, defends divine sovereignty in the context of contemporary science. His position takes modern physics into account, but it is not as radical or comprehensive a departure from traditional views of nature as that developed in process philosophy. We include this volume in our first major group because its basic understanding of God's sovereignty seems closest to the classical view, though its suggestions about the mode of divine activity are not unlike those of many process philosophers.

Pollard uses as his starting point *the indeterminacy of the atomic world*. Within science such irreducible unpredictability is called chance, but the Christian can look on it as a place where God's *providential control* is exercised. This is not a new natural theology, but a possible sphere for the activity of the God known on other grounds. Providence is not overtly visible, and its operation violates no natural law. For God determines only which actual value among the naturally determined probabilities is to occur. The scientist can give no reason (except "chance," which is the absence of a reason) why one possibility among the alternatives is selected in an individual case. This selection, for which no natural cause can be assigned, appears to the eye of faith to be God's doing.

God can thus influence events *without acting as a physical force*. We must not imagine God as pushing electrons around. The outcome in a particular unrepeatable event is different from what it would have been otherwise, yet we have not violated the scientific description, for "what it might have been" can never be ascertained except as a set of alternatives. God does not have to apply "some sort of extranatural spiritual force akin to an electromagnetic field,"[15] nor does he intervene to manipulate "natural" probability patterns. One would ordinarily assume that anything which influences the position of an object would have to be some sort of physical force. But this assumption rests on common sense and classical physics rather than quantum modes of thought; in the new view, an electron in a probability distribution just does not have a definite position, so no force at all is required to influence the outcome.

In the light of atomic indeterminacy, it is thus not self-contradictory to say that *God's action*: (a) makes a difference in events, (b) is not scientifically discernible, and (c) is not a physical force or a mechanical form of causation. Pollard does not elaborate the structure of such action, or how it differs from natural causation. Perhaps it could be said that natural forces at the atomic level exert what Northrop calls "a weak form of causality,"[16] leaving alternatives among which God's action supplies the final choice. Or it could be said that God does not act as a physical cause, but rather actualizes one among a set of alternative potentialities; the whole set, but not any one outcome, is causally connected to the antecedents. By a coordinated influence on many atoms, God could control events.

Several questions may be raised about the way Pollard presents his thesis. First, he refers to God as having *total control over the world*. He maintains "the essentially providential character of all events," and defends the idea of predestination. We have already indicated that the reality of human freedom and the character of God's act in Christ lead us to question such a concept of divine omnipotence.

Second, Pollard's position might be taken to imply that God's will is achieved through *unlawful* but not through *lawful* aspects of nature. "The more an event or sequence of events makes manifest the providential character of history, the more chaotic and fortuitous they will appear to those who seek to discover universal law."[17] Here God's activity is seen in "gaps" in the causal account, but of course these are gaps of a much more fundamental sort

---

15. Pollard, *Chance and Providence*, p. 95.
16. See Chapter 10, Section III, above.
17. Pollard, *Chance and Providence*, p. 113.

than those exploited for theological purposes in previous centuries. For atomic indeterminacies, we have argued, exist in nature itself, and not in the limitations in our knowledge. But perhaps it needs to be stated that (as in Whitehead's view) God is the source of both order and novelty.

Third, Pollard pictures God's action as occurring primarily *at the atomic level*. His argument could be extended if, as process philosophers maintain, there is novelty and freedom as well as lawfulness at all levels of reality. God's action would then occur on various levels, perhaps primarily on the higher levels which would in turn influence others "from the top down," rather than acting "from the bottom up." We will see later how some of Pollard's ideas might be developed further along the lines of process thought. In particular, he tries to correlate theological and scientific terms, such as providence and indeterminacy, without using philosophical middle terms. But an elaborated metaphysics is needed if we want to relate rather than simply to juxtapose divine causation, natural causation, and free human causation. If we talk only about God and the electrons, the distance between the two languages is almost too great for common discourse. It is perhaps partly for this reason that Pollard ends by moving the argument to a new area, as follows.

The idea of *complementarity* in Pollard's concluding chapters represents a shift to a different approach, in which not the events themselves but the viewpoint of the observer is discussed. The paradox of chance and providence is said to arise, like the wave-particle paradox and the Complementarity Principle, from the employment of two perspectives in viewing a single reality. If one adopts this line of reasoning, Pollard's earlier chapters on the importance of indeterminacy seem unnecessary. For there could be two perspectives on a deterministic world, wherein faith discerns providence in strictly lawful patterns. If chance in science is compatible with providence in theology because they belong to "distinct and sharply contrasted dimensions," would not law and providence be equally compatible? In emphasizing two contrasting *perspectives* on one reality, rather than two *aspects* of one reality, the argument has moved from God's control of nature to the interpretive perspective of the observer. The interpretation, not the events, becomes religiously significant. This portion of Pollard's volume leads us into the second major approach.

II. EXISTENTIALIST AND LINGUISTIC VIEWS

In the classical view above, God is *the sovereign ruler of the created order*; Barth, neo-Thomism, and Pollard agree on this, though they portray this sovereign control in diverse ways. In the existentialist view, God is *the transformer of personal existence*. Bultmann maintains that we must not speak of God as acting in the objective and impersonal order of nature, but only in the sphere of man's personal existence. Heim refers to this realm as a distinctive "dimension" or "space." Here man and his history are depicted in discontinuity from nature, which is viewed as a mechanical system, an impersonal stage for the drama of human and divine action. Linguistic philosophers start by analyzing the functions of language about providence (as a personal confession that the pattern of events has significance for one's own life); these functions are unrelated to the functions of scientific theories (as useful fictions for correlating observations). All these thinkers end by denying God's activity in nature.

1. God in the Sphere of Selfhood (Bultmann)

Rudolph Bultmann is a forceful exponent of the proposition that God does not act in the objective arena of nature but *in man's existential self-understanding*. He considers nature to be a rigidly determined mechanical order. What he takes to be the scientific view of the universe, as a completely closed system of cause-and-effect laws, excludes belief in God's action in the world. Moreover, the idea that God produces external changes in space and time is held to be theologically objectionable. It will be recalled from Chapter 5 that a *myth*, in Bultmann's definition, is any representation of divine activity as if it were an objective occurrence in the world. The transcendent is falsely objectified when it is spoken of in the language of space and time, or imagined as a supernatural cause. To refer to God as "up there," for example, is to employ spatial distance instead of qualitative difference as a portrayal of transcendence. Biblical myths also usually incorporated a pre-scientific world-view. Thus the three-decker view of heaven-earth-hell is at once a spatial representation of the divine—which is theologically inadequate—and an expression of an ancient cosmology—which is scientifically inadequate. Miracles and "supernatural events" objectify the divine as a cause, and at the same time run counter to the scientific understanding of the world as law-abiding. But Bultmann holds that rather than simply rejecting these mythical elements *in toto*, as earlier liberals did, we must recover their deeper meaning. If mythical imagery misrepresented the transcendent as if it were an external objective occurrence, we must translate it back to the language of personal experience.

To *"demythologize"* thus means to reinterpret existentially in terms of man's self-understanding. All along, the real function of myths was to provide new insight into man's existence, his fears and hopes and decisions, the meaning of his life and death. Bultmann holds that he is not imposing an alien idea on the biblical message, but rather seeing it for what it was, a call to repentance, faith, and obedience. He wants us to ask of any myth what it says about our relation to God now, and what new possibilities it suggests for our lives. All religious formulations must be statements about a new understanding of *personal existence*. The resurrection, for example, was not an observable event, but the rebirth of faith in Christ among the disciples, a transformation which is repeated anew throughout the history of the church. In response to Christ men find the possibility of achieving authentic existence, overcoming despair and gaining an openness to the future and to other persons.

In this framework, can one say that *God acts in history or nature?* We must take great care, says Bultmann, to avoid referring to God's action as something objective and external to us:

> God as acting does not refer to an event which can be perceived by me without myself being drawn into the event as into God's action, [and] myself taking part in it as being acted upon. . . . When we speak of God as acting we mean that we are confronted by God, addressed, asked, judged, or blessed by God.[18]

Does this mean that we must deny the traditional assertion that God acted in Christ? Bultmann's critics have said that to associate God with any objective occurrence, such as a historical event, is on his own terms a remnant of mythology. (Fritz Buri, for example, holds that a more complete demythologizing would rely entirely on existential analysis, without reference to Christ, to disclose the possibilities of authentic human existence.) Bultmann replies that while the Christ-event is in history, it is hiddenly and

18. Bultmann, *Jesus Christ and Mythology*, p. 68. Used by permission of Charles Scribner's Sons and SCM Press.

not objectively present, its significance remaining unrecognized apart from encounter with God in the present; so one can avoid the type of objective claim which characterizes myths. Thus God's action, for Bultmann, always occurs in *the present transformation of man's life.* Christ becomes God's act only when men respond to him, so "the incarnation is being continuously re-enacted in the events of the proclamation."[19] But, the critic wonders, if the preaching of the gospel is simply the occasion for re-orientation and faith, why do we need to refer to any past involvement of God in the world? Are we not in effect saying that God acts in our interpretation of events, not in the events themselves? The logic of Bultmann's position seems to move toward a dehistoricized faith in which Christ is deprived of all independent reality, except as a parable of the possibilities for present existence. "God's acts" appear to be transactions in the life of the believer. They are not purely "private," for they have to do with aspects of human existence that all men encounter (death, guilt, and so forth), and they are not "merely psychological"; but neither are they objective events in history. In the last chapter we cited Bultmann's insistence that the doctrine of creation is not a neutral statement about God and the world, but a personal confession of dependence, an acknowledgement of one's life as a gift.

Can Bultmann find any place for *God's activity in nature?* Any reference to observable events would be a reversion to myth. Moreover, God does not violate the closed system of natural causality. Thus the idea of providence is comprised entirely in the way a man *looks at* natural events:

> In faith I can understand an accident with which I meet as a gracious gift of God or as his punishment, or as his chastisement. On the other hand, I can understand the same accident as a link in the chain of the natural course of events. If, for example, my child has recovered from a dangerous illness, I give thanks because he has saved my child. . . . I need to see the worldly events as linked by cause and effect, not only as a scientific observer, but also in my daily living. In doing so there remains room for God's working. This is the paradox of faith, that faith "nevertheless" understands as God's action here and now an event which is completely intelligible in the natural or historical connection of events.[20]

19. Rudolph Bultmann, *Kerygma and Myth,* ed., H. Bartsch (London: S.P.C.K., 1953; Harper PB°), p. 209, n. 1.
20. Bultmann, *Jesus Christ and Mythology,* pp. 62, 65. Used by permission of Charles Scribner's Sons, and SCM Press.

Presumably he cannot say that God's action influenced the outcome of the child's illness, for that would be to identify divine action with an objective event. Is the difference then only in how he takes an outcome which was itself determined by inexorable and impersonal causal laws? What does he mean, then, when he thanks God rather than nature or the doctor for saving his child?

Bultmann's reluctance to affirm God's activity in the world, and his retreat to the inner realm of personal existence, arises in part from his *view of nature* as an inviolable and mechanically determined causal system—a view more consonant, we have suggested, with nineteenth-century than with contemporary science. A recent critic deplores his acceptance of "the Kantian bifurcation of reality into nature and spirit and the expulsion of God's activity from the realm of nature. ... God was banished from the world of nature and history in order to secure for man's scientific conquest an unembarrassed right of way, and for faith a sanctuary."[21] One wonders also whether he has not made from the epistemological contrast between personal and impersonal relationships an unbridgeable division within reality itself. It is one thing to say that God is not *known* apart from personal involvement; it is another matter to say he does not *act* except in the sphere of selfhood. God's action need not be confined to man's personal existence in the present moment, though its recognition does indeed depend on the inner transformation and reorientation on which Bultmann insists.

2. *God in a Distinctive Dimension (Heim)*

The German theologian Karl Heim develops the contrast between the impersonal, objective world studied in science, and the distinctive "dimensions" of human and divine existence; God's action occurs primarily *in the "space" of selfhood*. Like Bultmann, Heim says that to imagine God as "up there" or as "breaking into" natural causes is inconsistent with the scientific world-view. Unlike Bultmann, however, Heim holds that there is one scientific concept, namely the idea of "dimensions" or "spaces," which can provide a powerful analogy for expressing God's role in the world. To understand the analogy that he proposes we must first indicate the scientific meaning of these terms.

21. Robert Cushman, "Is the Incarnation a Symbol?" *Theology Today*, Vol. 15 (1958), 179.

A *dimension*, in scientific usage, is a way of ordering events. Time, distance, and temperature are different dimensions, for a given set of events may be arranged according to temporal order, location, or temperature. A *space* is a continuum in one or more dimensions, that is, a framework within which events can be dimensionally specified. The range of all possible temperatures is a one-dimensional space. A plane is two-dimensional, as is a spherical surface specified by latitude and longitude. Each space involves both a rule of ordering and a characteristic structure. Newton assumed a universe of three linear dimensions obeying Euclidian geometry, plus an independent temporal dimension; in relativity, three non-Euclidian spatial dimensions are united with time in a four-dimensional continuum.

We may formulate as follows *the characteristics of physical spaces* that are important for Heim's thesis: (a) The same set of events can be differently ordered in different spaces. Thus spaces are not mutually exclusive, and may be thought of as permeating each other, since they refer to various aspects of the same events. (b) There are no boundaries between spaces. All the events in the universe may, with regard to a particular dimension, be included in the infinite continuum of a given space. (By contrast, segments of any one space—such as past and future time—are bounded and mutually exclusive.) Dimensional differentiation is qualitative rather than quantitative, and reflects distinctions of form rather than content. (c) A space is a relational term involving subject and object. It is "a form in which the whole of reality or else a part of it presents itself to a particular subject."[22] (d) What is impossible in one space may be possible in another (for example, on a Euclidian plane, parallel lines do not meet; on a sphere or a non-Euclidian plane they do).

In the light of these characteristics, Heim suggests that *the realm of selfhood* may be referred to as a "*space*." The objective world and the realm of the ego are two disparate "orders of reality"— or, we may now say, two different "dimensions" or "spaces." Heim's actual comparison of the two orders follows existentialist lines. Science can study only public objects; the ego is not objectifiable and is known only from within. Science analyzes events already crystallized into the definite past; the ego lives in the molten undetermined present of decision. I-It interactions are impersonal and

22. Heim, *Christian Faith and Natural Science*, p. 133.

detached; I-Thou interactions are personal and direct. Yet the same events enter both realms, and we may appropriately call them two different spaces.

Heim applies the concept of spaces also to the new "space" revealed in religious encounter. The concept is useful as a way of conceiving of God's relation to the world, especially in reinterpreting *transcendence* and *immanence*. Within one space, transcendence can only mean quantitative enlargement; God is either indistinguishable from the world (as in pantheism), or is separated from it by a "boundary" which he has to cross to invade it (as in Deism). Separation and nearness are incompatible within one space. But two spaces can be separated by an "infinite qualitative distinction," involving totally incommensurable dimensions, and yet permeate and interpenetrate with no boundaries of separation. Transcendence as difference of dimension is compatible with immanence.

Several comments are in order. First, we suggest[23] that Heim's use of the concept of spaces should be regarded as *analogical*. He is not making an inference from science to God, but proposing an analogy for talking about the God who is known in revelation and personal encounter. His concern is not the proof of transcendence and immanence, but their conceivability today. Second, the symbolism of spaces can supplement *biblical symbols* but need not replace them. The idea of "dimensional transcendence," like Bultmann's "demythologizing," is a valid protest against "one-space" literalism in theology. But many writers, long before modern science, recognized that the traditional imagery of transcendence is symbolic. And Heim's terminology, like the older terms, uses an analogy drawn from the objective world. Third, his particular description of the three "spaces"—self, world, and God—stresses their *discontinuity* (the contrast of dimensions) more than their interrelatedness (the interpenetration of spaces). Transcendence is forcefully represented, but less is said about God's mode of immanence. Existentialist categories describe man and nature in strongly contrasting terms. The net result is a separation of spheres between science and religion, and between man and the objective world.

Finally, how does Heim treat *God's activity in the world?* In one space, God's acts were interventions from above into an autono-

---

23. A more extensive discussion of Heim is given in I. G. Barbour, *The Christian Scholar*, Vol. 39 (1956), 229.

mous natural process, violating its laws. But in two spaces the *same* events can be differently ordered in accordance with different structural laws, so "an occurrence of which we fully understand the natural causes . . . at the same time appears to us as an act of God." To see an event as providential means to locate it in the pattern of God's space. Natural and divine activity no longer appear mutually exclusive, and we do not need to seek gaps in the natural order through which God can act. But does God influence natural events, or only the way we order events? Presumably a space is neither simply a mode of perception nor a mode of being, but a combination of both. "We cannot ask whether the structure of a space has its origin in the subject or in the object."[24]

Now such attention to both subject and object is commendable; but where our own "critical realism" emphasizes the referential function of language in representing the object, Heim's existential-ism leads him to emphasize *the role of the subject.* Thus for Heim "spaces" tend to be equated with different perspectives on the same events. Presumably one could not speak of God as causally related to events in the world, since world-events form a complete causal chain, and since temporal causality is a concept belonging to objective space. (In other volumes Heim sometimes speaks of God's action in causal terms, for example, in discussing miracles,[25] but there he invokes not the concept of spaces but atomic inde-terminacy and a "psychic substratum akin to will.") As Heim uses the concept of spaces, then, God's action seems to occur, as it does for others in this second major group, in the transformation of personal interpretive perspectives, rather than in the control of events in nature.

3. God and Man's Attitude Toward Events (Linguistic Analysis)

Existentialists prescribe that all reference to God must reflect a context of personal involvement; there can be no statements about God's activity apart from man's relation to him. Somewhat similar conclusions have been reached by several linguistic philosophers. In Chapter 9 we explored the view that *religious language* is not true about anything, but is a useful guide to living and an expres-sion of worship, self-commitment, and decision. An application of

---

24. Heim, *Christian Faith and Natural Science,* p. 166.
25. Karl Heim, *The Transformation of the Scientific World-View* (New York: Harper and Brothers, 1953).

this view was given in Evans' analysis of the doctrine of creation as a self-involving acknowledgement of one's creaturely status, dependence, and gratitude. Along the same lines, the doctrine of providence can be interpreted as a way of looking at and responding to events *as if* they were from the hand of God—a personal confession that a pattern of events has significance for one's own life. The idea of providence does not provide an explanation of occurrences in the world; rather it changes our *attitudes* toward events and commends certain types of response. Its result is not cognitive information but the transformation of personal attitudes.

It will be recalled from Chapter 6 that for most linguistic analysts the so-called *"laws of nature"* are useful fictions for correlating observations and making predictions. Laws and theories are mental constructs that serve strictly scientific purposes; they are "principles of procedure," "regulative maxims," organizing guides for further experimentation, or tools for achieving technical control. Ever since Hume argued that causality is simply man's habit of associating phenomena, the positivistic interpreters of science have denied any kind of necessary connection between events in nature. Where Bultmann takes nature to be mechanistic and deterministic, the linguistic analyst avoids making any statements about the world itself. Now it might appear that one could assert that God's activity in nature is unhindered by any laws, if laws are only human constructs; but the instrumentalist also denies that religious language can make any assertions about reality. (Not all analysts are instrumentalists, of course, but such a viewpoint is rather common.) We are left with two unrelated languages, serving totally different functions. As was pointed out earlier, the *Complementarity Principle* in physics is sometimes invoked to support such a dichotomy. The physicist views electrons as waves or as particles, depending on the experiment; the same events are viewed as providential or as following scientific laws, depending on the context.

Some *general criticisms of this approach* were offered in Part Two. It was suggested that most scientists are realists and assume that laws are discovered rather than invented. We concluded also that while religious language does express and evoke personal attitudes, it also purports to refer cognitively to reality. In particular, propositions about providence, immanence, and God's activity in nature claim to be statements about God and the world, not about the sphere of selfhood. Granting the epistemological importance of personal involvement, we must still face the ontological question: *does God's action make a difference in nature?* The linguistic analyst might reply: yes, there is a difference reflected in those statements about nature that serve religious purposes, but not in statements about nature that serve scientific purposes. Some existentialists, in a similar vein, find considerable religious significance in nature, but not in nature as the scientist studies it. (Buber, for example, holds that it is possible to be in I-Thou rapport with a tree.) But is the nature with which man is personally involved, and in which God is seen to act, totally unrelated to the nature whose laws and structures the scientist investigates?

Thus neither existentialism nor this form of linguistic analysis can make the classical affirmation of *God's sovereignty over nature.* God's rule over space and time is replaced by his lordship in the hearts of the faithful who acknowledge him. As in Deism, the world goes its independent way apart from God. Even those who try to avoid the concept of causality seem to assume that events in the world are the product of finite forces of whose operation science will eventually give an exhaustive explanation. What was God doing, then, in the history of the cosmos before man? Is the world in any sense an expression of the divine purpose, or is it in itself devoid of significance? In sum, where classical theism attributes to God such complete control of nature that human freedom is jeopardized and evil is ascribed to God, existentialist and linguistic authors end by denying him any influence at all on the natural order. We will find that process philosophy defends God's influence in the world, but not his absolute sovereignty.

III. PROCESS VIEWS

For the first group, God is *sovereign ruler of the created order.* For the second, he is *transformer of personal existence.* We turn to a third group for whom God is *influence on the world process.* As in the first approach, divine activity in nature is affirmed, but the view of God is modified: divine omnipotence is qualified and immanence within the process receives greater stress. Moreover, a distinctive view of nature is presented: a dynamic organic process in which there is spontaneity and novelty as well as openness to God's action. In interrelating the activity of God and nature, these authors provide metaphysical analyses of such concepts as action, cause, and law. We will first look at Whitehead, the formative influence in this group, and will then outline the views of Hartshorne and others.

1. God as Creative Persuasion (Whitehead)

Whitehead develops a set of categories that allow for lawfulness, spontaneity, and divine influence in the unfolding of events. In earlier discussion (Chapter 5), some of his basic ideas were outlined: the primacy of time, the interfusion of events, the organic character of processes, and the self-creation of each event. We have also set forth (Chapter 11) Whitehead's view of every new occurrence as a present response (self-cause) to past events (efficient cause) in terms of potentialities grasped (final cause). Each event is represented as a moment of experience under the guidance of its "subjective aim"; every entity has a "mental" pole, though the contribution of the latter may be vanishingly small.

Concerning this "subjective" side of things we must recall that in process thought "mind" and "matter" are not two separate substances. What we call *mental* and *physical* patterns of events are abstractions from the complex unity of activities. For some entities, such as atoms, physical patterns obviously predominate; for others, such as men, integration follows patterns that we call mental. Whitehead wants a unified scheme, not a mind-matter dualism; but this unity is achieved, not by reducing mind to matter (materialism) or matter to mind (idealism), but by making organic process primary. He thus views an atom as an exceedingly low-grade organism, rather than viewing man as a complex machine. Again, he holds that there is *novelty* and *law* at all levels, though in some cases law predominates and novelty is negligible. Freedom is always accompanied by a structure of order, for the components of each novel occurrence are provided in part by the antecedents out of which it grows.

We must now ask how Whitehead represents God's role in this process. First, God is *the primordial ground of order*. He embodies within himself the order of possibilities, the potential forms of relationship that are not chaotic but orderly even before they are actualized. This aspect of God is an answer to the question: why does the world have the particular type of order it has (for example, three spatial dimensions) rather than some other type? This function of God seems to be automatic, passive, and unchanging; he is an abstract metaphysical principle, the impersonal structure of the world, "the inevitable ordering of things conceptually realized in the nature of God." But Whitehead's God is more than just the timeless source of order, for he also has specific purposes for the realization of maximum value. God has an active role in ordering potential forms "with graded relevance to concrete situations"; he selects possibilities for the initial "subjective aims" of particular entities. Such relevance presupposes God's knowledge of and responsiveness to the world.

God is also *the ground of novelty*. Here the question is: why do new kinds of things come into existence (in evolutionary history, for instance) rather than merely repeat the patterns of their predecessors? "Apart from God," Whitehead writes, "there would be nothing new in the world, and no order in the world."[26] God presents novel possibilities, but there are many of these, so there are alternatives left open. He elicits the self-creation of individual entities, and thus allows for freedom as well as structure and directionality; the process does show an upward trend, a teleological aspect —but not a simple one. By valuing particular potentialities to which creatures respond, God influences the world without determining it. On the level of man, this influence is the lure of ideals to be actualized, the persuasive vision of the good. In his contribution to the self-creation of each entity, God has the unchanging goal of promoting the harmonious achievement of value. There are new possibilities open even for "inanimate" objects, as their evolution into animate beings has disclosed.

A third characteristic of God is that *he is influenced by events in the world* (Whitehead calls this "the consequent nature of God"). The central categories of process philosophy (temporality, interaction, mutual relatedness) apply also to God; he is understood to be temporal in the sense that his experience changes, for he both receives from the world and contributes to it. God's purposes and character are eternal, but his knowledge of events changes as those events unfold. He takes the life of the world into his own life. In this interaction God receives from the world and unifies the diversity of his experience in his own way, so that his own freedom is maintained, along with that of the world. And in presenting himself to his creatures, in being part of the data to which they respond,

---

26. Whitehead, *Process and Reality*, p. 377.

he influences them. In his supreme sensitivity to the world, and his ability to supplement its accomplishments by seeing them in relation to the infinite resources of potential forms, he reflects back to the world a specific and relevant influence. Whitehead uses personal images to portray this action:

> But the principle of universal relativity is not to be stopped at the consequent nature of God. This nature itself passes into the temporal world according to its gradation of relevance to the various concrescent occasions. . . . For the perfected actuality passes back into the temporal world, and qualifies this world so that each temporal actuality includes it as an immediate fact of relevant experience. For the kingdom of heaven is with us today. The action of the fourth phase is the love of God for the world. It is the particular providence for particular occasions. What is done in the world is transformed into a reality in heaven, and the reality in heaven passes back into the world. By reason of this reciprocal relation, the love in the world passes into the love in heaven, and floods back again into the world. In this sense, God is the great companion—the fellow-sufferer who understands."[27]

God acts *by being experienced by the world*, influencing the constitution of successive moments. All pairs of entities—including God and any other being—are mutually immanent in each other. More specifically, God's vision of the ideal possibilities for particular situations changes the world. Moreover, God conserves whatever is achieved, with "tender care that nothing be lost"; he saves whatever can be saved. Even the evil he transmutes by supplying its ideal counterparts and envisaging how it can contribute to a larger good. His concern for value is felt by the world, and it is not inappropriate to speak of it as divine love, unlimited sympathy and participation. His greatest gift consists simply in being the object of our experience. In relation to man, "the power of God is the worship he inspires."[28]

God's activity is thus more akin to *persuasion* than to compulsion. He does not determine the outcome of events or violate the self-creation of all beings; he is never the sole cause, but one influence among others. God's love, like love between men, is a significant influence which is causally effective, making a difference in the activity of other beings but not sacrificing their freedom. The power of love consists in its ability to evoke a response while yet

27. *Ibid.*, p. 532. Used by permission of The Macmillan Company.
28. Whitehead, *Science and the Modern World*, p. 276.

respecting the integrity of the other. Thus causality within inter-personal relationships, rather than mechanical force, seems to provide the basic analogy for God's relation to the world. Whitehead strongly rejects the coercive element he finds in traditional theism, the image of the "divine tyrant." The rejection appears to be partly based on moral grounds (coercion as on a lower ethical plane than persuasion) and partly on metaphysical grounds (divine determination as incompatible with creaturely freedom, and arbitrary action as incompatible with rationality).

Whitehead does stress God's *immanence*, but he does not omit *transcendence*. Between God and the world there is genuine reciprocity, interdependence, and mutual immanence; there is a two-way interaction—but it is by no means symmetrical. For the world is more radically dependent on God than he is on the world. As William Christian puts it: "God does what no temporal actuality can do either for another actuality or for itself. He evokes novel actuality into being."[29] He is the source of every initial subjective aim, for he orders possibilities relevantly to each event. God's freedom is defended by Whitehead. Every entity—and God preeminently—has its own individuality, privacy, and self-creativity as a subject. God is distinct from the world and not, as in pantheism, identified with it. He is omnipresent, a universal influence; he experiences all actualities and all possibilities and preserves their achievements eternally.

The traditional view of *God as creator* is drastically modified in Whitehead's writings, but it is not totally repudiated. He disavows creation "out of nothing" in an act of absolute origination. In the preceding chapter we indicated that the idea of an initial instant of creation may prove to be questionable on scientific grounds; Whitehead rejects it on metaphysical grounds, and substitutes his version of "continuous creation." Nothing comes into being apart from God, and there are no materials given to him from some other source. "He is not *before* all creation but *with* all creation."[30] God always acts along with other causes, and yet everything depends on him for its existence. He initially provides all subjective aims, and "in this sense he can be termed the creator of each temporal actual entity."[31] He evokes new subjects into being and preserves their

29. Christian, *An Interpretation of Whitehead's Metaphysics*, p. 379.
30. Whitehead, *Process and Reality*, p. 521.
31. *Ibid.*, p. 343.

achievements and thus is both the source and conserver of all finite values. While *creativity* is universally present in the self-creation of every entity, God is the primary instance of creativity and he is active in all its instances. Although Whitehead's God does not have temporal priority, he clearly has *priority of status* over all else. To be sure, there is no act of creation *ex nihilo*, and in every moment there is given to God a world that has to some extent determined itself. But this does not represent an ultimate dualism; this is not Plato's God struggling to impose form on recalcitrant matter, doing the best he can with the materials that happen to be on hand. Cobb points out that "Whitehead attributes to God the all-decisive role in the creation of each new occasion," namely provision of its initial aim. In terms of the total system, "God's role is more radical and fundamental than Whitehead's own language usually suggests."[32] Every occasion is dependent on God for its existence, as well as for the order of possibilities it can actualize. Though God is influenced by the world, he is radically different from all other beings; he alone is "everlasting" and his primordial aim is not changed by the passing flux of events. Although Whitehead says at one point that God is no exception to the metaphysical principles that apply to all entities, he does in fact defend a number of exceptions (God alone does not perish and does not change in subjective aim).[33] We will return shortly to some criticisms of this concept of God.

2. God as Sympathetic Participant (Hartshorne)

Charles Hartshorne's viewpoint is strongly influenced by Whitehead. His position is developed in part as an elaboration of the categories of process philosophy, but also as an attempt to remove what he considers *the logical inconsistencies of traditional theism.* As he sees it, medieval thought tried to combine two incompatible concepts of God: the timeless, self-sufficient Absolute of Greek philosophy, and the living God of the Bible who acts in history in dynamic interaction with man. But the Absolute strain was dominant in the scholastic exposition of God's attributes; permanence predominated over change, being over becoming, eternity over

---

32. John B. Cobb, *A Christian Natural Theology: Based on the Thought of Alfred North Whitehead* (Philadelphia: Westminster Press, 1965), pp. 205, 212.

33. Christian, *An Interpretation of Whitehead's Metaphysics,* pp. 292–94.

temporality, necessity over contingency, self-sufficiency over relatedness.[34] God was static and immutable perfection, unaffected
by the world. If he knows the future, there is no change in his
knowledge and ultimately no contingency in the world.

Hartshorne maintains that Christian thought since the Middle
Ages has mistakenly attributed a one-sided perfection to God in
exalting *permanence* over *change*. If the future is genuinely open,
if there are real alternatives for choice, then God's knowledge of
the world must vary and his experience is dependent on events as
they develop. God is thus temporal—but he is also eternal. While
Hartshorne wants to make room for the "dynamic" attributes which
the traditional view slights, he does not go to the opposite extreme
and ignore the "absolute" attributes. He is critical of Wieman's
purely temporalistic deity who is part of the creative process itself;
he rejects pantheism, in which God is in no respect independent of
the world. We may summarize Hartshorne's view by saying that
God is *changing* in the content of his experience but *eternal* in his
character and purpose. God is not dependent on any particular
world for his essential nature; he will exist, and will always be perfect in love, goodness, and wisdom, whatever happens. He is omniscient in knowing all reality, though not the future which is unde-
cided and hence inherently unknowable. Even those aspects of the
divine which change have a perfection of their own. He is not
merely influenced by the world, but is "infinitely sensitive" and
"ideally responsive." Divine love is supremely sympathetic participation in the world process.

Hartshorne, like Whitehead, maintains that every event is the
joint product of *lawful causes, self-creation,* and *God's influence.*
The definiteness of an event is almost entirely provided by its antecedents, which completely determine a well-defined and usually
narrow range of alternatives. But the final restriction to a single
outcome is the work of the event itself. There is continuity of past
and future, which can be called causation, but (as in the "weak
causality" of quantum physics) there remains a limited set of potentialities—which is reduced to one by the actual occurrence, not by
the previous causes or by God. The transition from potential to
actual includes the addition of "a new definiteness not contained in
the antecedently obtaining alternatives." Now God's action, like

---

34. Charles Hartshorne and William L. Reese, *Philosophers Speak of God*
(Chicago: University of Chicago Press, 1953; PB), pp. 1–25.

natural causation, is not coercive determination but an influence
that still leaves room for alternatives. "Providence can reasonably
be conceived, not as a simple alternative to chance, its mere nega-
tion or prevention, but only as a channeling of chance between
banks less than infinitely close together."[35]

As compared to traditional theologians, Hartshorne does indeed
qualify *God's sovereignty over nature*. God participates in the self-
creation of other beings, but they have effective power too. Yet
God is adequate to all needs—including the need of the creatures
to make their own decisions. He does all that it would be good for
him to do, but not all that it would be good for us in our freedom
to do. He has power sufficient to control the universe in the best
way consistent with his purposes. The risks of evil might have been
reduced by eliminating freedom, but positive opportunities for creative value would have been lost; God balances risk against opportunity. He thus provides both control and flexibility, giving the
world unity and yet considerable independence.

God's complete *knowledge of the world*, and the world's *awareness of God*, however dim, are important media of mutual influence. Here the basic analogy is that of interpersonal relationships,
in which one man's knowledge of another influences his own responses. Knowledge can be considered a form of causality, for a
mind is influenced by what it knows—in some respects even constituted by what it knows. Through God's omniscient knowledge of
reality, and his ability to restructure this knowledge in his own
perfect way and reflect it back through the world's awareness of
him, his influence is supreme:

> God orders the universe by taking into his own life all the currents
> of feeling in existence. He is the most irresistible of influences pre-
> cisely because he is in himself most open to influence. . . . His reaction
> to the world's action absorbs and transmutes all influences into coun-
> terinfluence, integrative and harmonizing in tendency.[36]

As analogy for God's relation to the world, Hartshorne uses not
only the influence of mind on mind, but also of *mind* on *body*. He
is even willing to call the universe God's body, provided we remember that a person's character can remain unchanged amid
major bodily changes, and that God's essence is uniquely indepen-

35. Hartshorne, *Reality as Social Process*, p. 107.
36. Charles Hartshorne, *The Divine Relativity* (New Haven, Conn.: Yale
University Press, 1948; PB), pp. xv, 50.

dent of the particulars of the universe. In addition, there are portions of our bodies and of our past of which we have only dim
awareness, whereas God knows the world completely at every point,
and forgets nothing. The mind-body analogy, however, if appropriately extended, provides an image of God's infinitely sympathetic
and all-embracing participation in the world process, a mode of
influence that is internal rather than external.

3. Discussion of Process Views

Let us now consider some criticisms of these views of God's action
in the world—from the standpoint first of theology and then of science. We will examine Whitehead's position, though similar observations would be applicable to Hartshorne's. Compared with the
biblical God, it is clear that Whitehead's God is *limited in his
power to act.* He is always one factor among many, and particularly
with respect to low-level beings, in which self-creativity is minimal,
his influence seems to be small. Insofar as natural agents exercise
causal efficacy, God's ability to compel changes is thereby restricted.
But we must remember that God is not absent from events that
monotonously repeat their past, for he is the ground of order and
the source of all "initial subjective aims." Whereas some theologians
identify God's role with order, and others with violations of order,
for Whitehead God is involved in both order and novelty; but in
neither is he the only factor. For *order* arises from God's structuring
of possibilities *and* from the event's conformation to its past; and
novelty arises from God's offering of alternative possibilities *and*
from the event's self-creation. This means that there is no event
which can be attributed solely to God, and that his acts in the
world are *not readily detectable.* This is a conclusion with which
many theologians would agree. In discussing Whitehead's view of
God, Daniel Williams writes as follows:

> God's causality is exercised in, through, and with all other causes
> operating. There is no demand here to factor out what God is adding
> to the stream of events apart from those events. But there is the
> assignment of specific functions to God's causality. . . . Every "act of
> God" is presented to us in, through, and with the complex of nature
> and life in which we are. When we say God elected Israel, or that he
> sends his rain on the just and the unjust, we must not ignore the
> complex analysis of assignable causes and factors in Israel's history
> or in the cosmic record of rainfall. We have no way of extricating
> the acts of God from their involvement in the activities of the world.

To assign any particular historical event to God's specific action in the world is to risk ultimate judgment on our assertions. Faith leads us to take the risk.[37]

There are many themes in Christian thought that support Whitehead's portrayal of *a God of persuasion and love* rather than of coercion and power. We noted Bonhoeffer's assertion that the power of love shown in the cross appears as powerlessness. God acts in the Word, the communication of meaning; we have freedom to respond or not, for grace is not "irresistible." Moreover, by limiting God's power, Whitehead absolves him of responsibility for evil—though at the expense of his ability to overcome it.[38] For in this representation God lacks both the sovereign control and the moral intensity of the biblical Jehovah. Whitehead's God can, however, turn evil to good account by envisaging the larger patterns into which it can be integrated. He preserves all that occurs, transmutes it, and reflects it back to the world. He is omniscient, infinitely sensitive to events, responding to them with perfect adequacy. This is a God of wisdom and compassion who shares in the world's suffering and is a transforming influence in it, even if he is not omnipotent.

For Whitehead, God's action is *the evocation of response*, the lure of ideals whose actualization is dependent on the world's activity. Since man's capacity for response far exceeds that of other beings, it is in human life that God's creative influence can be most effective—or most willfully opposed. God's ability to engender creative change in lower beings seems to be very limited. But even in the case of man, one wonders whether Whitehead's God is *too powerless* to inspire worship. Perhaps in addition to the "persuasive" aspects of God there are more active and authoritative aspects, to which the sense of inescapable judgment and overwhelming awe in religious experience testify.[39]

Though Whitehead relies predominantly on the requirements of his general metaphysical system in formulating his concept of God,

---

37. Daniel Williams, "How Does God Act? An Essay in Whitehead's Metaphysics," in Reese and Freeman, eds., *Process and Divinity*, pp. 179–80. Used by permission of the Open Court Publishing Company.

38. See Stephen Ely, *The Religious Availability of Whitehead's God* (Madison: University of Wisconsin Press PB, 1942).

39. See Daniel Williams, "Deity, Monarchy and Metaphysics: Whitehead's Critique of the Theological Tradition," in Ivor Leclerc, ed., *The Relevance of Whitehead* (New York: Macmillan and Co., 1961).

he does suggest at several points that *religious experience* can make an important contribution. "Religion contributes its own independent evidence which metaphysics must take account of in framing its description."[40] "Any cogency of argument entirely depends upon elucidation of somewhat exceptional elements in our conscious experience—those elements which may roughly be classed together as religious and moral intuitions."[41] As Whitehead turns from God as the "primordial" ground of order to God's "consequent" nature interacting with the world, he makes more frequent reference to religious as against purely philosophical considerations. Moreover, he recognizes the ability of particular events to illuminate reality:

> Religion claims that its concepts, though derived primarily from special experiences, are yet of universal validity, to be applied by faith to the ordering of all experience. Rational religion appeals to the direct intuition of special occasions and to the elucidatory power of its concepts for all occasions. It arises from that which is special, but it extends to what is general.[42]

In addition, Whitehead allows for the idea of *divine freedom and initiative* in particular events; God provides specifically ordered potentialities for individual occasions, and responds creatively and in novel ways to the changing needs of the world. Thus a doctrine of revelation in history, although not developed by Whitehead himself, would not be inconsistent with his metaphysics. There is nothing in his system to rule out God's more particular acts, if the evidence seems to require us to acknowledge them—and Whitehead always insisted that general metaphysical principles are abstractions that must not hinder us from confronting concrete particulars. Such an adaptation of process thought is necessary if we are to be faithful to the biblical conviction that God is Redeemer as well as Creator; a number of theologians have attempted such a synthesis of process philosophy and Christian thought.[43]

40. Whitehead, *Religion in the Making*, p. 76.
41. Whitehead, *Process and Reality*, p. 521.
42. Whitehead, *Religion in the Making*, p. 31. Used by permission of The Macmillan Company and Cambridge University Press.
43. Among American theologians strongly influenced by Whitehead (in addition to Hartshorne, Williams, and Cobb) is Bernard Meland, e.g., *The Realities of Faith* (New York: Oxford University Press, 1962). The writings of several Anglicans are indebted to process thought: Temple, *Nature, Man and God*; Lionel Thornton, *The Incarnate Lord* (London: Longman's Green, 1928); W. Norman Pittenger, *The Word Incarnate* (New York: Harper and Brothers, 1959). A few process themes are taken up by Nels F. S. Ferré, *The*

Finally, this interpretation of God's action in the world must be evaluated *from the standpoint of science*. Whitehead, it will be recalled, sees science as abstractive and symbolic; it deals with real patterns among events, but represents only partial and limited aspects of the world. He calls the tendency to treat scientific abstractions as if they were an exhaustive description of reality "the fallacy of misplaced concreteness." He also notes that many *scientific laws* are statistical in character and yield exact predictions only for large numbers; there is indeterminacy in individual events. Furthermore, in many situations, especially in the inanimate world, God's action is almost entirely confined to the maintenance of the order whose regularities are precisely those studied by the scientist. God's purpose for low-level beings is that they be orderly; his gift is the structuredness of the possibilities they exemplify. At lower levels, where physical patterns predominate over mental ones, law over freedom, and efficient over final causes, God's novel action may be beyond detection—though perhaps in cosmic history and emergent evolution there are signs of his action even in the inanimate. Moreover, even when God does contribute to novelty he always acts along with other causes, qualifying but not abrogating their operation. We can never extricate the "acts of God" from their involvement in the complex of natural processes through which he works.

In Whitehead's scheme, all of the influences producing order and novelty come together in *events* or *"actual occasions,"* which are the fundamental units of becoming. God acts not *on* things or substances, but *in* events, which are individual integrated acts; an event may involve a network of atoms or other components, but it is an act of the whole. This means that there is no opportunity for novelty in a stone (a "corpuscular society" as Whitehead calls it), in which there are no integrated events, no patterns of activity of the whole, no unified organization (except the mere physical cohesion of the parts). If the stone is considered as a collection of virtually independent atoms, the "law of large numbers" leads to highly predictable behavior; the stone is essentially inert and passive. Even a tree is a relatively loose aggregate with a less complex

Christian Understanding of God (New York: Harper and Brothers, 1951). Whereas these authors all defend personalistic theism, a more naturalistic viewpoint, drawing from Whitehead at certain points, is evident in Henry N. Wieman, *The Source of Human Good* (Chicago: University of Chicago Press, 1946; Southern Illinois University PB).

integration than the cells that compose it; Whitehead compares it to "a democracy" or a swarm of bees, which has no subjective experience as a whole. On the other hand, an atom *is* a highly integrated unity; the wave-equation applies to the whole atom, and its component electrons have lost their identity (Chapter 10). Individual atoms, even in stones, are unpredictable, and there are, in Whiteheadian terms, unitary "atomic events." There are unified events also in aggregates of atoms having *higher levels of organization.* Here patterns of the whole influence the parts without violating their measure of independence. For example, a cell is a complex community with its own internal laws, and yet it participates in the activity of the larger organism. Whitehead suggests that cells, and even atoms in cells, are affected by their wider context.[44] The unified events that man experiences as conscious aims depend on lawful regularities at various levels of biological activity. It is these individual moments of experience in integrated systems—and their analogues at lower levels—that are the locus of creativity.

The feature of process philosophy which at first sight may seem dubious to many scientists is this ascription of at least a rudimentary *"mental pole"* or *"subjective aim"* to all "actual occasions." But we must avoid reading too much into these terms. A stone has no "subjective aim" for it is not the scene of any unified events. Events in a cell have only an incipient mental aspect whose contribution is negligible in practice; it is an organism of such low grade that any novelty or creativity is effectively absent; and its aim is simply to transmit its past patterns, unimaginatively and repetitively. Its mode of inheriting its past is only remotely analogous to human memory; its response to a structure of possibilities and its sensitivity to changing stimuli can at most be seen as reflecting an exceedingly attenuated form of aim or purpose. Whitehead attributes consciousness to the higher animals only, and acknowledges a number of distinctive characteristics of man (self-awareness, language, scope of memory and anticipation, variety of levels of experience, and so forth). Moreover, "mental" and "physical" poles are abstractions from the unity of the event. Some passages in Whitehead could even be interpreted as a "two-language" rendition: that which is "matter" when seen from without is "mind" when seen from within, or imagined as a center of experience. But clearly Whitehead would not be content with useful fictions or unrelated

44. E.g., Whitehead, *Science and the Modern World*, p. 81.

languages; he takes events-in-process to be ontologically real, and he tries to relate the two languages by his description of the dynamics of events—in a metaphysics that avoids both materialism and the dualism of mind and matter as separate substances.

Some of the motives for *postulating rudimentary forms of experience* in low-grade entities were suggested in Chapter 11. Among these were the conviction that our own immediate experience is an important clue to the character of reality, and the assumption that there is continuity among the levels of being. Human experience, as an extreme case of an event in nature, is taken to exhibit the generic features of all events. Man is linked to simpler forms by a continuous evolutionary history; no sharp line can be drawn setting the limits at which the basic features of human experience—or something remotely akin to them—may be present. But above all it is for the sake of the coherence and generality of metaphysical categories that the mental pole is postulated. In Whitehead's definition a category must be universally applicable to all events; the diversity among the characteristics of events must then be accounted for by the diversity of the modes in which these basic categories are exemplified. Mechanical interactions can be viewed as low-grade organismic events (since organisms always have a mechanical aspect), whereas no extrapolation of mechanical concepts can yield the concepts needed to describe subjective experience. However, we suggested earlier that perhaps Whitehead's concern for continuity, coherence, and generality led him to give too little attention to the contrasts between events at various levels, or to the differences between distinctively human experience and the experience of other creatures.

IV. CONCLUSIONS: TOWARD A THEOLOGY OF NATURE

Drawing also from the discussion in previous chapters, we may now venture some conclusions concerning five issues in this chapter:

1. THE PLACE OF NATURE IN THEOLOGY: A THEOLOGY OF NATURE. In Part Two we concluded that theology should not be based primarily on nature, and we criticized the approach of natural theology. With neo-orthodoxy, we pointed to Christ as the central event in which God is revealed; with existentialism, we found personal involvement to be a prerequisite of religious understanding; with linguistic analysis, we held that the distinctive functions of reli-

gious language are worship, self-commitment, and life-orientation. In earlier chapters the centrality of religious experience and the life of the community were stressed; man's repentance and faith in response to judgment and redemption were seen to be at the heart of biblical religion. These distinctive aspects of historical revelation and present experience must not be replaced by arguments starting from science, nor assimilated into a general metaphysics (as sometime happens among process thinkers). The context of theological discourse is always the worshiping community.

In the biblical tradition, faith in *God as Redeemer* is more important than faith in God as Creator. Let us acknowledge that it has been through confrontation with historical events that we have found renewal. Here we have known release from guilt and insecurity, from anxiety and despair; and here we have discovered, at least in a fragmentary way, the power of reconciliation overcoming alienation. Here we have come to know the meaning of repentance and forgiveness, and of the new self-understanding and release from self-centeredness which are the beginning of the capacity for love. We can only confess what has occurred in our lives: that we have made a mess of things, but that in Christ something happened which opens up new possibilities in human existence. The purpose of creation is made known to us in Christ, "the new creation," who is at the same time the full flowering of the created order and the manifestation of continuing creation. In the image of the "suffering servant," the power of God is revealed as the power of love. God is thus encountered in historical events and human relationships, in the creative renewal of personal and social life, in grace redeeming estrangement. It is, above all, in man's response to his neighbor in need that the biblical God is known and served.

But we have urged that while theology must start from historical revelation and personal experience, it must also include *a theology of nature*[45] which does not disparage or neglect the natural order.

---

45. Our proposal differs somewhat from that of Cobb's *A Christian Natural Theology*, which (1) unlike traditional natural theology, recognizes that its fundamental perspective is indebted to the Christian community, but (2) like traditional natural theology, limits itself to arguments based on general experience and subject only to the norms of philosophy, setting aside any particular Christian beliefs. Cobb holds that such an enterprise should be presented in complete independence of what he calls "theology proper"; it is essentially a part of *philosophy* (though it acknowledges that all philosophers stand in a cultural context). The "theology of nature" which we are urging makes no

In neo-orthodoxy, nature remains the unredeemed stage for the drama of human redemption. In existentialism, the world is the impersonal setting for man's personal existence. In linguistic analysis, discourse about phenomena in the natural order has no functions in common with discourse about God. These positions minimize the continuity between nature and grace, between impersonal and personal realms, and between language about nature and about God. But the Bible itself takes a predominantly affirmative attitude toward the natural world; it declares that God is Lord of all of life, not of some separate "religious" realm. Moreover, it is this same world, whose regularities the scientist studies, which the theologian declares to be the scene of providential action. "Critical realism" will not allow us to be content with two unrelated languages. Especially in the doctrines of creation and providence, a theology of nature is essential.

In asserting that *God acts in nature* we side with classical and process positions against existentialist views. To be sure, theologians have in past centuries "had their fingers burned" by claiming divine action at points which were later explained in scientific terms; there is an understandable desire today to avoid any possible conflict by assigning nature to the scientist and confining religion to the realm of man's inward life. But if Christianity is radically interiorized, nature is left devoid of meaning, and the stretches of cosmic history before man's appearance are unrelated to God. We can accept the existentialist thesis that religious problems should not be approached in the detached objectivity of theoretical speculation, but this does not mean that we must avoid reference to nature. God makes a difference in events, not just in our way of looking at them. If the ideas of "complementarity" or "spaces" are to be introduced, they should be taken to refer to different aspects of reality, rather than to different interpretive perspectives; and we should go on to explore the relationship between these aspects, rather than accept too readily a sharp dualism of isolated spheres. We suggest, then, that statements about nature do have an important though always secondary place in theology.[46]

---

attempt to set aside Christian beliefs, for it is an integral part of *theology.* It is closer to the suggestions of Joseph Sittler, e.g., "A Theology for Earth," *The Christian Scholar,* Vol. 37 (1954), 367; Sittler, however, is more concerned about implications for ethics, such as stewardship of natural resources, than about the metaphysics of God's action in nature.

46. We should point out again that there is a whole area of interaction between science and theology which has been excluded from consideration in

2. THE CHARACTER OF NATURE: NATURE AS DYNAMIC PROCESS. Through most of its history, Christianity assumed an essentially static view of the world, with all things created in their present forms. Under the impact of early physics, a conception of nature as deterministic and mechanical was widely adopted. The analogy of watch and watchmaker seemed appropriate. We have seen above that contemporary existentialists tend to perpetuate this deistic image of nature; Bultmann considers the world to be a rigid mechanical order, a completely closed system of cause-and-effect laws that God does not violate. On the other hand, neo-Thomists, Pollard, and Whitehead all hold that nature has flexibility as well as structure, openness and novelty as well as regularity; our own conclusions have been along similar lines. It was suggested in Chapter 10 that *atomic indeterminacy* is a characteristic of nature, and not simply of our limited human knowledge or of disturbances introduced by the observer; in Heisenberg's words, "the concept of potentiality has been restored," since genuine alternatives are open. Scientific laws in many areas are statistical and do not allow prediction of individual events. *Time* is constitutive rather than incidental; the temporality of process has been one of our recurrent themes.

The concept of levels was central in Chapter 11, in which an organismic view was defended against mechanistic and vitalistic alternatives. We argued for distinctive biological concepts, purposive behavior, mental aspects of events, and human freedom. In each case we rejected both reductionism and dualism and indicated the advantages of the "two-language" views proposed by linguistic analysts (teleology-mechanism, mind-body, freedom-determinism). We ended, however, by advocating a *metaphysics of levels* as more consonant with "critical realism." We suggested that "levels of activity," like "levels of analysis," are not mutually exclusive. But we claimed that there are activities occurring in wholes which cannot be analyzed adequately in terms of the laws of their parts. Purpose, mind, and freedom were thus seen as aspects of the activities of unified wholes.

---

this volume, namely the analysis of ethical problems arising from applied science. Ethical decisions faced by the scientist, public policy issues involving the applications of science, and the influence of a technological orientation on human values are discussed in Ian G. Barbour, *Christianity and the Scientist*; C. A. Coulson, *Science, Technology and the Christian* (Nashville: Abingdon Press, 1960); Hugh White, ed., *Christians in a Technological Era* (New York: Seabury Press, 1964).

Again, an *evolutionary* understanding of nature was presented. Nature has a history; we can acknowledge the distinctive features of human history without making an absolute contrast between "natural" and "historical" orders, as existentialists do. We can, with Teilhard, picture a single continuous process in which there are threshold transitions from matter to life and thence to mind and society; but the rudiments of higher levels are already present in the lower. Teilhard's "within of things" is very similar to the "subjective" side postulated by Whitehead, though it is not expressed in the categories of a developed metaphysical system. Hardy and others have shown that the activity of a species does influence its own evolutionary development. Organisms may first adopt novel patterns of behavior, and then subsequent mutations which aid this pattern will be useful and will be preserved. Thus without reverting to Lamarckianism we can assert the importance of *the internal life* of organisms as it affects their total behavior and thence their evolutionary course. We do not have to assume that random mutations are the primary factor in the initiation of change. In Whiteheadian terminology, we may say that higher-level events can introduce "conceptual novelty" which is then inherited physically; teleological activity passes over into efficient causality.

We have criticized the idea that "*laws of nature*" are only human constructs. Barth adopts a Kantian interpretation in which scientific laws are an order imposed on events by man's mind. Such an ordering system, says Barth, is no obstacle to God, who can act on the real world of "things-in-themselves" that are inaccessible to human knowledge. Many linguistic analysts contend that laws are useful fictions or calculational devices for achieving limited scientific purposes; if laws do not describe reality, their use in scientific language does not conflict with the use of religious language about divine providence, which serves existential functions in man's life-orientation. But we have maintained that laws are symbolic representations of the structure of the world. They are, to be sure, abstractions from the complex fabric of events, but they are intended to express patterns in nature. It was urged, moreover, that religious language does include statements about God's action in the world. Thus we concluded that our understanding of the particular character of nature is relevant to the doctrine of providence.

3. GOD'S SOVEREIGNTY IN NATURE: CONTINUING CREATION. If existentialism ends by abandoning God's sovereignty over nature, neo-

orthodoxy, neo-Thomism, and Pollard, at the opposite extreme, have overemphasized *divine omnipotence*. For them, God's will is the ultimate cause of all events—including, according to the logic of the case, contingent and evil ones (though valiant efforts are made to escape the latter conclusion). We have argued, however, that foreordination is not compatible with the existence of open alternatives. Time is not the unrolling of a previously written scroll, but passage into a novel and indeterminate future. Man is free to reject God's purposes; such freedom is a prerequisite of man's voluntary love and uncoerced response. Not all that happens is God's will. Providence does not mean that "everything will turn out for the best"; there is in the gospel no promise of immunity from suffering. In creating a world of freedom and of stable order God has limited himself. But these conditions are God's purposeful self-limitation, not the imposition of restrictions by something external to God.

The existence of evil and the tragic element in all of life must be taken with utmost seriousness. It constitutes a problem for any doctrine of divine omnipotence, and equally for any natural theology which is too glib in claiming detailed design in nature. The early Deists saw God's beneficence everywhere, and the modernists turned evolution into a guarantee of inevitable progress. But evolution resembles not so much a simple and direct ascent as a long, slow travail. We must acknowledge, with Luther and Calvin, that providential action is not clearly and unambiguously visible. We need to recover the biblical motif that God's sovereignty is *the power of love*—coupled always with the righteousness, holiness, and judgment without which love becomes sentimentality. If Christ is our model of God, we must think of power in terms of the power of the Word, of the Cross, and of the Spirit, rather than omnipotence imagined as coercive force.

Whitehead and Hartshorne portray God as *a persuasive influence* on the world. They insist that the interaction between God and the world is two-directional but not symmetrical. God is affected by the world, and hence cannot be unchanging; but he is also transcendent, according to process thought. He is an integral participant in the world, but he is not simply a part of the process itself. The world makes a difference to God, and time is significant in his experience; he responds to new events and is a continuing influence contributing to both order and novelty. Perhaps the process tradition has gone too far in qualifying the classical idea of God's sovereignty; if Barth tends to jeopardize man's freedom, Whitehead tends to jeopardize God's. We have proposed, however, that a stronger doctrine of divine initiative and moral judgment, as suggested by religious experience and historical revelation, would not be incompatible with the basic framework of process metaphysics. This would make God a more effective influence but not an omnipotent ruler.

If, as we have proposed, the doctrines of creation and providence are combined in a concept of continuing creation, we do not have to abandon the idea of *dependence on God*, which both doctrines have traditionally affirmed. We may have to give up *creatio ex nihilo* as an initial act of absolute origination, but God's priority in status can be maintained apart from priority in time. We can even preserve some of the classical intent of *ex nihilo* by saying that novelty is as such not traceable to its antecedents. Each human being, for example, is truly a new creation, and every poem, painting, or symphony is a novel event which cannot be completely accounted for by its past. Creation is not just the rearrangement of the given, but the origination of the genuinely new. Yet creativity always works in what exists to bring into being what did not exist. Thus the Whiteheadian can say at the same time that God always acts along with other causes, and that nothing comes into being apart from God. Every creature is indeed radically dependent on God for its existence.

Perhaps the most serious danger in the idea of continuing creation is that its representation of *divine immanence* will seem to preclude *transcendence*. We need new symbols of transcendence which do not imply priority in space and time; we have tended to spatialize and temporalize God, putting him outside, alongside, or before the world.[47] When the universe was imagined to be like a watch, God was pictured as external to it and temporally earlier; such an image seemed to guarantee transcendence but rule out immanence (except by "divine intervention"). If the world is more like an organism, its principle of order and growth seems to be internal and cotemporal, and transcendence seems to be precluded. But in both cases the spatial imagery is misleading. We have indicated Heim's defense of "dimensional transcendence," which de-

---

47. Bultmann's treatment of this theme has been given wide circulation by John A. T. Robinson, *Honest to God* (Philadelphia: Westminster Press, 1963; PB).

scribes the realms of world, selfhood and God as interpenetrating but distinct "spaces." His proposal helps us to avoid identifying transcendence with geographical location, though it too relies on an analogy drawn from physical dimensions. A Whiteheadian conception of transcendence would stress the priority of God's status and his role in world events, his freedom and everlasting purpose. We have also indicated that transcendence refers to God's holiness and righteousness, and expresses man's experience of reverence, awe, and mystery. The distinctively Christian understanding of transcendence is defined by the radical character of judgement and redemption in Christ.[48]

4. THE ROLE OF METAPHYSICS: THE USE OF PROCESS PHILOSOPHY IN THEOLOGY. In defending the relevance of metaphysics we agree with neo-Thomism and process thought as against neo-orthodoxy, existentialism, and linguistic analysis. Because Barth tries to avoid metaphysics and relies entirely on the language of grace, providential action as he presents it seems to have no connection with nature as understood by the scientist. We have submitted, furthermore, that metaphysical categories are inescapably present, whether recognized or not; even the personalistic language of scripture has ontological implications, which should be explicitly analyzed. In Pollard's case, the absence of philosophical concepts as a bridge between theology and science hinders communication between these realms of discourse; there are simply no common terms between scientific language about electrons and biblical language about God. The linguistic analyst is willing to live with two unrelated languages and give up the quest for a unified account of the world.

Our defense of *the use of philosophical categories in theology* is of course not a new proposal. Augustine was indebted to Plato, Aquinas to Aristotle, nineteenth-century Protestantism to Kant. In each case the theologian had to adapt the philosopher's ideas to the theological task; correspondingly, the theologian's philosophical commitments made him more sensitive to some aspects of the biblical witness than to others. The components of any creative synthesis are themselves transformed by being brought together. Now Whitehead, like Kant, was a philosopher already deeply influenced by the Christian vision of reality; both men were also thoroughly

---

48. See Edward Farley, *The Transcendence of God* (Philadelphia: Westminster Press, 1960), Chap. 7.

conversant with science—in Whitehead's case, with recent science. He was interested in many diverse areas of human experience, but recognized the tentative and partial character of his attempt at synthesis; he held that every philosophical system illuminates some types of experience more adequately than other types, and none attains to final truth.

The way in which metaphysics is used requires careful consideration. There have been times in the past when the imposition of a rigid philosophical system has hindered both scientific and theological development; we contended earlier that the dominance of the Aristotelian framework from the thirteenth to the seventeenth centuries was in some ways detrimental to science as well as to theology. Not without reason, many men in both fields today are apprehensive of metaphysics. In the search for unity and coherence, any premature or externally imposed synthesis must be avoided. We can expect no complete and final system; our endeavors must be tentative, exploratory, and open, allowing a measure of pluralism in recognition of the variety of experience. Christianity cannot be identified with any particular metaphysical system.

It may be objected that reference to God in *metaphysics* serves very different functions from reference to God in *worship*, and this is indeed the case. It is the strength of linguistic analysis and of existentialism that they do not neglect the primary context in which religious language is used. Even a theistic metaphysics is detached and speculative and its modes of thought are abstract and general —a long way from personal reorientation or the worshiping community. Nevertheless we argued in Part Two that religious statements do serve cognitive functions in providing a world-view and in making assertions about reality. Whitehead himself was concerned to connect metaphysics and worship; he insisted that the God who performs the general "secular" or metaphysical functions in the "housekeeping" of the universe is also the God who evokes worship and the sense of companionship in the religious life which man labels "sacred." While much of his writing dealt with more technical philosophical problems, it is clear that he was working out a basically religious vision of all human experience.

Our suggestion, then, is that the ideas of process philosophy may be *adapted to the expression of the biblical message* in the contemporary world. If metaphysics alone is the starting point, and the most general categories applicable to the structure of all areas of experience are sought, then impersonal philosophical language tends to predominate. But if only the classical language of salvation is employed, its personal and historical terms have limited applicability to nature. The position we are defending would employ metaphysical categories within the expression of the Christian message. Clearly, such metaphysical considerations make no contribution to science (except perhaps to support certain attitudes toward the world which are congenial to the scientific enterprise). Neither do they make any direct contribution to religious commitment or to theology in its most central doctrines. But they do contribute to *an integral world-view* which is required if modern man is to find religious beliefs credible. Their concern is the intelligibility and coherence of the total world process and of human experience in all its diversity. Metaphysics is not, as its critics hold, sheer speculation unrelated to experience; but it does attempt greater generality than specialized inquiry into particular types of experience.

5. GOD'S ACTION IN NATURE: GOD AS CREATIVE INFLUENCE. Does the neo-Thomist distinction of *primary* and *secondary* causality fulfill the specifications above for a theology of nature? It does indeed allow one to speak both of God's activity in nature and of the operation of natural forces. It does employ a carefully articulated metaphysics which deals with the whole range of human experience and the testimony of biblical religion. Some of the neo-Thomist categories which we have criticized in previous chapters (such as the dualism of body and soul, or the idea of unchanging substances with changing attributes) might be modified without altering the scheme of primary and secondary causes, which has much to commend it as a solution to the issues of this chapter. The idea of divine omnipotence, however, seems to constitute a more serious difficulty; if God is conceived as primary cause, one must conclude that he operates through all secondary causes.

What is the relation between *primary* and *secondary* causes in neo-Thomism? Primary causality might be emphasized to such a degree that natural forces have no independence and are purely instrumental to God's action. Or one might so emphasize secondary causality that God's role is simply to establish the natural order and then let it operate without interference. Actually Thomistic thought can make both assertions, since it insists that the two types of causality are on totally different planes and do not compete with each other; the presence of divine causality, it is said, does not diminish the effectiveness of natural causality, or vice versa. But if God's action is of a completely separate order, how is it related to natural forces? Does God only "sustain" and "concur with" the actions of temporal beings, in a general and uniform way? In this scheme, how can one represent God's initiative in particular events, except as a miraculous disruption of an established order of secondary causes?

Most authors in the classical tradition seem to end by representing God's action *as a coercive force*, even though they have tried to avoid this conclusion. Barth's insistence on "absolute determination," as well as the Thomist doctrine that God employs secondary causes "instrumentally," suggests a mechanical compulsion or metaphysical necessity that jeopardizes the autonomy of natural agents. A basically impersonal analogy of causation is used. In other aspects of Thomism, however, and in process thought, it is recognized that causality is complex; analogies derived not from physical forces but from interpersonal relationships are introduced. Here there is a mode of causal influence that does not compromise the independent activity and integrity of other beings.

Both Pollard and Whitehead make use of *indeterminacy in nature* in their representations of God's action, but they do so in somewhat different ways. For Pollard, indeterminacy allows an omnipotent God to actualize one particular potentiality from among the alternatives inherited from the past; for Whitehead, potentialities are actualized by the natural agents themselves, in response to both God and their past. For Pollard, God acts primarily at the atomic level and thereby controls all events; for Whitehead, God influences unified activities at various levels, especially the mental pole of events in whole organisms. For Pollard, God affects the world, but is not himself changed; for Whitehead the world also affects God. Pollard correlates providence with the control of atoms, and he shifts to a different approach when he comes to God's action in human life (for which he relies on the existentialist delineation of an I-Thou sphere independent of the world of I-It); Whitehead has God acting in the subjective aim of every entity, including man. In process thought the representation of God's action throughout nature is patterned after his action in human life. Whitehead's scheme already has built into it provisions for freedom, efficient causality, and divine action.

Now it might appear that both Pollard and Whitehead perpetuate *"the God of the gaps"*—but with many little gaps in the natural order, instead of the few big ones postulated in the older version that both scientists and theologians rejected. The critic may object that *any* mention of God's influence, whether large or small, sudden or gradual, runs counter to the modern assumption of the sufficiency of scientific explanations in terms of natural causes. The reply to this objection would recall that scientific laws are always selective and abstractive and often statistical. Moreover, while God has a clearly defined role in the Whiteheadian scheme, his contribution can never be separated out because he always acts with other causes. Yet Whitehead does affirm that God makes a difference in the world, not just in our attitudes toward the world. A critical realism acknowledges the symbolic character of all languages, but insists that they refer to a single world.

Does this restrict *God's power over nature*? As human beings our own action on stones is mechanical, whereas our action on other persons is personal; must we not hold that God, too, acts on stones mechanically or not at all? The parallel breaks down, however, because we are external to the stone, whereas God as source of all initial subjective aims is constitutive of its being. The stability of the stone is in accordance with God's purposes as source of order. Yet even in the inanimate there is an infinitesimal element of new potentiality, which only the long ages of cosmic history could disclose; "continuing creation" has been a slow process, if we take the scientific record seriously. It is in *human life*, however, that the greatest opportunities for God's influence exist today. And it is in religious experience and historical revelation, rather than in nature apart from man, that divine initiative is most clearly manifest; our conclusions on metaphysics and on theological method here support each other. Both experience and history point to a God who acts not by coercing but by evoking the response of his creatures. But these same sources remind us of the inadequacy of all our models —for there is no adequate analogy for God. Only in worship and reverence can we acknowledge the mystery of God and the pretensions of any human system that claims to have mapped out his ways.

Index of Selected Topics

Only topics discussed in more than one chapter are indexed. For detailed topical outline, see the Contents. (The symbol "f" means "and the following page.")

Index of Names

If the symbol "n" directly follows the page number (76n), the author is mentioned *only in the footnote*. If it is preceded by a comma (76,n), the author is mentioned *in the text and in a footnote which is the first citation of a work*, with full bibliographical data. (Subsequent citations of the same work are indicated by page number only if they appear on the same page as a reference in the text.)

470

Schoeck, H., 191n
Schrödinger, E., 278,
319,n
Schwann, T., 325
Scopes, T., 100
Scriven, M., 149,n, 349,n,
356n
Sellars, W., 195n
Sertillanges, A. D., 426n
Shakespeare, W., 387
Shapere, D., 154
Shapley, H., 133n
Sheer, D. E., 323n
Sherrington, C. S., 352n
Shils, E. A., 193n
Simpson, G. G., 331,n,
338,n, 369n, 371,
388, 391, 397,n, 411
Sinnott, E., 341, 342,n
Sittler, J., 454n
Skinner, B. F., 186,n,
306,n, 311n, 353
Skinner, J., 384n
Slukin, W., 348n
Smart, J. J. C., 169n,
355n
Smelser, N. J., 193n
Smethurst, A., 287n
Smith, H., 264n
Smith, N. K., 73n
Smuts, J., 327,n, 396
Snow, C. P., 175,n
Socrates, 47
Sommerhoff, G., 338n
Spencer, H., 94f, 99,
108,n, 109, 410, 413
Spener, P. J., 68
Spinoza, B., 32,n, 43, 69
Sprat, T., 37
Stebbing, L. S., 288,n
Stevenson, C., 241n
Strawson, P. F., 264n,
356,n
Sullivan, H. S., 190
Sullivan, J. W. N., 288,n

Taube, M., 349n
Tawney, R. H., 49,n
Tax, S., 374n
Taylor, C. W., 143n
Taylor, R., 311n
Teilhard de Chardin, P.,
133n, 391, 399,n,

400–406, 407,n, 408,
415, 417, 456
Temple, W., 230,n, 232,
449n
Tennant, F. R., 132n,
392, 414
Tennyson, A., 227
Terrien, S., 105n
Thomas, G. F., 73n
Thornton, L., 449n
Thorp, W., 67n
Tillich, P., 211,n, 212,n,
219,n, 258
Tindal, M., 60
Tomkins, S., 349n
Toulmin, S., 124, 145,n,
146, 150,n, 153, 156,
161, 164f, 181n,
411,n, 412, 415
Toynbee, A., 197
Tresmontant, C., 399n,
405
Turing, A. M., 348,n, 351
Tyrell, G., 104

University of California
Associates, 307n
Urey, H., 368
Urmson, J. O., 123n, 243
Ussher, J., 97

Van Buren, P., 244n
Van der Waal, J. D., 160
Van der Ziel, A., 119n,
292n
Voltaire, F. M., 62
Von Bertalanffy, L., 332,
333,n
Von Neumann, J., 300,
351,n
Von Weizsäcker, C. F.,
134n, 166, 266,n,
302, 368n
Vriezen, T. C., 361n,
384n

Waddington, C. H., 397,
398n, 403,n, 410,n
Wallace, A. R., 92,n
Walsh, W. H., 193,n, 198
Warnock, G. J., 243n
Watkins, J. N., 198,n
Watson, J. B., 353

Watson, J. D., 319,n
Weber, M., 49, 186,n
Weismann, A., 87
Wells, A. N., 123n
Werkmeister, W. H., 169
Wesley, J., 68
Westfall, R. S., 43,n
Wheelwright, P., 203n
White, A. D., 44n
White, H., 455n
White, M., 195,n
Whitehead, A. N., 6,
12,n, 24, 36, 46,
128,n, 129–31, 169f,
171,n, 206, 208,
262n, 265, 344f,
346,n, 347, 394,
399, 408, 440–44,
447–52, 455–63
Whitehouse, W. A., 119n
Whittaker, E. T., 167,n,
367n
Wieman, H. N., 445,
450n
Wiener, N., 338n, 351n
Wiener, P., 327n
Wiggins, J. W., 191n
Wilberforce, S., 97
Wilder, A., 362n
Willey, B., 30n, 61n, 66n
Williams, D. D., 230n,
447, 448n
Wilson, R. H., 323n
Winch, P., 187,n
Windelband, W., 194n
Wisdom, J., 249,n
Wittgenstein, L., 187n,
243
Wöhler, F., 325
Woodger, J. H., 329,
330,n
Woolsey, C. N., 323n
Wordsworth, W., 67,n
Wright, C., 108, 109,n
Wright, S., 343,n, 370

Yngve, V., 350n
Young, F., 215n

Zahn, J., 100
Zilsel, E., 45n
Zuurdeeg, W., 246,n, 247